JOHN DONNE
Poetry and Prose

Modern Library College Editions

JOHN DONNE
Poetry and Prose

Edited by FRANK J. WARNKE

University of Washington

MODERN LIBRARY · *New York*
Distributed by McGraw-Hill, Inc.

Acknowledgments

"The First Anniversarie," "A Funerall Elegie," and
"The Second Anniversarie" are reprinted from *The
Anniversaries*, edited by Frank Manley (Baltimore,
Md.: Johns Hopkins Press, 1963), by permission of
The Johns Hopkins Press.

The arrangement of the "Holy Sonnets" as proposed
by Helen Gardner from *Divine Poems*, edited by
Helen Gardner (Oxford: Clarendon Press, 1952),
is used by permission of The Clarendon Press.

The sermons, "Preached at Lincolns Inne" (Vol. III,
No. 3), "Preached at White-hall, March 8, 1621"
(Vol. IV, No. 1), and "Deaths Duell" (Vol. X,
No. 11), from *Sermons of John Donne*, edited
by G. R. Potter and E. M. Simpson
(Berkeley, Calif.: University of California Press, 1953-61),
are reprinted by permission of the University of
California Press.

Library of Congress Catalog Card Number 0-07-553663-3

THE MODERN LIBRARY
is published by Random House, Inc.

Manufactured in the United States of America

Contents

Introduction

by FRANK J. WARNKE

As WE MOVE into the last third of the twentieth
century, John Donne continues to be a poet and prose-
writer of unique significance for our time. That significance, which made itself fully apparent during the two
decades following 1912, the year of publication of Grierson's great edition of the *Poetical Works*, is rooted, it
must now be clear, in something more than the poet's
alleged "modernity." It was not always clear. During the
first stage of Donne's modern popularity, extending until
the mid-1930s, he was, despite the warnings of some
scholars, often praised for his seeming anticipations of the
modern temper—his intellectual toughness, his frequent
cynicism, his acute psychological perceptions, and his
"anti-Petrarchism," the last quality being one which many
readers of the 1920s equated with their own "anti-Vic-
torianism" in a manner which would have startled Vic-
toria and Petrarch alike.

Gradually, as more sober criticism and more probing
scholarship accumulated, the picture of Donne as a modern author before the fact began to give way to the picture of Donne as a man of his time. In drawing attention
to Donne's relationship to medieval thought and Renaissance science; to inherited habits of intellect and conventions of expression both amorous and religious; to
traditional rhetoric and to such practices as that of for-

mal devotional meditation; modern scholarship has done much to reclaim a great and original artist from the sometimes distorting enthusiasms of contemporary admirers. Nevertheless, the Donne reconstructed by informed historical study is not the whole Donne unless such study brings with it the imaginative sympathy necessary to transform the reading of any poet from an intellectual exercise into an aesthetic experience. With such sympathy, Donne becomes, like Shakespeare, larger than his own age without ceasing to be of that age; like any great poet, he includes his age rather than being included by it. Without becoming a modern poet, he is revealed as a poet of vital importance to modern men. In these terms, some of the perceptions of Donne's readers earlier in our century retain their validity as ways of approaching his art—although we would be wise to use such perceptions with the healthy caution engendered by the work of historical scholars.

It is instructive, for example, to look back from a distance of some forty-five years at the most influential single analysis of Donne's work produced during the first half of our century. That analysis is found in T. S. Eliot's essay "The Metaphysical Poets" (1921). At the heart of Eliot's view is the conviction that Donne and the other Metaphysical poets are distinguished by a capacity for synthesizing into an artistic unity the disparate elements of experience. Donne and the other poets practicing his style, according to Eliot, "feel their thought as immediately as the odor of a rose"; their fusion of thought and feeling accounts for their singular artistic power. Eliot goes on to posit a "dissociation of sensibility" which set in during the later seventeenth century and which afflicted English poetry until the twentieth, producing poets who, like Tennyson and Browning, separated the intellectual and emotive functions. This formulation has, as later writers have pointed out, something of the shape of myth (more specifically, the myth of the Golden Age), and it is true that the sweeping historical generalization Eliot engages in fails to hold up if we examine it critically. But it is not necessary to share Eliot's artistic and historical prejudices (perhaps necessary to him in 1921 for his own development as a poet) to recognize that he has ascertained one of the most compelling features of Donne's work—as noticeable in prose as in poetry—and has phrased his perception with admirable cogency.

The literature of any culture, viewed historically, seems to present us with a fairly regular alternation of two types of style. To one type, dominated by aspirations toward order, decorum, rationality, relative objectivity, and the realistic representation of observed nature, tradition has given the name *classicism*. For the other type, dominated by such qualities as formal asymmetry, deliberate violation of decorum, fantasy, relative subjectivity, and what amounts to the reworking of observed nature, tradition has found no name that elicits general agreement, though such period stylistic labels as *Gothic, Baroque,* and *Romanticism* have all at one time or another been pressed into service. The term *mannerism* will perhaps serve as well as any other to designate the recurrent stylistic constant which alternates with classicism. Donne is a great poet of the Baroque age, one of the major ages of European mannerism, and the Metaphysical style of which he is the chief exponent is an important manifestation of mannerism in its Baroque form. The qualities which Eliot found central to Metaphysical poetry are the qualities which are generally dominant in the Baroque.

Donne's "mechanism of sensibility," adapted to the synthesizing of different kinds of experience and, most of all, to the unification of passionate feeling and intricate thought (the "passionate paradoxical reasoning" of which H. J. C. Grierson speaks in the influential introduction to his anthology *Metaphysical Lyrics and Poems*, 1921), is fully characteristic of the Baroque temperament, though few authors of that or any other age have exercised that mechanism with such intensity and versatility. Such a lyric as "Lovers Infinitenesse" exemplifies the qualities which struck Eliot so forcibly. Its opening stanza, bringing into play a whole range of mundane imagery alien to the poetic decorum of the Elizabethans, applies the questioning, rational intellect to the attempted resolution of a problem in passionate experience:

> If yet I have not all thy love,
> Deare, I shall never have it all,
> I cannot breath one other sigh, to move,
> Nor can intreat one other teare to fall,

> And all my treasure, which should purchase thee,
> Sighs, teares, and oathes, and letters I have spent.
> Yet no more can be due to mee,
> Than at the bargaine made was ment,
> If then thy gift of love were partiall,
> That some to mee, some should to others fall,
>   Deare, I shall never have Thee All.

The texture of the verse, empty of sensuous physical description and obvious verbal melodiousness alike, enforces concentration on the intellectual process which is its content, and the imagery, primarily commercial and legal, directs our attention to the poet's argumentation rather than to the specific gravity of his desire. And yet, in at least two ways that are almost definitive for Donne's practice, the stanza makes itself felt as a passionate utterance of great power. To begin with, despite the absence of any facile smoothness of versification, the lines have a strange and original music, derived largely from a rhythmic imitation of the accents of emotionally heightened conversation. One of the most widespread misconceptions about Donne's poetry, from Ben Jonson's day almost to our own, is that he is somehow careless, maladroit, or harsh in his prosody; in fact, Donne's metrical control is of an astounding virtuosity, although that virtuosity is generally in the service of drama rather than of song.

The mention of drama leads to the second quality notable in the quoted stanza: it evokes a dramatic situation, with a characterized speaker and a figure to whom the poem is addressed. Much—perhaps most—Elizabethan lyric poetry has what one might call a public quality about it. Whether the subject is God or profane love, the typical Renaissance poet habitually addresses an uncharacterized audience—us, the readers—whom he tells *about* the beauty or cruelty of his mistress, the intensity of his passion, or his desire for salvation. Donne, like Herbert and Marvell after him, almost always operates in the manner of drama, evoking, usually in his first line, a precisely defined human situation, normally one with an enormous and immediate emotional potential. In their amorous sonnets, such Elizabethan poets as Spenser and Sidney frequently begin with some generalization, maxim, mythological reference, or apostrophe, in the light of which private emotional experience is scrutinized or explicated. Donne, on the other hand, usually begins his *Songs and Sonets* (and, for that matter, his *Divine Poems*) with an abrupt scrap of conversation—"I wonder by my troth, what thou, and I/Did, till we lov'd?," or "For Godsake hold your tongue, and let me love," or "Batter my heart, three person'd God"—which at once makes us unseen witnesses to a private drama unfolding in the present. In Spenser's lyrics we hear an address directed at us, an audience. In Donne's we overhear a conversation directed at another individual in circumstances of the utmost intimacy. The "naked thinking heart" which Donne claimed for himself in "The Blossome" expresses itself in an art which is simultaneously governed by the intellect and the passions.

To return to "Lovers Infinitenesse," one finds in the second stanza a continuation of the intellectual argumentation of the first:

> Or if then thou gavest mee all,
> All was but All, which thou hadst then;
> But if in thy heart, since, there be or shall,
> New love created bee, by other men,
> Which have their stocks intire, and can in teares,
> In sighs, in oathes, and letters outbid mee,
> This new love may beget new feares,
> For, this love was not vowed by thee.
> And yet it was, thy gift being generall,
> The ground, thy heart is mine, what ever shall
>   Grow there, deare, I should have it all.

Although the stanza complicates as well as continues the argument, the poem is in no danger of becoming a mere exercise in amorous casuistry (as sometimes occurs in the thirteenth-century Italian poetry of the *dolce stil novo*). The new fear of a new love and its attempted exorcism both exist not so much as problems to be solved by the intellect as forms assumed by the lover's desperate desire for complete possession. It is no accident that commercial metaphor continues to dominate the poem. The final stanza fails to solve the logical problems raised by the first two, but it succeeds in rendering those problems irrelevant to the lover's desire. As so often in Donne, its success derives from paradox, from the perception framed by the mind on the evidence supplied by the heart:

Yet I would not have all yet,
Hee that hath all can have no more,
And since my love doth every day admit
New growth, thou shouldst have new rewards in store;
Thou canst not every day give me thy heart,
If thou canst give it, then thou never gavest it:
Loves riddles are, that though thy heart depart,
It stayes at home, and thou with losing savest it:
But wee will have a way more liberall,
Than changing hearts, to joyne them, so wee shall
    Be one, and one anothers All.

In particular, the imagery of this stanza transcends the language of commerce, replacing it with the language of religious experience. The great paradox, central not only to Christianity but also to other higher religions—that one gains one's life by losing it—supplies the model by which the lover understands the nature of his own desire. This is not to say that the poem is a religious allegory, still less that it is a literal elevation of amorous experience to the status of divine; it is rather to say that a part of the poem's meaning is a recognition of the basis shared by all transcendent desire (in the words of Arnold Stein, whose *John Donne's Lyrics* contains an excellent interpretation of this poem, "the love of the finite for the infinite").

The presentation of amorous experience in religious terms, like the later presentation of devotional experience in erotic terms, may serve as a clue to an understanding of Donne's style and the vision which it embodies. (One might note, for other examples of religious language applied to amorous subjects, such poems as "The Canonization," "The Extasie," and "The Relique.")

Donne's poetry, like most Metaphysical poetry and like much of the Baroque literature of which such poetry is an important manifestation, characteristically views personal emotional experience in the context of ultimate reality, or what we may conjecture of ultimate reality—in a setting, then, of speculation which, like all metaphysical speculation, is concerned with the paradoxical and the self-contradictory, and, ultimately, with the materials of religious contemplation. The relation of this kind of vision to what was noted earlier about the qualities of a mannerist style as opposed to those of a classical style is clear:

whereas classical style represents human actions and emotions within an accepted context of limitations—limitations deriving from a concept of rationality, a sense of practicality, or, very frequently, an adherence to a given artistic decorum—mannerist art, whether Baroque, Romantic, or Surrealistic, pursues the most unrealizable human aspirations beyond all limits of reason or decorum. In much Baroque literature, as in much modern literature, such pursuit leads to the dominance of fantasy or dream; in Donne's work it leads to the dominance of paradox, irony, and ambiguity, and to the exploitation of these features in a way which is either religious or quasi-religious: *Le cœur a ses raisons que la raison ne connaît point.*

In many obvious and more superficial respects Donne's art shares the general qualities of the Baroque age. For example, the concept of form underlying his practice as a lyric poet contrasts with that of the Elizabethan sonneteers and songwriters in that it accepts as a necessity the unique creation of a particular form to suit each poetic utterance. It would be unhistorical to see in Donne's lyric poetry (or in Herbert's) an anticipation of Coleridge's concept of organic form, and yet, from the point of view of the twentieth-century reader, the operation of Donne's poetic form is sometimes surprisingly similar. (It is worth noting that Coleridge admired Donne in an age in which Metaphysical poetry was generally held in low esteem.) Renaissance poetry, like eighteenth-century poetry, tends to operate as if it thought of poetic form as a preexistent vessel, into which the content of poetic vision might be poured. The sonnet, the Spenserian stanza, ottava rima, rhyme royal—all have an existence anterior to the individual poems to which they give shape, and, as one result, Renaissance poetry tends to fall into categories of both form and genre more readily than does Baroque poetry. Donne's lyrics, like much seventeenth-century poetry, tend to create a novel stanzaic form which serves as the vehicle for one poem and is then discarded. Even in his *Holy Sonnets,* where Donne does employ a conventional form, he treats that form with a high-handed lack of respect for its traditional manipulation (one might note, for example, the freedom and variety with which the "turn" is located in these sonnets).

Moving from the lyrics to the large body of Donne's poetic work that is composed in pentameter couplets, one notes the same qualities of flexibility and license: freely enjambed, marked by great variety in rhythm and in the location of caesuras, Donne's couplets establish as their unit of expression neither the line nor the single couplet (as in Pope) but rather an extended series of couplets, the separate identity of which is felt as a function of the thought expressed rather than of the metrical form employed. In their creation of a structure of verse-paragraphs, Donne's finer couplet poems (such as the "Anniversaries") supply some of the few examples of similarity in practice, even purely technical practice, between Donne and the other giant of English Baroque poetry, John Milton, who is in most respects Donne's opposite but whose blank verse compositions also tend to fall into verse-paragraphs.

At this point I would like to caution that the observations in the foregoing paragraphs are in no sense meant to imply that the kind of poetry written by Donne and the Metaphysical poets is better than the kind of poetry written by Spenser and the Elizabethans. It is not. But in terms of stylistic history the two kinds of poetry are significantly different, and an awareness of that difference is helpful in reading Donne's poetry and responding to it as it deserves.

In his prose, as clearly as in his poetry, Donne belongs to the Baroque age. The themes of his prose—the transience of existence, the vivid but theatrical illusoriness of the phenomenal world, the certainty of death and dissolution, the promise of resurrection—are definitive for the Baroque, while his prose style, whether in the *Devotions upon Emergent Occasions* or the *Sermons*, is no less Baroque. Like the other great masters of English Baroque prose, Sir Francis Bacon, Robert Burton, and Sir Thomas Browne, Donne eschews the traditional Ciceronian period, with its qualities of balance and antithesis, its rhythmic regularity, and its polished smoothness, in favor of a sentence which is asymmetrical in structure, irregular in rhythm, and harshly dramatic in texture. Ciceronian prose, which dominated the high Renaissance, produces an overall impression appropriate to an oratorical style—that of a sequence of thought completed unalterably some time in the past and now presented as persuasively as possible to an audience. Baroque prose, which is, whatever its public purpose, private rather than public in its manner, offers the reader not completed thought but thought in the process of formulation, thought in the very moment that it is being thought. The immediacy, irregularity, and dramatic excitement of Donne's prose ally it unmistakably to his poetry, and the general tendencies of Baroque prose explain how it is that Donne's *Sermons*, delivered, of course, to a congregation, are as personal in tone, and as desperately committed as are the great private *Devotions* elicited by his illness of 1623.

Donne's poetry and prose alike, then, exhibit in both their concept of form and their characteristic texture some of the features of the new period style which emerged in European literature at the end of the sixteenth century. Viewed from the perspective of stylistic history, some of the aspects of Donne's lyric poetry which have often excited critical comment take on a new meaning. The abrupt, often cynical rejection of the commonplaces of Petrarchan and Platonic tradition in the *Songs and Sonets* is a case in point. Although the professed scorn for both Petrarchan conventions (see, for example, "The Indifferent") and Platonic ("The Blossome") is an aspect of the poet's serious speculation on the subject of love, that scorn fulfills a more important function as a symptom of a new convention in the process of formation. The rejection of standard Petrarchism and Platonism is, like the rejection of Augustan meter and diction by Wordsworth and Keats, or the rejection of Romantic attitudes by Eliot and Pound, a manifestation of the parent-destroying instinct which marks the early stages of any new period style. In short, the youthful Donne's argument is with an artistic tradition, a style, rather than with a philosophical tradition; his poetic thought remains within the Petrarchan and Platonic heritage, although with some differences.

One might consider, for example, "The Canonization," in which Donne pulls off the virtuoso feat of burlesquing the Petrarchan conventions and revivifying them at the same time. The second stanza, with its semisatiric use of the wornout formulas of Renaissance amorous verse, nevertheless affirms the truth asserted by those formulas through the simple but brilliant trick of inflating the hyperbole to the point of absurdity, while at the same time denying the literal truth of that hyperbole. The modest affirmation of the lover remains, and remains believable:

> Alas, alas, who's injur'd by my love?
>   What merchants ships have my sighs drown'd?
> Who saies my teares have overflow'd his ground?
>   When did my colds a forward spring remove?
>   When did the heats which my veines fill
>   Adde one more to the plaguie Bill?
> Soldiers finde warres, and Lawyers finde out still
>   Litigious men, which quarrels move,
>   Though she and I do love.

The great and complex "Anniversaries" also, from one point of view, constitute the most extreme imaginable profession of the religion of the worship of woman which is at the heart of the tradition that Petrarch inherited and perfected.

Similarly, although Donne has a good deal of fun at the expense of the doctrine of Platonic love which had become so fashionable and so tarnished in Elizabethan society, in many of his lyrics he expounds that doctrine with conviction, subtlety, and power. "Love's not so pure, and abstract, as they use/ To say, which have no Mistresse but their Muse," he writes in "Loves Growth," but "The Extasie," one of the finest of the *Songs and Sonets,* is a rhapsody on the Platonic theme which Donne states near the end of the poem:

> Loves mysteries in soules doe grow,
> But yet the body is his booke.

The love Donne celebrates is never abstract, but it can be dazzling in its purity.

Donne's constant preoccupation with the interrelationship of the spiritual and the physical, first in erotic experience, later in religious experience, brings us again to Eliot's *aperçu* concerning the unified sensibility and to the whole question of the role which, as Donne's poetry demonstrates, speculative thought can play in passionate utterance. It brings us, in short, to the question of what is "metaphysical" in Metaphysical poetry. The term owes its currency to Dr. Johnson, whose "Life of Cowley," in his *Lives of the English Poets* (1779–81) contains a famous hostile analysis of "a race of writers that may be termed the *metaphysical poets*," among whom the critic classed Donne. The perception of some kind of connection between metaphysics and Donne's poetry is, however, considerably older than Johnson. John Dryden, in his *Discourse Concerning the Original and Progress of Satire* (1693), observed that Donne:

> affects the metaphysics, not only in his satires, but in his amorous verses, where nature only should reign; and perplexes the minds of the fair sex with nice speculations of philosophy, when he should engage their hearts, and entertain them with the softnesses of love.

In Donne's own lifetime the traditionalist poet William Drummond of Hawthornden complained of the new poetic style in a letter to a friend. Speaking of poetry, he wrote:

> In vain have some Men of late (Transformers of every Thing) consulted upon her Reformation, and endeavoured to abstract her to *Metaphysical* ideas, and *Scholastical* Quiddities, denuding her of her own Habits, and those Ornaments with which she hath amused the whole World some Thousand Years.

Drummond, Dryden, and Johnson, all spokesmen for a classical stylistic tradition, censure Donne and similar poets for inadequate decorum and inappropriate diction. "The metaphysics," for these critics, designates a vocabulary employed by Donne in poetic contexts where such a vocabulary is out of place. Such critics, even when as perceptive and profoundly intelligent as Dryden and Johnson, are incapable, because of temperament and training, of responding relevantly to an art which, like Donne's, habitually breaks through the established limits of decorum, even of genre, and employs "the metaphysics," for example, not for its own sake but as a means of contemplating the mysteries of passionate engagement. The technical language of philosophy which aroused the disapproval of Drummond and Dryden is present in Donne's lyrics neither because of affectation nor because of any abstract interest in metaphysics per se, but simply because it enables the poet to understand the nature of his experience as more than either a physical impulse or a social convention.

Without sharing the disapproval expressed by the classicist critics, many modern readers have failed to recognize just how apt the term metaphysical is as applied to Donne. Grierson, though ultimately justifying the term, notes that the work of Donne and his contemporaries is not "Metaphysical Poetry, in the full sense of the term," poetry which, "like that of the *Divina Commedia*, the *De Natura Rerum*, perhaps Goethe's *Faust*, has been inspired by a philosophical conception of the universe and the role assigned to the human spirit in the great drama of existence" ("Introduction" to *Metaphysical Lyrics and Poems of the Seventeenth Century,* 1921). And later critics have proposed that the term be replaced by some other—psychological, perhaps, or dialectical. Their proposals have not met with general acceptance, perhaps because most readers of Donne recognize, even if not consciously, that, as James Smith points out, his poetry views emotional experience in terms of its implicit metaphysical and theological mysteries, "problems either deriving from, or closely resembling in the nature of their difficulty, the problem of the Many and the One" ("On Metaphysical Poetry," *Scrutiny*, 2, No. 3, 1933).

Metaphysical poetry is a great and fully typical manifestation of the Baroque style in literature, and like most Baroque literature it is marked by dramatic tension, contradiction, extravagance, and vigor. Donne, the greatest of the Metaphysical poets, led a life which displayed many of these qualities—though it would be, as we shall see, naive to posit too close and too literal a relationship between the life and the art which emerged from it.

John Donne was born in London in 1572, the son of a Catholic family which had suffered much for its adherence to the old religion. It was a family distinguished for both wit and piety; the poet's grandfather was the early Tudor writer John Heywood, and two of his uncles were Jesuits. Donne studied at Oxford and possibly also at Cambridge, but did not take a degree at either university, his religion preventing him from swearing the required oath of allegiance to the Protestant crown. By the early 1590s he was studying law at Lincoln's Inn in London, at the same time initiating an intensive study of theology in order to satisfy himself as to the opposed claims of Protestantism and

Catholicism. During this time, he was also absorbing a wide variety of experiences both intellectual and sensual. To the period of his young adulthood belong such varied utterances as many of the *Songs and Sonets*, the cynical *Paradoxes and Problemes* in prose, and the five *Satyres*, including *Satyre V*, with its serious religious perplexity. Before the composition of many of these works, however, Donne had already added significant foreign experiences to those of his student years in London. At some point in the early 1590s he may have spent some time in travel on the Continent; it is certain that he accompanied the Earl of Essex on the latter's expeditions against Cadiz in 1596 and the Azores in 1597. These naval exploits are referred to in the poet's *Epigrams* and in "The Storme" and "The Calme," the earliest of his *Verse Letters*. They seem also to have left their mark on *Satyre V*. In 1598 Donne became secretary to Sir Thomas Egerton, Lord Keeper of the Great Seal, by which time he had probably at least nominally become an Anglican. In 1601 he fell in love with Anne More, niece of Sir Thomas and daughter of Sir George More, Chancellor of the Garter. Donne's clandestine marriage to Anne led immediately to his dismissal from his post, imprisonment for a short time, and the complete destruction of his prospects for a brilliant career in the public service. Donne's marriage was, as his first biographer Izaak Walton observes, the crucial episode of his life, and it marks the close of his first period of artistic creation.

That first period, to which belong many of the *Songs and Sonets*, the *Satyres*, the *Epigrams*, most of the *Elegies*, the earlier *Verse Letters*, and the youthful prose, has been much misunderstood by posterity. The attitudes expressed in these works, ranging from exuberant lustfulness to exquisite tenderness, from all-encompassing cynicism to profound attempts at religious commitment, have led some readers to be so incautious as to attempt to reconstruct Donne's inner life from the texts themselves, positing the story of a young libertine reclaimed for virtue and sobriety by the love of a good woman. Others, daunted perhaps by the unavailability of any certain evidence for dating most of the work exactly, have seen Donne as a young man of wildly fluctuating moods, gifted with the ability to find nearly perfect expression for each fleeting personal disposition. Both approaches to the early Donne are essentially unhistorical, depending as they do on an unexamined post-Romantic assumption about the nature of art. Donne, like any Renaissance or Baroque poet, is first of all a craftsman, concerned with making a poem rather than with laying bare his personal attitudes. This is not to say that Donne's love poems by definition have nothing to do with his personal experience; on the contrary, such poems as "The Good-Morrow," "Breake of Day," "The Canonization," and "A Valediction: Forbidding Mourning" may well have been inspired by the poet's consuming love for Anne More (my own private suspicion is that they were). The point is rather that the extreme sophistication of Donne's artistic method and of his whole conception of art makes it impossible for anyone to be sure. The materials of his life went into his poetry, but those materials were arranged and transfigured into the finally impersonal substance of art.

The point is worth remembering in approaching such poems as the *Elegies* and the *Satyres*, poems which, by their very adherence to specific genres, imply a particular persona as speaker. The coarse, savage protagonist of the *Satyres* is largely decreed by the Elizabethan conception of the genre of satire, and the brutal rake who appears as the speaker in *Elegies I, IV*, and *VII*, though he may owe a little to the personal experience of young John Donne, owes far more to the poet's model in Ovid's *Amores* and the poet's reading in the French *libertin* thinkers of the late sixteenth century. The *Elegies*, like the *Songs and Sonets*, try on different attitudes for size. We cannot say which attitudes are those of the "real" John Donne and which are poses, for in a sense none of them are and all of them are. Both groups of poems center around the mystery of sexual love, and, in the exposition of that mystery, even the most radically opposed conceptions can claim validity. Paradox, in Donne's love poetry as in his devotional poetry, is not a mere device of rhetoric; it is an absolutely essential instrument of vision, expressing as it does the recognition that truths of experience are balanced by equal and opposite truths of experience.

From the time of his marriage until 1615, the year of

his ordination into the Anglican church, Donne's life was one of desperation and penury. Denied the worldly advancement that both his gifts and his ambitions indicated as natural, he and his growing family were obliged to subsist on the charity of friends and the sporadic generosity of noble patrons. During the latter part of this period the poet found some employment as a religious controversialist. *Pseudo-Martyr*, a tract urging English Catholics to take the oath of allegiance, was published in 1610, and in 1611 appeared *Ignatius His Conclave*, a witty and satirical attack on the Jesuits which is also interesting for the light it casts on Donne's attitude toward the new science. One of the most interesting of his prose works, however, did not see print until 1646. *Biathanatos*, "a declaration of that paradox . . . that self-homicide is not so naturally a sin that it may never be otherwise," is a grimmer manifestation of the sportive love for paradox which dominated the youthful poetry and prose. Here it suggests the despair which at times haunted Donne during his years of struggle.

Whatever the quality of his spiritual depression during this time, Donne's poetic creativity remained at a high peak. Scholars have often associated Donne's years of penury primarily with the *Verse Letters*, generally rather frigid exercises in compliment addressed to friends and noble patronesses (exercises which are often redeemed by flashes of brilliant wit or surprising tenderness). Modern studies, however, have made us aware of the probability that a good many of the *Songs and Sonets* were composed after 1601 and of the virtual certainty that most of the great *Holy Sonnets* were written between 1609 and 1611. Furthermore, the "Anniversaries," Donne's most ambitious poems, were published in 1611 and 1612.

The "Anniversaries" were the product of Donne's relationship with the wealthy and prominent Sir Robert Drury. The origins of Donne's acquaintance with Drury are not known, but when the latter's only daughter Elizabeth died in 1610 at the age of fourteen, Donne responded with "The First Anniversarie" and "A Funerall Elegie," followed a year later by "The Second Anniversarie." The length, complexity, and extravagance of these poems have elicited a good deal of confusion and some hostility from Donne's readers, who have found a disturbing lack of proportion between the poems' ostensible subject and the poet's treatment of it. Some readers have been troubled further by Donne's apparent motive in writing: although his father-in-law had finally, in 1609, paid Anne's dowry, the poet was still in need of a patron who might be flattered into generosity. Such an objection is both narrow and anachronistic, given the Renaissance traditions of compliment and the facts of artistic creation itself. Elizabeth Drury became for Donne the "occasion" of serious contemplation and high artistic expression, and his personal motives or their absence are equally irrelevant to the merits of the poems themselves—merits which give them a place among the greatest of Baroque literary achievements. In the chronology of Donne's works they also occupy an important place; as Louis L. Martz has demonstrated, they foreshadow in their strict meditative structure the great religious poetry and prose of Donne's final period.

That final period may be seen as beginning in 1615, with Donne's ordination. The suggestion that he enter the clergy of the Church of England had been made to Donne years before by Bishop Morton, but he had resisted the idea for a long time—possibly because the memory of youthful sins made him feel unworthy of the cloth; possibly because he was reluctant to give up the hopes, so stubbornly held, of secular preferment, replacing those hopes with the humble reality of a clergyman's role; possibly because of lingering doubts as to the relative truths of the Anglican and Roman churches. Whatever the case, James I, who had commissioned *Pseudo-Martyr*, was convinced that the brilliant polemicist belonged in the Anglican church, and he saw to it that every other avenue of advancement was closed to him. In 1615 Donne was ordained. In 1617 Anne Donne died.

The final period of Donne's life was taken up almost wholly by "things divine." Almost from the time of his ordination he was recognized as one of the greatest of English preachers, and the sermons later collected in three folio volumes constitute, with the *Devotions upon Emergent Occasions* of 1624, his principal claim to a position as one of the major prose artists of seventeenth-century England. He continued to write some poetry as well. The three most private of the *Holy Sonnets*—one of them mourning the death of the poet's wife, another questioning the identity of the true church—were composed after 1617, and the three great "Hymnes" were composed between 1619 and 1631, the year of Donne's death. Some incidental epistolary verse also belongs to this period, but the poet seems to have felt that his ecclesiastical position made the practice of verse a triviality. Particularly was this true after 1621, the year in which he was named Dean of St. Paul's Cathedral, a post which he exercised with extraordinary devotion and fervor. Nevertheless, the two last "Hymnes" show neither a slackening of his poetic power nor any actual change in his poetic attitudes. Here, as in the amorous poems and the *Holy Sonnets*, his poetic gift is in the service of a tortuous and passionate quest through paradox and contradiction; a quest which has as its object the same principle of transcendence and permanence which the young poet had sought beneath the multiple disguises of physical passion.

His major prose works, as well, reveal the final unity of temperament behind the apparent vivid contrasts of Donne's personality. The *Devotions upon Emergent Occasions* are formal meditations, examples of those strenuous spiritual exercises, Catholic in origin, which exerted a powerful influence on Donne and other Baroque poets. Meditation, with its advocacy, for devotional purposes, of a combination of imaginative concreteness, intellectual analysis, and dramatic immediacy, constitutes, as Martz has observed, a kind of program for achieving that quality of sensibility which Eliot labels "undissociated." The *Devotions*, indeed, exercise upon their readers, regardless of their specific religious beliefs, an effect very like that of Donne's poetry, and for similar reasons.

The emphases of Donne's religion indicate further links with the temperament of the love poet. Distinguished among the religious writings of an age of virulent controversy by virtue of their relative breadth of view and moderation of tone, their concentration on the essentials of Christianity to the virtual exclusion of controversial points of doctrine, Donne's *Sermons* breathe a spirit of charity which serves to remind us that this is the work of a man always obsessed, one way or another, with love. Sometimes, as in the *Devotions,* charity takes the form of a profound investigation of the theme of human brotherhood, as in the often-quoted meditation on the bell tolling the death of a fellow-human being, or in the speculation on the symbolic function of society, or in the following passage, wherein the narrator's sickness approaches its crisis:

> How many are sicker (perchance) than I, and laid on their wofull straw at home (if that corner be a home) and have no more hope of helpe, though they die, than of preferment, though they live? Nor doe no more expect to see a *Phisician* then, than to bee an *Officer* after; of whome, the first that takes knowledge, is the *Sexten* that buries them; who buries them in *oblivion* too? For they doe but fill up the number of the dead in the Bill, but we shall never heare their *Names,* till wee reade them in the Booke of life, with our owne. How many are sicker (perchance) than I, and thrown into *Hospitals,* where, (as a fish left upon the Sand, must stay the tide) they must stay the *Phisicians* houre of visiting, and then can bee but *visited?* How many are sicker (perchaunce) than all wee, and have not this *Hospitall* to cover them, not this straw, to lie in, to die in, but have their *Grave-stone* under them, and breathe out their soules in the eares, and in the eies of passengers, harder than their bed, the flint of the street? That taste of no part of our *Phisick,* but a *sparing dyet;* to whom ordinary porridge would bee *Julip* enough, the refuse of our servants, *Bezar* enough, and the off-scouring of our Kitchen tables *Cordiall* enough. O my *soule,* when thou art not enough awake, to blesse thy *God* enough for his plentifull mercy, in affoording thee many *Helpers,* remember how many lacke them, and helpe them to them, or to those other things, which they lacke as much as them.

The *Sermons,* like the *Devotions,* are obsessed by death and dissolution, and Donne's imagination falls readily into an almost masochistic evocation of the details of bodily disintegration. Nevertheless, his writings seldom show any of that fervent contempt for the body which crops up so frequently among other Christian writers. For the man who had written "The Extasie," the body remains always a temple of the Holy Ghost, and the reality of decay is constantly countered in the *Sermons* by the promise of bodily resurrection, a promise on the belief in which Donne's whole faith rests. In the words of the preacher as in the words of the poet, we encounter an insistence on the unity of the human person, a unity which, even when it is realized beyond time and change, in union with God, will still consist of both soul and body.

Seized by his final illness in 1631, Donne made his death one of exemplary piety. After his last appearance in the pulpit, he was declared, according to Walton, to have "preached his own funeral sermon." On his deathbed he donned his shroud and had his portrait painted in that melancholy garment, keeping the finished portrait by his bedside for his contemplation. A few days later he died, expressing to the end his eagerness to meet death.

There is something dramatic, indeed something theatrical, about Donne's death as reported by Walton, and not all of Donne's modern readers may share Walton's un-equivocal admiration for such a death, suspecting in it both the manipulation of a showman and the self-conscious display of an egotist. But caution is required of the modern reader if he would understand either Donne's life or his art. "This is my playes last scene, here heavens appoint/My pilgrimages last mile," he had written years before in the *Holy Sonnets*, and there and elsewhere he had rehearsed in his meditative imagination the scene which in 1631 he was concerned with playing as well as possible. The con-ception of life as theatre and of death as the final scene of a play is important, for it helps to define not only Donne but also the age in which he lived and created. For Donne as for Shakespeare (in whose work the metaphor of life as theatre is equally obsessive) the theatre-metaphor op-erates not as a term for unreality and illusion, but rather as a term for reality insofar as our earthly existence partici-pates in reality. If life is a play, an "insubstantial pageant," as Shakespeare phrases it, then the play in turn is life, and the theatrical performance, although only a shadowy simu-lacrum of an ineffable and transcendent reality, is no more shadowy, no less "real," than the acts which we perform, as we think, offstage. In making of his death a theatrical performance, Donne was, we may conjecture, both sup-plying a good example to the Christian observers who would survive him and enabling himself to experience the reality of his own death in the fullest sense possible.

The concept of life as theatre is relevant not only to the last scene of Donne's life but also to the art which it had been the major business of that life to create. The concept brings us back once again to the qualities of paradox and irony, of witty juxtaposition and dramatic projection, which characterize Donne's poetry and prose from the beginning to the end. All art, in the great age of western European drama, had something of the nature of a play and, beyond that, something of the nature of "play" itself—that curious activity which, embracing levity, make-believe, and contest, largely defines our humanity. Donne once wrote in a letter to a friend, "I did best when I had least truth for my subjects," and the statement is neither a witty piece of cynicism nor a rejection of artistic responsibility. It is rather an implicit recognition that the artist arrives at his truth not by documenting his private experiences but by transcending them, by creating his own personality as an actor on the stage of the enlivened imagination.

It is no accident that Donne's poetry has had a profound influence on such a large number of the finest poets in twentieth-century England and America—Yeats, Eliot, Auden, and many others. In his work they have found a ratification of the claims of the imagination and of the autonomy of art, a recognition of the paradoxical truth that poetry engages life most significantly when it stands at a certain ironic distance from it and that the emotions find their deepest expression when filtered through the inquiring intellect. In an age largely ignorant of art and hostile to it, they have learned from a poet dead for three centuries much that has helped them to be modern artists. Donne's "modernity" finally rests not in any fancied confirmation which he provides for our own presuppositions but in the fact that he teaches us how to question those presuppositions and how to turn our questioning into significant and fully realized expression.

SELECTED
BIBLIOGRAPHY

IMPORTANT MODERN EDITIONS OF DONNE:

Poetical Works. H. J. C. Grierson (ed.). 2 vols., Oxford, 1912.
The Songs and Sonets. T. Redpath (ed.). London, 1956.
The Elegies and the Songs and Sonets. H. Gardner (ed.). Oxford, 1965.
The Divine Poems. H. Gardner (ed.). Oxford, 1952.
The Anniversaries. F. Manley (ed.). Baltimore, Md., 1963.
Devotions upon Emergent Occasions. J. Sparrow (ed.). Cambridge, 1923.
The Sermons. G. R. Potter and E. M. Simpson (eds.). 10 vols., Berkeley, Calif., 1953–62.

SCHOLARSHIP AND CRITICISM:

A. Alvarez. *The School of Donne.* New York, 1961.
R. C. Bald. *Donne's Influence in English Literature.* Morpeth, Eng., 1932.
———. *Donne and the Drurys.* Cambridge, 1959.
J. Bennett. *Four Metaphysical Poets.* Cambridge, 1934.
L. I. Bredvold. "The Naturalism of Donne in Relation to Some Renaissance Traditions," *Journal of English and Germanic Philology,* XXII (1923).
———. "The Religious Thought of Donne in Relation to Medieval and Later Traditions," *Studies in Shakespeare, Milton, and Donne.* University of Michigan Publications, New York, 1925.
C. Brooks. *Modern Poetry and the Tradition.* Chapel Hill, N.C., 1939.
———. *The Well Wrought Urn.* New York, 1947.
C. M. Coffin. *John Donne and the New Philosophy.* New York, 1937.
R. Colie. *Paradoxia Epidemica.* Princeton, 1966.

H. C. Combs and Z. R. Sullens. *A Concordance to the English Poetry of John Donne*. Chicago, Ill., 1940.

T. S. Eliot. "The Metaphysical Poets," *Selected Essays*. New York, 1950.

E. Gosse. *The Life and Letters of John Donne*. 2 vols., London and New York, 1899.

K. W. Gransden. *John Donne*. London, 1954.

D. L. Guss. *John Donne, Petrarchist*. Detroit, Mich., 1966.

E. Hardy. *John Donne: a spirit in conflict*. London, 1942.

V. H. Harris. *All Coherence Gone*. Chicago, Ill., 1949.

M. Y. Hughes. "The Lineage of *The Extasie*," *Modern Language Review*, XXVII (1932).

———. "Kidnapping Donne," *Essays in Criticism. Second Series*, Berkeley, Calif., and Cambridge, 1934.

C. Hunt. *Donne's Poetry*. New Haven, Conn., 1954.

I. Husain. *The Dogmatic and Mystical Theology of John Donne*. New York, 1938.

S. Johnson. "Abraham Cowley," *The Lives of the Poets*. London, 1779–81.

F. Kermode. *John Donne*. London, 1957.

A. Kernan. *The Cankered Muse*. New Haven, Conn., 1959.

G. Keynes. *A Bibliography of Dr. John Donne*. 2nd ed., Cambridge, 1932.

E. LeComte. *Grace to a Witty Sinner: A Life of Donne*. New York, 1965.

P. Legouis. *Donne the Craftsman*. Paris, 1928.

J. B. Leishman. *The Metaphysical Poets*. Oxford, 1934.

———. *The Monarch of Wit*. London, 1951.

D. Louthan. *The Poetry of John Donne*. New York, 1951.

L. L. Martz. *The Poetry of Meditation*. Rev. ed., New Haven, Conn., 1962.

J. A. Mazzeo. *Renaissance and Seventeenth-Century Studies*. New York, 1964.

W. F. Mitchell. *English Pulpit Oratory from Andrewes to Tillotson*. London, 1932.

M. F. Moloney. *John Donne: His Flight from Mediaevalism*. Urbana, Ill., 1944.

M. H. Nicolson. *The Breaking of the Circle*. Rev. ed., New York, 1960.

M. Praz. *Secentismo e marinismo in Inghilterra*. Florence, 1925.

K. Raine. "John Donne and the Baroque Doubt," *Horizon* (June 1945).

M. P. Ramsay. *Les Doctrines médiévales chez Donne*. Rev. ed., Paris, 1924.

M. A. Rugoff. *Donne's Imagery*. New York, 1939.

Seventeenth-Century Studies Presented to Sir Herbert Grierson. Oxford, 1938.

R. L. Sharp. *From Donne to Dryden: the Revolt against Metaphysical Poetry.* Chapel Hill, N.C., 1940.

E. M. Simpson. *A Study of the Prose Works of John Donne* Rev. ed., Oxford, 1948.

T. Spencer (ed.). *A Garland for John Donne.* Cambridge, Mass., 1932.

A. Stein. *John Donne's Lyrics.* Minneapolis, Minn., 1962.

R. Tuve. *Elizabethan and Metaphysical Imagery.* Chicago, Ill., 1947.

L. Unger. *Donne's Poetry and Modern Criticism.* New York, 1950.

I. Walton. *Life of Dr. John Donne,* in S. B. Carter (ed.), *Lives.* London, 1951. (Walton's *Life of Donne* was published in 1640 and, in an enlarged form, in 1658.)

J. Webber. *Contrary Music.* Madison, Wis., 1963.

H. C. White. *The Metaphysical Poets.* New York, 1936.

G. Williamson. *The Donne Tradition.* Cambridge, Mass., 1930

THE BASIC TEXT in this volume, with a number of additions, omissions, and changes, is that of the *Complete Poetry and Selected Prose* edited by John Hayward (London: Nonesuch Press, 1929), which is based on that of the *Poetical Works of John Donne* edited by H. J. C. Grierson (Oxford: Clarendon Press, 1912). The exceptions from the Hayward edition are as follows:

Some rearrangement in Hayward's order has been made throughout and prefatory material from seventeenth-century editions has been added to the "Songs and Sonets."

The texts of "The First Anniversarie," "A Funerall Elegie," and "The Second Anniversarie" are those established by Frank Manley in his edition of *The Anniversaries* (Baltimore, Md.: Johns Hopkins Press, 1963).

The "Holy Sonnets" appear in the order proposed by Helen Gardner in her edition of the *Divine Poems* (Oxford: Clarendon Press, 1952).

"Problems V and VIII," the "Epistle Dedicatorie" to the *Devotions upon Emergent Occasions,* and the "Expostulation" and "Prayer" of the nineteenth "Meditation" (thereby giving the whole of one devotion) have been added to the prose.

The three complete sermons which have been added, "Preached at Lincolns Inne," "Preached at White-hall, March 8, 1621," and "Deaths Duell," are from the definitive modern edition, *Sermons of John Donne* edited by G. R. Potter and E. M. Simpson, 10 vols. (Berkeley, Calif.: University of California Press, 1953–62).

JOHN DONNE
Poetry and Prose

Songs and Sonets

DONNE'S LOVE LYRICS appeared scattered at random throughout the first edition (1633) of his poems. The next edition (1635) grouped them together under the title *Songs and Sonets*, a designation which has been retained in almost all subsequent editions. The 1635 editors employed the term "sonet" in the very general sense common in the Renaissance, meaning by it nothing more precise than "short poem": The *Songs and Sonets* contain no "sonnets" in the accepted modern sense.

Donne's love poems gave him a reputation in his own time, and it is on them, together with his *Divine Poems*, that his popularity with modern readers mainly rests. During the poet's lifetime the love poems, like most of his poetry, circulated only in manuscript form. Since they were not printed until after his death, the problem of dating them with any accuracy is effectively insoluble. His contemporary Ben Jonson remarked that Donne had "written all his best pieces ere he was twenty-five years old," an assertion which would establish 1598 as a terminal date for his lyric work. Internal evidence, however, proves many of the *Songs and Sonets* to be of later composition, and Jonson's estimate of what Donne's "best pieces" are is, in any case, demonstrably different from that of posterity. Most modern scholars would hold that the *Songs and Sonets* were written over a period extending from the early 1590s to 1614, possibly even to 1617. There has been a tendency among literary historians to attribute the lighter and more cynical pieces to the 1590s and the more serious love poems to a later period, but one cannot do so with complete confidence: Donne was, from beginning to end, remarkable for the variety and complexity of his poetic personality.

The *Songs and Sonets* have elicited much critical attention. They supplied many of the examples on which Dr. Johnson, in the eighteenth century, based his discussion of "metaphysical poetry," and they helped provide T. S. Eliot, in 1921, with his conception of the "unified sensibility," influential in the development of modern poetry.

Among the works listed in the Selected Bibliography, the studies by C. Hunt, J. B. Leishman, and A. Stein may be singled out as particularly useful for the study of the *Songs and Sonets* (Stein's work is devoted exclusively to these poems). T. Redpath's copiously annotated edition of the *Songs and Sonets* is subject to some question in its textual and interpretive decisions, but it focuses attention on many crucial passages. H. Gardner's recent edition of *The Elegies and the Songs and Sonets* contains, in addition to valuable annotations, a number of verbal and formal emendations, many of which will, if accepted, alter significantly the reading of the poems.

The Printer to the Understanders

For this time I must speake only to you: at another, *Readers* may perchance serve my turne; and I thinke this a way very free from exception, in hope that very few will have a minde to confesse themselves ignorant.

The Printer to the Understanders: This prefatory note appeared in the first edition of Donne's poems, published posthumously in 1633. The use of the term *understanders* indicates Donne's reputation for recondite wit.

If you looke for an Epistle, as you have before ordinary publications, I am sory that I must deceive you; but you will not lay it to my charge, when you shall consider that this is not ordinary, for if I should say it were the best in this kinde, that ever this Kingdome hath yet seene; he that would doubt of it must goe out of the Kingdome to enforme himselfe, for the best judgments, within it, take it for granted.

You may imagine (if it please you) that I could endeare it unto you, by saying, that importunity drew it on; that had it not beene presented here, it would have come to us from beyond the Seas; (which perhaps is true enough), That my charge and paines in procuring of it hath beene such, and such. I could adde hereto, a promise of more correctnesse, or enlargement in the next Edition, if you shall in the meane time content you with this. But these things are so common, as that I should profane this Peece by applying them to it; A Peece which who so takes not as he findes it, in what manner soever, he is unworthy of it, sith a scattered limbe of this Author, hath more amiablenesse in it, in the eye of a discerner, than a whole body of some other; Or (to expresse him best by himselfe),

> —A hand, or eye,
> By Hilyard drawne, is worth a history
> By a worse Painter made;—

In the
Storme

If any man (thinking I speake this to enflame him for the vent of the Impression) be of another opinion, I shall as willingly spare his money as his judgement. I cannot lose so much by him as hee will by himselfe. For I shall satisfie my selfe with the conscience of well doing, in making so much good common.

Howsoever it may appeare to you, it shall suffice mee to enforme you, that it hath the best warrant that can bee, publique authority, and private friends.

There is one thing more wherein I will make you of my counsell, and that is, That whereas it hath pleased some, who had studyed and did admire him, to offer to the memory of the Author, not long after his decease, I have thought I should do you service in presenting them unto you now; onely whereas, had I placed them in the beginning, they might have serv'd for so many Encomiums of the Author (as is usuall in other workes, where perhaps there is need of it, to prepare men to digest such stuffe as follows after), you shall here finde them in the end, for whosoever reades the rest so farre, shall perceive that there is no occasion to use them to that purpose; yet there they are, as an attestation for their sakes that knew not so much before, to let them see how much honour was attributed to this worthy man, by those that are capable to give it. *Farewell.*   [1633]

HEXASTICHON BIBLIOPOLAE

I see in his last preach'd, and printed Booke,
His Picture in a sheet; in *Pauls* I looke,
And see his Statue in a sheete of stone,
And sure his body in the grave hath one:
Those sheetes present him dead, these if you buy,
You have him living to Eternity.

Jo[hn] Mar[riot]
[1633]

HEXASTICHON AD BIBLIOPOLAM

Incerti

In thy Impression of Donnes *Poems rare,*
For his Eternitie thou hast ta'ne care:
'Twas well, and pious; And for ever may
He live: Yet shew I thee a better way;
Print but his Sermons, and if those we buy,
He, We, and Thou shall live t'Eternity.

[1635]

Hexastichon Bibliopolae: six-lined stanza of the bookseller (Greek). John Marriot was the publisher of the 1633 edition. The lines refer to Donne's last sermon, *Death's Duell,* and to its frontispiece, a representation of the poet in his shroud, as he is also represented in his statue in St. Paul's Cathedral.

Hexastichon ad Bibliopolam: six-lined stanza to the bookseller. These anonymous lines were added in the 1635 edition.

THE GOOD-MORROW

I wonder by my troth, what thou, and I
Did, till we lov'd? were we not wean'd till then?
But suck'd on countrey pleasures, childishly?
Or snorted we in the seaven sleepers den?
T'was so; But this, all pleasures fancies bee.
If ever any beauty I did see,
Which I desir'd, and got, t'was but a dreame of thee.

And now good morrow to our waking soules,
Which watch not one another out of feare;
For love, all love of other sights controules,
And makes one little roome, an every where.   10
Let sea-discoverers to new worlds have gone,
Let Maps to other, worlds on worlds have showne,
Let us possesse one world, each hath one, and is one.

My face in thine eye, thine in mine appeares,
And true plaine hearts doe in the faces rest,
Where can we finde two better hemispheares
Without sharpe North, without declining West?
What ever dyes, was not mixt equally;
If our two loves be one, or, thou and I   20
Love so alike, that none doe slacken, none can die

SONG

Goe, and catche a falling starre,
  Get with child a mandrake roote,
Tell me, where all past yeares are,

l.4 *seaven sleepers den:* According to legend, seven Christian youths, fleeing persecution by the emperor Decius in the third century, hid in a cave. There they fell into a miraculous sleep from which they awakened two centuries later.

l.5 *But:* except.

l.14 *one:* Gardner emends to our.

ll.19–21 *What . . . die:* Scholastic philosophy held that corruption cannot occur in simple substances or in substances composed of elements mixed in perfect proportion.

l.2 *mandrake roote:* a fork-shaped root, whose resemblance to the human body inspired numerous superstitions.

Or who cleft the Divels foot,
Teach me to heare Mermaides singing,
Or to keep off envies stinging,
      And finde
      What winde
Serves to advance an honest minde.

If thou beest borne to strange sights,   10
  Things invisible to see,
Ride ten thousand daies and nights,
  Till age snow white haires on thee,
Thou, when thou retorn'st, wilt tell mee
All strange wonders that befell thee,
      And sweare
      No where
Lives a woman true, and faire.

If thou findst one, let mee know,
  Such a Pilgrimage were sweet;   20
Yet doe not, I would not goe,
  Though at next doore wee might meet,
Though shee were true, when you met her,
And last, till you write your letter,
      Yet shee
      Will bee
False, ere I come, to two, or three.

WOMANS CONSTANCY

Now thou hast lov'd me one whole day,
To morrow when thou leav'st, what wilt thou say?
Wilt thou then Antedate some new made vow?
      Or say that now
We are not just those persons, which we were?
Or, that oathes made in reverentiall feare
Of Love, and his wrath, any may forsweare?
Or, as true deaths, true maryages untie,
So lovers contracts, images of those,
Binde but till sleep, deaths image, them unloose?   10
      Or, your owne end to Justifie,

[handwritten marginalia: Someone who worships the moon Diana - women + insanity]

For having purpos'd change, and falsehood; you
   Can have no way but falsehood to be true?
Vaine lunatique, against these scapes I could
       Dispute, and conquer, if I would,
        Which I abstaine to doe,
For by to morrow, I may thinke so too.

[handwritten marginalia: ambiguous - both men's women can be inconstant]

THE UNDERTAKING

I have done one braver thing
   Than all the *Worthies* did,
And yet a braver thence doth spring,
   Which is, to keepe that hid.

It were but madnes now t'impart
   The skill of specular stone,
When he which can have learn'd the art
   To cut it, can finde none.

So, if I now should utter this,
   Others (because no more
Such stuffe to worke upon, there is,)
   Would love but as before.

But he who lovelinesse within
   Hath found, all outward loathes,
For he who colour loves, and skinne,
   Loves but their oldest clothes.

If, as I have, you also doe
   Vertue'attir'd in woman see,

10

l.1 braver: more handsome, or splendid.
l.2 Worthies: The Nine Worthies—three Jews, three Pagans, and three Christians—were, in medieval tradition, the supreme heroes of antiquity.
ll.6-8 skill . . . none: a crux in Donne criticism. The most likely explanation is given by Redpath, who, following Don Cameron Allen, contends that "specular stone" refers to *old selenite,* a stone used in ancient times for glazing. It was believed in Donne's time that this stone could no longer be found and that the secret of cutting it into thin sheets had been lost.

And dare love that, and say so too,
　　And forget the Hee and Shee;　　　　　　　　　20

And if this love, though placed so,
　　From prophane men you hide,
Which will no faith on this bestow,
　　Or, if they doe, deride:

Then you have done a braver thing
　　Than all the *Worthies* did;
And a braver thence will spring,
　　Which is, to keepe that hid.

THE SUNNE RISING

　　　Busie old foole, unruly Sunne,
　　　　Why dost thou thus,
Through windowes, and through curtaines call on us?
Must to thy motions lovers seasons run?
　　　　Sawcy pedantique wretch, goe chide
　　　　Late schoole boyes and sowre prentices,
　　Goe tell Court-huntsmen, that the King will ride,
　　Call countrey ants to harvest offices;
Love, all alike, no season knowes, nor clyme,
Nor houres, dayes, moneths, which are the rags of
time.　　　　　　　　　　　　　　　　　　10

　　　Thy beames, so reverend, and strong
　　　　Why shouldst thou thinke?
I could eclipse and cloud them with a winke,
But that I would not lose her sight so long:
　　　　If her eyes have not blinded thine,
　　　　Looke, and to morrow late, tell mee,
　　Whether both the'India's of spice and Myne
　　Be where thou leftst them, or lie here with mee.
Aske for those Kings whom thou saw'st yesterday,
And thou shalt heare, All here in one bed lay.　　　20

l.7 the . . . ride: James I was an enthusiastic hunter. This line probably dates the poem as 1603 or later, since James became king in
1603.
l.17 both . . . 'India's: the East Indies and the West Indies.

She'is all States, and all Princes, I,
    Nothing else is.
Princes doe but play us; compar'd to this,
All honor's mimique; All wealth alchimie.
    Thou sunne art halfe as happy'as wee,
    In that the world's contracted thus;
  Thine age askes ease, and since thy duties bee
  To warme the world, that's done in warming us.
Shine here to us, and thou art every where;
This bed thy center is, these walls, thy spheare.   30

THE INDIFFERENT

I can love both faire and browne,
Her whom abundance melts, and her whom want be-
  traies,
Her who loves lonenesse best, and her who maskes and
  plaies,
Her whom the country form'd, and whom the town,
Her who beleeves, and her who tries,
Her who still weepes with spungie eyes,
And her who is dry corke, and never cries;
I can love her, and her, and you and you,
I can love any, so she be not true.

Will no other vice content you?   10
Will it not serve your turn to do, as did your mothers?
Or have you all old vices spent, and now would finde
  out others?
Or doth a feare, that men are true, torment you?
Oh we are not, be not you so,
Let mee, and doe you, twenty know.

l.24 alchimie: Alchemy, in this case, implies counterfeit.
l.30 This . . . spheare: The reference is to Ptolemaic astronomy, wherein
  the earth was conceived as the center of the universe, around which
  revolved the sun and the other planets, each embedded in its crystal-
  line sphere.

The Indifferent: Indifferent means, of course, all-embracing in taste.
l.5 tries: tests.

Rob mee, but binde me not, and let me goe.
Must I, who came to travaile thorow you,
Grow your fixt subject, because you are true?

Venus heard me sigh this song,
And by Loves sweetest Part, Variety, she swore,   20
She heard not this till now; and that it should be so no
  more.
She went, examin'd, and return'd ere long,
And said, alas, Some two or three
Poore Heretiques in love there bee,
Which thinke to stablish dangerous constancie.
But I have told them, since you will be true,
You shall be true to them, who'are false to you.

LOVES USURY

For every houre that thou wilt spare mee now,
    I will allow,
Usurious God of Love, twenty to thee,
When with my browne, my gray haires equall bee;
Till then, Love, let my body raigne, and let
Mee travell, sojourne, snatch, plot, have, forget,
Resume my last yeares relict: thinke that yet
    We'had never met.

Let mee thinke any rivalls letter mine,
    And at next nine   10
Keepe midnights promise; mistake by the way
The maid, and tell the Lady of that delay;
Onely let mee love none, no, not the sport;
From country grasse, to comfitures of Court,
Or cities quelque choses, let report
    My minde transport.

l.17 travaile: incorporates a pun on travel and travail, the latter word
meaning both sorrow and physical effort.
ll.26–27 since . . . you: ought probably to be taken as an internal quotation, reporting the words spoken by Venus to the heretical girls.

l.13 the sport: the physical pleasure of love.
l.15 quelque choses: dainties. In Renaissance thought, court, city, and
country represented the three divisions of society.

This bargaine's good; if when I'am old, I bee
    Inflam'd by thee,
If thine owne honour, or my shame, or paine,
Thou covet, most at that age thou shalt gaine.   20
Doe thy will then, then subject and degree,
And fruit of love, Love I submit to thee,
Spare mee till then, I'll beare it, though she bee
    One that loves mee.

THE CANONIZATION

For Godsake hold your tongue, and let me love,
  Or chide my palsie, or my gout,
My five gray haires, or ruin'd fortune flout,
  With wealth your state, your minde with Arts im-
    prove
    Take you a course, get you a place,
    Observe his honour, or his grace,
Or the Kings reall, or his stamped face
  Contemplate, what you will, approve,
  So you will let me love.

Alas, alas, who's injur'd by my love?   10
  What merchants ships have my sighs drown'd?
Who saies my teares have overflow'd his ground?
  When did my colds a forward spring remove?
    When did the heats which my veines fill
    Adde one more to the plaguie Bill?
Soldiers finde warres, and Lawyers finde out still
  Litigious men, which quarrels move,
  Though she and I do love.

Call us what you will, wee are made such by love;
Call her one, mee another flye,
We'are Tapers too, and at our owne cost die,   20
  And wee in us finde the'Eagle and the Dove.

l.5 *Take . . . course:* follow a career.
l.7 *Kings:* The reference to the king seems to date this poem as post-
    1603, see p. 10, note to line 7.
l.15 *Bill:* weekly list of those dead of the Plague.

The Phœnix ridle hath more wit   *— beginning of paradox*
  By us, we two being one, are it.   *indicate that the*
So to one neutrall thing both sexes fit,   *lovers will have*
  Wee dye and rise the same, and prove *some sort of*
  Mysterious by this love.   *immortality*

Wee can dye by it, if not live by love,
  And if unfit for tombes and hearse
Our legend bee, it will be fit for verse;   *→ one is*   30
  And if no peece of Chronicle wee prove,   *proving*
    We'll build in sonnets pretty roomes;   *it by writing*
    As well a well wrought urne becomes   *this*
The greatest ashes, as halfe-acre tombes,
  And by these hymnes, all shall approve
  Us *Canoniz'd* for Love: *— these verses*   *will be our record*
    to become a saint

And thus invoke us; You whom reverend love
  Made one anothers hermitage;
You, to whom love was peace, that now is rage;
  Who did the whole worlds soule contract, and
    drove   40
    Into the glasses of your eyes
    (So made such mirrors, and such spies,
That they did all to you epitomize,)
  Countries, Townes, Courts: Beg from above
  A patterne of your love!

who is your God?

---

ll.19–27 Call . . . love: Much in this stanza requires comment: the fly
is a conventional symbol of lust; the eagle and the dove symbolize
the masculine and the feminine; the phoenix is the mythical Arabian
bird which, unique in its existence, lives for a thousand years and
then immolates itself on a pyre, from the ashes of which a new
phoenix arises. The verb *die,* throughout the poem, carries the Renaissance colloquial meaning, to experience sexual climax.

ll.37–45 And . . . love: The entire stanza, after the words, "And thus
invoke us," is a quotation of the appeal which will be made by the
lovers of the future to the spirits of the ideal lovers, canonized for
love. In that appeal they will beg the saints of love to beseech a pat-
tern of ideal love from God. For the significance of "Countries,
Townes, Courts," see p. 12, note to line 15.

THE TRIPLE FOOLE

I am two fooles, I know,
For loving, and for saying so
  In whining Poëtry;
But where's that wiseman, that would not be I,
  If she would not deny?
Then as th'earths inward narrow crooked lanes
Do purge sea waters fretfull salt away,
  I thought, if I could draw my paines,
Through Rimes vexation, I should them allay.
Griefe brought to numbers cannot be so fierce,   10
For, he tames it, that fetters it in verse.

  But when I have done so,
Some man, his art and voice to show,
  Doth Set and sing my paine,
And, by delighting many, frees againe
  Griefe, which verse did restraine.
To Love, and Griefe tribute of Verse belongs,
But not of such as pleases when'tis read,
  Both are increased by such songs:
For both their triumphs so are published,
And I, which was two fooles, do so grow three;   20
Who are a little wise, the best fooles bee.

LOVERS INFINITENESSE

If yet I have not all thy love,
Deare, I shall never have it all,
I cannot breath one other sigh, to move,
Nor can intreat one other teare to fall,
And all my treasure, which should purchase thee,
Sighs, teares, and oathes, and letters I have spent.
Yet no more can be due to mee,
Than at the bargaine made was ment,
If then thy gift of love were partiall,

l.10 numbers: poetic meter.
l.14 Set: set to music.

That some to mee, some should to others fall,   10
   Deare, I shall never have Thee All.

Or if then thou gavest mee all,
All was but All, which thou hadst then;
But if in thy heart, since, there be or shall,
New love created bee, by other men,
Which have their stocks intire, and can in teares,
In sighs, in oathes, and letters outbid mee,
This new love may beget new feares,
For, this love was not vowed by thee.
And yet it was, thy gift being generall,   20
The ground, thy heart is mine, what ever shall
   Grow there, deare, I should have it all.

Yet I would not have all yet,
Hee that hath all can have no more,
And since my love doth every day admit
New growth, thou shouldst have new rewards in store;
Thou canst not every day give me thy heart,
If thou canst give it, then thou never gavest it:
Loves riddles are, that though thy heart depart,
It stayes at home, and thou with losing savest it: 30
But wee will have a way more liberall,
Than changing hearts, to joyne them, so wee shall
   Be one, and one anothers All.

SONG

Sweetest love, I do not goe,
   For wearinesse of thee,
Nor in hope the world can show
   A fitter Love for mee;
     But since that I
Must dye at last, 'tis best,
To use my selfe in jest
   Thus by fain'd deaths to dye;

Yesternight the Sunne went hence,
   And yet is here to day,   10

He hath no desire nor sense,
  Nor halfe so short a way·
    Then feare not mee,
But beleeve that I shall make
Speedier journeyes, since I take
  Mòre wings and spurres than hee.

O how feeble is mans power,
  That if good fortune fall,
Cannot adde another houre,
  Nor a lost houre recall!
    But come bad chance,
And wee joyne to'it our strength,
And wee teach it art and length,
  It selfe o'r us to'advance.

When thou sigh'st, thou sigh'st not winde,
  But sigh'st my soule away,
When thou weep'st, unkindly kinde,
  My lifes blood doth decay.
    It cannot bee
That thou lov'st mee, as thou say'st,
If in thine my life thou waste,
  That art the best of mee.

Let not thy divining heart
  Forethinke me any ill,
Destiny may take thy part,
  And may thy feares fulfill;
    But thinke that wee
Are but turn'd aside to sleepe;
They who one another keepe
  Alive, ne'r parted bee.

20

3〇

40

l.27 kinde: means both natural and affectionate. The phrase is thus
  highly ambiguous.
l.33 divining: prophetic.

THE LEGACIE

When I dyed last, and, Deare, I dye
  As often as from thee I goe,
  Though it be but an houre agoe,
And Lovers houres be full eternity,
I can remember yet, that I
  Something did say, and something did bestow;
Though I be dead, which sent mee, I should be
Mine owne executor and Legacie.

I heard mee say, Tell her anon,
  That my selfe, (that is you, not I,)
  Did kill me, and when I felt mee dye,
I bid mee send my heart, when I was gone,
But I alas could there finde none,
  When I had ripp'd me, 'and search'd where hearts
    did lye;
It kill'd mee againe, that I who still was true,
In life, in my last Will should cozen you.

Yet I found something like a heart,
  But colours it, and corners had,
  It was not good, it was not bad,
It was intire to none, and few had part.
As good as could be made by art
  It seem'd; and therefore for our losses sad,
I meant to send this heart in stead of mine,
But oh, no man could hold it, for twas thine.

A FEAVER

Oh doe not die, for I shall hate
  All women so, when thou art gone,
That thee I shall not celebrate,
  When I remember, thou wast one.

l.18 colours . . . had: In having colors and corners, the heart indicates
its falsity and imperfection. In Donne's time the circle was considered
the symbol of perfection.
l.20 It . . . part: It belonged to no one, and few shared in its affection.

But yet thou canst not die, I know,
    To leave this world behinde, is death,
But when thou from this world wilt goe,
    The whole world vapors with thy breath.

Or if, when thou, the worlds soule, goest,
    It stay, tis but thy carkasse then,
The fairest woman, but thy ghost,
    But corrupt wormes, the worthyest men.   10

O wrangling schooles, that search what fire
    Shall burne this world, had none the wit
Unto this knowledge to aspire,
    That this her feaver might be it?

And yet she cannot wast by this,
    Nor long beare this torturing wrong,
For such corruption needfull is
    To fuell such a feaver long.   20

These burning fits but meteors bee,
    Whose matter in thee is soone spent.
Thy beauty,'and all parts, which are thee,
    Are unchangeable firmament.

Yet t'was of my minde, seising thee,
    Though it in thee cannot persever.
For I had rather owner bee
    Of thee one houre, than all else ever.

AIRE AND ANGELS

Twice or thrice had I loved thee,
Before I knew thy face or name;
So in a voice, so in a shapeless flame,
Angells affect us oft, and worship'd bee;
    Still when, to where thou wert, I came,

l.13 schooles: schools of philosophy.

ll.1–4 Twice . . . bee: The speaker has loved the idea of his beloved,
  as imperfectly manifested in other women, before meeting her.

Some lovely glorious nothing I did see.
  But since my soule, whose child love is,
Takes limmes of flesh, and else could nothing doe,
  More subtile than the parent is,
Love must not be, but take a body too,   10
  And therefore what thou wert, and who,
      I bid Love aske, and now
That it assume thy body, I allow,
And fixe it selfe in thy lip, eye, and brow.

Whilst thus to ballast love, I thought,
And so more steddily to have gone,
With wares which would sinke admiration,
I saw, I had loves pinnace overfraught,
  Ev'ry thy haire for love to worke upon   20
Is much too much, some fitter must be sought;
  For, nor in nothing, nor in things
Extreme, and scatt'ring bright, can love inhere;
  Then as an Angell, face, and wings
Of aire, not pure as it, yet pure doth weare,
  So thy love may be my loves spheare;
      Just such disparitie
As is twixt Aire and Angells puritie,
Twixt womens love, and mens will ever bee.

BREAKE OF DAY

'Tis true, 'tis day; what though it be?
O wilt thou therefore rise from me?
Why should we rise, because 'tis light?
Did we lie downe, because 'twas night?
Love which in spight of darknesse brought us hether,
Should in despight of light keepe us together.

l.13 assume thy body: Just as the soul assumes a body, so must love, the
child of the soul. He first thinks of having his love assume the body
of the beloved.
ll.23–24 as . . . aire: In scholastic philosophy angels, who are bodiless
spirits, assume a body of air in order to become visible to men.

Breake of Day: The speaker in this poem is a woman.

Light hath no tongue, but is all eye;
If it could speake as well as spie,
This were the worst, that it could say,
That being well, I faine would stay,   10
And that I lov'd my heart and honor so,
That I would not from him, that had them, goe.

Must businesse thee from hence remove?
Oh, that's the worst disease of love,
The poore, the foule, the false, love can
Admit, but not the busied man.
He which hath businesse, and makes love, doth doe
Such wrong, as when a maryed man doth wooe.

THE ANNIVERSARIE

All Kings, and all their favorites,
    All glory of honors, beauties, wits,
The Sun it selfe, which makes times, as they passe,
Is elder by a yeare, now, than it was
When thou and I first one another saw:
All other things, to their destruction draw,
    Only our love hath no decay;
This, no to morrow hath, nor yesterday,
Running it never runs from us away,
But truly keepes his first, last, everlasting day.   10

    Two graves must hide thine and my coarse,
    If one might, death were no divorce.
Alas, as well as other Princes, wee,
(Who Prince enough in one another bee,)
Must leave at last in death, these eyes, and eares,
Oft fed with true oathes, and with sweet salt teares;
    But soules where nothing dwells but love
(All other thoughts being inmates) then shall prove
This, or a love increased there above,
When bodies to their graves, soules from their graves
    remove.   20

l.11 coarse: corpse.
l.18 inmates: as opposed to permanent dwellers.
l.18 prove: experience.

And then wee shall be throughly blest,
  But wee no more, than all the rest;
Here upon earth, we'are Kings, and none but wee
Can be such Kings, nor of such subjects bee.
Who is so safe as wee? where none can doe
Treason to us, except one of us two.

  True and false feares let us refraine,
Let us love nobly, and live, and adde againe
Yeares and yeares unto yeares, till we attaine
To write threescore: this is the second of our raigne.   30

A VALEDICTION: OF MY
NAME, IN THE WINDOW

I

My name engrav'd herein,
Doth contribute my firmnesse to this glasse,
  Which, ever since that charme, hath beene
  As hard, as that which grav'd it, was;
Thine eye will give it price enough, to mock
  The diamonds of either rock.

II

'Tis much that glasse should bee
As all confessing, and through-shine as I,
  'Tis more, that it shewes thee to thee,
  And cleare reflects thee to thine eye.   10
But all such rules, loves magique can undoe,
  Here you see me, and I am you.

III

As no one point, nor dash,
Which are but accessaries to this name,
  The showers and tempests can outwash,
  So shall all times finde mee the same;
You this intirenesse better may fulfill,
  Who have the patterne with you still.

l.6 diamonds . . . rock: diamonds from whatever source.
l.8 through-shine: transparent.
l.17 this intirenesse: this complete devotion.

IV

Or if too hard and deepe
This learning be, for a scratch'd name to teach,   20
  It, as a given deaths head keepe,
  Lovers mortalitie to preach,
Or thinke this ragged bony name to bee
    My ruinous Anatomie.

V

Then, as all my soules bee,
Emparadis'd in you, (in whom alone
  I understand, and grow and see,)
  The rafters of my body, bone
Being still with you, the Muscle, Sinew, and Veine,
    Which tile this house, will come againe.   30

VI

Till my returne, repaire
And recompact my scattered body so.
  As all the vertuous powers which are
  Fix'd in the starres, are said to flow
Into such characters, as graved bee
    When these starres have supremacie:

VII

So since this name was cut
When love and griefe their exaltation had,
  No doore 'gainst this names influence shut
  As much more loving, as more sad,   40
'Twill make thee; and thou shouldst, till I returne,
    Since I die daily, daily mourne.

l.21 given . . . keepe: a reference to the pious custom of presenting a *memento mori,* a ring or similar object with a carved death's head.
l.24 Anatomie: skeleton.
l.25 all . . . soules: Renaissance thought held that, in addition to the intellectual soul which distinguished him, man possessed a vegetative soul (like that of plants and animals) and a sensitive soul (like that of animals).
l.36 starres . . . supremacie: a reference to the influence of the stars on words written during their ascendancy.

VIII

When thy inconsiderate hand
Flings ope this casement, with my trembling name,
   To looke on one, whose wit or land,
   New battry to thy heart may frame.
Then thinke this name alive, and that thou thus
     In it offendst my Genius.

IX

And when thy melted maid,
Corrupted by thy Lover's gold, and page,   50
   His letter at thy pillow'hath laid,
   Disputed it, and tam'd thy rage,
And thou begin'st to thaw towards him, for this,
     May my name step in, and hide his.

X

And if this treason goe
To an overt act, and that thou write againe;
   In superscribing, this name flow
   Into thy fancy, from the pane.
So, in forgetting thou remembrest right,
     And unaware to mee shalt write.   60

XI

But glasse, and lines must bee,
No meanes our firme substantiall love to keepe;
   Neere death inflicts this lethargie,
   And this I murmure in my sleepe;
Impute this idle talke, to that I goe,
     For dying men talke often so.

TWICKNAM GARDEN

Blasted with sighs, and surrounded with teares,
   Hither I come to seeke the spring,
   And at mine eyes, and at mine eares,

l.48 Genius: guardian spirit.

Twicknam Garden: Twickenham was the home of Donne's friend and patroness Lucy, Countess of Bedford.
l.1 surrounded: carries the meaning of overflowed, as Grierson points out.

Receive such balmes, as else cure every thing;
    But O, selfe traytor, I do bring
The spider love, which transubstantiates all,
    And can convert Manna to gall,
And that this place may thoroughly be thought
    True Paradise, I have tne serpent brought.
'Twere wholsomer for mee, that winter did   10
    Benight the glory of this place,
    And that a grave frost did forbid
These trees to laugh, and mocke mee to my face;
    But that I may not this disgrace
Indure, nor yet leave loving, Love let mee
    Some senslesse peece of this place bee;
Make me a mandrake, so I may groane here,
    Or a stone fountaine weeping out my yeare.
Hither with christall vyals, lovers come,
    And take my teares, which are loves wine,   20
    And try your mistresse Teares at home,
For all are false, that tast not just like mine;
    Alas, hearts do not in eyes shine,
Nor can you more judge womans thoughts by teares
    Than by her shadow, what she weares.
O perverse sexe, where none is true but shee,
    Who's therefore true, because her truth kills mee.

A VALEDICTION: OF THE BOOKE

I'll tell thee now (deare Love) what thou shalt doe
    To anger destiny, as she doth us,
How I shall stay, though she Esloygne me thuɔ
And how posterity shall know it too;
      How thine may out-endure
      Sybills glory, and obscure
      Her who from Pindar could allure,

l.6 spider: Spiders were widely believed to be poisonous.

l.7 Manna: a reference to the miraculous food on which the Israelites were fed (Exodus 16:14-21).

l.17 mandrake . . . here: The mandrake root was said to cry out when pulled from the earth.

l.3 Esloygne: take away (cf. French *éloigner*).

And her, through whose helpe *Lucan* is not lame,
And her, whose booke (they say) *Homer* did finde,
  and name.

Study our manuscripts, those Myriades   10
  Of letters, which have past twixt thee and mee,
  Thence write our Annals, and in them will bee
To all whom loves subliming fire invades,
    Rule and example found;
    There, the faith of any ground
    No schismatique will dare to wound,
  That sees, how Love this grace to us affords,
To make, to keep, to use, to be these his Records.

This Booke, as long-liv'd as the elements,
  Or as the worlds forme, this all-graved tome   20
  In cypher writ, or new made Idiome,
Wee for loves clergie only'are instruments:
    When this booke is made thus,
    Should againe the ravenous
    Vandals and Goths inundate us,
  Learning were safe; in this our Universe
Schooles might learne Sciences, Spheares Musick, An-
  gels Verse.

Here Loves Divines, (since all Divinity
  Is love or wonder) may finde all they seeke,
  Whether abstract spirituall love they like,   30
Their Soules exhal'd with what they do not see,
    Or, loth so to amuze
    Faiths infirmitie, they chuse
    Something which they may see and use.
  For, though minde be the heaven, where love doth
    sit,
Beauty a convenient type may be to figure it.

ll.6–9 Sybills . . . name: references to various ancient traditions: to the
  Cumaean sibyl, a famous prophetess of legend; to the Greek poetess
  Corinna, reputed to have defeated the great Pindar in poetic compe-
  titions; to the wife of the Roman poet Lucan, said to have assisted
  her husband in writing his epic; and to the legendary female scribe
  reputed to have been Homer's source.
l.31 exhal'd: drawn out.
l.36 figure: represent.

Here more than in their bookes may Lawyers finde,
  Both by what titles Mistresses are ours,
  And how prerogative these states devours,
Transferr'd from Love himselfe, to womankinde,   40
    Who though from heart, and eyes,
    They exact great subsidies,
  Forsake him who on them relies,
  And for the cause, honour, or conscience give,
Chimeraes, vaine as they, or their prerogative.

Here Statesmen, (or of them, they which can reade,)
  May of their occupation finde the grounds:
  Love and their art alike it deadly wounds,
If to consider what 'tis, one proceed,
    In both they doe excell   50
    Who the present governe well,
  Whose weaknesse none doth, or dares tell;
  In this thy booke, such will their nothing see,
As in the Bible some can finde out Alchimy.

Thus vent thy thoughts; abroad I'll studie thee,
  As he removes farre off, that great heights takes;
  How great love is, presence best tryall makes,
But absence tryes how long this love will bee;
    To take a latitude
    Sun, or starres, are fitliest view'd   60
    At their brightest, but to conclude
Of longitudes, what other way have wee,
But to marke when, and where the darke eclipses bee?

l.39 prerogative . . . devours: The reference is to the feudal custom
(prerogative) by which the lord might demand of his vassal more
dues than those customarily owing to him.
l.53 nothing see: They will see the nothingness of statesmen and lovers.
ll.59–63 latitude . . . bee: An extravagant comparison with, as Grierson
points out, "a purely verbal basis": latitude literally means breadth;
longitude means length. It is possible, however, to determine longitude
by comparing the times at which an eclipse is observed from different
points.

COMMUNITIE

Good wee must love, and must hate ill,
For ill is ill, and good good still,
   But there are things indifferent,
Which wee may neither hate, nor love,
But one, and then another prove,
   As wee shall finde our fancy bent.

If then at first wise Nature had
Made women either good or bad,
   Then some wee might hate, and some chuse,
But since shee did them so create,   10
That we may neither love, nor hate,
   Onely this rests, All, all may use.

If they were good it would be seene,
Good is as visible as greene,
   And to all eyes it selfe betrayes:
If they were bad, they could not last
Bad doth it selfe, and others wast,
   So they deserve nor blame, nor praise

But they are ours as fruits are ours,
He that but tasts, he that devours,   20
   And he that leaves all, doth as well:
Chang'd loves are but chang'd sorts of meat,
And when hee hath the kernell eate,
   Who doth not fling away the shell?

LOVES GROWTH

I scarce beleeve my love to be so pure
    As I had thought it was,
    Because it doth endure
Vicissitude, and season, as the grasse;
Me thinkes I lyed all winter, when I swore,

l.2 still: always.
l.5 prove: try.

My love was infinite, if spring make'it more.
But if this medicine, love, which cures all sorrow
With more, not onely bee no quintessence,
But mixt of all stuffes, paining soule, or sense,
And of the Sunne his working vigour borrow,   10
Love's not so pure, and abstract, as they use
To say, which have no Mistresse but their Muse,
But as all else, being elemented too,
Love sometimes would contemplate, sometimes do.

And yet no greater, but more eminent,
 Love by the Spring is growne;
  As, in the firmament,
Starres by the Sunne are not inlarg'd, but showne.
Gentle love deeds, as blossomes on a bough,
From loves awakened root do bud out now.   20
If, as in water stir'd more circles bee
Produc'd by one, love such additions take,
Those like so many spheares, but one heaven make,
For, they are all concentrique unto thee.
And though each spring doe adde to love new heate,
As princes doe in times of action get
New taxes, and remit them not in peace,
No winter shall abate the springs encrease.

LOVES EXCHANGE

Love, any devill else but you,
Would for a given Soule give something too.
At Court your fellowes every day,
Give th'art of Riming, Huntsmanship, or Play,
For them which were their owne before;
Onely I have nothing which gave more,
But am, alas, by being lowly, lower.

ll.8-9 bee . . . stuffes: According to Paracelsus, the famous sixteenth-
 century alchemist and physician, the quintessence, or fifth element,
 of ancient philosophy could be extracted from all natural substances
 and used for effecting cures.
l.13 elemented: composed of various elements.
l.18 Starres . . . showne: Grierson interprets this difficult line as meaning that the stars appear larger at sunrise.

1 aske no dispensation now
To falsifie a teare, or sigh, or vow,
I do not sue from thee to draw   10
A *non obstante* on natures law,
These are prerogatives, they inhere
In thee and thine; none should forsweare
Except that hee *Loves* minion were.

Give mee thy weaknesse, make mee blinde,
Both wayes, as thou and thine, in eies and minde;
Love, let me never know that this
Is love, or, that love childish is.
Let me not know that others know
That she knowes my paines, lest that so   20
A tender shame make me mine owne new woe.

If thou give nothing, yet thou'art just,
Because I would not thy first motions trust;
Small townes which stand stiffe, till great shot
Enforce them, by warres law *condition* not.
Such in loves warfare is my case,
I may not article for grace,
Having put Love at last to shew this face.

This face, by which he could command
And change the Idolatrie of any land,   30
This face, which wheresoe'r it comes,
Can call vow'd men from cloisters, dead from tombes,
And melt both Poles at once, and store
Deserts with cities, and make more
Mynes in the earth, than Quarries were before.

For this, Love is enrag'd with mee,
Yet kills not. If I must example bee
To future Rebells; If th'unborne
Must learne, by my being cut up, and torne:

l.11 non obstante: an exemption from the law.
l.14 minion: favorite.
ll.24–25 Small . . . not: Towns which refuse to surrender to a siege do
  not, when forced to surrender, have the right to make conditions.

Kill, and dissect me, Love; for this   40
Torture against thine owne end is,
Rack't carcasses make ill Anatomies.

CONFINED LOVE

Some man unworthy to be possessor
Of old or new love, himselfe being false or weake,
   Thought his paine and shame would be lesser,
If on womankind he might his anger wreake,
        And thence a law did grow,
        One might but one man know;
        But are other creatures so?

   Are Sunne, Moone, or Starres by law forbidden,
To smile where they list, or lend away their light?
   Are birds divorc'd, or are they chidden   10
If they leave their mate, or lie abroad a-night?
        Beasts doe no joyntures lose
        Though they new lovers choose,
        But we are made worse than those.

   Who e'r rigg'd faire ship to lie in harbors,
And not to seeke new lands, or not to deale withall?
   Or built faire houses, set trees, and arbors,
Only to lock up, or else to let them fall?
        Good is not good, unlesse
        A thousand it possesse,   20
        But doth wast with greedinesse.

THE DREAME

Deare love, for nothing lesse than thee
Would I have broke this happy dreame,
      It was a theame   *physical sensation acting itself out*
For reason, much too strong for phantasie,
Therefore thou wakd'st me wisely; yet   *you continued*
My Dreame thou brok'st not, but continued'st it,   *my happy dream by waking me —*

l.42 Rack't . . . Anatomies: Tortured bodies are not good for dissection.   *(a wet dream perhaps?)*

Thou art so truth, that thoughts of thee suffice,
To make dreames truths; and fables histories;
Enter these armes, for since thou thoughtst it best,
Not to dreame all my dreame, let's act the rest.　　10

[handwritten: phallic symbol let's act out my dream (sex?)]

As lightning, or a Tapers light,
Thine eyes, and not thy noise wak'd mee;
　　　　Yet I thought thee
(For thou lovest truth) an Angell, at first sight,

[handwritten: compares his lover to an angel at first sight]

But when I saw thou sawest my heart,
And knew'st my thoughts, beyond an Angels art,
When thou knew'st what I dreamt, when thou knew'st

[handwritten: when you know what I dream]

Excesse of joy would wake me, and cam'st then,
I must confesse, it could not chuse but bee
Prophane, to thinke thee any thing but thee.　　20

[handwritten: sexual connotation]

Comming and staying show'd thee, thee,
But rising makes me doubt, that now,
　　　　Thou art not thou.

[handwritten: waking in doubt]

That love is weake, where feare's as strong as hee;
'Tis not all spirit, pure, and brave,
If mixture it of *Feare, Shame, Honor*, have.
Perchance as torches which must ready bee,
Men light and put out, so thou deal'st with mee,
Thou cam'st to kindle, goest to come; Then I
Will dreame that hope againe, but else would die　　30

[handwritten left margin: she gives up & leaves]
[handwritten: she "torches" him - leaves him]
[handwritten: wants the hope of love not the reality]

A VALEDICTION: OF WEEPING

　　　Let me powre forth
My teares before thy face, whil'st I stay here,
For thy face coines them, and thy stampe they beare,

---

l.7 Thou . . . suffice: As Grierson points out, the speaker endows his
beloved with one of the divine attributes. This reading is important to
an understanding of the second stanza.

l.16 knew'st . . . art: To know a person's thoughts is a capacity of God,
not of the angels.

ll.27–28 torches . . . out: Torches were frequently lighted and then extinguished so that, being dry, they could easily be lighted when
needed.

l.3 For . . . beare: The sight of his lady's face is the cause of the speaker's tears, and those tears in turn reflect her face.

And by this Mintage they are something worth,
      For thus they bee
      Pregnant of thee;
Fruits of much griefe they are, emblemes of more,
When a teare falls, that thou falls which it bore,
So thou and I are nothing then, when on a divers shore.

      On a round ball   10
A workeman that hath copies by, can lay
An Europe, Afrique, and an Asia,
And quickly make that, which was nothing, *All*:
      So doth each teare,
      Which thee doth weare,
A globe, yea world by that impression grow,
Till thy teares mixt with mine doe overflow
This world, by waters sent from thee, my heaven dis-
  solved so.

      O more than Moone,
Draw not up seas to drowne me in thy spheare,   20
Weepe me not dead, in thine armes, but forbeare
To teach the sea, what it may doe too soone;
      Let not the winde
      Example finde,
To doe me more harme, than it purposeth;
Since thou and I sigh one anothers breath,
Who e'r sighes most, is cruellest, and hastes the others
  death.

LOVES ALCHYMIE ~magical chemistry

Some that have deeper digg'd loves Myne than I,
Say, where his centrique happinesse doth lie:
      I have lov'd, and got, and told,
But should I love, get, tell, till I were old,
I should not finde that hidden mysterie;
      Oh, 'tis imposture all:

l.27 Who . . . death: It was widely believed that every sigh diminishes
  the life span of the person who sighs.

l.3 told: counted.

And as no chymique yet th'Elixar got,
    But glorifies his pregnant pot,
    If by the way to him befall
Some odoriferous thing, or medicinall,   10
  So, lovers dreame a rich and long delight,
  But get a winter-seeming summers night.

Our ease, our thrift, our honor, and our day,
Shall we, for this vaine Bubles shadow pay?
    Ends love in this, that my man,
Can be as happy'as I can; If he can
Endure the short scorne of a Bridegroomes play?
    That loving wretch that sweares,
    'Tis not the bodies marry, but the mindes,
    Which he in her Angelique findes,
    Would sweare as justly, that he heares
In that dayes rude hoarse minstralsey, the spheares.
  Hope not for minde in women; at their best
Sweetnesse and wit, they'are but *Mummy*, possest.

THE FLEA

Marke but this flea, and marke in this,
How little that which thou deny'st me is;
It suck'd me first, and now sucks thee,
And in this flea, our two bloods mingled bee;
Thou know'st that this cannot be said
A sinne, nor shame, nor losse of maidenhead,
  Yet this enjoyes before it wooe,
  And pamper'd swells with one blood made of two.
  And this, alas, is more than wee would doe.

Oh stay, three lives in one flea spare,   10
Where wee almost, yea more than maryed are.

l.7 Elixar: refers to the *Elixir Vitae* sought by the alchemists, who believed that this potion would cure all diseases.

l.15 man: servant.

l.22 the spheares: the music of the spheres.

l.24 Mummy: The powdered flesh of mummies was esteemed as medicinal.

This flea is you and I, and this
Our mariage bed, and mariage temple is;
Though parents grudge, and you, w'are met,
And cloysterd in these living walls of Jet.
   Though use make you apt to kill mee,
   Let not to that, selfe murder added bee,
   And sacrilege, three sinnes in killing three.

Cruell and sodaine, hast thou since
Purpled thy naile, in blood of innocence?   20
Wherein could this flea guilty bee,
Except in that drop which it suckt from thee?
Yet thou triumph'st, and saist that thou
Find'st not thy selfe, nor mee the weaker now;
   'Tis true, then learne how false, feares bee;
   Just so much honor, when thou yeeld'st to mee,
   Will wast, as this flea's death tooke life from thee.

THE CURSE

Who ever guesses, thinks, or dreames he knowes
Who is my mistris, wither by this curse;
     His only, and only his purse
     May some dull heart to love dispose,
And shee yeeld then to all that are his foes;
   May he be scorn'd by one, whom all else scorne,
   Forsweare to others, what to her he'hath sworne,
   With feare of missing, shame of getting, torne:

Madnesse his sorrow, gout his cramp, may hee
Make, by but thinking, who hath made him such: 10
     And may he feele no touch
     Of conscience, but of fame, and bee
Anguish'd, not that'twas sinne, but that'twas shee:
   In early and long scarcenesse may he rot,
   For land which had been his, if he had not
   Himselfe incestuously an heire begot:

l.12 fame: reputation.
l.14 scarcenesse: poverty.

May he dreame Treason, and beleeve, that hee
Meant to performe it, and confesse, and die,
  And no record tell why:
   His sonnes, which none of his may bee,   20
Inherite nothing but his infamie:
 Or may he so long Parasites have fed,
 That he would faine be theirs, whom he hath bred,
And at the last be circumcis'd for bread:

The venom of all stepdames, gamsters gall,
What Tyrans, and their subjects interwish,
  What Plants, Myne, Beasts, Foule, Fish,
  Can contribute, all ill which all
Prophets, or Poets spake; And all which shall
 Be annex'd in schedules unto this by mee,   30
 Fall on that man; For if it be a shee
Nature beforehand hath out-cursed mee.

THE MESSAGE

Send home my long strayd eyes to mee,
Which (Oh) too long have dwelt on thee;
Yet since there they have learn'd such ill,
  Such forc'd fashions,
  And false passions,
   That they be
   Made by thee
Fit for no good sight, keep them still.

Send home my harmlesse heart againe,
Which no unworthy thought could staine;   10
But if it be taught by thine
  To make jestings
  Of protestings,
   And crosse both
   Word and oath,

l.24 circumcis'd . . . bread: This line probably means, "May he finally become a Jew in order to benefit from the mutual assistance customary in the Jewish community."

l.14 crosse: violate.

Keepe it, for then 'tis none of mine.

Yet send me back my heart and eyes,
That I may know, and see thy lyes,
And may laugh and joy, when thou
    Art in anguish   20
    And dost languish
       For some one
       That will none,
Or prove as false as thou art now.

A NOCTURNALL UPON
S. LUCIES DAY,

BEING THE SHORTEST DAY

Tis the yeares midnight, and it is the dayes,
Lucies, who scarce seaven houres herself unmaskes,
   The Sunne is spent, and now his flasks
   Send forth light squibs, no constant rayes;
     The worlds whole sap is sunke:
The generall balme th'hydroptique earth hath drunk,
Whither, as to the beds-feet, life is shrunke,
Dead and enterr'd; yet all these seeme to laugh,
Compar'd with mee, who am their Epitaph.

Study me then, you who shall lovers bee   10
At the next world, that is, at the next Spring:
   For I am every dead thing,

A Nocturnall upon S. Lucies Day: St. Lucy's day fell on December 13
in the old calendar in use in Donne's time. Some scholars believe that
the poem was occasioned by the serious illness of the Countess of
Bedford in 1612; others, with more justice, hold that it refers to the
death of Donne's wife in 1617.

l.3 flasks: containers for gunpowder. The reference is to the stars.

l.4 squibs: firecrackers.

l.6 balme: a preservative substance believed to exist in all organic bodies.
The line suggests the ancient belief that the earth is an organism.

l.7 Whither . . . shrunke: probably a reference to a dying man's tendency to huddle toward the foot of his bed.

In whom love wrought new Alchimie.
    For his art did expresse
A quintessence even from nothingnesse,
From dull privations, and leane emptinesse:
He ruin'd mee, and I am re-begot
Of absence, darknesse, death; things which are not

All others, from all things, draw all that's good,
Life, soule, forme, spirit, whence they beeing have;   20
    I, by loves limbecke, am the grave
    Of all, that's nothing. Oft a flood
    Have wee two wept, and so
Drownd the whole world, us two; oft did we grow
To be two Chaosses, when we did show
Care to ought else; and often absences
Withdrew our soules, and made us carcasses.

But I am by her death, (which word wrongs her)
Of the first nothing, the Elixer grown;
    Were I a man, that I were one,   30
    I needs must know; I should preferre,
    If I were any beast,
Some ends, some means; Yea plants, yea stones detest,
And love; All, all some properties invest;
If I an ordinary nothing were,
As shadow, a light, and body must be here.

But I am None; nor will my Sunne renew.
You lovers, for whose sake, the lesser Sunne
    At this time to the Goat is runne
    To fetch new lust, and give it you,   40
    Enjoy your summer all;

l.14 expresse: press out.
l.15 quintessence: refers, as in "Loves Growth," to the fifth element held
    to be present in all matter.
l.21 limbecke: alembic, alchemical retort for distilling.
l.29 Elixer: general panacea sought by the alchemists.
l.33 plants . . . detest: plants choose their sustenance and some stones
    have magnetic qualities.
l.34 all . . . invest: All existing things have some distinguishing quali-
    ties.
l.39 Goat: both the zodiacal sign of Capricorn and a traditional figure of
    lust.

Since shee enjoyes her long nights festivall,
Let mee prepare towards her, and let mee call
This houre her Vigill, and her Eve, since this
Both the yeares, and the dayes deep midnight is.

WITCHCRAFT BY A PICTURE

I fixe mine eye on thine, and there
   Pitty my picture burning in thine eye,
My picture drown'd in a transparent teare,
   When I looke lower I espie;
     Hadst thou the wicked skill
By pictures made and mard, to kill,
How many wayes mightst thou performe thy will?

But now I have drunke thy sweet salt teares,
   And though thou poure more I'll depart;
My picture vanish'd, vanish feares,   10
   That I can be endamag'd by that art;
     Though thou retaine of mee
One picture more, yet that will bee,
Being in thine owne heart, from all malice free.

THE BAITE

Come live with mee, and bee my love,
And wee will some new pleasures prove
Of golden sands, and christall brookes,
With silken lines, and silver hookes.

There will the river whispering runne
Warm'd by thy eyes, more than the Sunne.
And there the'inamor'd fish will stay,
Begging themselves they may betray.

l.44 Vigill . . . Eve: along with "festivall," are terms associated with the celebration of a saint's day.

l.6 By . . . kill: The reference is to the reputed practice of witches—killing a person by destroying his picture.

The Baite: This poem is a parody of Christopher Marlowe's well-known lyric, "The Passionate Shepherd to His Love."

When thou wilt swimme in that live bath,
Each fish, which every channell hath,   10
Will amorously to thee swimme,
Gladder to catch thee, than thou him.

If thou, to be so seene, beest loath,
By Sunne, or Moone, thou darknest both,
And if my selfe have leave to see,
I need not their light, having thee.

Let others freeze with angling reeds,
And cut their legges, with shells and weeds,
Or treacherously poore fish beset,
With strangling snare, or windowie net: 20

Let coarse bold hands, from slimy nest
The bedded fish in banks out-wrest,
Or curious traitors, sleavesilke flies
Bewitch poore fishes wandring eyes.

For thee, thou needst no such deceit,
For thou thy selfe art thine owne bait;
That fish, that is not catch'd thereby,
Alas, is wiser farre than I.

THE APPARITION

you murdered me

When by thy scorne, O murdresse, I am dead,
And that thou thinkst thee free   *you think you are*
From all solicitation from mee,   *free of me but*
Then shall my ghost come to thy bed,   *my ghost will come*
And thee, fain'd vestall, in worse armes shall see;
another sexual pun?   Then thy sicke taper will begin to winke,
And he, whose thou art then, being tyr'd before,
Will, if thou stirre, or pinch to wake him, thinke
        Thou call'st for more,
And in false sleepe will from thee shrinke,   10
And then poore Aspen wretch, neglected thou
Bath'd in a cold quicksilver sweat wilt lye
        A veryer ghost than I;

l.23 sleavesilke: a particularly fine variety of silk thread.

What I will say, I will not tell thee now,
Lest that preserve thee'; and since my love is spent,
I'had rather thou shouldst painfully repent,
Than by my threatnings rest still innocent.

— if he can't bring her to use grief because she would still be innocent? he won't disturb her

THE BROKEN HEART

He is starke mad, who ever sayes,
   That he hath been in love an houre,
Yet not that love so soone decayes,
   But that it can tenne in lesse space devour;
Who will beleeve mee, if I sweare
That I have had the plague a yeare?
   Who would not laugh at mee, if I should say,
   I saw a flaske of *powder burne a day?*

Ah, what a trifle is a heart,
   If once into loves hands it come!   10
All other griefes allow a part
   To other griefes, and aske themselves but some;
They come to us, but us Love draws,
Hee swallows us, and never chawes:
   By him, as by chain'd shot, whole rankes doe dye,
   He is the tyran Pike, our hearts the Frye.

If 'twere not so, what did become
   Of my heart, when I first saw thee?
I brought a heart into the roome,
      But from the roome, I carried none with mee: 20
If it had gone to thee, I know
Mine would have taught thine heart to show
   More pitty unto mee: but Love, alas,
   At one first blow did shiver it as glasse.

Yet nothing can to nothing fall,
   Nor any place be empty quite,
Therefore I thinke my breast hath all
   Those peeces still, though they be not unite;
And now as broken glasses show
A hundred lesser faces, so   30
   My ragges of heart can like, wish, and adore,
   But after one such love, can love no more.

woman is fixed foot of a couple the man is the wandering foot

A VALEDICTION: FORBIDDING MOURNING

As virtuous men passe mildly away,
   And whisper to their soules, to goe,
Whilst some of their sad friends doe say,
   The breath goes now, and some say, no:

So let us melt, and make no noise,
   No teare-floods, nor sigh-tempests move,
T'were prophanation of our joyes
   To tell the layetie our love.

let us part w/o tears?

Moving of th'earth brings harmes and feares,
   Men reckon what it did and meant,   10
But trepidation of the spheares,
   Though greater farre, is innocent.

Dull sublunary lovers love
   (Whose soule is sense) cannot admit
Absence, because it doth remove
   Those things which elemented it.

But we by a love, so much refin'd,
   That our selves know not what it is,
Inter-assured of the mind,
   Care lesse, eyes, lips, and hands to misse.   20

Our two soules therefore, which are one,
   Though I must goe, endure not yet
A breach, but an expansion,
   Like gold to ayery thinnesse beate.

If they be two, they are two so
   As stiffe twin compasses are two,

A Valediction: Forbidding Mourning: According to Izaak Walton, Donne's earliest biographer, the poet presented this poem to his wife before leaving on a trip to the Continent in 1611.
l.11 trepidation . . . spheares: shaking of the spheres was assumed in order to account for the precession of the equinoxes, a phenomenon otherwise inexplicable by Ptolemaic astronomy.
l.14 sense: either sensuality or simply an undue reliance on the senses.

[handwritten: woman is fixed in place]

Thy soule the fixt foot, makes no show
    To move, but doth, if the'other doe.

And though it in the center sit,
    Yet when the other far doth rome, *[handwritten: he wanders]* 30
It leanes, and hearkens after it,
    And growes erect, as that comes home.

Such wilt thou be to mee, who must
    Like th'other foot, obliquely runne; *[handwritten: would this be about a man's sexuality roaming?]*
Thy firmnes drawes my circle just,
    And makes me end, where I begunne. *[handwritten: infidelity]*

[handwritten: transcending bodies? ecstasis to stand outside of]

THE EXTASIE

[handwritten: compares to bed]

Where, like a pillow on a bed, *[handwritten: where are the lovers? river bank what are they doing?]*
    A Pregnant banke swel'd up, to rest
The violets reclining head, *[handwritten: have they had sex or not?]*
    Sat we two, one anothers best.
Our hands were firmely cimented *[handwritten: scientific conception of what eyes did]*
    With a fast balme, which thence did spring,
Our eye-beames twisted, and did thred *[handwritten: is it important?]*
    Our eyes, upon one double string;
So to'entergraft our hands, as yet
    Was all the meanes to make us one, 10
And pictures in our eyes to get
    Was all our propagation.
As 'twixt two equall Armies, Fate *[handwritten: souls out of bodies]*
    Suspends uncertaine victorie,
Our soules, (which to advance their state,
    Were gone out,) hung 'twixt her, and mee.
And whil'st our soules negotiate there, *[handwritten: 2 lovers on a bank like statues of dead people]*
    Wee like sepulchrall statues lay;
All day, the same our postures were,
    And wee said nothing, all the day. 20
If any, so by love refin'd,
    That he soules language understood,

The Extasie: The title has reference to the mystical state in which the
  soul, temporarily separated from the body, is vouchsafed a direct experience of divine truth, the so-called *beatific vision.*
l.11 get: beget.

[handwritten: complicated poem of seduction]

And by good love were growen all minde,
  Within convenient distance stood,
He (though he knew not which soul spake,
  Because both meant, both spake the same)
Might thence a new concoction take,
  And part farre purer than he came.
This Extasie doth unperplex
  (We said) and tell us what we love,   30
Wee see by this, it was not sexe,
  Wee see, we saw not what did move:
But as all severall soules containe
  Mixture of things, they know not what,
Love, these mixt soules, doth mixe againe,
  And makes both one, each this and that.
A single violet transplant,
  The strength, the colour, and the size,
(All which before was poore, and scant,)
  Redoubles still, and multiplies.   40
When love, with one another so
  Interinanimates two soules,
That abler soule, which thence doth flow,
  Defects of lonelinesse controules.
Wee then, who are this new soule, know,
  Of what we are compos'd, and made,
For, th'Atomies of which we grow,
  Are soules, whom no change can invade.
But O alas, so long, so farre
  Our bodies why doe wee forbeare?   50
They are ours, though they are not wee, Wee are
  The intelligences, they the spheares.
We owe them thankes, because they thus,
  Did us, to us, at first convay,
Yeelded their forces, sense, to us,
  Nor are drosse to us, but allay.
On man heavens influence workes not so,
  But that it first imprints the ayre,

l.27 concoction: purification (an alchemical term).
l.33 severall: separate.
l.47 Atomies: atoms.
l.52 intelligences: refers to the angels who were supposed to move the
  spheres in Ptolemaic astronomy.
l.56 allay: alloy.

Soe soule into the soule may flow,
  Though it to body first repaire.   60
As our blood labours to beget
  Spirits, as like soules as it can,
Because such fingers need to knit
  That subtile knot, which makes us man:
So must pure lovers soules descend
  T'affections, and to faculties,
Which sense may reach and apprehend,
  Else a great Prince in prison lies.
To'our bodies turne wee then, that so
  Weake men on love reveal'd may looke;   70
Loves mysteries in soules doe grow,
  But yet the body is his booke.
And if some lover, such as wee,
  Have heard this dialogue of one,
Let him still marke us, he shall see
  Small change, when we'are to bodies gone.

LOVES DEITIE

I long to talke with some old lovers ghost,
  Who dyed before the god of Love was borne:
I cannot thinke that hee, who then lov'd most,
  Sunke so low, as to love one which did scorne.
But since this god produc'd a destinie,
And that vice-nature, custome, lets it be;
  I must love her, that loves not mee.

Sure, they which made him god, meant not so much,
  Nor he, in his young godhead practis'd it.
But when an even flame two hearts did touch,   10
  His office was indulgently to fit
Actives to passives. Correspondencie
Only his subject was; It cannot bee
  Love, till I love her, that loves mee.

ll.58–60 imprints . . . repaire: It was believed that the stars exerted
their influence on man by first influencing the air; Donne argues that
the souls of the lovers reach union by way of their bodies.

l.62 Spirits: the delicate vapors believed to arise from the blood and
serve as a link between soul and body.

But every moderne god will now extend
   His vast prerogative, as far as Jove.
To rage, to lust, to write to, to commend,
   All is the purlewe of the God of Love.
Oh were wee wak'ned by this Tyrannie
To ungod this child againe, it could not bee   20
   I should love her, who loves not mee.

Rebell and Atheist too, why murmure I,
   As though I felt the worst that love could doe?
Love might make me leave loving, or might trie
   A deeper plague, to make her love mee too,
Which, since she loves before, I'am loth to see;
Falshood is worse than hate; and that must bee,
   If shee whom I love, should love mee.

LOVES DIET

To what a combersome unwieldinesse
And burdenous corpulence my love had growne,
   But that I did, to make it lesse,
   And keepe it in proportion,
Give it a diet, made it feed upon
That which love worst endures, *discretion*.

Above one sigh a day I'allow'd him not,
Of which my fortune, and my faults had part;
   And if sometimes by stealth he got
   A she sigh from my mistresse heart,   10
And thought to feast on that, I let him see
'Twas neither very sound, nor meant to mee.

If he wroung from mee'a teare, I brin'd it so
With scorne or shame, that him it nourish'd not;
   If he suck'd hers, I let him know
   'Twas not a teare, which hee had got,
His drinke was counterfeit, as was his meat;
For, eyes which rowle towards all, weepe not, but sweat.

l.18 purlewe: disafforested outskirts of a forest, subject to royal authority; hence, any sphere of authority or influence.

What ever he would dictate, I writ that,
But burnt my letters; When she writ to me,   20
   And that that favour made him fat,
   I said, if any title bee
Convey'd by this, Ah, what doth it availe,
To be the fortieth name in an entaile?

Thus I reclaim'd my buzard love, to flye
At what, and when, and how, and where I chuse;
   Now negligent of sport I lye,
   And now as other Fawkners use,
I spring a mistresse, sweare, write, sigh and weepe:
And the game kill'd, or lost, goe talke, and sleepe.   30

THE WILL

Before I sigh my last gaspe, let me breath,
Great love, some Legacies; Here I bequeath
Mine eyes to *Argus*, if mine eyes can see,
If they be blinde, then Love, I give them thee;
   My tongue to Fame; to'Embassadours mine eares;
     To women or the sea, my teares.
   Thou, Love, hast taught mee heretofore
  By making mee serve her who'had twenty more,
That I should give to none, but such, as had too much
before.

My constancie I to the planets give;   10
My truth to them, who at the Court doe live;
   Mine ingenuity and opennesse,
   To Jesuites; to Buffones my pensivenesse;
   My silence to'any, who abroad hath beene;
     My mony to a Capuchin.
   Thou Love taught'st me, by appointing mee
  To love there, where no love receiv'd can be,
Onely to give to such as have an incapacitie.

l.28 Fawkners: falconers.

l.3 Argus: a hundred-eyed monster, in Greek mythology.
l.12 ingenuity: ingenuousness.

My faith I give to Roman Catholiques;
All my good works unto the Schismaticks   20
Of Amsterdam: my best civility
And Courtship, to an Universitie;
My modesty I give to souldiers bare;
    My patience let gamesters share.
  Thou Love taughtst mee, by making mee
 Love her that holds my love disparity,
Onely to give to those that count my gifts indignity.

I give my reputation to those
Which were my friends; Mine industrie to foes;
To Schoolemen I bequeath my doubtfulnesse;   30
My sicknesse to Physitians, or excesse;
To Nature, all that I in Ryme have writ;
    And to my company my wit.
  Thou Love, by making mee adore
 Her, who begot this love in mee before,
Taughtst me to make, as though I gave, when I did but
restore.

To him for whom the passing bell next tolls,
I give my physick bookes; my writen rowles
Of Morall counsels, I to Bedlam give;
My brazen medals, unto them which live   40
In want of bread; To them which passe among
    All forrainers, mine English tongue.
  Thou, Love, by making mee love one
 Who thinkes her friendship a fit portion
For yonger lovers, dost my gifts thus disproportion.

Therefore I'll give no more; But I'll undoe
The world by dying; because love dies too.
Then all your beauties will be no more worth
Than gold in Mines, where none doth draw it
    forth;

l.20 Schismaticks: a reference to a point of religious doctrine much controverted in the seventeenth century: the Catholics maintained that
good works, as well as faith, are necessary to salvation; most Protestants held that good works are useless and that man is saved through
faith alone.

And all your graces no more use shall have   50
    Than a Sun dyall in a grave.
  Thou Love taughtst mee, by making mee
 Love her, who doth neglect both mee and thee,
To'invent, and practise this one way, to'annihilate all
 three.

[handwritten: Contrast to Stanley's The Bracelet in grave]

THE FUNERALL

Who ever comes to shroud me, do not harme
    Nor question much
That subtile wreathe of haire, which crowns my arme;
The mystery, the signe you must not touch,
    For'tis my outward Soule,
[handwritten: magistrate]
Viceroy to that, which then to heaven being gone,
    Will leave this to controule,
And keep these limbes, her Provinces, from dissolution.

[handwritten: the bracelet will keep him from decomposing]

For if the sinewie thread my braine lets fall
    Through every part,
Can tye those parts, and make mee one of all;   10
These haires which upward grew, and strength and art
    Have from a better braine,
Can better do'it; Except she meant that I
    By this should know my pain,
As prisoners then are manacled, when they'are con-
 demn'd to die.

[handwritten: she owns his body + is smarter than him]

What ere shee meant by'it, bury it with me,
    For since I am
Loves martyr, it might breed idolatrie,
If into others hands these Reliques came;   20
    As'twas humility
To afford to it all that a Soule can doe,
    So,'tis some bravery,
That since you would save none of mee, I bury some
 of you.

[handwritten: bitter caustic]

l.9 sinewie thread: a reference to the nervous system.
l.14 Except: unless.
l.23 bravery: bravado.

THE BLOSSOME

Little think'st thou, poore flower,
  Whom I have watch'd sixe or seaven dayes,
And seene thy birth, and seene what every houre
Gave to thy growth, thee to this height to raise,
And now dost laugh and triumph on this bough,
        Little think'st thou
That it will freeze anon, and that I shall
To morrow finde thee falne, or not at all.

Little think'st thou poore heart
  That labour'st yet to nestle thee,
And think'st by hovering here to get a part
In a forbidden or forbidding tree,
And hop'st her stiffenesse by long siege to bow:
        Little think'st thou,
That thou to morrow, ere that Sunne doth wake,
Must with this Sunne, and mee a journey take.

But thou which lov'st to bee
  Subtile to plague thy selfe, wilt say,
Alas, if you must goe, what's that to me?
Here lyes my businesse, and here I will stay:
You goe to friends, whose love and meanes present
        Various content
To your eyes, eares, and tongue, and every part.
If then your body goe, what need you a heart?

Well then, stay here; but know,
  When thou hast stayd and done thy most;
A naked thinking heart, that makes no show,
Is to a woman, but a kinde of Ghost;
How shall shee know my heart; or having none,
        Know thee for one?
Practise may make her know some other part,
But take my word, shee doth not know a Heart.

Meet mee at London, then,
  Twenty dayes hence, and thou shalt see
Mee fresher, and more fat, by being with men,

Than if I had staid still with her and thee.
For Gods sake, if you can, be you so too:
    I would give you
There, to another friend, whom wee shall finde
As glad to have my body, as my minde.   40

THE PRIMROSE. BEING AT
MONTGOMERY CASTLE, UPON
THE HILL, ON WHICH IT IS
SITUATE

    Upon this Primrose hill,
        Where, if Heav'n would distill
A shoure of raine, each severall drop might goe
To his owne primrose, and grow Manna so;
And where their forme, and their infinitie
        Make a terrestriall Galaxie,
        As the small starres doe in the skie:
I walke to finde a true Love; and I see
That'tis not a mere woman, that is shee,
But must, or more, or lesse than woman bee.   10

        Yet know I not, which flower
            I wish; a sixe, or foure;
For should my true-Love lesse than woman bee,
She were scarce any thing; and then, should she

The Primrose: The reference to Montgomery Castle, the residence of
the Herbert family, first appeared in the second edition of Donne's
poems (1635). It has led some scholars to assume that the poem is
addressed to Magdalen Herbert. If so, "The Funerall," "The Blossome," and "The Relique," which appear near it in the early editions and display a similar concern with the fashionable doctrines of
Platonic love, may be addressed to the same woman.
l.6 terrestriall Galaxie: The reference suggests that the poem was written
after the dissemination of Galileo's view that the galaxy is composed
of stars.
ll.11–12 which . . . foure: According to Redpath, a four-petalled or a
six-petalled primrose was considered a symbol of true love. The
speaker, looking for such a flower, is disturbed by further symbolic
implications, which he presents in the next stanza.

Be more than woman, shee would get above
    All thought of sexe, and thinke to move
    My heart to study her, and not to love;
Both these were monsters; Since there must reside
Falshood in woman, I could more abide,
She were by art, than Nature falsify'd.   20

    Live Primrose then, and thrive
    With thy true number five;
And women, whom this flower doth represent,
With this mysterious number be content;
Ten is the farthest number; if halfe ten
    Belonge unto each woman, then
    Each woman may take halfe us men;
Or if this will not serve their turne, Since all
Numbers are odde, or even, and they fall
First into this, five, women may take us all.   30

THE RELIQUE

    When my grave is broke up againe
    Some second ghest to entertaine,
    (For graves have learn'd that woman-head
    To be to more than one a Bed)
        And he that digs it, spies
A bracelet of bright haire about the bone,
        Will he not let'us alone,
And thinke that there a loving couple lies,
Who thought that this device might be some way
To make their soules, at the last busie day,
Meet at this grave, and make a little stay?   10

ll.21–30 Live . . . all: The wit of this stanza depends on numerological
    traditions: ten is regarded as the perfect number, but five also, the
    combination of odd and even, may make a claim to symbolic per-
    fection. There may also be a reference to the five-petalled rose as a
    symbol of the Blessed Virgin, the perfect woman.

If this fall in a time, or land,
Where mis-devotion doth command,
Then, he that digges us up, will bring
Us, to the Bishop, and the King,
    To make us Reliques; then
Thou shalt be a Mary Magdalen, and I
    A something else thereby;
All women shall adore us, and some men;
And since at such time, miracles are sought,
I would have that age by this paper taught   20
What miracles wee harmlesse lovers wrought.

First, we lov'd well and faithfully,
Yet knew not what wee lov'd, nor why,
Difference of sex no more wee knew,
Than our Guardian Angells doe;
    Comming and going, wee
Perchance might kisse, but not between those meales;
    Our hands ne'r toucht the seales,
Which nature, injur'd by late law, sets free: 30
These miracles wee did; but now alas,
All measure, and all language, I should passe,
Should I tell what a miracle shee was.

THE DAMPE

When I am dead, and Doctors know not why,
    And my friends curiositie
Will have me cut up to survay each part,
When they shall finde your Picture in my heart,
    You thinke a sodaine dampe of love
    Will through all their senses move,

---

l.13 mis-devotion: Donne means Catholicism, thus making the familiar
    Protestant charge that such Catholic practices as the veneration of
    relics constitute idolatry.
l.28 might . . . meales: In Donne's England the kiss of salutation or
    parting was common social custom.
l.29 seales: colloquially, the sexual organs.

The Dampe: refers to a noxious vapor believed to cause disease.

And worke on them as mee, and so preferre
Your murder, to the name of Massacre.

Poore victories! But if you dare be brave,
   And pleasure in your conquest have,   10
First kill th'enormous Gyant, your *Disdaine*,
And let th'enchantresse *Honor*, next be slaine,
   And like a Goth and Vandall rize,
   Deface Records, and Histories
Of your owne arts and triumphs over men,
And without such advantage kill me then.

For I could muster up as well as you
   My Gyants, and my Witches too,
Which are vast *Constancy*, and *Secretnesse*,
But these I neyther looke for, nor professe;   20
   Kill mee as Woman, let mee die
   As a meere man; doe you but try
Your passive valor, and you shall finde then,
Naked you'have odds enough of any man.

THE DISSOLUTION

Shee' is dead; And all which die
  To their first Elements resolve;
And wee were mutuall Elements to us,
  And made of one another.
My body then doth hers involve,
And those things whereof I consist, hereby
In me abundant grow, and burdenous,
  And nourish not, but smother.
  My fire of Passion, sighes of ayre,

l.7 preferre: promote.
l.12 Honor: chastity.
l.21 Kill . . . die: As so often in Donne's poetry, the verbs *kill* and
die carry the contemporary colloquial meaning: to experience sexual
climax.

ll.9–10 fire . . . despaire: The reference is to the four elements of
classical science—earth, water, air, and fire—which were believed
to make up the entire physical world, including the body of man.

Water of teares, and earthly sad despaire,   10
    Which my materialls bee,
But neere worne out by loves securitie,
Shee, to my losse, doth by her death repaire,
    And I might live long wretched so
But that my fire doth with my fuell grow.
      Now as those Active Kings
    Whose foraine conquest treasure brings,
Receive more, and spend more, and soonest breake:
This (which I am amaz'd that I can speake)
      This death, hath with my store   20
        My use encreas'd.
And so my soule more earnestly releas'd,
Will outstrip hers; as bullets flowen before
A latter bullet may o'rtake, the pouder being more.

A JEAT RING SENT

    Thou art not so black, as my heart,
    Nor halfe so brittle, as her heart, thou art;
What would'st thou say? shall both our properties by
  thee bee spoke,
    Nothing more endlesse, nothing sooner broke?

    Marriage rings are not of this stuffe;
Oh, why should ought lesse precious, or lesse tough
Figure our loves? Except in thy name thou have bid
  it say,
    I'am cheap, and nought but fashion, fling me'away.

    Yet stay with mee since thou art come,
    Circle this fingers top, which did'st her thombe.   10
Be justly proud, and gladly safe, that thou dost dwell
  with me,
    She that, Oh, broke her faith, would soon breake
  thee.

ll.1–4 Thou . . . broke: Implicit in this stanza is the traditional conception of the circle as the symbol of perfection. (See Nicolson.)
l.10 Circle . . . thombe: Thumb-rings were common in Donne's England.

NEGATIVE LOVE

I never stoop'd so low, as they
Which on an eye, cheeke, lip, can prey,
   Seldome to them, which soare no higher
   Than vertue or the minde to'admire,
For sense, and understanding may
   Know, what gives fuell to their fire:
My love, though silly, is more brave,
For may I misse, when ere I crave,
If I know yet, what I would have.

If that be simply perfectest
Which can by no way be exprest
   But *Negatives*, my love is so.
   To All, which all love, I say no.
If any who deciphers best,
   What we know not, our selves, can know,
Let him teach mee that nothing; This
As yet my ease, and comfort is,
Though I speed not, I cannot misse.

10

THE PROHIBITION

   Take heed of loving mee,
At least remember, I forbade it thee;
Not that I shall repaire my 'unthrifty wast
Of Breath and Blood, upon thy sighes, and teares,
By being to thee then what to me thou wast;
But, so great Joy, our life at once outweares,
Then, lest thy love, by my death, frustrate bee,
If thou love mee, take heed of loving mee.

Negative Love: This poem is based on the witty application to love of
the doctrines of the so-called "negative theology," which held that,
since God cannot be understood by finite human minds, the best ap-
proximation of an approach to an understanding of His nature is to
recognize that He is none of those things which we may conceive Him
to be.

Take heed of hating mee,
Or too much triumph in the Victorie.   10
Not that I shall be mine owne officer,
And hate with hate againe retaliate;
But thou wilt lose the stile of conquerour,
If I, thy conquest, perish by thy hate.
Then, lest my being nothing lessen thee,
If thou hate mee, take heed of hating mee.

Yet, love and hate mee too,
So, these extreames shall neithers office doe;
Love mee, that I may die the gentler way;
Hate mee, because thy love is too great for mee;   20
Or let these two, themselves, not me decay;
So shall I, live, thy Stage, not triumph bee;
Lest thou thy love and hate and mee undoe,
To let mee live, O love and hate mee too.

THE EXPIRATION

So, so, breake off this last lamenting kisse,
   Which sucks two soules, and vapors Both away,
Turne thou ghost that way, and let mee turne this,
   And let our selves benight our happiest day,
We ask'd none leave to love; nor will we owe
   Any, so cheape a death, as saying, Goe;

Goe; and if that word have not quite kil'd thee,
   Ease mee with death, by bidding mee goe too.
Oh, if it have, let my word worke on mee,
   And a just office on a murderer doe.   10
Except it be too late, to kill me so,
   Being double dead, going, and bidding, goe.

THE COMPUTATION

For the first twenty yeares, since yesterday,
   I scarce beleev'd, thou could'st be gone away,
For forty more, I fed on favours past,

l.11 Except: unless.

And forty'on hopes, that thou would'st, they might
    last.
Teares drown'd one hundred, and sighes blew out two,
    A thousand, I did neither thinke, nor doe,
    Or not divide, all being one thought of you;
    Or in a thousand more, forgot that too.
Yet call not this long life; But thinke that I
Am, by being dead, Immortall; Can ghosts die?   10

THE PARADOX

No Lover saith, I love, nor any other
    Can judge a perfect Lover;
Hee thinkes that else none can, nor will agree
    That any loves but hee:
I cannot say I lov'd, for who can say
    Hee was kill'd yesterday?
Love with excesse of heat, more yong than old,
    Death kills with too much cold;
Wee dye but once, and who lov'd last did die,
    Hee that saith twice, doth lye: 10
For though hee seeme to move, and stirre a while,
    It doth the sense beguile.
Such life is like the light which bideth yet
    When the lights life is set,
Or like the heat, which fire in solid matter
    Leaves behinde, two houres after.
Once I lov'd and dy'd; and am now become
    Mine Epitaph and Tombe.
Here dead men speake their last, and so do I;
    Love-slaine, loe, here I lye.   20

FAREWELL TO LOVE

    Whilst yet to prove,
I thought there was some Deitie in love
    So did I reverence, and gave

l.14 lights . . . set: a reference to the sun.
l.19 dead . . . I: The sense is that dead men speak their last in their
epitaphs.
l.1 Whilst . . . prove: while yet inexperienced.

Worship; as Atheists at their dying houre
Call, what they cannot name, an unknowne power,
  As ignorantly did I crave:
       Thus when
Things not yet knowne are coveted by men,
  Our desires give them fashion, and so
As they waxe lesser, fall, as they sise, grow.   10

      But, from late faire
His highnesse sitting in a golden Chaire,
  Is not lesse cared for after three dayes
By children, than the thing which lovers so
Blindly admire, and with such worship wooe;
  Being had, enjoying it decayes:
      And thence,
What before pleas'd them all, takes but one sense,
  And that so lamely, as it leaves behinde
A kinde of sorrowing dulnesse to the minde.   20

      Ah cannot wee,
As well as Cocks and Lyons jocund be,
  After such pleasures? Unlesse wise
Nature decreed (since each such Act, they say.
Diminisheth the length of life a day)
  This, as shee would man should despise
      The sport,
Because that other curse of being short,
  And onely for a minute made to be
Eager, desires to raise posterity.   30

      Since so, my minde
Shall not desire what no man else can finde,
  I'll no more dote and runne

l.10 sise: increase in size.
l.12 His . . . Chaire: probably a reference to a gingerbread figure bought
for a child.
l.22 Cocks . . . be: a reference to the ancient belief that the cock and
the lion are the only male creatures which do not feel melancholy
after coitus.
ll.21–30 Ah . . . posterity: This difficult passage may perhaps be para-
phrased: Since each act of love shortens life by a day, nature causes
men to feel melancholy so that, although they repeat the act often
enough to perpetuate the race, they don't do so often enough to
shorten their lives to a dangerous degree.

To pursue things which had indammag'd me.
And when I come where moving beauties be,
    As men doe when the summers Sunne
        Growes great,
Though I admire their greatnesse, shun their heat;
    Each place can afford shadowes. If all faile,
'Tis but applying worme-seed to the Taile.   40

A LECTURE UPON
THE SHADOW

Stand still, and I will read to thee
A Lecture, love, in Loves philosophy.
    These three houres that we have spent,
    Walking here, Two shadowes went
Along with us, which we our selves produc'd;
But, now the Sunne is just above our head,
    We doe those shadowes tread;
    And to brave clearnesse all things are reduc'd.
So whilst our infant loves did grow,
Disguises did, and shadowes, flow,   10
From us, and our cares; but, now 'tis not so.

That love hath not attain'd the high'st degree,
Which is still diligent lest others see.

Except our loves at this noone stay,
We shall new shadowes make the other way.
    As the first were made to blinde
    Others; these which come behinde
Will worke upon our selves, and blind our eyes.
If our loves faint, and westwardly decline;
    To me thou, falsly, thine,   20
    And I to thee mine actions shall disguise.
The morning shadowes weare away,
But these grow longer all the day,
But oh, loves day is short, if love decay.

Love is a growing, or full constant light;
And his first minute, after noone, is night.

l.40 worme-seed: used as an anaphrodisiac.

SONNET. THE TOKEN

Send me some token, that my hope may live,
  Or that my easelesse thoughts may sleep and rest;
Send me some honey to make sweet my hive,
  That in my passion I may hope the best.
I beg noe ribbond wrought with thine owne hands,
  To knit our loves in the fantastick straine
Of new-toucht youth; nor Ring to shew the stands
  Of our affection, that as that's round and plaine,
So should our loves meet in simplicity.
  No, nor the Coralls which thy wrist infold,   10
Lac'd up together in congruity,
  To shew our thoughts should rest in the same hold;
No, nor thy picture, though most gracious,
  And most desir'd, because best like the best;
Nor witty Lines, which are most copious,
  Within the Writings which thou hast addrest.

Send me nor this, nor that, t'increase my store,
But swear thou thinkst I love thee, and no more.

SELFE LOVE

He that cannot chuse but love,
And strives against it still,
Never shall my fancy move;
For he loves 'gaynst his will;
Nor he which is all his own,
And can att pleasure chuse,
When I am caught he can be gone,
And when he list refuse.
Nor he that loves none but faire,
For such by all are sought;   10
Nor he that can for foul ones care,

Sonnet. The Token: I agree with Redpath and with Gardner that this
  poem seems untypical of Donne and may be falsely ascribed to him.
  It first appeared in the 1649 edition of Donne's poems.

Selfe Love: The lines are spoken by a woman.

For his Judgement then is nought:
Nor he that hath wit, for he
Will make me his jest or slave;
Nor a fool, for when others . . . ,
He can neither . . . . . .
Nor he that still his Mistresse payes,
For she is thrall'd therefore:
Nor he that payes not, for he sayes
Within, shee's worth no more.   20
Is there then no kinde of men
Whom I may freely prove?
I will vent that humour then
In mine own selfe love.

ll.15–16 neither . . . . . . : The gap occurs in all versions of the poem
    available to us.

Elegies and
Heroicall Epistle

THE TWENTY poems by Donne traditionally grouped together as the *Elegies* bear that title by virtue not of content but of metrical form. In the Renaissance, as in classical antiquity, the term designated not, as it does for us, a poem of lament, but simply a poem composed in the elegiac meter—that is, for the ancients, a distich composed of alternating lines of hexameter and pentameter, for the English Renaissance and Baroque poets, rhymed couplets of iambic pentameter. In Roman literature the elegiac meter was used conspicuously for love poems, as in Ovid's *Amores*, which constitute the principal inspiration for Donne's love elegies. Such elegies as numbers I, IV, VII, and XIX are clearly Ovidian in their frank eroticism, their masculinity of tone, and their occasional brutality and selfishness. Although the young John Donne led a life that was far from celibate, it would be incautious to regard the poems as autobiographical in any strict sense; the obvious literary source in Ovid should warn us from such a mistaken approach, as should our awareness of Donne's characteristically dramatic method. In part, in these elegies, the young poet is dramatically projecting the philosophy of "naturalism," fashionable in some late-Renaissance intellectual circles.

Apart from "Elegie IX: The Autumnall," which was probably composed around 1600, all of the elegies which are unquestionably authentic can be ascribed to the period 1593–1596. H. Gardner, the most recent editor of the *Elegies*, denies the authenticity of numbers XII, XIII, XIV, XV, and XVII, as well as of the "Heroicall Epistle: Sapho to Philaenis," an uncharacteristic excursion into a genre which enjoyed great popularity among the Elizabethans and actually survived until the time of Pope's "Eloisa to Abelard" (1717). In addition, Gardner points out that "Elegie X: The Dreame" belongs in both form and content with the *Songs and Sonets* rather than with the *Elegies*.

Gardner's edition is of primary importance to the student of the *Elegies*. Among other critical treatments, that of J. B. Leishman, *The Monarch of Wit*, has particular value, as does L. I. Bredvold's article "The Naturalism of Donne in Relation to Some Renaissance Traditions."

ELEGIE I

JEALOSIE

Fond woman, which would'st have thy husband die,
And yet complain'st of his great jealousie;
If swolne with poyson, hee lay in his last bed,
His body with a sere-barke covered,
Drawing his breath, as thick and short, as can
The nimblest crocheting Musitian,
Ready with loathsome vomiting to spue
His Soule out of one hell, into a new,
Made deafe with his poore kindreds howling cries,
Begging with few feign'd teares, great legacies,   10
Thou would'st not weepe, but jolly,'and frolicke bee,
As a slave, which to morrow should be free;
Yet weep'st thou, when thou seest him hungerly
Swallow his owne death, hearts-bane jealousie.
O give him many thanks, he'is courteous,
That in suspecting kindly warneth us.

Wee must not, as wee us'd, flout openly,
In scoffing ridles, his deformitie;
Nor at his boord together being satt,
With words, nor touch, scarce lookes adulterate.   20
Nor when he swolne, and pamper'd with great fare
Sits downe, and snorts, cag'd in his basket chaire,
Must wee usurpe his owne bed any more,
Nor kisse and play in his house, as before.
Now I see many dangers; for that is
His realme, his castle, and his diocesse.
But if, as envious men, which would revile
Their Prince, or coyne his gold, themselves exile
Into another countrie,'and doe it there,
Wee play'in another house, what should we feare?   30
There we will scorne his houshold policies,
His seely plots, and pensionary spies,
As the inhabitants of Thames right side
Do Londons Major; or Germans, the Popes pride.

ELEGIE II

The Anagram

Marry, and love thy *Flavia*, for, shee
Hath all things, whereby others beautious bee,
For, though her eyes be small, her mouth is great,
Though they be Ivory, yet her teeth be jeat,
Though they be dimme, yet she is light enough,
And though her harsh haire fall, her skinne is rough;
What though her cheeks be yellow, her haire's red,
Give her thine, and she hath a maydenhead.
These things are beauties elements, where these
Meet in one, that one must, as perfect, please.   10
If red and white and each good quality
Be in thy wench, ne'r aske where it doth lye.
In buying things perfum'd, we aske; if there

l.32 seely: silly, in its obsolete meaning of ineffective, futile.
l.33 Major: mayor. The south bank of the Thames was beyond the jurisdiction of the city of London.

l.11 red and white: the colors of a beautiful complexion were used by
Renaissance poets to designate female beauty in general.

Be muske and amber in it, but not where.
Though all her parts be not in th'usuall place,
She'hath yet an Anagram of a good face.
If we might put the letters but one way,
In the leane dearth of words, what could wee say?
When by the Gamut some Musitions make
A perfect song, others will undertake,   20
By the same Gamut chang'd, to equall it.
Things simply good, can never be unfit.
She's faire as any, if all be like her,
And if none bee, then she is singular.
All love is wonder; if wee justly doe
Account her wonderfull, why not lovely too?
Love built on beauty, soone as beauty, dies,
Chuse this face, chang'd by no deformities.
Women are all like Angels; the faire be
Like those which fell to worse; but such as thee,   30
Like to good Angels, nothing can impaire:
'Tis lesse griefe to be foule, than to'have beene faire.
For one nights revels, silke and gold we chuse,
But, in long journeyes, cloth, and leather use.
Beauty is barren oft; best husbands say,
There is best land, where there is foulest way.
Oh what a soveraigne Plaister will shee bee,
If thy past sinnes have taught thee jealousie!
Here needs no spies, nor eunuches; her commit
Safe to thy foes; yea, to a Marmosit.   40
When Belgiaes citties, the round countries drowne,
That durty foulenesse guards, and armes the towne:
So doth her face guard her; and so, for thee,
Which, forc'd by businesse, absent oft must bee,
Shee, whose face, like clouds, turnes the day to night,
Who, mightier than the sea, makes Moores seem white,
Who, though seaven yeares, she in the Stews had laid,
A Nunnery durst receive, and thinke a maid,
And though in childbeds labour she did lie,

l.19 Gamut: musical scale.
l.40 Marmosit: ape.
ll.41–42 round . . . towne: a reference to the opening of the dikes
  by the Dutch in order to flood the land in times of invasion.
l.47 Stews: brothels.

Midwifes would sweare,'twere but a tympanie,   50
Whom, if shee accuse her selfe, I credit lesse
Than witches, which impossibles confesse,
Whom Dildoes, Bedstaves, and her Velvet Glasse
Would be as loath to touch as Joseph was:
One like none, and lik'd of none, fittest were,
For, things in fashion every man will weare.

ELEGIE III

CHANGE

Although thy hand and faith, and good workes too,
Have seal'd thy love which nothing should undoe,
Yea though thou fall backe, that apostasie
Confirme thy love; yet much, much I feare thee.
Women are like the Arts, forc'd unto none,
Open to'all searchers, unpriz'd, if unknowne.
If I have caught a bird, and let him flie,
Another fouler using these meanes, as I,
May catch the same bird; and, as these things bee,
Women are made for men, not him, nor mee.   10
Foxes and goats; all beasts change when they please,
Shall women, more hot, wily, wild than these,
Be bound to one man, and did Nature then
Idly make them apter to'endure than men?
They'are our clogges, not their owne; if a man bee
Chain'd to a galley, yet the galley'is free;
Who hath a plow-land, casts all his seed corne there,
And yet allowes his ground more corne should beare;
Though Danuby into the sea must flow,
The sea receives the Rhene, Volga, and Po.   20
By nature, which gave it, this liberty
Thou lov'st, but Oh! canst thou love it and mee?
Likenesse glues love: and if that thou so doe,
To make us like and love, must I change too?

l.50 tympanie: swelling (like a kettledrum).
l.53 Dildoes: phalluses. The line refers to objects used for autoerotic
   stimulation.
l.54 Joseph: a reference to the story of Joseph and Potiphar's wife.

l.8 fouler: fowler.

More than thy hate, I hate'it, rather let mee
Allow her change, than change as oft as shee,
And soe not teach, but force my'opinion
To love not any one, nor every one.
To live in one land, is captivitie,
To runne all countries, a wild roguery;   30
Waters stincke soone, if in one place they bide
And in the vast sea are more putrifi'd:
But when they kisse one banke, and leaving this
Never looke backe, but the next banke doe kisse,
Then are they purest; Change'is the nursery
Of musicke, joy, life, and eternity.

ELEGIE IV

THE PERFUME

Once, and but once found in thy company,
All thy suppos'd escapes are laid on mee;
And as a thiefe at barre, is question'd there
By all the men, that have beene rob'd that yeare,
So am I, (by this traiterous meanes surpriz'd)
By thy Hydroptique father catechiz'd.
Though he had wont to search with glazed eyes,
As though he came to kill a Cockatrice,
Though hee hath oft sworne, that hee would remove
Thy beauties beautie, and food of our love,   10
Hope of his goods, if I with thee were seene,
Yet close and secret, as our soules, we'have beene.
Though thy immortall mother which doth lye
Still buried in her bed, yet will not dye,
Takes this advantage to sleepe out day-light,
And watch thy entries, and returnes all night,
And, when she takes thy hand, and would seeme kind,
Doth search what rings, and armelets she can finde,
And kissing notes the colour of thy face,

l.6 Hydroptique: suffering from dropsy, that is, from an extreme thirst.
l.8 Cockatrice: a mythical monster reputed to kill with a glance; hence, as Grierson points out, the eye of a man who comes to kill a cockatrice would be glazed with fear.
l.10 beauties beautie: The speaker regards the girl's wealth as her beauty's beauty.

And fearing least thou'art swolne, doth thee embrace;   20
To trie if thou long, doth name strange meates,
And notes thy palenesse, blushing, sighs, and sweats;
And politiquely will to thee confesse
The sinnes of her owne youths ranke lustinesse;
Yet love these Sorceries did remove, and move
Thee to gull thine owne mother for my love.
Thy little brethren, which like Faiery Sprights
Oft skipt into our chamber, those sweet nights,
And kist, and ingled on thy fathers knee,
Were brib'd next day, to tell what they did see: 30
The grim eight-foot-high iron-bound serving-man,
That oft names God in oathes, and onely then,
He that to barre the first gate, doth as wide
As the great Rhodian Colossus stride,
Which, if in hell no other paines there were,
Makes mee feare hell, because he must be there:
Though by thy father he were hir'd to this,
Could never witnesse any touch or kisse.
But Oh, too common ill, I brought with mee
That, which betray'd mee to my enemie: 40
A loud perfume, which at my entrance cryed
Even at thy fathers nose, so were wee spied.
When, like a tyran King, that in his bed
Smelt gunpowder, the pale wretch shivered.
Had it beene some bad smell, he would have thought
That his owne feet, or breath, that smell had wrought.
But as wee in our Ile emprisoned,
Where cattell onely,'and diverse dogs are bred,
The pretious Unicornes, strange monsters call,
So thought he good, strange, that had none at all.   50
I taught my silkes, their whistling to forbeare,
Even my opprest shoes, dumbe and speechlesse were,
Onely, thou bitter sweet, whom I had laid
Next mee, mee traterously hast betraid,
And unsuspected hast invisibly
At once fled unto him, and staid with mee.
Base excrement of earth, which dost confound

l.49 Unicornes: The unicorn's horn was esteemed as medicinal. The
   unicorn, needless to say, was not native to England.
l.53 Onely . . . sweet: The speaker, at this point, changes from addressing his mistress and addresses the traitrous perfume.

Sense, from distinguishing the sicke from sound;
By thee the seely Amorous sucks his death
By drawing in a leprous harlots breath;   60
By thee, the greatest staine to mans estate
Falls on us, to be call'd effeminate;
Though you be much lov'd in the Princes hall,
There, things that seeme, exceed substantiall.
Gods, when yee fum'd on altars, were pleas'd well,
Because you'were burnt, not that they lik'd your smell;
You'are loathsome all, being taken simply alone,
Shall wee love ill things joyn'd, and hate each one?
If you were good, your good doth soone decay;
And you are rare, that takes the good away.   70
All my perfumes, I give most willingly
To'embalme thy fathers corse; What? will hee die?

ELEGIE V

HIS PICTURE

Here take my Picture; though I bid farewell,
Thine, in my heart, where my soule dwels, shall dwell.
'Tis like me now, but I dead, 'twill be more
When wee are shadowes both, than'twas before.
When weather-beaten I come backe; my hand,
Perhaps with rude oares torne, or Sun beams tann'd,
My face and brest of hairecloth, and my head
With cares rash sodaine stormes, being o'rspread,
My body'a sack of bones, broken within,
And powders blew staines scatter'd on my skinne;   10
If rivall fooles taxe thee to'have lov'd a man,
So foule, and course, as, Oh, I may seeme then,
This shall say what I was: and thou shalt say,
Doe his hurts reach mee? doth my worth decay?
Or doe they reach his judging minde, that hee
Should now love lesse, what hee did love to see?
That which in him was faire and delicate,
Was but the milke, which in loves childish state
Did nurse it: who now is growne strong enough
To feed on that, which to disus'd tasts seemes tough.   20

l.12 course: coarse.

ELEGIE VI

Oh, let mee not serve so, as those men serve
Whom honours smoakes at once fatten and sterve;
Poorely enrich't with great mens words or lookes;
Nor so write my name in thy loving bookes
As those Idolatrous flatterers, which still
Their Princes stiles, with many Realmes fulfill
Whence they no tribute have, and where no sway.
Such services I offer as shall pay
Themselves, I hate dead names: O then let mee
Favorite in Ordinary, or no favorite bee.   10
When my Soule was in her owne body sheath'd,
Nor yet by oathes betroth'd, nor kisses breath'd
Into my Purgatory, faithlesse thee,
Thy heart seem'd waxe, and steele thy constancie:
So, carelesse flowers strow'd on the waters face,
The curled whirlepooles suck, smack, and embrace,
Yet drowne them; so, the tapers beamie eye
Amorously twinkling, beckens the giddie flie,
Yet burnes his wings; and such the devill is,
Scarce visiting them, who are intirely his.   20
When I behold a streame, which, from the spring,
Doth with doubtfull melodious murmuring,
Or in a speechlesse slumber, calmely ride
Her wedded channels bosome, and then chide
And bend her browes, and swell if any bough
Do but stoop downe, or kisse her upmost brow:
Yet, if her often gnawing kisses winne
The traiterous banke to gape, and let her in,
She rusheth violently, and doth divorce
Her from her native, and her long-kept course,   30
And rores, and braves it, and in gallant scorne,
In flattering eddies promising retorne,
She flouts the channell, who thenceforth is drie;
Then say I; that is shee, and this am I.

ll.6-7 Their . . . sway: a reference to monarchs who claim, in their
   titles, sovereignty over lands in which they exert no *de facto* power.
l.10 Favorite in Ordinary: regular favorite. The phrase burlesques an
   official title.

Yet let not thy deepe bitternesse beget
Carelesse despaire in mee, for that will whet
My minde to scorne; and Oh, love dull'd with paine
Was ne'r so wise, nor well arm'd as disdaine.
Then with new eyes I shall survay thee,'and spie
Death in thy cheekes, and darknesse in thine eye.   40
Though hope bred faith and love: thus taught, I shall
As nations do from Rome, from thy love fall.
My hate shall outgrow thine, and utterly
I will renounce thy dalliance: and when I
Am the Recusant, in that resolute state,
What hurts it mee to be'excommunicate?

ELEGIE VII

Natures lay Ideot, I taught thee to love,
And in that sophistrie, Oh, thou dost prove
Too subtile: Foole, thou didst not understand
The mystique language of the eye nor hand:
Nor couldst thou judge the difference of the aire
Of sighes, and say, this lies, this sounds despaire:
Nor by the'eyes water call a maladie
Desperately hot, or changing feaverously.
I had not taught thee then, the Alphabet
Of flowers, how they devisefully being set   10
And bound up, might with speechlesse secrecie
Deliver arrands mutely, and mutually.
Remember since all thy words us'd to bee
To every suitor; *I, if my friends agree;*
Since, household charmes, thy husbands name to teach,

l.45 Recusant: one who refuses to acknowledge existing ecclesiastical
authority.

l.1 Natures . . . Ideot: person ignorant by nature. The adjective *lay*
may imply specifically ignorance of such "sacred mysteries" as those
of love.

ll.10–12 flowers . . . mutually: a reference to the arrangement of flowers in a bouquet in such a manner as to convey amorous messages.

l.13 since: when.

l.14 I: aye.

l.15 thy . . . teach: a reference to girlish games to discover the identity
of the future husband.

Were all the love trickes, that thy wit could reach;
And since, an houres discourse could scarce have made
One answer in thee, and that ill arraid
In broken proverbs, and torne sentences.
Thou art not by so many duties his,   20
That from the worlds Common having sever'd thee,
Inlaid thee, neither to be seene, nor see,
As mine: who have with amorous delicacies
Refin'd thee'into a blis-full Paradise.
Thy graces and good words my creatures bee;
I planted knowledge and lifes tree in thee,
Which Oh, shall strangers taste? Must I alas
Frame and enamell Plate, and drinke in Glasse?
Chafe waxe for others seales? breake a colts force
And leave him then, beeing made a ready horse?   30

ELEGIE VIII

The Comparison

As the sweet sweat of Roses in a Still,
As that which from chaf'd muskats pores doth trill,
As the Almighty Balme of th'early East,
Such are the sweat drops of my Mistris breast,
And on her [brow] her skin such lustre sets,
They seeme no sweat drops, but pearle coronets.
Ranke sweaty froth thy Mistresse's brow defiles,
Like spermatique issue of ripe menstruous boiles,
Or like the skumme, which, by needs lawlesse law
Enforc'd, Sanserra's starved men did draw   10
From parboild shooes, and bootes, and all the rest
Which were with any soveraigne fatnes blest,
And like vile lying stones in saffrond tinne,
Or warts, or wheales, they hang upon her skinne.
Round as the world's her head, on every side,

l.22 Inlaid: concealed, with a play on placing a jewel in a setting.

ll.10–11 Sanserra's . . . rest: When the Protestant city of Sancerre was besieged by the Catholics in 1573, the inhabitants were reduced by starvation to eating shoes.

l.13 saffrond tinne: yellow-painted tin, imitation gold.

Like to the fatall Ball which fell on Ide,
Or that whereof God had such jealousie,
As, for the ravishing thereof we die.
Thy *head* is like a rough-hewne statue of jeat,
Where marks for eyes, nose, mouth, are yet scarce set;   20
Like the first Chaos, or flat seeming face
Of Cynthia, when th'earths shadowes her embrace.
Like Proserpines white beauty-keeping chest,
Or Joves best fortunes urne, is her faire brest.
Thine's like worme eaten trunkes, cloth'd in seals skin,
Or grave, that's dust without, and stinke within.
And like that slender stalke, at whose end stands
The wood-bine quivering, are her armes and hands.
Like rough bark'd elmboughes, or the russet skin
Of men late scurg'd for madnes, or for sinne,   30
Like Sun-parch'd quarters on the citie gate,
Such is thy tann'd skins lamentable state.
And like a bunch of ragged carrets stand
The short swolne fingers of thy gouty hand.
Then like the Chymicks masculine equall fire,
Which in the Lymbecks warme wombe doth inspire
Into th'earths worthlesse durt a soule of gold,
Such cherishing heat her best lov'd part doth hold.
Thine's like the dread mouth of a fired gunne,
Or like hot liquid metalls newly runne   40
Into clay moulds, or like to that Ætna
Where round about the grasse is burnt away.
Are not your kisses then as filthy, and more,
As a worme sucking an invenom'd sore?
Doth not thy fearefull hand in feeling quake,
As one which gath'ring flowers, still feares a snake?
Is not your last act harsh, and violent,
As when a Plough a stony ground doth rent?
So kisse good Turtles, so devoutly nice
Are Priests in handling reverent sacrifice,   50
And such in searching wounds the Surgeon is
As wee, when wee embrace, or touch, or kisse.

l.16 fatall . . . Ide: a reference to the golden apple which Paris was to
present to the most beautiful goddess in the mythical contest on Mt.
Ida.
l.19 Thy head: thy mistress' head.
l.36 Lymbecks: alembics, alchemical apparatus for distillation.

Leave her, and I will leave comparing thus,
She, and comparisons are odious.

ELEGIE IX

THE AUTUMNALL

No *Spring*, nor *Summer* Beauty hath such grace,
 As I have seen in one *Autumnall* face.
Yong *Beauties* force our love, and that's a *Rape*,
 This doth but *counsaile*, yet you cannot scape.
If t'were a *shame* to love, here t'were no *shame*,
 Affection here takes *Reverences* name.
Were her first yeares the *Golden Age*; That's true,
 But now she's *gold* oft tried, and ever new.
That was her torrid and inflaming time,
 This is her tolerable *Tropique clyme*.   10
Faire eyes, who askes more heate than comes from
 hence,
 He in a fever wishes pestilence.
Call not these wrinkles, *graves;* If *graves* they were,
 They were *Loves graves;* for else he is no where.
Yet lies not Love *dead* here, but here doth sit
 Vow'd to this trench, like an *Anachorit*.
And here, till hers, which must be his *death*, come,
 He doth not digge a *Grave*, but build a *Tombe*.
Here dwells he, though he sojourne ev'ry where
 In *Progresse*, yet his standing house is here.   20
Here, where still *Evening* is; not *noone*, nor *night;*
 Where no *voluptuousnesse*, yet all *delight*.
In all her words, unto all hearers fit,
 You may at *Revels*, you at *Counsaile*, sit.
This is loves timber, youth his under-wood;
 There he, as wine in *June*, enrages blood,
Which then comes seasonabliest, when our tast

Elegie IX: The Autumnall: Tradition holds that this poem, probably
 written later than the other elegies, was addressed to Donne's friend
 Mrs. Herbert.
l.16 Anachorit: anchorite, hermit.
ll.19–20 though . . . here: The contrast is between a monarch's permanent residence and his temporary dwellings while on a royal journey.
l.25 under-wood: bushy undergrowth.

And appetite to other things, is past.
Xerxes strange *Lydian* love, the *Platane* tree,
    Was lov'd for age, none being so large as shee,   30
Or else because, being yong, nature did blesse
    Her youth with ages glory, *Barrennesse*.
If we love things long sought, *Age* is a thing
    Which we are fifty yeares in compassing.
If transitory things, which soone decay,
    Age must be lovelyest at the latest day.
But name not *Winter-faces*, whose skin's slacke;
    Lanke, as an unthrifts purse; but a soules sacke;
Whose *Eyes* seeke light within, for all here's shade;
    Whose *mouthes* are holes, rather worne out, than
      made,   40
Whose every tooth to a severall place is gone,
    To vexe their soules at *Resurrection;*
Name not these living *Deaths-heads* unto mee,
    For these, not *Ancient*, but *Antique* be.
I hate extreames; yet I had rather stay
    With *Tombs* than *Cradles*, to weare out a day.
Since such loves naturall lation is, may still
    My love descend, and journey downe the hill,
Not panting after growing beauties, so,
    I shall ebbe out with them, who home-ward goe.   50

ELEGIE X

THE DREAME

Image of her whom I love, more than she,
    Whose faire impression in my faithfull heart,
Makes mee her *Medall*, and makes her love mee,
    As Kings do coynes, to which their stamps impart

ll.29–30 Xerxes . . . shee: Herodotus tells of Xerxes' extravagant admiration for a large and beautiful plane tree, which he had decorated
with golden ornaments.

Elegie X: The Dreame: Gardner believes that this poem should be
grouped with the *Songs and Sonets* rather than with the *Elegies.*
l.1 Image . . . she: The poem is based on the Neoplatonic idea that the
image of the beloved in the lover's heart is more beautiful than the
beloved herself.

The value: goe, and take my heart from hence,
  Which now is growne too great and good for me:
Honours oppresse weake spirits, and our sense
  Strong objects dull; the more, the lesse wee see.

When you are gone, and *Reason* gone with you,
  Then *Fantasie* is Queene and Soule, and all;   10
She can present joyes meaner than you do;
  Convenient, and more proportionall.
So, if I dreame I have you, I have you,
  For, all our joyes are but fantasticall.
And so I scape the paine, for paine is true;
  And sleepe which locks up sense, doth lock out all.

After a such fruition I shall wake,
  And, but the waking, nothing shall repent;
And shall to love more thankfull Sonnets make,
  Than if more *honour, teares,* and *paines* were spent.   20
But dearest heart, and dearer image stay;
  Alas, true joyes at best are *dreame* enough;
Though you stay here you passe too fast away:
  For even at first lifes *Taper* is a snuffe.

Fill'd with her love, may I be rather grown
Mad with much *heart,* than *ideott* with none.

ELEGIE XI

The Bracelet

UPON THE LOSSE OF HIS MISTRESSES CHAINE, FOR WHICH HE MADE SATISFACTION

Not that in colour it was like thy haire,
For Armelets of that thou maist let me weare:
Nor that thy hand it oft embrac'd and kist,
For so it had that good, which oft I mist:
Nor for that silly old moralitie,
That as these linkes were knit, our love should bee:
Mourne I that I thy seavenfold chaine have lost;

l.5 moralitie: symbolic significance.

Nor for the luck sake; but the bitter cost.
O, shall twelve righteous Angels, which as yet
No leaven of vile soder did admit;   10
Nor yet by any way have straid or gone
From the first state of their Creation;
Angels, which heaven commanded to provide
All things to me, and be my faithfull guide;
To gaine new friends, t'appease great enemies;
To comfort my soule, when I lie or rise;
Shall these twelve innocents, by thy severe
Sentence (dread judge) my sins great burden beare?
Shall they be damn'd, and in the furnace throwne,
And punisht for offences not their owne?   20
They save not me, they doe not ease my paines,
When in that hell they'are burnt and tyed in chains.
Were they but Crownes of France, I cared not,
For, most of these, their naturall Countreys rot
I think possesseth, they come here to us,
So pale, so lame, so leane, so ruinous;
And howsoe'r French Kings most Christian be,
Their Crownes are circumcis'd most Jewishly.
Or were they Spanish Stamps, still travelling,
That are become as Catholique as their King,   30
Those unlickt beare-whelps, unfil'd pistolets
That (more than Canon shot) availes or lets;
Which negligently left unrounded, looke
Like many angled figures, in the booke
Of some great Conjurer that would enforce
Nature, as these doe justice, from her course;

l.9 Angels: The entire poem is built on a pun on angel—a gold coin
common in Donne's day.

ll.23-26 Crownes . . . ruinous: crowne is another type of coin. With
a pun on *crown* as *head*, the passage incorporates the familiar English sneer at France as the home of the "French disease" (syphilis).

l.27 French . . . be: The French king was styled "Most Christian
Monarch."

l.29 Stamps: coins. This is a reference to the dissemination of Spanish
coins throughout Europe, with disastrous effects on local economy.

l.30 Catholique . . . King: The Spanish king was styled "Most Catholic Monarch."

l.31 pistolets: Spanish coins.

ll.34-36 Like . . . course: a reference to the conjuring of spirits through
the use of geometrical diagrams.

Which, as the soule quickens head, feet and heart,
As streames, like veines, run through th'earth's every
  part,
Visit all Countries, and have slily made
Gorgeous *France*, ruin'd, ragged and decay'd;   40
Scotland, which knew no State, proud in one day:
And mangled seventeen-headed *Belgia*.
Or were it such gold as that wherewithall
Almighty *Chymiques* from each minerall,
Having by subtle fire a soule out-pull'd;
Are dirtely and desperately gull'd:
I would not spit to quench the fire they'are in,
For, they are guilty of much hainous Sin.
But, shall my harmlesse angels perish? Shall
I lose my guard, my ease, my food, my all?   50
Much hope which they should nourish will be dead,
Much of my able youth, and lustyhead
Will vanish; if thou love let them alone,
For thou wilt love me lesse when they are gone;
And be content that some lowd squeaking Cryer
Well-pleas'd with one leane thred-bare groat, for hire,
May like a devill roare through every street;
And gall the finders conscience, if they meet.
Or let mee creepe to some dread Conjurer,
That with phantastique scheames fils full much paper;   60
Which hath divided heaven in tenements,
And with whores, theeves, and murderers stuft his rents,
So full, that though hee passe them all in sinne,
He leaves himselfe no roome to enter in.
But if, when all his art and time is spent,
Hee say 'twill ne'r be found; yet be content;
Receive from him that doome ungrudgingly,
Because he is the mouth of destiny.
    Thou say'st (alas) the gold doth still remaine,
Though it be chang'd, and put into a chaine;   70
So in the first falne angels, resteth still
Wisdome and knowledge; but,'tis turn'd to ill:
As these should doe good works; and should provide
Necessities; but now must nurse thy pride.
And they are still bad angels; Mine are none;

l.42 seventeen-headed Belgia: the seventeen provinces of the Netherlands,
  engaged at that time in war with Spain.

For, forme gives being, and their forme is gone:
Pitty these Angels; yet their dignities
Passe Vertues, Powers, and Principalities.
    But, thou art resolute; Thy will be done!
Yet with such anguish, as her onely sonne   80
The Mother in the hungry grave doth lay,
Unto the fire these Martyrs I betray.
Good soules, (for you give life to every thing)
Good Angels, (for good messages you bring)
Destin'd you might have beene to such an one,
As would have lov'd and worship'd you alone:
One that would suffer hunger, nakednesse,
Yea death, ere he would make your number lesse.
But, I am guilty of your sad decay;
May your few fellowes longer with me stay.   90
    But ô thou wretched finder whom I hate
So, that I almost pitty thy estate:
Gold being the heaviest metal amongst all,
May my most heavy curse upon thee fall:
Here fetter'd, manacled, and hang'd in chains,
First mayst thou bee; then chaind to hellish paines;
Or be with forraine gold brib'd to betray
Thy Countrey, and faile both of that and thy pay.
May the next thing thou stoop'st to reach, containe
Poyson, whose nimble fume rot thy moist braine;   100
Or libels, or some interdicted thing,
Which negligently kept, thy ruine bring.
Lust-bred diseases rot thee; and dwell with thee
Itchy desire, and no abilitie.
May all the evils that gold ever wrought;
All mischiefes that all devils ever thought;
Want after plenty; poore and gouty age;
The plagues of travellers; love; marriage
Afflict thee, and at thy lives last moment,
May thy swolne sinnes themselves to thee present.   110
    But, I forgive; repent thee honest man:
Gold is Restorative, restore it then:
But if from it thou beest loath to depart,
Because 'tis cordiall, would 'twere at thy heart.

l.112 Gold . . . Restorative: regarded as medicinal, particularly for the
heart ("cordiall").

ELEGIE XII

His Parting from Her

Since she must go, and I must mourn, come Night,
Environ me with darkness, whilst I write:
Shadow that hell unto me, which alone
I am to suffer when my Love is gone.
Alas the darkest Magick cannot do it,
Thou and greate Hell to boot are shadows to it.
Should *Cinthia* quit thee, *Venus*, and each starre,
It would not forme one thought dark as mine are.
I could lend thee obscureness now, and say,
Out of my self, There should be no more Day,   10
Such is already my felt want of sight,
Did not the fires within me force a light.
Oh Love, that fire and darkness should be mixt,
Or to thy Triumphs soe strange torments fixt!
Is't because thou thy self art blind, that wee
Thy Martyrs must no more each other see?
Or tak'st thou pride to break us on the wheel,
And view old Chaos in the Pains we feel?
Or have we left undone some mutual Rite,
Through holy fear, that merits thy despight?   20
No, no. The falt was mine, impute it to me,
Or rather to conspiring destinie,
Which (since I lov'd for forme before) decreed,
That I should suffer when I lov'd indeed:
And therefore now, sooner than I can say,
I saw the golden fruit, 'tis rapt away.
Or as I had watcht one drop in a vast stream,
And I left wealthy only in a dream.
Yet Love, thou'rt blinder than thy self in this,
To vex my Dove-like friend for my amiss: 30
And, where my own sad truth may expiate
Thy wrath, to make her fortune run my fate:
So blinded Justice doth, when Favorites fall,
Strike them, their house, their friends, their followers
  all.
Was't not enough that thou didst dart thy fires

l.7 Cinthia: the moon.

Into our blouds, inflaming our desires,
And made'st us sigh and glow, and pant, and burn,
And then thy self into our flame did'st turn?
Was't not enough, that thou didst hazard us
To paths in love so dark, so dangerous: 40
And those so ambush'd round with houshold spies,
And over all, thy husbands towring eyes
That flam'd with oylie sweat of jealousie:
Yet went we not still on with Constancie?
Have we not kept our guards, like spie on spie?
Had correspondence whilst the foe stood by?
Stoln (more to sweeten them) our many blisses
Of meetings, conference, embracements, kisses?
Shadow'd with negligence our most respects?
Varied our language through all dialects,   50
Of becks, winks, looks, and often under-boards
Spoak dialogues with our feet far from our words?
Have we prov'd all these secrets of our Art,
Yea, thy pale inwards, and thy panting heart?
And, after all this passed Purgatory,
Must sad divorce make us the vulgar story?
First let our eyes be rivited quite through
Our turning brains, and both our lips grow to
Let our armes clasp like Ivy, and our fear
Freese us together, that we may stick here,   60
Till Fortune, that would rive us, with the deed,
Strain her eyes open, and it make them bleed.
For Love it cannot be, whom hitherto
I have accus'd, should such a mischief doe.
Oh Fortune, thou'rt not worth my least exclame,
And plague enough thou hast in thy own shame.
Do thy great worst, my friend and I have armes,
Though not against thy strokes, against thy harmes.
Rend us in sunder, thou canst not divide
Our bodies so, but that our souls are ty'd,   70
And we can love by letters still and gifts,
And thoughts and dreams; Love never wanteth shifts.
I will not look upon the quickning Sun,
But straight her beauty to my sense shall run;
The ayre shall note her soft, the fire most pure;
Water suggest her clear, and the earth sure.
Time shall not lose our passages; the Spring

How fresh our love was in the beginning;
The Summer how it ripened in the eare;
And Autumn, what our golden harvests were. 80
The Winter I'll not think on to spite thee,
But count it a lost season, so shall shee.
And dearest Friend, since we must part, drown night
With hope of Day, burthens well born are light.
Though cold and darkness longer hang somewhere,
Yet *Phoebus* equally lights all the Sphere.
And what he cannot in like Portions pay,
The world enjoyes in Mass, and so we may.
Be then ever your self, and let no woe
Win on your health, your youth, your beauty: so 90
Declare your self base fortunes Enemy,
No less by your contempt than constancy:
That I may grow enamoured on your mind,
When my own thoughts I there reflected find,
For this to th'comfort of my Dear I vow,
My Deeds shall still be what my words are now;
The Poles shall move to teach me ere I start;
And when I change my Love, I'll change my heart;
Nay, if I wax but cold in my desire,
Think, heaven hath motion lost, and the world, fire: 100
Much more I could, but many words have made
That, oft, suspected which men would perswade;
Take therefore all in this: I love so true,
As I will never look for less in you.

ELEGIE XIII

JULIA

Harke newes, ô envy, thou shalt heare descry'd
My *Julia;* who as yet was ne'r envy'd.
To vomit gall in slander, swell her vaines
With calumny, that hell it selfe disdaines,
Is her continuall practice; does her best,
To teare opinion even out of the brest
Of dearest friends, and (which is worse than vilde)
Sticks jealousie in wedlock; her owne childe
Scapes not the showres of envie, To repeate

The monstrous fashions, how, were, alive, to eate   10
Deare reputation. Would to God she were
But halfe so loath to act vice, as to heare
My milde reproofe. Liv'd *Mantuan* now againe,
That fœmall Mastix, to limme with his penne
This she *Chymera*, that hath eyes of fire,
Burning with anger, anger feeds desire,
Tongued like the night-crow, whose ill boding cries
Give out for nothing but new injuries,
Her breath like to the juice in *Tenarus*
That blasts the springs, though ne'r so prosperous,   20
Her hands, I know not how, us'd more to spill
The food of others, than her selfe to fill.
But oh her minde, that *Orcus*, which includes
Legions of mischiefs, countlesse multitudes
Of formlesse curses, projects unmade up,
Abuses yet unfashion'd, thoughts corrupt,
Mishapen Cavils, palpable untroths,
Inevitable errours, self-accusing oaths:
These, like those Atoms swarming in the Sunne,
Throng in her bosome for creation.   30
I blush to give her halfe her due; yet say,
No poyson's halfe so bad as *Julia*.

ELEGIE XIV

A TALE OF A CITIZEN
AND HIS WIFE

I sing no harme good sooth to any wight,
To Lord or foole, Cuckold, begger or knight,
To peace-teaching Lawyer, Proctor, or brave
Reformed or reduced Captaine, Knave,

l.10 alive: Gardner's text has no comma after "alive," which makes
more sense of this obscure line.
l.14 Mastix: scourge of women; a reference to a misogynistic poem by
the fifteenth-century neo-Latin poet Mantuan.
l.19 Tenarus: a cavern in Greece believed to be an entrance to the un-
derworld.
l.23 Orcus: Hades.

Officer, Jugler, or Justice of peace,
Juror or Judge; I touch no fat sowes grease,
I am no Libeller, nor will be any,
But (like a true man) say there are too many.
I feare not *ore tenus;* for my tale,
Nor Count nor Counsellour will redd or pale.   10
A citizen and his wife the other day
Both riding on one horse, upon the way
I overtooke, the wench a pretty peate,
And (by her eye) well fitting for the feate.
I saw the lecherous Citizen turne backe
His head, and on his wifes lip steale a smacke,
Whence apprehending that the man was kinde,
Riding before, to kisse his wife behinde,
To get acquaintance with him I began
To sort discourse fit for so fine a man: 20
I ask'd the number of the Plaguy Bill,
Ask'd if the Custome Farmers held out still,
Of the Virginian plot, and whether Ward
The traffique of the I[n]land seas had marr'd.
Whether the Brittaine *Burse* did fill apace,
And likely were to give th'Exchange disgrace;
Of new-built *Algate*, and the *More-field* crosses,
Of store of Bankerouts, and poore Merchants losses
I urged him to speake; But he (as mute
As an old Courtier worne to his last suite)   30
Replies with onely yeas and nayes; At last
(To fit his element) my theame I cast
On Tradesmens gaines; that set his tongue agoing:
Alas, good sir (quoth he) *There is no doing*
In Court nor City now; she smil'd and I,
And (in my conscience) both gave him the lie
In one met thought: but he went on apace,

---

l.6 I . . . grease: I make no libellous reference to any rich man's acqui-
    sition of his wealth (Grierson).
l.9 ore tenus: report by word of mouth.
l.13 peate: darling.
l.21 Plaguy Bill: weekly list of those dead of the Plague.
l.22 Custome Farmers: collectors of customs.
l.23 Virginian plot: the plan to colonize Virginia.
l.23 Ward: a famous pirate.
l.24 I[n]land seas: the Mediterranean.

And at the present time with such a face
He rail'd, as fray'd me; for he gave no praise,
To any but my Lord of *Essex* dayes;   40
Call'd those the age of action; true (quoth Hee)
There's now as great an itch of bravery,
And heat of taking up, but cold lay downe,
For, put to push of pay, away they runne;
Our onely City trades of hope now are
Bawd, Tavern-keeper, Whore and Scrivener;
The much of priviledg'd kingsmen, and the store
Of fresh protections make the rest all poore;
In the first state of their Creation,
Though many stoutly stand, yet proves not one   50
A righteous pay-master. Thus ranne he on
In a continued rage: so void of reason
Seem'd his harsh talke, I sweat for feare of treason.
And (troth) how could I lesse? when in the prayer
For the protection of the wise Lord Major,
And his wise brethrens worships, when one prayeth,
He swore that none could say Amen with faith.
To get him off from what I glowed to heare,
(In happy time) an Angel did appeare,
The bright Signe of a lov'd and wel-try'd Inne,   60
Where many Citizens with their wives have bin
Well us'd and often; here I pray'd him stay,
To take some due refreshment by the way.
Looke how hee look'd that hid the gold (his hope)
And at's returne found nothing but a Rope,
So he on me, refus'd and made away,
Though willing she pleaded a weary day:
I found my misse, struck hands, and praid him tell
(To hold acquaintance still) where he did dwell;
He barely nam'd the street, promis'd the Wine,   70
But his kinde wife gave me the very Signe.

l.53 I . . . treason: The speaker feared that the merchant's angry talk,
if overheard, would sound like treason.

l.55 Major: mayor.

l.65 returne . . . Rope: Gardner traces this reference to an epigram in
the *Greek Anthology:* "A man finding gold left his halter, but the
man who had left the gold and did not find it, hanged himself with
the halter he found."

ELEGIE XV

The Expostulation

To make the doubt cleare, that no woman's true,
  Was it my fate to prove it strong in you?
Thought I, but one had breathed purest aire,
  And must she needs be false because she's faire?
Is it your beauties marke, or of your youth,
  Or your perfection, not to study truth?
Or thinke you heaven is deafe, or hath no eyes?
  Or those it hath, smile at your perjuries?
Are vowes so cheape with women, or the matter
  Whereof they are made, that they are writ in water,   10
And blowne away with winde? Or doth their breath
  (Both hot and cold at once) make life and death?
Who could have thought so many accents sweet
  Form'd into words, so many sighs should meete
As from our hearts, so many oathes, and teares
  Sprinkled among, (all sweeter by our feares
And the divine impression of stolne kisses,
  That seal'd the rest) should now prove empty blisses?
Did you draw bonds to forfet? signe to breake?
  Or must we reade you quite from what you speake,   20
And finde the truth out the wrong way? or must
  Hee first desire you false, would wish you just?
O I prophane, though most of women be
  This kinde of beast, my thought shall except thee;
My dearest love, though froward jealousie,
  With circumstance might urge thy'inconstancie,
Sooner I'll thinke the Sunne will cease to cheare
  The teeming earth, and *that* forget to beare,
Sooner that rivers will runne back, or Thames
  With ribs of Ice in June would bind his streames,   30
Or Nature, by whose strength the world endures,
  Would change her course, before you alter yours.
But O that treacherous breast to whom weake you
  Did trust our Counsells, and wee both may rue,

l.19 breake: go bankrupt.

Having his falshood found too late, 'twas hee
  That made me *cast* you guilty, and you me,
Whilst he, black wretch, betray'd each simple word
  Wee spake, unto the cunning of a third.
Curst may hee be, that so our love hath slaine,
  And wander on the earth, wretched as *Cain*,   40
Wretched as hee, and not deserve least pitty;
  In plaguing him, let misery be witty;
Let all eyes shunne him, and hee shunne each eye,
  Till hee be noysome as his infamie;
May he without remorse deny God thrice,
  And not be trusted more on his Soules price;
And after all selfe torment, when hee dyes,
  May Wolves teare out his heart, Vultures his eyes,
Swine eate his bowels, and his falser tongue
  That utter'd all, be to some Raven flung,   50
And let his carrion coarse be a longer feast
  To the Kings dogges, than any other beast.
Now have I curst, let us our love revive;
  In mee the flame was never more alive;
I could beginne againe to court and praise,
  And in that pleasure lengthen the short dayes
Of my lifes lease; like Painters that do take
  Delight, not in made worke, but whiles they make;
I could renew those times, when first I saw
  Love in your eyes, that gave my tongue the law   60
To like what you lik'd; and at maskes and playes
  Commend the self same Actors, the same wayes;
Aske how you did, and often with intent
  Of being officious, be impertinent;
All which were such soft pastimes, as in these
  Love was as subtilly catch'd, as a disease;
But being got it is a treasure sweet,
  Which to defend is harder than to get:
And ought not be prophan'd on either part,
  For though'tis got by *chance*,'tis kept by *art*.   70

l.36 cast: consider.

ELEGIE XVI

On His Mistris

By our first strange and fatall interview,
By all desires which thereof did ensue,
By our long starving hopes, by that remorse
Which my words masculine perswasive force
Begot in thee, and by the memory
Of hurts, which spies and rivals threatned me,
I calmly beg: But by thy fathers wrath,
By all paines, which want and divorcement hath,
I conjure thee, and all the oathes which I
And thou have sworne to seale joynt constancy,   10
Here I unsweare, and oversweare them thus,
Thou shalt not love by wayes so dangerous.
Temper, ô faire Love, loves impetuous rage,
Be my true Mistris still, not my faign'd Page;
I'll goe, and, by thy kinde leave, leave behinde
Thee, onely worthy to nurse in my minde,
Thirst to come backe; ô if thou die before,
My soule from other lands to thee shall soare.
Thy (else Almighty) beautie cannot move
Rage from the Seas, nor thy love teach them love,   20
Nor tame wilde Boreas harshnesse; Thou hast reade
How roughly hee in peeces shivered
Faire Orithea, whom he swore he lov'd.
Fall ill or good, 'tis madnesse to have prov'd
Dangers unurg'd; Feed on this flattery,
That absent Lovers one in th'other be.
Dissemble nothing, not a boy, nor change
Thy bodies habite, nor mindes; bee not strange
To thy selfe onely; All will spie in thy face

Elegie XVI: On His Mistris: Tradition connects this poem with Donne's
  love for Anne More, who later became his wife. If tradition is correct, the poem was composed at a rather later date than most of the
  elegies.
l.3 remorse: pity.
ll.21–23 Boreas . . . lov'd: According to mythology, Boreas, the north
  wind, fell in love with the maiden Orithea. In Donne's version, evidently, he destroyed her.
l.29 To . . . onely: The sense is: Do not deceive thyself.

A blushing womanly discovering grace;   30
Richly cloath'd Apes, are call'd Apes, and as soone
Ecclips'd as bright we call the Moone the Moone.
Men of France, changeable Camelions,
Spittles of diseases, shops of fashions,
Loves fuellers, and the rightest company
Of Players, which upon the worlds stage be,
Will quickly know thee, and no lesse, alas!
Th'indifferent Italian, as we passe
His warme land, well content to thinke thee Page,
Will hunt thee with such lust, and hideous rage,   40
As *Lots* faire guests were vext. But none of these
Nor spungy hydroptique Dutch shall thee displease,
If thou stay here. O stay here, for, for thee
England is onely a worthy Gallerie,
To walke in expectation, till from thence
Our greatest King call thee to his presence.
When I am gone, dreame me some happinesse,
Nor let thy lookes our long hid love confesse,
Nor praise, nor dispraise me, nor blesse nor curse
Openly loves force, nor in bed fright thy Nurse   50
With midnights startings, crying out, oh, oh,
Nurse, ô my love is slaine, I saw him goe
O'r the white Alpes alone; I saw him I,
Assail'd, fight, taken, stabb'd, bleed, fall, and die.
Augure me better chance, except dread *Jove*
Thinke it enough for me to'have had thy love.

ELEGIE XVII

VARIETY

The heavens rejoyce in motion, why should I
Abjure my so much lov'd variety,
And not with many youth and love divide?
Pleasure is none, if not diversifi'd:
The sun that sitting in the chaire of light
Sheds flame into what else soever doth seem bright,

l.34 Spittles: hospitals.
l.38 indifferent: to the question of which sex the disguised girl is.
l.42 hydroptique: dropsical, suffering from an unquenchable thirst.
l.44 Gallerie: antechamber.

Is not contented at one Signe to Inne,
But ends his year and with a new beginnes.
All things doe willingly in change delight,
The fruitfull mother of our appetite: 10
Rivers the clearer and more pleasing are,
Where their fair spreading streames run wide and farr;
And a dead lake that no strange bark doth greet,
Corrupts it self and what doth live in it.
Let no man tell me such a one is faire,
And worthy all alone my love to share.
Nature in her hath done the liberall part
Of a kinde Mistresse, and imploy'd her art
To make her loveable, and I aver
Him not humane that would turn back from her: 20
I love her well, and would, if need were, dye
To doe her service. But followes it that I
Must serve her onely, when I may have choice
Of other beauties, and in change rejoice?
The law is hard, and shall not have my voice.
The last I saw in all extreames is faire,
And holds me in the Sun-beames of her haire;
Her nymph-like features such agreements have
That I could venture with her to the grave:
Another's brown, I like her not the worse,   30
Her tongue is soft and takes me with discourse:
Others, for that they well descended are,
Do in my love obtain as large a share;
And though they be not fair, 'tis much with mee
To win their love onely for their degree.
And though they faile of my required ends,
The attempt is glorious and it selfe commends.
How happy were our Syres in ancient time,
Who held plurality of loves no crime!
With them it was accounted charity   40
To stirre up race of all indifferently;
Kindreds were not exempted from the bands:
Which with the Persian still in usage stands.
Women were then no sooner asked than won,
And what they did was honest and well done.
But since this title honour hath been us'd,
Our weake credulity hath been abus'd;

l.46 honour: chastity.

The golden laws of nature are repeald,
Which our first Fathers in such reverence held;
Our liberty's revers'd, our Charter's gone,   50
And we're made servants to opinion,
A monster in no certain shape attir'd,
And whose originall is much desir'd,
Formlesse at first, but growing on it fashions,
And doth prescribe manners and laws to nations.
Here love receiv'd immedicable harmes,
And was dispoiled of his daring armes.
A greater want than is his daring eyes,
He lost those awfull wings with which he flies;
His sinewy bow, and those immortall darts   60
Wherewith he'is wont to bruise resisting hearts.
Onely some few strong in themselves and free
Retain the seeds of antient liberty,
Following that part of Love although deprest,
And make a throne for him within their brest,
In spight of modern censures him avowing
Their Soveraigne, all service him allowing.
Amongst which troop although I am the least,
Yet equall in perfection with the best,
I glory in subjection of his hand,   70
Nor ever did decline his least command:
For in whatever forme the message came
My heart did open and receive the same.
But time will in his course a point discry
When I this loved service must deny,
For our allegiance temporary is,
With firmer age returnes our liberties.
What time in years and judgement we repos'd,
Shall not so easily be to change dispos'd,
Nor to the art of severall eyes obeying;   80
But beauty with true worth securely weighing,
Which being found assembled in some one,
Wee'l love her ever, and love her alone.

l.53 desir'd: sought after.
l.64 part: party, faction.

ELEGIE XVIII

LOVES PROGRESS

Who ever loves, if he do not propose
The right true end of love, he's one that goes
To sea for nothing but to make him sick:
Love is a bear-whelp born, if we o're lick
Our love, and force it new strange shapes to take,
We erre, and of a lump a monster make.
Were not a Calf a monster that were grown
Fac'd like a man, though better than his own?
Perfection is in unitie: preferr
One woman first, and then one thing in her.   10
I, when I value gold, may think upon
The ductilness, the application,
The wholsomeness, the ingenuitie,
From rust, from soil, from fire ever free:
But if I love it, 'tis because 'tis made
By our new nature (Use) the soul of trade.
    All these in women we might think upon
(If women had them) and yet love but one.
Can men more injure women than to say
They love them for that, by which they're not they?   20
Makes virtue woman? must I cool my bloud
Till I both be, and find one wise and good?
May barren Angels love so. But if we
Make love to woman; virtue is not she:
As beauty'is not nor wealth: He that strayes thus
From her to hers, is more adulterous,
Than if he took her maid. Search every sphear
And firmament, our *Cupid* is not there:
He's an infernal god and under ground,
With *Pluto* dwells, where gold and fire abound: 30
Men to such Gods, their sacrificing Coles
Did not in Altars lay, but pits and holes.
Although we see Celestial bodies move
Above the earth, the earth we Till and love:
So we her ayres contemplate, words and heart,

l.32 Did . . . holes: a reference to Pagan custom, in which sacrifices to
  the infernal gods were placed in trenches in the earth.

And virtues; but we love the Centrique part.
Nor is the soul more worthy, or more fit
For love, than this, as infinite as it.
But in attaining this desired place
How much they erre; that set out at the face?   40
The hair is of a Forest of Ambushes,
Of springes, snares, fetters and manacles:
The brow becalms us when 'tis smooth and plain,
And when 'tis wrinckled, shipwracks us again.
Smooth, 'tis a Paradice, where we would have
Immortal stay, and wrinkled 'tis our grave.
The Nose (like to the first Meridian) runs
Not 'twixt an East and West, but 'twixt two suns;
It leaves a Cheek, a rosie Hemisphere
On either side, and then directs us where   50
Upon the Islands fortunate we fall,
(Not faynte *Canaries*, but *Ambrosiall*)
Her swelling lips; To which when wee are come,
We anchor there, and think our selves at home,
For they seem all: there Syrens songs, and there
Wise Delphick Oracles do fill the ear;
There in a Creek where chosen pearls do swell,
The Remora, her cleaving tongue doth dwell.
These, and the glorious Promontory, her Chin
Ore past; and the streight *Hellespont* betweene   60
The *Sestos* and *Abydos* of her breasts,
(Not of two Lovers, but two Loves the neasts)
Succeeds a boundless sea, but yet thine eye
Some Island moles may scattered there descry;
And Sailing towards her *India*, in that way
Shall at her fair Atlantick Navell stay;
Though thence the Current be thy Pilot made,
Yet ere thou be where thou wouldst be embay'd,
Thou shalt upon another Forest set,
Where many Shipwrack, and no further get.   70
When thou art there, consider what this chace
Mispent by thy beginning at the face.
Rather set out below; practice my Art,

l.58 Remora: a fish which was believed to be capable of fastening itself to a ship and thus impeding its progress.
l.61 Sestos and Abydos: which were on opposite sides of the Hellespont,
were the abodes of the legendary lovers Hero and Leander.

Some Symetry the foot hath with that part
Which thou dost seek, and is thy Map for that
Lovely enough to stop, but not stay at:
Least subject to disguise and change it is;
Men say the Devil never can change his.
It is the Emblem that hath figured
Firmness; 'tis the first part that comes to bed.   80
Civilitie we see refin'd: the kiss
Which at the face began, transplanted is,
Since to the hand, since to the Imperial knee,
Now at the Papal foot delights to be:
If Kings think that the nearer way, and do
Rise from the foot, Lovers may do so too;
For as free Spheres move faster far than can
Birds, whom the air resists, so may that man
Which goes this empty and Ætherial way,
Than if at beauties elements he stay.   90
Rich Nature hath in women wisely made
Two purses, and their mouths aversely laid:
They then, which to the lower tribute owe,
That way which that Exchequer looks, must go:
He which doth not, his error is as great,
As who by Clyster gave the Stomack meat.

ELEGIE XIX

To His Mistris
Going to Bed

Come, Madam, come, all rest my powers defie,
Until I labour, I in labour lie.
The foe oft-times having the foe in sight,
Is tir'd with standing though he never fight.
Off with that girdle, like heavens Zone glistering,
But a far fairer world incompassing.
Unpin that spangled breastplate which you wear,

l.96 Clyster: enema.
l.96 meat: food in general.

l.5 girdle: sash.
l.5 heavens Zone: the sphere of the fixed stars, posited by Ptolemaic
astronomy.

That th'eyes of busie fooles may be stopt there.
Unlace your self, for that harmonious chyme,
Tells me from you, that now it is bed time. 10
Off with that happy busk, which I envie,
That still can be, and still can stand so nigh.
Your gown going off, such beautious state reveals,
As when from flowry meads th'hills shadow steales.
Off with that wyerie Coronet and shew
The haiery Diademe which on you doth grow:
Now off with those shooes, and then safely tread
In this loves hallow'd temple, this soft bed.
In such white robes, heaven's Angels us'd to be
Receavd by men; Thou Angel bringst with thee 20
A heaven like Mahomets Paradice; and though
Ill spirits walk in white, we easly know,
By this these Angels from an evil sprite,
Those set our hairs, but these our flesh upright.
    Licence my roaving hands, and let them go,
Before, behind, between, above, below.
O my America! my new-found-land,
My kingdome, safeliest when with one man man'd,
My Myne of precious stones, My Emperie,
How blest am I in this discovering thee! 30
To enter in these bonds, is to be free;
Then where my hand is set, my seal shall be.
    Full nakedness! All joyes are due to thee,
As souls unbodied, bodies uncloth'd must be,
To taste whole joyes. Gems which you women use
Are like Atlanta's balls, cast in mens views,
That when a fools eye lighteth on a Gem,
His earthly soul may covet theirs, not them.
Like pictures, or like books gay coverings made
For lay-men, are all women thus array'd; 40

l.9 chyme: a reference to the chiming watch worn by the girl.
l.32 seal: Donne's familiar pun on the colloquial meaning of seal as sexual organ.
ll.34–35 As . . . joyes: The reference is to the theological doctrine that the soul cannot enjoy the beatific vision until it is separated from the body.
ll.37–38 fools . . . them: In the myth, Atlanta loses the race to her suitor because she is distracted by the golden balls which he drops in her path; Donne alters the myth to make her the schemer.

Themselves are mystick books, which only wee
(Whom their imputed grace will dignifie)
Must see reveal'd. Then since that I may know;
As liberally, as to a Midwife, shew
Thy self: cast all, yea, this white lynnen hence,
[Here] is no pennance, much less innocence.
　　To teach thee, I am naked first; why then
What needst thou have more covering than a man.

ELEGIE XX
LOVES WARRE

Till I have peace with thee, warr other Men,
And when I have peace, can I leave thee then?
All other Warrs are scrupulous; Only thou
O fayr free Citty, maist thyselfe allow
To any one: In Flanders, who can tell
Whether the Master presse; or men rebell?
Only we know, that which all Ideots say,
They beare most blows which come to part the fray.
France in her lunatique giddines did hate
Ever our men, yea and our God of late;　　　　　　　　10
Yet she relyes upon our Angels well,
Which nere returne; no more than they which fell.
Sick Ireland is with a strange warr possest
Like to an Ague; now raging, now at rest;
Which time will cure: yet it must doe her good
If she were purg'd, and her head vayne let blood.
And Midas joyes our Spanish journeys give,
We touch all gold, but find no food to live.
And I should be in the hott parching clime,
To dust and ashes turn'd before my time.　　　　　　　　20
To mew me in a Ship, is to inthrall

---

l.42 imputed grace: a theological term: woman's love is like the divine
　　grace made available through Christ's sacrifice.

l.6 Whether . . . rebell: a reference to the war of rebellion of the
　　Netherlands (Flanders) against their Spanish rulers.
l.10 God of late: a reference to Henry IV's conversion to Catholicism.
l.11 Angels: gold coins, see "Elegie XI," note to line 9.
l.17 Midas: the mythical king whose touch turned all things to gold.

Mee in a prison, that weare like to fall;
Or in a Cloyster; save that there men dwell
In a calme heaven, here in a swaggering hell.
Long voyages are long consumptions,
And ships are carts for executions,
Yea they are Deaths; Is't not all one to flye
Into an other World, as t'is to dye?
Here let mee warr; in these armes lett mee lye;
Here lett mee parlee, batter, bleede, and dye.   30
Thyne armes imprison me, and myne armes thee,
Thy hart thy ransome is, take myne for mee.
Other men war that they their rest may gayne;
But wee will rest that wee may fight agayne.
Those warrs the ignorant, these th'experienc'd love,
There wee are alwayes under, here above.
There Engins farr off breed a just true feare,
Neere thrusts, pikes, stabs, yea bullets hurt not here.
There lyes are wrongs; here safe uprightly ly;
There men kil men, we'will make one by and by.   40
Thou nothing; I not halfe so much shall do
In these Warrs, as they may which from us two
Shall spring. Thousands wee see which travaile not
To warrs; But stay swords, armes, and shott
To make at home; And shall not I do then
More glorious service, staying to make men?

HEROICALL EPISTLE

Sapho to Philaenis

Where is that holy fire, which *Verse* is said
    To have? is that inchanting force decai'd?
Verse that drawes *Natures* workes, from *Natures* law,
    Thee, her best worke, to her worke cannot draw.

Heroicall Epistle: Sapho to Philaenis: In this type of poem, first intro-
    duced by Ovid, a lover is presented as addressing his or her beloved
    in a letter. The genre was popularized in Elizabethan England by
    Daniel and Drayton.
ll.3–4 Verse . . . draw: The speaker laments the fact that verse, which
    imitates the works of nature, cannot induce the beloved to participate
    in the work of nature, i.e., love.

Have my teares quench'd my old *Poetique* fire;
  Why quench'd they not as well, that of *desire?*
Thoughts, my mindes creatures, often are with thee,
  But I, their maker, want their libertie.
Onely thine image, in my heart, doth sit,
  But that is waxe, and fires environ it.   10
My fires have driven, thine have drawne it hence;
  And I am rob'd of *Picture, Heart,* and *Sense.*
Dwells with me still mine irksome *Memory,*
  Which, both to keepe, and lose, grieves equally.
That tells me'how faire thou art: Thou art so faire,
  As, *gods,* when *gods* to thee I doe compare,
Are grac'd thereby; And to make blinde men see,
  What things *gods* are, I say they'are like to thee.
For, if we justly call each silly *man*
  A *litle world,* What shall we call thee then?   20
Thou art not soft, and cleare, and strait, and faire,
  As *Down,* as *Stars, Cedars,* and *Lillies* are,
But thy right hand, and cheek, and eye, only
  Are like thy other hand, and cheek, and eye.
Such was my *Phao* awhile, but shall be never,
  As thou, wast, art, and, oh, maist be ever.
Here lovers sweare in their *Idolatrie,*
  That I am such; but *Griefe* discolors me.
And yet I grieve the lesse, lest *Griefe* remove
  My beauty, and make me'unworthy of thy love.   30
Plaies some soft boy with thee, oh there wants yet
  A mutuall feeling which should sweeten it.
His chinne, a thorny hairy unevennesse
  Doth threaten, and some daily change possesse.
Thy body is a naturall *Paradise,*
  In whose selfe, unmanur'd, all pleasure lies,
Nor needs *perfection;* why shouldst thou then
  Admit the tillage of a harsh rough man?
Men leave behinde them that which their sin showes,
  And are as theeves trac'd, which rob when it snows.   40
But of our dallyance no more signes there are,

l.20 litle world: a reference to the ancient belief that man, the microcosm or little world, corresponds in every respect to the macrocosm
or great world.
ll.37–38 why . . . man: Sappho, the female speaker of the poem, is
addressing another woman.

Than *fishes* leave in streames, or *Birds* in aire.
And betweene us all sweetnesse may be had;
    All, all that *Nature* yields, or *Art* can adde.
My two lips, eyes, thighs, differ from thy two,
    But so, as thine from one another doe;
And, oh, no more; the likenesse being such,
    Why should they not alike in all parts touch?
Hand to strange hand, lippe to lippe none denies;
    Why should they brest to brest, or thighs to thighs?   50
Likenesse begets such strange selfe flatterie,
    That touching my selfe, all seemes done to thee.
My selfe I embrace, and mine owne hands I kisse,
    And amorously thanke my selfe for this.
Me, in my glasse, I call thee; But alas,
    When I would kisse, teares dimme mine *eyes*, and
    glasse.
O cure this loving madnesse, and restore
    Me to mee; thee, my *halfe*, my *all*, my *more*.
So may thy cheekes red outweare scarlet dye,
    And their white, whitenesse of the *Galaxy*,   60
So may thy mighty, amazing beauty move
    Envy'in all *women*, and in all *men*, *love*,
And so be *change*, and *sicknesse*, farre from thee,
    As thou by comming neere, keep'st them from me.

Epigrams

THE EPIGRAM, as a classical form, was revived during the Renaissance and practiced with enthusiasm by poets all over Europe. Donne's epigrams play almost no role in contemporary estimates of the poet's achievement, but they were highly esteemed by many readers and fellow poets in Donne's own time.

Hero and Leander

Both rob'd of aire, we both lye in one ground,
Both whom one fire had burnt, one water drownd.

Pyramus and Thisbe

Two, by themselves, each other, love and feare
Slaine, cruell friends, by parting have joyn'd here.

Niobe

By childrens births, and death, I am become
So dry, that I am now mine owne sad tombe.

A Burnt Ship

Out of a fired ship, which, by no way
But drowning, could be rescued from the flame,
Some men leap'd forth, and ever as they came
Neere the foes ships, did by their shot decay;

So all were lost, which in the ship were found,
  They in the sea being burnt, they in the burnt ship
  drown'd.

FALL OF A WALL

Under an undermin'd, and shot-bruis'd wall
A too-bold Captaine perish'd by the fall,
Whose brave misfortune, happiest men envi'd,
That had a towne for tombe, his bones to hide.

A LAME BEGGER

I am unable, yonder begger cries,
To stand, or move; if he say true, hee *lies*.

CALES AND GUYANA

If you from spoyle of th'old worlds farthest end
To the new world your kindled valors bend,
What brave examples then do prove it trew
That one things end doth still beginne a new.

SIR JOHN WINGEFIELD

Beyond th'old Pillers many have travailed
Towards the Suns cradle, and his throne, and bed.
A fitter Piller our Earle did bestow
In that late Island; for he well did know
Farther than Wingefield no man dares to goe.

A SELFE ACCUSER

Your mistris, that you follow whores, still taxeth you:
'Tis strange that she should thus confesse it, though'it
  be true.

A LICENTIOUS PERSON

Thy sinnes and haires may no man equall call,
For, as thy sinnes increase, thy haires doe fall.

Cales: Cadiz. Grierson believes that this epigram, together with the
  three preceding and the one following it, have reference to the English expedition against Cadiz in 1596, in which Donne took part.
  The suggestion, as well as the style of the poems, would date the
  epigrams as 1596–1597.

Sir John Wingefield: killed in the Cadiz exploit.
l.1 Pillers: the Pillars of Hercules, that is, the Straits of Gibraltar.

ANTIQUARY

If in his Studie he hath so much care
To'hang all old strange things, let his wife beware.

DISINHERITED

Thy father all from thee, by his last Will,
Gave to the poore; Thou hast good title still.

PHRYNE

Thy flattering picture, *Phryne*, is like thee,
Onely in this, that you both painted be.

AN OBSCURE WRITER

Philo, with twelve yeares study, hath beene griev'd
To be understood; when will hee be beleev'd?

KLOCKIUS

Klockius so deeply hath sworne, ne'r more to come
In bawdie house, that hee dares not goe home.

RADERUS

Why this man gelded *Martiall* I muse,
Except himselfe alone his tricks would use,
As *Katherine*, for the Courts sake, put down Stewes.

MERCURIUS
GALLO-BELGICUS

Like *Esops* fellow-slaves, O *Mercury*,
Which could do all things, thy faith is; and I
Like *Esops* selfe, which nothing; I confesse
I should have had more faith, if thou hadst lesse;
Thy credit lost thy credit: 'Tis sinne to doe,
In this case, as thou wouldst be done unto,
To beleeve all: Change thy name: thou art like
Mercury in stealing, but lyest like a *Greeke*.

Raderus: Matthew Rader, the German editor of the works of Martial, who censored his author (Grierson).
l.3 Stewes: brothels.

Mercurius Gallo-Belgicus: a publication, originating at Cologne, which may be regarded as one of the precursors of the modern newspaper.
l.8 Mercury: the god of thieves.

RALPHIUS

Compassion in the world againe is bred:
Ralphius is sick, the broker keeps his bed.

THE LIER

Thou in the fields walkst out thy supping howers
   And yet thou swear'st thou hast supp'd like a king:
Like Nebuchadnezar perchance with grass and flowers,
   A sallet worse than Spanish dyeting.

Satyres

TO THE Elizabethans, verse satire meant something rather different from what it was to mean a century later to the Augustan poets. Such satiric poets of the 1590s as Donne, John Marston, and Joseph Hall conceived of the genre as general in its abuse, deliberately rough in its meter, and obscure and cacophonous in its diction. As a result they created an art form which contrasts strongly with that which was to emerge from the practice of Dryden and Pope—particularized in its targets, clear in its construction, viciously polished in its style. In part the willful ruggedness of Elizabethan satire may be traced to a false etymology current at the time: believing that the term *satire* was derived from *satyr* (rather than, as is the case, from the Latin *satura*, "medley"), Elizabethan poets cultivated a style which they felt might appropriately proceed from a savage, uncivilized wood creature, delivering diatribes against the hypocritically concealed vices of the age. In pursuit of their goals of harshness and obscurity, they took the Roman satirists Juvenal and, especially, Persius as their models, eschewing the manner of the milder and more urbane Horace.

The vogue of formal satire in Elizabethan England was destined to be short. In 1599 Elizabeth's Court of High Commission, concerned over possible political reverberations, prohibited the further printing of satires without specific permission.

Donne's five numbered satires were composed during the period 1593–1598, as is indicated by various topical references; the first three are among the earliest of English formal satires based on Latin models. The high-spirited lines dedicated to Coryat's *Crudities* date from 1611 and differ in tone from the formal satires. Donne's satiric targets in these poems are, in general, the standard ones of the age—courtiers, fops, poetasters, lawyers, *nouveaux riches*. A recurrent theme is the persecution of the Catholics. Although Donne had, by the time of the satires, abandoned his Catholic faith ("Satyre III" is the best indication of the poet's religious attitudes during the 1590s), his obsessive concern with informers and "pursevants" suggests his continuing emotional identification with his oppressed former coreligionists.

J. B. Leishman has a helpful treatment of the *Satyres* in *The Monarch of Wit*. For Elizabethan satire in general, see A. Kernan, *The Cankered Muse*.

SATYRE I

Away thou fondling motley humorist,
Leave mee, and in this standing woodden chest,
Consorted with these few bookes, let me lye
In prison, and here be coffin'd, when I dye;
Here are Gods conduits, grave Divines; and here
Natures Secretary, the Philosopher;
And jolly Statesmen, which teach how to tie
The sinewes of a cities mistique bodie;
Here gathering Chroniclers, and by them stand
Giddie fantastique Poëts of each land.   10
Shall I leave all this constant company,
And follow headlong, wild uncertaine thee?
First sweare by thy best love in earnest

l.1 humorist: foolish, changeable person.

(If thou which lov'st all, canst love any best)
Thou wilt not leave mee in the middle street,
Though some more spruce companion thou dost meet,
Not though a Captaine do come in thy way
Bright parcell gilt, with forty dead mens pay,
Not though a briske perfum'd piert Courtier
Deigne with a nod, thy courtesie to answer.   20
Nor come a velvet Justice with a long
Great traine of blew coats, twelve, or fourteen strong,
Wilt thou grin or fawne on him, or prepare
A speech to Court his beautious sonne and heire!
For better or worse take mee, or leave mee:
To take, and leave mee is adultery.
Oh monstrous, superstitious puritan,
Of refin'd manners, yet ceremoniall man,
That when thou meet'st one, with enquiring eyes
Dost search, and like a needy broker prize   30
The silke, and gold he weares, and to that rate
So high or low, dost raise thy formall hat:
That wilt comfort none, untill thou have knowne
What lands hee hath in hope, or of his owne,
As though all thy companions should make thee
Jointures, and marry thy deare company.
Why should'st thou (that dost not onely approve,
But in ranke itchie lust, desire, and love
The nakednesse and barenesse to enjoy,
Of thy plumpe muddy whore, or prostitute boy)   40
Hate vertue, though shee be naked, and bare?
At birth, and death, our bodies naked are;
And till our Soules be unapparrelled
Of bodies, they from blisse are banished.
Mans first blest state was naked, when by sinne
Hee lost that, yet hee was cloath'd but in beasts skin,
And in this course attire, which I now weare,
With God, and with the Muses I conferre.
But since thou like a contrite penitent,
Charitably warn'd of thy sinnes, dost repent   50

l.18 Bright . . . gilt: clad in armor.
l.18 dead . . . pay: a reference to the pay owed to men no longer on
    the muster-roll of a company, a certain portion of which belonged
    to the perquisites of the captain.
l.47 course: coarse.

These vanities, and giddinesse, loe
I shut my chamber doore, and come, lets goe.
But sooner may a cheape whore, who hath beene
Worne by as many severall men in sinne,
As are black feathers, or musk-colour hose,
Name her childs right true father, 'mongst all those:
Sooner may one guesse, who shall beare away
The Infanta of London, Heire to an India;
And sooner may a gulling weather Spie
By drawing forth heavens Scheme tell certainly   60
What fashioned hats, or ruffes, or suits next yeare
Our subtile-witted antique youths will weare;
Than thou, when thou depart'st from mee, canst show
Whither, why, when, or with whom thou wouldst go.
But how shall I be pardon'd my offence
That thus have sinn'd against my conscience?
Now we are in the street; He first of all
Improvidently proud, creepes to the wall,
And so imprisoned, and hem'd in by mee
Sells for a little state his libertie;   70
Yet though he cannot skip forth now to greet
Every fine silken painted foole we meet,
He them to him with amorous smiles allures,
And grins, smacks, shrugs, and such an itch endures,
As prentises, or schoole-boyes which doe know
Of some gay sport abroad, yet dare not goe.
And as fidlers stop lowest, at highest sound,
So to the most brave, stoops hee nigh'st the ground.
But to a grave man, he doth move no more
Than the wise politique horse would heretofore,   80
Or thou O Elephant or Ape wilt doe,
When any names the King of Spaine to you.

l.58 The . . . India: This may be a specific reference to some wealthy heiress.

l.59 gulling: cheating.

l.62 antique: antic.

ll.68–70 creepes . . . libertie: In Donne's England it was customary for the person of higher social rank to "take to the wall," that is, to walk as far as possible from the muddy center of the street. The speaker's companion is trying to assert his superiority.

l.81 Elephant . . . Ape: performing animals which were exhibited in London in 1594 (Grierson).

Now leaps he upright, Joggs me, and cryes, Do you see
Yonder well favoured youth? Oh, 'tis hee
That dances so divinely; Oh, said I,
Stand still, must you dance here for company?
Hee droopt, wee went, till one (which did excell
Th'Indians, in drinking his Tobacco well)
Met us; they talk'd; I whispered, let'us goe,
'T may be you smell him not, truely I doe;   90
He heares not mee, but, on the other side
A many-coloured Peacock having spide,
Leaves him and mee; I for my lost sheep stay;
He followes, overtakes, goes on the way,
Saying, him whom I last left, all repute
For his device, in hansoming a sute,
To judge of lace, pinke, panes, print, cut, and pleate
Of all the Court, to have the best conceit;
Our dull Comedians want him, let him goe;
But Oh, God strengthen thee, why stoop'st thou so?   100
Why? he hath travayld; Long? No, but to me
(Which understand none,) he doth seeme to be
Perfect French, and Italian; I replyed,
So is the Poxe; He answered not, but spy'd
More men of sort, of parts, and qualities;
At last his Love he in a windowe spies,
And like light dew exhal'd, he flings from mee
Violently ravish'd to his lechery.
Many were there, he could command no more;
Hee quarrell'd, fought, bled; and turn'd out of dore   110
    Directly came to mee hanging the head,
    And constantly a while must keepe his bed.

SATYRE II

Sir; though (I thanke God for it) I do hate
Perfectly all this towne, yet there's one state
In all ill things so excellently best,
That hate, toward them, breeds pitty towards the rest.
Though Poëtry indeed be such a sinne
As I thinke that brings dearth, and Spaniards in,
Though like the Pestilence and old fashion'd love,
Ridlingly it catch men; and doth remove

Never, till it be sterv'd out; yet their state
Is poore, disarm'd, like Papists, not worth hate.   10
One, (like a wretch, which at Barre judg'd as dead,
Yet prompts him which stands next, and cannot reade,
And saves his life) gives ideot actors meanes
(Starving himselfe) to live by his labor'd sceanes;
As in some Organ, Puppits dance above
And bellows pant below, which them do move.
One would move Love by rithmes; but witchcrafts
 charms
Bring not now their old feares, nor their old harmes:
Rammes, and slings now are seely battery,
Pistolets are the best Artillerie.   20
And they who write to Lords, rewards to get,
Are they not like singers at doores for meat?
And they who write, because all write, have still
That excuse for writing, and for writing ill;
But hee is worst, who (beggarly) doth chaw
Others wits fruits, and in his ravenous maw
Rankly digested, doth those things out-spue,
As his owne things; and they are his owne, 'tis true,
For if one eate my meate, though it be knowne
The meate was mine, th'excrement is his owne: 30
But these do mee no harme, nor they which use
To out-swive Dildoes, and out-usure Jewes;
To out-drinke the sea, to out-sweare the Letanie;
Who with sinnes all kindes as familiar bee
As Confessors; and for whose sinfull sake,
Schoolemen new tenements in hell must make:
Whose strange sinnes, Canonists could hardly tell
In which Commandements large receit they dwell.
But these punish themselves; the insolence
Of Coscus onely breeds my just offence,   40
Whom time (which rots all, and makes botches poxe,
And plodding on, must make a calfe an oxe)
Hath made a Lawyer, which was (alas) of late
But a scarce Poët; jollier of this state,

l.13 saves . . . life: a reference to the custom of benefit of clergy, which
  spared from capital punishment a condemned person who could read.
l.19 seely: silly, in its obsolete sense as ineffective, futile.
l.32 Dildoes: phalluses.
l.37 Canonists: specialists in canon law.

Than are new benefic'd ministers, he throwes
Like nets, or lime-twigs, wheresoever he goes,
His title of Barrister, on every wench,
And wooes in language of the Pleas, and Bench:
A motion, Lady; Speake Coscus; I have beene
In love, ever since *tricesimo* of the Queene,   50
Continuall claimes I have made, injunctions got
To stay my rivals suit, that hee should not
Proceed; spare mee; In Hillary terme I went,
You said, If I return'd next size in Lent,
I should be in remitter of your grace;
In th'interim my letters should take place
Of affidavits: words, words, which would teare
The tender labyrinth of a soft maids eare,
More, more, than ten Sclavonians scolding, more
Than when winds in our ruin'd Abbeyes rore.   60
When sicke with Poëtrie, and possest with muse
Thou wast, and mad, I hop'd; but men which chuse
Law practise for meere gaine, bold soule, repute
Worse than imbrothel'd strumpets prostitute.
Now like an owlelike watchman, hee must walke
His hand still at a bill, now he must talke
Idly, like prisoners, which whole months will sweare
That onely suretiship hath brought them there,
And to every suitor lye in every thing,
Like a Kings favourite, yea like a King;   70
Like a wedge in a blocke, wring to the barre,
Bearing-like Asses; and more shamelesse farre
Than carted whores, lye, to the grave Judge; for
Bastardy abounds not in Kings titles, nor
Symonie and Sodomy in Churchmens lives,
As these things do in him; by these he thrives.
Shortly (as the sea) hee will compasse all our land,
From Scots, to Wight; from Mount, to Dover strand.
And spying heires melting with luxurie,

ll.48–57 language . . . teare: These lines abound in technical legal terms.

ll.71–72 wring . . . Asses: This obscure passage probably means that the poet-turned-lawyer specializes in bringing suspected Catholics to trial (Grierson).

l.73 carted whores: prostitutes bound to the back of a cart and publicly whipped.

Satan will not joy at their sinnes, as hee.   80
For as a thrifty wench scrapes kitching-stuffe,
And barrelling the droppings, and the snuffe,
Of wasting candles, which in thirty yeare
(Relique-like kept) perchance buyes wedding geare;
Peecemeale he gets lands, and spends as much time
Wringing each Acre, as men pulling prime.
In parchments then, large as his fields, hee drawes
Assurances, bigge, as gloss'd civill lawes,
So huge, that men (in our times forwardnesse)
Are Fathers of the Church for writing lesse.   90
These hee writes not; nor for these written payes,
Therefore spares no length; as in those first dayes
When Luther was profest, He did desire
Short *Pater nosters*, saying as a Fryer
Each day his beads, but having left those lawes,
Addes to Christs prayer, the Power and glory clause.
But when he sells or changes land, he'impaires
His writings, and (unwatch'd) leaves out, *ses heires*,
As slily as any Commenter goes by
Hard words, or sense; or in Divinity   100
As controverters, in vouch'd Texts, leave out
Shrewd words, which might against them cleare the
 doubt.
Where are those spred woods which cloth'd hertofore
Those bought lands? not built, nor burnt within dore.
Where's th'old landlords troops, and almes? In great
 hals
Carthusian fasts, and fulsome Bachanalls
Equally I hate; meanes blesse; in rich mens homes
I bid kill some beasts, but no Hecatombs,
None starve, none surfet so; But (Oh) we allow,
Good workes as good, but out of fashion now,   110
Like old rich wardrops; but my words none drawes
Within the vast reach of th'huge statute lawes.

---

l.86 pulling prime: drawing for a winning hand in a card game.
l.96 Addes . . . clause: a reference to the phrase which distinguishes
 the Protestant version of the Lord's Prayer from the Catholic version.
l.111 wardrops: wardrobes.

SATYRE III

Kinde pitty chokes my spleene; brave scorn forbids
Those teares to issue which swell my eye-lids;
I must not laugh, nor weepe sinnes, and be wise,
Can railing then cure these worne maladies?
Is not our Mistresse faire Religion,
As worthy of all our Soules devotion,
As vertue was to the first blinded age?
Are not heavens joyes as valiant to asswage
Lusts, as earths honour was to them? Alas,
As wee do them in meanes, shall they surpasse   10
Us in the end, and shall thy fathers spirit
Meete blinde Philosophers in heaven, whose merit
Of strict life may be imputed faith, and heare
Thee, whom hee taught so easie wayes and neare
To follow, damn'd? O if thou dar'st, feare this;
This feare great courage, and high valour is.
Dar'st thou ayd mutinous Dutch, and dar'st thou lay
Thee in ships woodden Sepulchers, a prey
To leaders rage, to stormes, to shot, to dearth?
Dar'st thou dive seas, and dungeons of the earth?   20
Hast thou couragious fire to thaw the ice
Of frozen North discoveries? and thrise
Colder than Salamanders, like divine
Children in th'oven, fires of Spaine, and the line,
Whose countries limbecks to our bodies bee,
Canst thou for gaine beare? and must every hee
Which cryes not, Goddesse, to thy Mistresse, draw,
Or eat thy poysonous words? courage of straw!
O desperate coward, wilt thou seeme bold, and
To thy foes and his (who made thee to stand   30
Sentinell in his worlds garrison) thus yeeld,
And for the forbidden warres, leave th'appointed field?

l.10 As . . . meanes: We surpass the ancients in means because we
  have the revealed truth of the Christian religion.
ll.12-13 whose . . . faith: The life of the virtuous ancients may be
  counted as faith by God, and they may thus be saved.
l.25 limbecks: alembics, apparatus for distillation. The conceit refers
  wittily to both the hot climate of Spain and the burning of Protestants
  there as heretics.

Know thy foes: The foule Devill (whom thou
Strivest to please,) for hate, not love, would allow
Thee faine, his whole Realme to be quit; and as
The worlds all parts wither away and passe,
So the worlds selfe, thy other lov'd foe, is
In her decrepit wayne, and thou loving this,
Dost love a withered and worne strumpet; last,
Flesh (it selfes death) and joyes which flesh can taste,   40
Thou lovest; and thy faire goodly soule, which doth
Give this flesh power to taste joy, thou dost loath.
Seeke true religion. O where? Mirreus
Thinking her unhous'd here, and fled from us,
Seekes her at Rome; there, because hee doth know
That shee was there a thousand yeares agoe,
He loves her ragges so, as wee here obey
The statecloth where the Prince sate yesterday,
Crantz to such brave Loves will not be inthrall'd,
But loves her onely, who at Geneva is call'd   50
Religion, plaine, simple, sullen, yong,
Contemptuous, yet unhansome; As among
Lecherous humors, there is one that judges
No wenches wholsome, but course country drudges.
Graius stayes still at home here, and because
Some Preachers, vile ambitious bauds, and lawes
Still new like fashions, bid him thinke that shee
Which dwels with us, is onely perfect, hee
Imbraceth her, whom his Godfathers will
Tender to him, being tender, as Wards still   60
Take such wives as their Guardians offer, or
Pay valewes. Carelesse Phrygius doth abhorre
All, because all cannot be good, as one
Knowing some women whores, dares marry none.
Graccus loves all as one, and thinkes that so
As women do in divers countries goe

l.43 Mirreus: the Catholic.
l.49 Crantz: the Calvinist.
l.55 Graius: the Anglican.
l.62 Phrygius: the freethinker, or, to use the term common in Donne's
    day, libertine.
l.65 Graccus: the so-called Erastian, who believed in the principle that
    the religion of the monarch should determine the religion of the
    country.

In divers habits, yet are still one kinde,
So doth, so is Religion; and this blind-
nesse too much light breeds; but unmoved thou
Of force must one, and forc'd but one allow;   70
And the right; aske thy father which is shee,
Let him aske his; though truth and falshood bee
Neare twins, yet truth a little elder is;
Be busie to seeke her, beleeve mee this,
Hee's not of none, nor worst, that seekes the best.
To adore, or scorne an image, or protest,
May all be bad; doubt wisely; in strange way
To stand inquiring right, is not to stray;
To sleepe, or runne wrong, is. On a huge hill,
Cragged, and steep, Truth stands, and hee that will   80
Reach her, about must, and about must goe;
And what the hills suddennes resists, winne so;
Yet strive so, that before age, deaths twilight,
Thy Soule rest, for none can worke in that night.
To will, implyes delay, therefore now doe:
Hard deeds, the bodies paines; hard knowledge too
The mindes indeavours reach, and mysteries
Are like the Sunne, dazling, yet plaine to all eyes.
Keepe the truth which thou hast found; men do not
  stand
In so ill case here, that God hath with his hand   90
Sign'd Kings blanck-charters to kill whom they hate.
Nor are their Vicars, but hangmen to Fate.
Foole and wretch, wilt thou let thy Soule by tyed
To mans lawes, by which she shall not be tryed
At the last day? Oh, will it then boot thee
To say a Philip, or a Gregory,
A Harry, or a Martin taught thee this?
Is not this excuse for mere contraries,
Equally strong? cannot both sides say so?
That thou mayest rightly obey power, her bounds
  know;   100
Those past, her nature, and name is chang'd; to be
Then humble to her is idolatrie.

ll.96–97 Philip . . . Martin: The references are to Philip II of Spain,
  Pope Gregory XIII or Pope Gregory XIV, Henry VIII of England, and
  Martin Luther; that is, to political and spiritual representatives of
  Catholicism and Protestantism.

As streames are, Power is; those blest flowers that
  dwell
At the rough streames calme head, thrive and do well,
But having left their roots, and themselves given
To the streames tyrannous rage, alas are driven
Through mills, and rockes, and woods, and at last, al-
  most
Consum'd in going, in the sea are lost:
So perish Soules, which more chuse mens unjust
Power from God claym'd, than God himselfe to trust.   110

SATYRE IV

Well; I may now receive, and die; My sinne
Indeed is great, but I have beene in
A Purgatorie, such as fear'd hell is
A recreation to, and scarse map of this.
My minde, neither with prides itch, nor yet hath been
Poyson'd with love to see, or to bee seene,
I had no suit there, nor new suite to shew,
Yet went to Court; But as Glaze which did goe
To'a Masse in jest, catch'd, was faine to disburse
The hundred markes, which is the Statutes curse,   10
Before he scapt; So'it pleas'd my destinie
(Guilty of my sin of going), to thinke me
As prone to all ill, and of good as forget-
full, as proud, as lustfull, and as much in debt,
As vaine, as witlesse, and as false as they
Which dwell at Court, for once going that way.
Therefore I suffered this; Towards me did runne
A thing more strange, than on Niles slime, the Sunne
E'r bred; or all which into Noahs Arke came;
A thing, which would have pos'd Adam to name;   20
Stranger than seaven Antiquaries studies,
Than Africks Monsters, Guianaes rarities.

l.11 scapt: Glaze, that is, was fined for attending a clandestine Mass,
  even though he had done so only as a joke.
ll.18–19 Niles . . . bred: a reference to the ancient belief that the snakes
  and other reptiles of Egypt were bred by the action of the sun on
  the mud of the Nile.

Stranger than strangers; One, who for a Dane,
In the Danes Massacre had sure beene slaine,
If he had liv'd then; And without helpe dies,
When next the Prentises 'gainst Strangers rise.
One, whom the watch at noone lets scarce goe by,
One, to whom, the examining Justice sure would cry,
Sir, by your priesthood tell me what you are.
His cloths were strange, though coarse; and black,
   though bare;   30
Sleeveless his jerkin was, and it had beene
Velvet, but 'twas now (so much ground was seene)
Become Tufftaffatie; and our children shall
See it plaine Rashe awhile, then nought at all.
This thing hath travail'd, and saith, speakes all tongues
And only knoweth what to all States belongs.
Made of th'Accents, and best phrase of all these,
He speakes one language; If strange meats displease,
Art can deceive, or hunger force my tast,
But Pedants motley tongue, souldiers bumbast,   40
Mountebankes drugtongue, nor the termes of law
Are strong enough preparatives, to draw
Me to beare this: yet I must be content
With his tongue, in his tongue, call'd complement:
In which he can win widdowes, and pay scores,
Make men speake treason, cosen subtlest whores,
Out-flatter favorites, or outlie either
Jovius, or both together.
He names mee, and comes to mee; I whisper, God!
How have I sinn'd, that thy wraths furious rod,   50
This fellow chuseth me? He saith, Sir,
I love your judgement; Whom doe you prefer,
For the best linguist? And I seelily
Said, that I thought Calepines Dictionarie;
Nay, but of men, most sweet Sir; Beza then,

---

l.23 Stranger . . . strangers: Donne means the numerous foreigners
who were living in London in the 1590s and whose unpopularity
with the natives is referred to in lines 25–26.

l.46 Make . . . treason: The phrase suggests that the grotesque creature
who is the object of this satire is a professional informer, one who
tries to trick his victims into saying something suspiciously pro-
Catholic, or otherwise treasonable.

l.54 Calepines Dictionarie: a well-known polyglot dictionary.

Some other Jesuites, and two reverend men
Of our two Academies, I named; There
He stopt mee, and said; Nay, your Apostles were
Good pretty linguists, and so Panurge was;
Yet a poore gentleman, all these may passe   60
By travaile. Then, as if he would have sold
His tongue, he prais'd it, and such wonders told
That I was faine to say, If you'had liv'd, Sir,
Time enough to have beene Interpreter
To Babells bricklayers, sure the Tower had stood.
He adds, If of court life you knew the good,
You would leave lonenesse. I said, not alone
My lonenesse is, but Spartanes fashion,
To teach by painting drunkards, doth not last
Now; Aretines pictures have made few chast;   70
No more can Princes courts, though there be few
Better pictures of vice, teach me vertue;
He, like to a high strecht lute string squeakt, O Sir,
'Tis sweet to talke of Kings. At Westminster,
Said I, The man that keepes the Abbey tombes,
And for his price doth with who ever comes,
Of all our Harries, and our Edwards talke,
From King to King and all their kin can walke:
Your eares shall heare nought, but Kings; your eyes
    meet
Kings only; The way to it, is Kingstreet.   80
He smack'd, and cry'd, He's base, Mechanique, coarse,
So are all your Englishmen in their discourse.
Are not your Frenchmen neate? Mine? as you see,
I have but one Frenchman, looke, hee followes mee.
Certes they are neatly cloth'd; I, of this minde am,
Your only wearing is your Grogaram.
Not so Sir, I have more. Under this pitch
He would not flie; I chaff'd him; But as Itch
Scratch'd into smart, and as blunt iron ground
Into an edge, hurts worse: So, I (foole) found,   90
Crossing hurt mee; To fit my sullennesse,
He to another key, his stile doth addresse,

l.59 Panurge: in Rabelais.
l.70 Aretines: Pietro Aretino (1492–1556), an Italian writer well known
    for his satiric and licentious poems.

And askes, what newes? I tell him of new playes.
He takes my hand, and as a Still, which staies
A Sembriefe, 'twixt each drop, he nigardly,
As loth to enrich mee, so tells many a lie.
More than ten Hollensheads, or Halls, or Stowes,
Of triviall houshold trash he knowes; He knowes
When the Queene frown'd, or smil'd, and he knowes
  what
A subtle States-man may gather of that;   100
He knowes who loves; whom; and who by poyson
Hasts to an Offices reversion;
He knowes who'hath sold his land, and now doth beg
A licence, old iron, bootes, shooes, and egge-
shels to transport; Shortly boyes shall not play
At span-counter, or blow-point, but they pay
Toll to some Courtier; And wiser than all us,
He knowes what Ladie is not painted; Thus
He with home-meats tries me; I belch, spue, spit,
Looke pale, and sickly, like a Patient; Yet   110
He thrusts on more; And as if he'd undertooke
To say Gallo-Belgicus without booke
Speakes of all States, and deeds, that have been since
The Spaniards came, to the losse of Amyens.
Like a bigge wife, at sight of loathed meat,
Readie to travaile: So I sigh, and sweat
To heare this Makeron talke: In vaine; for yet,
Either my humour, or his owne to fit,
He like a priviledg'd spie, whom nothing can
Discredit, Libells now 'gainst each great man.   120
He names a price for every office paid;
He saith, our warres thrive ill, because delai'd;
That offices are entail'd, and that there are
Perpetuities of them, lasting as farre
As the last day; And that great officers,
Doe with the Pirates share, and Dunkirkers.
Who wasts in meat, in clothes, in horse, he notes;

l.95 Sembriefe: a pause the length of a whole note in music.
l.97 Hollensheads . . . Stowes: sixteenth-century English chroniclers.
l.106 span-counter . . . blow-point: children's games.
l.112 Gallo-Belgicus: a well-known newsletter.
l.117 Makeron: dandy.
l.124 Perpetuities: inalienable rights.

Who loves whores, who boyes, and who goats.
I more amas'd than Circes prisoners, when
They felt themselves turne beasts, felt my selfe then   130
Becomming Traytor, and mee thought I saw
One of our Giant Statutes ope his jaw
To sucke me in; for hearing him, I found
That as burnt venome Leachers do grow sound
By giving others their soares, I might growe
Guilty, and he free: Therefore I did shew
All signes of loathing; But since I am in,
I must pay mine, and my forefathers sinne
To the last farthing; Therefore to my power
Toughly and stubbornly I beare this crosse; But
   the'houre   140
Of mercy now was come; He tries to bring
Me to pay a fine to scape his torturing,
And saies, Sir, can you spare me; I said, willingly;
Nay, Sir, can you spare me a crowne? Thankfully I
Gave it, as Ransome; But as fidlers, still,
Though they be paid to be gone, yet needs will
Thrust one more jigge upon you: so did hee
With his long complementall thankes vexe me.
But he is gone, thankes to his needy want,
And the prerogative of my Crowne: Scant   150
His thankes were ended, when I, (which did see
All the court fill'd with more strange things than hee)
Ran from thence with such or more haste, than one
Who feares more actions, doth make from prison.
At home in wholesome solitarinesse
My precious soule began, the wretchednesse
Of suiters at court to mourne, and a trance
Like his, who dreamt he saw hell, did advance
It selfe on mee. Such men as he saw there,
I saw at court, and worse, and more; Low feare   160
Becomes the guiltie, not the accuser; Then,
Shall I, nones slave, of high borne, or rais'd men
Feare frownes? And, my Mistresse Truth, betray thee
To th'huffing braggart, puft Nobility?
No, no, Thou which since yesterday hast beene

l.133 To . . . in: see note to line 46.
l.158 who . . . hell: Dante.

Almost about the whole world, hast thou seene,
O Sunne, in all thy journey, Vanitie,
Such as swells the bladder of our court? I
Thinke he which made your waxen garden, and
Transported it from Italy to stand   170
With us, at London, flouts our Presence, for
Just such gay painted things, which no sappe, nor
Tast have in them, ours are; And naturall
Some of the stocks are, their fruits, bastard all.
'Tis ten a clock and past; All whom the Mews,
Baloune, Tennis, Dyet, or the stewes,
Had all the morning held, now the second
Time made ready, that day, in flocks, are found
In the Presence, and I, (God pardon mee.)
As fresh, and sweet their Apparrells be, as bee   180
The fields they sold to buy them; For a King
Those hose are, cry the flatterers; And bring
Them next weeke to the Theatre to sell;
Wants reach all states; Me seemes they doe as well
At stage, as court; All are players; who e'r lookes
(For themselves dare not goe) o'r Cheapside books,
Shall finde their wardrops Inventory. Now,
The Ladies come; As Pirats, which doe know
That there came weak ships fraught with Cutchannel,
The men board them; and praise, as they thinke, well,   190
Their beauties; they the mens wits; Both are bought.
Why good wits ne'r weare scarlet gownes, I thought
This cause, These men, mens wits for speeches buy,
And women buy all reds which scarlets die.
He call'd her beauty limetwigs, her haire net;
She feares her drugs ill laid, her haire loose set.
Would not Heraclitus laugh to see Macrine,
From hat to shooe, himselfe at doore refine,
As if the Presence were a Moschite, and lift

ll.169–171 waxen . . . London: artificial gardens of wax were exhibited
   by Italians in London.
l.175 Mews: stables.
l.176 Baloune: a game rather like football.
l.186 Cheapside: a market district of London.
l.187 wardrops: wardrobe's.
l.189 Cutchannel: cochineal.
l.199 Moschite: Moscovite.

His skirts and hose, and call his clothes to shrift,   200
Making them confesse not only mortall
Great staines and holes in them; but veniall
Feathers and dust, wherewith they fornicate:
And then by *Durers* rules survay the state
Of his each limbe, and with strings the odds trye
Of his neck to his legge, and wast to thighe.
So in immaculate clothes, and Symetrie
Perfect as circles, with such nicetie
As a young Preacher at his first time goes
To preach, he enters, and a Lady which owes   210
Him not so much as good will, he arrests,
And unto her protests protests protests
So much as at Rome would serve to have throwne
Ten Cardinalls into the Inquisition;
And whisperd by Jesu, so often, that A
Pursevant would have ravish'd him away
For saying of our Ladies psalter; But 'tis fit
That they each other plague, they merit it.
But here comes Glorius that will plague them both,
Who, in the other extreme, only doth   220
Call a rough carelessenesse, good fashion;
Whose cloak his spurres teare; whom he spits on
He cares not, His ill words doe no harme
To him; he rusheth in, as if arme, arme,
He meant to crie; And though his face be as ill
As theirs which in old hangings whip Christ, still
He strives to looke worse, he keepes all in awe;
Jeasts like a licenc'd foole, commands like law.
Tyr'd, now I leave this place, and but pleas'd so
As men which from gaoles to'execution goe,   230
Goe through the great chamber (why is it hung
With the seaven deadly sinnes?). Being among
Those Askaparts, men big enough to throw
Charing Crosse for a barre, men that doe know
No token of worth, but Queenes man, and fine
Living, barrells of beefe, flaggons of wine,

l.204 Durers rules: a reference to Albrecht Dürer's studies of proportion.
l.216 Pursevant: an officer whose task was to hunt out suspected Roman
    Catholics.
l.233 Askaparts: The name is taken from a giant in medieval romance.
ll.233–236 men . . . wine: The description of the royal guards sug-
    gests their familiar appellation as beefeaters.

I shooke like a spyed Spie. Preachers which are
Seas of Wit and Arts, you can, then dare,
Drowne the sinnes of this place, for, for mee
Which am but a scarce brooke, it enough shall bee   240
To wash the staines away; Although I yet
With *Macchabees* modestie, the knowne merit
Of my worke lessen: yet some wise man shall,
I hope, esteeme my writs Canonicall.

SATYRE V

Thou shalt not laugh in this leafe, Muse, nor they
Whom any pitty warmes; He which did lay
Rules to make Courtiers, (hee being understood
May make good Courtiers, but who Courtiers good?)
Frees from the sting of jests all who in extreme
Are wreched or wicked: of these two a theame
Charity and liberty give me. What is hee
Who Officers rage, and Suiters misery
Can write, and jest? If all things be in all,
As I thinke, since all, which were, are, and shall   10
Bee, be made of the same elements:
Each thing, each thing implyes or represents.
Then man is a world; in which, Officers
Are the vast ravishing seas; and Suiters,
Springs; now full, now shallow, now drye; which, to
That which drownes them, run: These selfe reasons do
Prove the world a man, in which, officers
Are the devouring stomacke, and Suiters
The excrements, which they voyd. All men are dust;
How much worse are Suiters, who to mens lust   20
Are made preyes? O worse than dust, or wormes meat,
For they do eate you now, whose selves wormes shall
  eate.
They are the mills which grinde you, yet you are
The winde which drives them; and a wastfull warre
Is fought against you, and you fight it; they
Adulterate lawe, and you prepare their way
Like wittals; th'issue your owne ruine is.

l.242 Macchabees modestie: a reference to a claim of modesty in the
  apocryphal Books of the Maccabees.

Greatest and fairest Empresse, know you this?
Alas, no more than Thames calme head doth know
Whose meades her armes drowne, or whose corne
  o'rflow: 30
You Sir, whose righteousnes she loves, whom I
By having leave to serve, am most richly
For service paid, authoriz'd, now beginne
To know and weed out this enormous sinne.
O Age of rusty iron! Some better wit
Call it some worse name, if ought equall it;
The iron Age *that* was, when justice was sold; now
Injustice is sold dearer farre. Allow
All demands, fees, and duties, gamsters, anon
The mony which you sweat, and sweare for, is gon 40
Into other hands: So controverted lands
Scape, like Angelica, the strivers hands.
If Law be the Judges heart, and hee
Have no heart to resist letter, or fee,
Where wilt thou appeale? powre of the Courts below
Flow from the first maine head, and these can throw
Thee, if they sucke thee in, to misery,
To fetters, halters; But if the injury
Steele thee to dare complaine, Alas, thou go'st
Against the stream, when upwards: when thou art
  most   50
Heavy and most faint; and in these labours they,
'Gainst whom thou should'st complaine, will in the
  way
Become great seas, o'r which, when thou shalt bee
Forc'd to make golden bridges, thou shalt see
That all thy gold was drown'd in them before;
All things follow their like, only who have may have
  more.
Judges are Gods; he who made and said them so,
Meant not that men should be forc'd to them to goe,
By meanes of Angels; When supplications
We send to God, to Dominations, 60

l.28 Empresse: Queen Elizabeth I.
l.31 Sir: The poem is addressed to Donne's patron, Sir Thomas Egerton.
l.42 Angelica: the heroine of Ariosto's *Orlando Furioso*, who was sought
  by many suitors.
l.59 Angels: Donne's familiar pun on the name of the coin.

Powers, Cherubins, and all heavens Courts, if wee
Should pay fees as here, Daily bread would be
Scarce to Kings; so 'tis. Would it not anger
A Stoicke, a coward, yea a Martyr,
To see a Pursivant come in, and call
All his cloathes, Copes; Bookes, Primers; and all
His Plate, Challices; and mistake them away,
And aske a fee for comming? Oh, ne'r may
Faire lawes white reverend name be strumpeted,
To warrant thefts: she is established   70
Recorder to Destiny, on earth, and shee
Speakes Fates words, and but tells us who must bee
Rich, who poore, who in chaires, who in jayles:
Shee is all faire, but yet hath foule long nailes,
With which she scracheth Suiters; In bodies
Of men, so in law, nailes are th'extremities,
So Officers stretch to more than Law can doe,
As our nailes reach what no else part comes to.
Why barest thou to yon Officer? Foole, Hath hee
Got those goods, for which erst men bar'd to thee?   80
Foole, twice, thrice, thou hast bought wrong, and now
  hungerly
Beg'st right; But that dole comes not till these dye.
Thou had'st much, and lawes Urim and Thummim trie
Thou wouldst for more; and for all hast paper
Enough to cloath all the great Carricks Pepper.
Sell that, and by that thou much more shalt leese,
Than Haman, when he sold his Antiquities.
O wretch that thy fortunes should moralize
Esops fables, and make tales, prophesies.
Thou'art the swimming dog whom shadows cosened,   90
And div'st, neare drowning, for what's vanished.

l.65 Pursivant: see "Satyre IV," note to line 216.
l.73 chaires: The reference is to sedan-chairs.

UPON MR. THOMAS CORYATS
CRUDITIES

Oh to what heighth will love of greatnesse drive
Thy leavened spirit, *Sesqui-superlative?*
Venice vast lake thou hadst seen, and wouldst seek
 then
Some vaster thing, and found'st a Curtizan.
That inland Sea having discovered well,
A Cellar gulfe, where one might saile to hell
From Heydelberg, thou longdst to see: And thou
This Booke, greater than all, producest now.
Infinite worke, which doth so far extend,
That none can study it to any end.   10
'Tis no one thing, it is not fruit nor roote;
Nor poorely limited with head or foot.
If man be therefore man, because he can
Reason, and laugh, thy booke doth halfe make man.
One halfe being made, thy modestie was such,
That thou on th'other half wouldst never touch.
When wilt thou be at full, great Lunatique?
Not till thou exceed the world? Canst thou be like
A prosperous nose-borne wenne, which sometimes
 growes
To be farre greater than the Mother-nose?   20
Goe then; and as to thee, when thou didst go,
Munster did Townes, and *Gesner* Authors show,
Mount now to *Gallo-belgicus;* appear
As deepe a States-man, as a Gazettier.
Homely and familiarly, when thou com'st back,
Talke of *Will. Conquerour,* and *Prester Jack.*
Go bashfull man, lest here thou blush to looke

Upon Mr. Thomas Coryats Crudities: Coryat was a notable English
traveler, one of the first to visit Asia and parts of the Near East.
Coryats Crudities, the eccentrically written account of his earlier
European travels, was published in 1611, preceded by a group of
witty mock-encomiastic poems, of which Donne's was one.
l.22 Munster . . . Gesner: encyclopedic authorities of the Renaissance.
l.23 Gallo-belgicus: the well-known newsletter.
l.26 Prester Jack: Prester John was the legendary ruler of Ethiopia.

Upon the progresse of thy glorious booke,
To which both Indies sacrifices send;
The West sent gold, which thou didst freely spend,   30
(Meaning to see't no more) upon the presse.
The East sends hither her deliciousnesse;
And thy leaves must imbrace what comes from thence,
The Myrrhe, the Pepper, and the Frankincense.
This magnifies thy leaves; but if they stoope
To neighbour wares, when Merchants do unhoope
Voluminous barrels; if thy leaves do then
Convey these wares in parcels unto men;
If for vast Tons of Currans, and of Figs,
Of Medicinall and Aromatique twigs,   40
Thy leaves a better method do provide,
Divide to pounds, and ounces sub-divide;
If they stoope lower yet, and vent our wares,
Home-*manufactures*, to thick popular Faires,
If *omni-praegnant* there, upon warme stalls,
They hatch all wares for which the buyer calls;
Then thus thy leaves we justly may commend,
That they all kinde of matter comprehend.
Thus thou, by means which th'Ancients never took,
A Pandect makest, and Universall Booke.   50
The bravest Heroes, for publike good,
Scattered in divers Lands their limbs and blood.
Worst malefactors, to whom men are prize,
Do publike good, cut in Anatomies;
So will thy booke in peeces; for a Lord
Which casts at Protescues, and all the board,
Provide whole books; each leafe enough will be
For friends to passe time, and keep company.
Can all carouse up thee? no, thou must fit
Measures; and fill out for the half-pint wit: 60
Some shall wrap pils, and save a friends life so,
Some shall stop muskets, and so kill a foe.
Thou shalt not ease the Criticks of next age

l.50 Pandect: comprehensive digest.
l.56 Protescues: One explanation for this puzzling phrase is supplied by
 Grierson, who, following Grosart, identifies Protescue, or Portescue,
 as his text has it, with a Portuguese coin. The passage then would
 refer to gentlemen at play cutting up pages of Coryat's book to use
 as pledges for money.

So much, at once their hunger to asswage:
Nor shall wit-pirats hope to finde thee lye
All in one bottome, in one Librarie.
Some Leaves may paste strings there in other books,
And so one may, which on another looks,
Pilfer, alas, a little wit from you;
But hardly* much; and yet I think this true;   70
As *Sibyls* was, your booke is mysticall,
For every peece is as much worth as all.
Therefore mine impotency I confesse,
The healths which my braine bears must be far lesse:
Thy Gyant-wit 'orethrowes me, I am gone;
And rather than read all, I would reade none.

IN EUNDEM MACARONICON

Quot, dos haec, **Linguists** *perfetti, Disticha* fairont,
Tot cuerdos **States-men.** *hic livre fara tuus.*
Es *sat* a my l'honneur estre hic inteso; Car **I leaue**
L'honra, de personne nestre creduto, *tibi.*

Explicit Joannes Donne.

* I meane from one page which shall paste strings in a booke. [Donne's
note.]

In Eundem Macaronicon: Grierson provides the following translation of
this multilingual jest:

 "As many perfect linguists as these two distichs make,
 So many prudent statesmen will this book of yours produce.
 To me the honour is sufficient of being understood: for I leave
 To you the honour of being believed by no one."

Metempsychosis:
The Progresse of the Soule

THIS EXTRAVAGANT fragment, written in 1601, marks approximately the end of Donne's first poetic period. Related to the *Satyres* in tone and attitude, it also recalls the more cynical of the *Elegies* and *Songs and Sonets* in its espousal of a libertine naturalism and in its display of wit for what often seems wit's own sake (in this latter respect it also resembles such early verse letters as "The Storme" and "The Calme").

In his *Conversations* with Drummond of Hawthornden, Ben Jonson made the following observations:

> The conceit of Dones Transformation or Μετεμψύχωσις was that he sought the soule of that aple which Eve pulled and thereafter made it the soule of a bitch, then of a shee wolf, and so of a woman; his general purpose was to have brought in all the bodies of the Hereticks from the soule of Cain, and at last left in the bodie of Calvin.

If Donne was the source of Jonson's information, it is likely that the author of *Metempsychosis* was taking care to avoid imputations of treason, for the poem itself indicates that the last residence of the soul of heresy is to be not Calvin but rather Queen Elizabeth I, "the great soule which here amongst us now / Doth dwell." (H. Gardner, in her recent edition of the *Elegies and Songs and Sonets*, expresses some doubt as to the validity of this otherwise generally accepted interpretation.)

The poem has received relatively little critical attention. It is discussed in some detail by E. LeComte and tangentially by others, including M. H. Nicolson.

INFINITATI SACRUM,[1]
16. Augusti 1601.
METEMPSYCHOSIS.
POÊMA SATYRICON.

EPISTLE

Others at the Porches and entries of their Buildings set their Armes; I, my picture; if any colours can deliver a minde so plaine, and flat, and through-light[2] as mine. Naturally at a new Author, I doubt, and sticke, and doe not say quickly, good. I censure much and taxe; And this liberty costs mee more than others, by how much my owne things are worse than others. Yet I would not be so rebellious against my selfe, as not to doe it, since I love it; nor so unjust to others, to do it *sine talione*.[3] As long as I give them as good hold upon mee, they must pardon mee my bitings. I forbid no reprehender, but him that like the Trent Councell forbids not bookes, but Authors, damning what ever such a name hath or shall write. None writes so ill, that he gives not some thing exemplary, to follow, or flie. Now when I beginne this booke, I have no purpose to come into any mans debt; how my stocke will hold out I know not; perchance waste, perchance increase in use; if I doe borrow any thing of Antiquitie, besides that I make account that I pay it to posterity, with as much and as

1. *Infinitati Sacrum:* sacred to infinity.
2. *through-light:* transparent.
3. *sine talione:* without retribution.

good: You shall still finde mee to acknowledge it, and to thanke not him onely that hath digg'd out treasure for mee, but that hath lighted mee a candle to the place. All which I will bid you remember, (for I will have no such Readers as I can teach) is, that the Pithagorian doctrine[4] doth not onely carry one soule from man to man, nor man to beast, but indifferently to plants also: and therefore you must not grudge to finde the same soule in an Emperour, in a Post-horse, and in a Mucheron,[5] since no unreadinesse in the soule, but an indisposition in the organs workes this. And therefore though this soule could not move when it was a Melon, yet it may remember, and now tell mee, at what lascivious banquet it was serv'd. And though it could not speake, when it was a spider, yet it can remember, and now tell me, who used it for poyson to attaine dignitie. How ever the bodies have dull'd her other faculties, her
memory hath ever been her owne, which makes
me so seriously deliver you by her relation all her passages from her
first making when shee was
that apple which Eve eate,
to this time when shee is
hee, whose life you shall
finde in the end of
this booke

THE PROGRESSE OF THE SOULE

FIRST SONG

I

I sing the progresse of a deathlesse soule,
Whom Fate, which God made, but doth not controule,
Plac'd in most shapes; all times before the law
Yoak'd us, and when, and since, in this I sing.
And the great world to his aged evening;
From infant morne, through manly noone I draw.

4. *Pithagorian doctrine:* the transmigration of the soul.
5. *Mucheron:* mushroom.

What the gold Chaldee, or silver Persian saw,
Greeke brasse, or Roman iron, is in this one;
A worke t'outweare *Seths* pillars, bricke and stone,
   And (holy writt excepted) made to yeeld to none.   10

II

Thee, eye of heaven, this great Soule envies not,
By thy male force, is all wee have, begot.
In the first East, thou now beginst to shine,
Suck'st early balme, and Iland spices there,
And wilt anon in thy loose-rein'd careere
At Tagus, Po, Sene, Thames, and Danow dine,
And see at night thy Westerne land of Myne,
Yet hast thou not more nations seene than shee,
That before thee, one day beganne to bee,
   And thy fraile light being quench'd, shall long, long
   out live thee.   20

III

Nor, holy *Janus*, in whose soveraigne boate
The Church, and all the Monarchies did floate;
That swimming Colledge, and free Hospitall
Of all mankinde, that cage and vivarie
Of fowles, and beasts, in whose wombe, Destinie
Us, and our latest nephewes did install
(From thence are all deriv'd, that fill this All,)
Did'st thou in that great stewardship embarke
So diverse shapes into that floating parke,
   As have beene moved, and inform'd by this heavenly
   sparke.   30

IV

Great Destiny the Commissary of God,
That hast mark'd out a path and period

l.9 Seths pillars: Seth was one of the sons of Adam. His progeny, according to Josephus, erected two pillars to commemorate his astronomical discoveries.
l.11 eye of heaven: the sun.
l.16 Sene: the Seine.
l.16 Danow: the Danube.
l.21 Janus: In medieval tradition, the Pagan deity Janus was regarded as a type of Noah.

For every thing; who, where wee of-spring tooke,
Our wayes and ends seest at one instant; Thou
Knot of all causes, thou whose changelesse brow
Ne'r smiles nor frownes, O vouch thou safe to looke
And shew my story, in thy eternall booke:
That (if my prayer be fit) I may'understand
So much my selfe, as to know with what hand,
    How scant, or liberall this my lifes race is spand.   40

V

To my sixe lustres almost now outwore,
Except thy booke owe mee so many more,
Except my legend be free from the letts
Of steepe ambition, sleepie povertie,
Spirit-quenching sicknesse, dull captivitie,
Distracting businesse, and from beauties nets,
And all that calls from this, and to others whets.
O let me not launch out, but let mee save
Th'expense of braine and spirit; that my grave
    His right and due, a whole unwasted man may have.   50

VI

But if my dayes be long, and good enough,
In vaine this sea shall enlarge, or enrough
It selfe; for I will through the wave, and fome,
And shall, in sad lone wayes a lively spright,
Make my darke heavy Poëm light, and light.
For though through many streights, and lands I roame,
I launch at paradise, and I saile towards home;
The course I there began, shall here be staid,
Sailes hoised there, stroke here, and anchors laid
    In Thames, which were at Tigrys, and Euphrates
      waide.   60

VII

For the great soule which here amongst us now
Doth dwell, and moves that hand, and tongue, and brow,

l.41 lustres: lustrums, five-year periods.
l.43 letts: obstacles.
l.61 For . . . now: Donne seems to have made Queen Elizabeth I the
   ultimate satiric subject of this poem: The soul which began in the
   fatal apple in Eden was to be traced through its various transmigra-

Which, as the Moone the sea, moves us; to heare
Whose story, with long patience you will long;
(For 'tis the crowne, and last straine of my song)
This soule to whom *Luther*, and *Mahomet* were
Prisons of flesh; this soule which oft did teare,
And mend the wracks of th'Empire, and late Rome,
And liv'd when every great change did come,
   Had first in paradise, a low, but fatall roome.   70

VIII

Yet no low roome, nor than the greatest, lesse,
If (as devout and sharpe men fitly guesse)
That Crosse, our joy, and griefe, where nailes did tye
That All, which alwayes was all, every where;
Which could not sinne, and yet all sinnes did beare;
Which could not die, yet could not chuse but die;
Stood in the selfe same roome in Calvarie,
Where first grew the forbidden learned tree,
For on that tree hung in security
   This Soule, made by the Makers will from pulling
    free.   80

IX

Prince of the orchard, faire as dawning morne,
Fenc'd with the law, and ripe as soone as borne
That apple grew, which this Soule did enlive,
Till the then climing serpent, that now creeps
For that offence, for which all mankinde weepes,
Tooke it, and t'her whom the first man did wive
(Whom and her race, only forbiddings drive)
He gave it, she, t'her husband, both did eate;
So perished the eaters, and the meate:
   And wee (for treason taints the blood) thence die
    and sweat.   90

X

Man all at once was there by woman slaine,
And one by one we'are here slaine o'er againe

tions until it took up residence in the body of the Queen who had
persecuted the religion to which Donne's family belonged and who
had, more recently, executed Donne's former commander, the Earl
of Essex.

By them. The mother poison'd the well-head,
The daughters here corrupt us, Rivolets;
No smalnesse scapes, no greatnesse breaks their nets;
She thrust us out, and by them we are led
Astray, from turning, to whence we are fled.
Were prisoners Judges, 'twould seeme rigorous,
Shee sinn'd, we beare; part of our paine is, thus
    To love them, whose fault to this painfull love yoak'd
    us.   100

XI

So fast in us doth this corruption grow,
That now wee dare aske why wee should be so.
Would God (disputes the curious Rebell) make
A law, and would not have it kept? Or can
His creatures will, crosse his? Of every man
For one, will God (and be just) vengeance take?
Who sinn'd? t'was not forbidden to the snake
Nor her, who was not then made; nor is't writ
That Adam cropt, or knew the apple; yet
    The worme and she, and he, and wee endure for it.   110

XII

But snatch mee heavenly Spirit from this vaine
Reckoning their vanities, lesse is their gaine
Than hazard still, to meditate on ill,
Though with good minde; their reasons, like those
  toyes
Of glassie bubbles, which the gamesome boyes
Stretch to so nice a thinnes through a quill
That they themselves breake, doe themselves spill:
Arguing is heretiques game, and Exercise
As wrastlers, perfects them; Not liberties
    Of speech, but silence; hands, not tongues, end
    heresies.   120

XIII

Just in that instant when the serpents gripe,
Broke the slight veines, and tender conduit-pipe,

---

ll.92–93 And . . . them: As so often in the *Songs and Sonets*, Donne
plays on the colloquial meaning of dying as experiencing sexual
climax.

Through which this soule from the trees root did draw
Life, and growth to this apple, fled away
This loose soule, old, one and another day.
As lightning, which one scarce dares say, he saw,
'Tis so soone gone, (and better proofe the law
Of sense, than faith requires) swiftly she flew
To a darke and foggie Plot; Her, her fates threw
   There through th'earths pores, and in a Plant hous'd
     her anew.   130

XIV

The plant thus abled, to it selfe did force
A place, where no place was; by natures course
As aire from water, water fleets away
From thicker bodies, by this root thronged so
His spungie confines gave him place to grow:
Just as in our streets, when the people stay
To see the Prince, and have so fill'd the way
That weesels scarce could passe; when she comes nere
They throng and cleave up, and a passage cleare,
   As if, for that time, their round bodies flatned were.   140

XV

His right arme he thrust out towards the East,
West-ward his left; th'ends did themselves digest
Into ten lesser strings, these fingers were:
And as a slumberer stretching on his bed,
This way he this, and that way scattered
His other legge, which feet with toes upbeare.
Grew on his middle parts, the first day, haire,
To show, that in loves businesse hee should still
A dealer bee, and be us'd well, or ill:
   His apples kindle, his leaves, force of conception kill.   150

XVI

A mouth, but dumbe, he hath; blinde eyes, deafe eares,
And to his shoulders dangle subtile haires;
A young *Colossus* there hee stands upright,

l.129 foggie: marshy.
l.137 Prince: The reference, as the next line makes clear, is to the Queen.
  As Grierson points out, the term *prince* might be applied to a female
  monarch.

And as that ground by him were conquered
A leafie garland weares he on his head
Enchas'd with little fruits, so red and bright
That for them you would call your Loves lips white;
So, of a lone unhaunted place possest,
Did this soules second Inne, built by the guest,
 This living buried man, this quiet mandrake, rest. 160

XVII

No lustfull woman came this plant to grieve,
But 'twas because there was none yet but Eve:
And she (with other purpose) kill'd it quite;
Her sinne had now brought in infirmities,
And so her cradled child, the moist red eyes
Had never shut, nor slept since it saw light;
Poppie she knew, she knew the mandrakes might,
And tore up both, and so coold her childs blood;
Unvirtuous weeds might long unvex'd have stood;
 But hee's short liv'd, that with his death can doe
 most good. 170

XVIII

To an unfetterd soules quick nimble haste
Are falling stars, and hearts thoughts, but slow pac'd:
Thinner than burnt aire flies this soule, and she
Whom foure new comming, and foure parting Suns
Had found, and left the Mandrakes tenant, runnes
Thoughtlesse of change, when her firme destiny
Confin'd, and enjayld her, that seem'd so free,
Into a small blew shell, the which a poore
Warme bird orespread, and sat still evermore,
 Till her inclos'd child kickt, and pick'd it selfe a
 dore. 180

XIX

Outcrept a sparrow, this soules moving Inne,
On whose raw armes stiffe feathers now begin,
As childrens teeth through gummes, to breake with
 paine,
His flesh is jelly yet, and his bones threds,

ll.161–170 No . . . good: As this stanza indicates, the mandrake was
 esteemed both as a source of love potions and as a narcotic.

All a new downy mantle overspreads,
A mouth he opes, which would as much containe
As his late house, and the first houre speaks plaine,
And chirps alowd for meat. Meat fit for men
His father steales for him, and so feeds then
   One, that within a moneth, will beate him from his
     hen.   190

XX

In this worlds youth wise nature did make haste,
Things ripened sooner, and did longer last;
Already this hot cocke, in bush and tree,
In field and tent oreflutters his next hen;
He asks her not, who did so last, nor when,
Nor if his sister, or his neece shee be;
Nor doth she pule for his inconstancie
If in her sight he change, nor doth refuse
The next that calls; both liberty doe use;
   Where store is of both kindes, both kindes may
     freely chuse.   200

XXI

Men, till they tooke laws which made freedome lesse,
Their daughters, and their sisters did ingresse;
Till now unlawfull, therefore ill, 'twas not.
So jolly, that it can move, this soule is,
The body so free of his kindnesses,
That selfe-preserving it hath now forgot,
And slackneth so the soules, and bodies knot,
Which temperance streightens; freely on his she friends
He blood, and spirit, pith, and marrow spends,
   Ill steward of himself, himselfe in three yeares ends.   210

XXII

Else might he long have liv'd; man did not know
Of gummie blood, which doth in holly grow,
How to make bird-lime, nor how to deceive
With faind calls, hid nets, or enwrapping snare,
The free inhabitants of the Plyant aire.

l.210 Ill . . . ends: According to Renaissance belief, each sexual act
   diminishes life by a day; hence the sparrow's rapid demise.

Man to beget, and woman to conceive
Askt not of rootes, nor of cock-sparrowes, leave:
Yet chuseth hee, though none of these he feares,
Pleasantly three, than streightned twenty yeares
    To live, and to encrease his race, himselfe outweares.   220

XXIII

This cole with overblowing quench'd and dead,
The Soule from her too active organs fled
T'a brooke. A female fishes sandie Roe
With the males jelly, newly lev'ned was,
For they had intertouch'd as they did passe,
And one of those small bodies, fitted so,
This soule inform'd, and abled it to rowe
It selfe with finnie oares, which she did fit:
Her scales seem'd yet of parchment, and as yet
    Perchance a fish, but by no name you could call it.   230

XXIV

When goodly, like a ship in her full trim,
A swan, so white that you may unto him
Compare all whitenesse, but himselfe to none,
Glided along, and as he glided watch'd,
And with his arched necke this poore fish catch'd.
It mov'd with state, as if to looke upon
Low things it scorn'd, and yet before that one
Could thinke he sought it, he had swallowed cleare
This, and much such, and unblam'd devour'd there
    All, but who too swift, too great, or well armed were.   240

XXV

Now swome a prison in a prison put,
And now this Soule in double walls was shut,
Till melted with the Swans digestive fire,
She left her house the fish, and vapour'd forth;
Fate not affording bodies of more worth
For her as yet, bids her againe retire
T'another fish, to any new desire
Made a new prey; For, he that can to none
Resistance make, nor complaint, sure is gone.
    Weaknesse invites, but silence feasts oppression.   250

XXVI

Pace with her native streame, this fish doth keepe,
And journeyes with her, towards the glassie deepe,
But oft retarded, once with a hidden net
Though with great windowes, for when Need first
  taught
These tricks to catch food, then they were not wrought
As now, with curious greedinesse to let
None scape, but few, and fit for use, to get,
As, in this trap a ravenous pike was tane,
Who, though himselfe distrest, would faine have slain
  This wretch; So hardly are ill habits left again.   260

XXVII

Here by her smallnesse shee two deaths orepast,
Once innocence scap'd, and left the oppressor fast.
The net through-swome, she keepes the liquid path,
And whether she leape up sometimes to breath
And suck in aire, or finde it underneath,
Or working parts like mills or limbecks hath
To make the water thinne and airelike, faith
Cares not; but safe the Place she's come unto
Where fresh, with salt waves meet, and what to doe
  She knowes not, but betweene both makes a boord
    or two.   270

XXVIII

So farre from hiding her guests, water is,
That she showes them in bigger quantities
Than they are. Thus doubtfull of her way,
For game and not for hunger a sea Pie
Spied through this traiterous spectacle, from high,
The seely fish where it disputing lay,
And t'end her doubts and her, beares her away:
Exalted she'is, but to the exalters good,
As are by great ones, men which lowly stood.
  It's rais'd, to be the Raisers instrument and food.   280

l.266 limbecks: alembics.
l.274 sea Pie: sea-bird.

XXIX

Is any kinde subject to rape like fish?
Ill unto man, they neither doe, nor wish:
Fishers they kill not, nor with noise awake,
They doe not hunt, nor strive to make a prey
Of beasts, nor their young sonnes to beare away;
Foules they pursue not, nor do undertake
To spoile the nests industrious birds do make;
Yet them all these unkinde kinds feed upon,
To kill them is an occupation,
   And lawes make Fasts, and Lents for their destruc-
     tion.   290

XXX

A sudden stiffe land-winde in that selfe houre
To sea-ward forc'd this bird, that did devour
The fish; he cares not, for with ease he flies,
Fat gluttonies best orator: at last
So long hee hath flowen, and hath flowen so fast
That many leagues at sea, now tir'd hee lyes,
And with his prey, that till then languisht, dies;
The soules no longer foes, two wayes did erre,
The fish I follow, and keepe no calender
   Of the other; he lives yet in some great officer.   300

XXXI

Into an embrion fish, our Soule is throwne,
And in due time throwne out againe, and growne
To such vastness as, if unmanacled
From Greece, Morea were, and that by some
Earthquake unrooted, loose Morea swome,
Or seas from Africks body had severed
And torne the hopefull Promontories head,
This fish would seeme these, and, when all hopes faile,
A great ship overset, or without saile
   Hulling, might (when this was a whelp) be like this
     whale.   310

XXXII

At every stroake his brazen finnes do take,
More circles in the broken sea they make

l.304 Morea: the Peloponnesus.

Than cannons voices, when the aire they teare:
His ribs are pillars, and his high arch'd roofe
Of barke that blunts best steele, is thunder-proofe:
Swimme in him swallow'd Dolphins, without feare,
And feele no sides, as if his vast wombe were
Some inland sea, and ever as hee went
Hee spouted rivers up, as if he ment
   To joyne our seas, with seas above the firmament.   320

XXXIII

He hunts not fish, but as an officer,
Stayes in his court, at his owne net, and there
All suitors of all sorts themselves enthrall;
So on his backe lyes this whale wantoning,
And in his gulfe-like throat, sucks every thing
That passeth neare. Fish chaseth fish, and all,
Flyer and follower, in this whirlepoole fall;
O might not states of more equality
Consist? and is it of necessity
   That thousand guiltlesse smals, to make one great,
     must die?   330

XXXIV

Now drinkes he up seas, and he eates up flocks,
He justles Ilands, and he shakes firme rockes.
Now in a roomefull house this Soule doth float,
And like a Prince she sends her faculties
To all her limbes, distant as Provinces.
The Sunne hath twenty times both crab and goate
Parched, since first lanch'd forth this living boate;
'Tis greatest now, and to destruction
Nearest; There's no pause at perfection;
   Greatnesse a period hath, but hath no station.   340

XXXV

Two little fishes whom hee never harm'd,
Nor fed on their kinde, two not throughly arm'd
With hope that they could kill him, nor could doe
Good to themselves by his death (they did not eate
His flesh, nor suck those oyles, which thence outstreat)
Conspir'd against him, and it might undoe
The plot of all, that the plotters were two,

But that they fishes were, and could not speake.
How shall a Tyran wise strong projects breake,
   If wreches can on them the common anger wreake?   350

XXXVI

The flaile-finn'd Thresher, and steel-beak'd Sword-fish
Onely attempt to doe, what all doe wish.
The Thresher backs him, and to beate begins;
The sluggard Whale yeelds to oppression,
And t'hide himselfe from shame and danger, downe
Begins to sinke; the Swordfish upward spins,
And gores him with his beake; his staffe-like finnes,
So well the one, his sword the other plyes,
That now a scoffe, and prey, this tyran dyes,
   And (his owne dole) feeds with himselfe all com-
     panies.   360

XXXVII

Who will revenge his death? or who will call
Those to account, that thought, and wrought his fall?
The heires of slaine kings, wee see are often so
Transported with the joy of what they get,
That they, revenge and obsequies forget,
Nor will against such men the people goe,
Because h'is now dead, to whom they should show
Love in that act; Some kings by vice being growne
So needy of subjects love, that of their own
   They thinke they lose, if love be to the dead Prince
     shown.   370

XXXVIII

This Soule, now free from prison, and passion,
Hath yet a little indignation
That so small hammers should so soone downe beat
So great a castle. And having for her house
Got the streight cloyster of a wreched mouse
(As basest men that have not what to eate,
Nor enjoy ought, doe farre more hate the great
Than they, who good repos'd estates possesse)
This Soule, late taught that great things might by lesse
   Be slaine, to gallant mischiefe doth herselfe addresse.   380

XXXIX

Natures great master-peece, an Elephant,
The onely harmlesse great thing; the giant
Of beasts; who thought, no more had gone, to make
  one wise
But to be just, and thankfull, loth to offend,
(Yet nature hath given him no knees to bend)
Himselfe he up-props, on himselfe relies,
And foe to none, suspects no enemies,
Still sleeping stood; vex't not his fantasie
Blacke dreames; like an unbent bow, carelessly
    His sinewy Proboscis did remisly lie: 390

XL

In which as in a gallery this mouse
Walk'd, and surveid the roomes of this vast house,
And to the braine, the soules bedchamber, went,
And gnaw'd the life cords there; Like a whole towne
Cleane undermin'd, the slaine beast tumbled downe;
With him the murtherer dies, whom envy sent
To kill, not scape, (for, only hee that ment
To die, did ever kill a man of better roome,)
And thus he made his foe, his prey, and tombe:
    Who cares not to turn back, may any whither come.   400

XLI

Next, hous'd this Soule a Wolves yet unborne whelp,
Till the best midwife, Nature, gave it helpe,
To issue. It could kill, as soone as goe.
Abel, as white, and milde as his sheepe were,
(Who, in that trade, of Church, and kingdomes, there
Was the first type) was still infested soe,
With this wolfe, that it bred his losse and woe;
And yet his bitch, his sentinell attends
The flocke so neere, so well warnes and defends,
    That the wolfe, (hopelesse else) to corrupt her,
    intends.   410

---

ll.381–385 Natures . . . bend: a characteristic example of Elizabethan
  "unnatural natural history," as LeComte remarks.
l.406 still: always.

XLII

Hee tooke a course, which since, successfully,
Great men have often taken, to espie
The counsels, or to breake the plots of foes.
To Abels tent he stealeth in the darke,
On whose skirts the bitch slept; ere she could barke,
Attach'd her with streight gripes, yet hee call'd those,
Embracements of love; to loves worke he goes,
Where deeds move more than words; nor doth she show,
Nor much resist, nor needs hee streighten so
   His prey, for, were shee loose, she would nor barke,
    nor goe.   420

XLIII

Hee hath engag'd her; his, she wholy bides;
Who not her owne, none others secrets hides.
If to the flocke he come, and Abell there,
She faines hoarse barkings, but she biteth not,
Her faith is quite, but not her love forgot.
At last a trap, of which some every where
Abell had plac'd, ends all his losse, and feare,
By the Wolves death; and now just time it was
That a quick soule should give life to that masse
   Of blood in Abels bitch, and thither this did passe.   430

XLIV

Some have their wives, their sisters some begot,
But in the lives of Emperours you shall not
Reade of a lust the which may equall this;
This wolfe begot himselfe, and finished
What he began alive, when hee was dead;
Sonne to himselfe, and father too, hee is
A ridling lust, for which Schoolemen would misse
A proper name. The whelpe of both these lay
In Abels tent, and with soft Moaba,
   His sister, being yong, it us'd to sport and play.   440

XLV

Hee soone for her too harsh, and churlish grew,
And Abell (the dam dead) would use this new

l.439 Moaba: Donne gets the name from post-scriptural Jewish tradition.

For the field. Being of two kindes thus made,
He, as his dam, from sheepe drove wolves away,
And as his Sire, he made them his owne prey.
Five yeares he liv'd, and cosened with his trade,
Then hopelesse that his faults were hid, betraid
Himselfe by flight, and by all followed,
From dogges, a wolfe; from wolves, a dogge he fled;
    And, like a spie to both sides false, he perished.   450

XLVI

It quickned next a toyfull Ape, and so
Gamesome it was, that it might freely goe
From tent to tent, and with the children play.
His organs now so like theirs hee doth finde,
That why he cannot laugh, and speake his minde,
He wonders. Much with all, most he doth stay
With Adams fift daughter *Siphatecia*,
Doth gaze on her, and, where she passeth, passe,
Gathers her fruits, and tumbles on the grasse,
    And wisest of that kinde, the first true lover was.   460

XLVII

He was the first that more desir'd to have
One than another; first that ere did crave
Love by mute signes, and had no power to speake;
First that could make love faces, or could doe
The valters sombersalts, or us'd to wooe
With hoiting gambolls, his owne bones to breake
To make his mistresse merry; or to wreake
Her anger on himselfe. Sinnes against kinde
They easily doe, that can let feed their minde
    With outward beauty; beauty they in boyes and
    beasts do find.   470

XLVIII

By this misled, too low things men have prov'd,
And too high; beasts and angels have beene lov'd.
This Ape, though else through-vaine, in this was wise,
He reach'd at things too high, but open way

l.457 Siphatecia: a name derived, like Moaba, from Jewish tradition.
l.468 kinde: nature.
l.471 prov'd: experienced.

There was, and he knew not she would say nay;
His toyes prevaile not, likelier meanes he tries,
He gazeth on her face with teare-shot eyes,
And up lifts subtly with his russet pawe
Her kidskinne apron without feare or awe
   Of Nature; Nature hath no gaole, though shee hath
    law.   480

XLIX

First she was silly and knew not what he ment.
That vertue, by his touches, chaft and spent,
Succeeds an itchie warmth, that melts her quite;
She knew not first, nowe cares not what he doth,
And willing halfe and more, more than halfe loth,
She neither puls nor pushes, but outright
Now cries, and now repents; when *Tethlemite*
Her brother, enterd, and a great stone threw
After the Ape, who, thus prevented, flew.
   This house thus batter'd downe, the Soule possest a
   new.   490

L

And whether by this change she lose or win,
She comes out next, where the Ape would have gone in.
Adam and *Eve* had mingled bloods, and now
Like Chimiques equall fires, her temperate wombe
Had stew'd and form'd it: and part did become
A spungie liver, that did richly allow,
Like a free conduit, on a high hils brow,
Life-keeping moisture unto every part;
Part hardned it selfe to a thicker heart,
   Whose busie furnaces lifes spirits do impart.   500

L I

Another part became the well of sense,
The tender well-arm'd feeling braine, from whence,
Those sinowie strings which do our bodies tie,
Are raveld out; and fast there by one end,
Did this Soule limbes, these limbes a soule attend;
And now they joyn'd; keeping some quality
Of every past shape, she knew treachery,
Rapine, deceit, and lust, and ills enow

To be a woman. *Themech* she is now,
  Sister and wife to *Caine*, *Caine* that first did plow.   510

LII

Who ere thou beest that read'st this sullen Writ,
Which just so much courts thee, as thou dost it,
Let me arrest thy thoughts; wonder with mee,
Why plowing, building, ruling and the rest,
Or most of those arts, whence our lives are blest,
By cursed *Cains* race invented be,
And blest *Seth* vext us with Astronomie.
Ther's nothing simply good, nor ill alone,
Of every quality comparison,
  The onely measure is, and judge, opinion.   520

Verse Letters

DONNE'S VERSE letters, some of the best of which appear in the following pages, were written over a period of time extending from 1597 to 1614, and they fall, as H. J. C. Grierson observes, into two fairly well-defined groups. The first and larger group consists of those epistles which Donne wrote to the friends of his youth—Christopher Brooke, Sir Henry Wotton, Rowland Woodward, and Thomas Woodward. The earliest of these were written in 1597, at the time of Essex's expedition against the Azores, in which Donne took part; the last of them were written around 1608. The second group, written between 1608 and 1614, is dominated by ingenious poems of compliment addressed to the great ladies—Lucy, Countess of Bedford; Catherine, Countess of Salisbury; Elizabeth, Countess of Huntingdon; Mrs. Magdalen Herbert—who were at once the poet's patronesses and the recipients of his Platonic devotion.

For the modern reader the verse letters, marked as they are by a conspicuous and rather labored ingenuity, are not among the most attractive or accessible of Donne's writings. Nevertheless, they are indispensable to a full knowledge of the poet and the society in which he lived and worked.

THE STORME
To MR. CHRISTOPHER
BROOKE

Thou which art I, ('tis nothing to be soe)
Thou which art still thy selfe, by these shalt know
Part of our passage; And, a hand, or eye
By *Hilliard* drawne, is worth an history,
By a worse painter made; and (without pride)
When by thy judgment they are dignifi'd,
My lines are such: 'Tis the preheminence
Of friendship onely to'impute excellence.
England to whom we'owe, what we be, and have,
Sad that her sonnes did seeke a forraine grave   10
(For, Fates, or Fortunes drifts none can soothsay,
Honour and misery have one face and way.)
From out her pregnant intrailes sigh'd a winde
Which at th'ayres middle marble roome did finde
Such strong resistance, that it selfe it threw
Downeward againe; and so when it did view
How in the port, our fleet deare time did leese,
Withering like prisoners, which lye but for fees,
Mildly it kist our sailes, and, fresh and sweet,
As to a stomack sterv'd, whose insides meete,   20
Meate comes, it came; and swole our sailes, when wee
So joyd, as *Sara*'her swelling joy'd to see.
But 'twas but so kinde, as our countrimen,
Which bring friends one dayes way, and leave them
   then.
Then like two mighty Kings, which dwelling farre
Asunder, meet against a third to warre,

The Storme: To Mr. Christopher Brooke: one of Donne's closest friends
   in the poet's earlier years.
l.4 Hilliard: Nicholas Hilliard (1537–1619), a famous English painter
   of miniatures.
l.14 ayres . . . roome: According to one school of thought, the middle
   region of the air was solid; hence Donne's epithet, marble. It is
   also possibly a reference to the blue color of the sky.
l.17 leese: lose.
l.18 fees: sums due to the jailer.

The South and West winds joyn'd, and, as they blew,
Waves like a rowling trench before them threw.
Sooner than you read this line, did the gale,
Like shot, not fear'd till felt, our sailes assaile;   30
And what at first was call'd a gust, the same
Hath now a stormes, anon a tempests name.
Jonas, I pitty thee, and curse those men,
Who when the storm rag'd most, did wake thee then;
Sleepe is paines easiest salve, and doth fulfill
All offices of death, except to kill.
But when I wakt, I saw, that I saw not;
Ay, and the Sunne, which should teach mee'had forgot
East, West, Day, Night, and I could onely say,
If'the world had lasted, now it had been day.   40
Thousands our noyses were, yet wee'mongst all
Could none by his right name, but thunder call:
Lightning was all our light, and it rain'd more
Than if the Sunne had drunke the sea before.
Some coffin'd in their cabbins lye,'equally
Griev'd that they are not dead, and yet must dye;
And as sin-burd'ned soules from graves will creepe,
At the last day, some forth their cabbins peepe:
And tremblingly'aske what newes, and doe heare so,
Like jealous husbands, what they would not know.   50
Some sitting on the hatches, would seeme there,
With hideous gazing to feare away feare.
Then note they the ships sicknesses, the Mast
Shak'd with this ague, and the Hold and Wast
With a salt dropsie clog'd, and all our tacklings
Snapping, like too-high-stretched treble strings.
And from our totterd sailes, ragges drop downe so,
As from one hang'd in chaines, a yeare agoe.
Even our Ordinance plac'd for our defence,
Strive to breake loose, and scape away from thence.   60
Pumping hath tir'd our men, and what's the gaine?
Seas into seas throwne, we suck in againe;
Hearing hath deaf'd our saylers; and if they
Knew how to heare, there's none knowes what to say.
Compar'd to these stormes, death is but a qualme,

l.59 Ordinance: ordnance.

Hell somewhat lightsome, and the'Bermuda calme.
Darknesse, lights elder brother, his birth-right
Claims o'er this world, and to heaven hath chas'd light.
All things are one, and that one none can be,
Since all formes, uniforme deformity   70
Doth cover, so that wee, except God say
Another *Fiat*, shall have no more day.
So violent, yet long these furies bee,
That though thine absence sterve me,'I wish not thee.

[1597]

THE CALME

Our storme is past, and that storms tyrannous rage,
A stupid calme, but nothing it, doth swage.
The fable is inverted, and farre more
A blocke afflicts, now, than a storke before.
Stormes chafe, and soon weare out themselves, or us;
In calmes, Heaven laughs to see us languish thus.
As steady'as I can wish, that my thoughts were,
Smooth as thy mistresse glasse, or what shines there,
The sea is now. And, as the Iles which wee
Seeke, when wee can move, our ships rooted bee.   10
As water did in stormes, now pitch runs out:
As lead, when a fir'd Church becomes one spout.
And all our beauty, and our trimme, decayes,
Like courts removing, or like ended playes.
The fighting place now seamens ragges supply;
And all the tackling is a frippery.

l.66 Bermuda: used as a plural. The Bermudas were famous for their
storms.

The Calme: This poem was probably also addressed to Christopher
Brooke.
l.2 swage: assuage.
ll.3–4 The . . . before: a reference to Aesop's fable of the log and the
stork.
l.9 Iles: This poem, like its companion piece, describes Donne's participa-
tion in the expedition of Essex and Raleigh against the Azores.
l.16 frippery: a place where old clothing is sold.

No use of lanthornes; and in one place lay
Feathers and dust, to day and yesterday.
Earths hollownesses, which the worlds lungs are,
Have no more winde than the upper valt of aire.   20
We can nor lost friends, nor sought foes recover,
But meteorlike, save that wee move not, hover.
Onely the Calenture together drawes
Deare friends, which meet dead in great fishes jawes:
And on the hatches as on Altars lyes
Each one, his owne Priest, and owne Sacrifice.
Who live, that miracle do multiply
Where walkers in hot Ovens, doe not dye.
If in despite of these, wee swimme, that hath
No more refreshing, than our brimstone Bath,   30
But from the sea, into the ship we turne,
Like parboyl'd wretches, on the coales to burne.
Like *Bajazet* encag'd, the shepheards scoffe,
Or like slacke sinew'd *Sampson*, his haire off,
Languish our ships. Now, as a Miriade
Of Ants, durst th'Emperours lov'd snake invade,
The crawling Gallies, Sea-gaols, finny chips,
Might brave our Pinnaces, now bed-ridde ships.
Whether a rotten state, and hope of gaine,
Or to disuse mee from the queasie paine   40
Of being belov'd, and loving, or the thirst
Of honour, or faire death, out pusht mee first,
I lose my end: for here as well as I
A desperate may live, and a coward die.
Stagge, dogge, and all which from, or towards flies,
Is paid with life, or pray, or doing dyes.

l.17 lanthornes: hung on the sterns of the ships in order to keep the
fleet together.
l.23 Calenture: a tropical fever which was reputed to cause its sufferers
to throw themselves into the sea in delirium.
l.27 Who: those who.
l.33 Like . . . scoffe: an allusion to Marlowe's *Tamburlaine,* in which
the Turkish emperor Bajazet is imprisoned in a cage by the hero, "the
Scythian shepherd."
l.36 Of . . . invade: According to Suetonius, the emperor Tiberius had
a pet snake which was devoured by ants, an episode which was taken
as an omen that the emperor should beware the mob.
l.46 pray: prey.

Fate grudges us all, and doth subtly lay
A scourge,'gainst which wee all forget to pray,
He that at sea prayes for more winde, as well
Under the poles may begge cold, heat in hell.   50
What are wee then? How little more alas
Is man now, than before he was? he was
Nothing; for us, wee are for nothing fit;
Chance, or our selves still disproportion it.
Wee have no power, no will, no sense; I lye,
I should not then thus feele this miserie.

                                                    [1597]

TO SIR HENRY WOTTON

Sir, more than kisses, letters mingle Soules;
For, thus friends absent speake. This ease controules
The tediousnesse of my life: But for these
I could ideate nothing, which could please,
But I should wither in one day, and passe
To'a bottle'of Hay, that am a locke of Grasse.
Life is a voyage, and in our lifes wayes
Countries, Courts, Towns are Rockes, or Remoraes;
They breake or stop all ships, yet our state's such,
That though than pitch they staine worse, wee must
    touch.   10
If in the furnace of the even line,
Or under th'adverse icy poles thou pine,
Thou know'st two temperate Regions girded in,
Dwell there: But Oh, what refuge canst thou winne
Parch'd in the Court, and in the country frozen?
Shall cities, built of both extremes, be chosen?
Can dung and garlike be'a perfume? or can
A Scorpion and Torpedo cure a man?
Cities are worst of all three; of all three

l.8 Remoraes: According to popular belief, the remora, or sucking-fish,
    was capable of stopping the motion of a ship to which it attached
    itself.
l.11 even line: the equator.
l.18 Torpedo: the electric ray (fish), sometimes known as the *crampfish*
    or *numbfish*.

(O knottie riddle) each is worst equally.   20
Cities are Sepulchers; they who dwell there
Are carcases, as if such there were.
And Courts are Theaters, where some men play
Princes, some slaves, all to one end, and of one clay.
The Country is a desert, where no good,
Gain'd (as habits, not borne,) is understood.
There men become beasts, and prone to more evils;
In cities blockes, and in a lewd court, devills.
As in the first Chaos confusedly
Each elements qualities were in the'other three;   30
So pride, lust, covetize, being severall
To these three places, yet all are in all,
And mingled thus, their issue incestuous.
Falshood is denizon'd. Virtue is barbarous.
Let no man say there, Virtues flintie wall
Shall locke vice in mee, I'll do none, but know all.
Men are spunges, which to poure out, receive,
Who know false play, rather than lose, deceive.
For in best understandings, sinne beganne,
Angels sinn'd first, then Devills, and then man.   40
Onely perchance beasts sinne not; wretched wee
Are beasts in all, but white integritie.
I thinke if men, which in these places live
Durst looke for themselves, and themselves retrive,
They would like strangers greet themselves, seeing then
Utopian youth, growne old Italian.
    Be thou thine owne home, and in thy selfe dwell;
Inne any where, continuance maketh hell.
And seeing the snaile, which every where doth rome,
Carrying his owne house still, still is at home,   50
Follow (for he is easie pac'd) this snaile,
Bee thine owne Palace, or the world's thy gaole.
And in the worlds sea, do not like corke sleepe
Upon the waters face; nor in the deepe
Sinke like a lead without a line: but as
Fishes glide, leaving no print where they passe,
Nor making sound; so closely thy course goe,
Let men dispute, whether thou breathe, or no.
Onely'in this one thing, be no Galenist: To make
Courts hot ambitions wholesome, do not take   60

A dramme of Countries dulnesse; do not adde
Correctives, but as chymiques, purge the bad.
But, Sir, I advise not you, I rather doe
Say o'er those lessons, which I learn'd of you:
Whom, free from German schismes, and lightnesse
Of France, and faire Italies faithlesnesse,
Having from these suck'd all they had of worth,
And brought home that faith, which you carried forth,
I throughly love. But if my selfe, I'have wonne
To know my rules, I have, and you have   70

                                         DONNE.
                                    [c. 1597-8]

TO SIR HENRY WOOTTON

Here's no more newes, than vertue,'I may as well
Tell you *Cales*, or *Saint Michaels* tale for newes, as tell
That vice doth here habitually dwell.

Yet, as to'get stomachs, we walke up and downe,
And toyle to sweeten rest, so, may God frowne,
If, but to loth both, I haunt Court, or Towne.

For here no one is from the'extremitie
Of vice, by any other reason free,
But that the next to'him, still, is worse than hee.

In this worlds warfare, they whom rugged Fate,   10
(Gods Commissary,) doth so throughly hate,
As in'the Courts Squadron to marshall their state:

ll.59–62 be . . . bad: According to the classical medicine of Galen, illness was due to some disproportion in the four humours, or fluids, of
the body. Therapy consisted of augmenting the defective humour or
humours with appropriate drugs. The new, or "chymique" medicine
of Paracelsus (1493–1541) depended instead on the purgation of
disease by the administration of antipathetic remedies.

l.2 Cales: Cadiz.
l.2 Saint Michaels: The Azores.
l.11 Commissary: deputy.

If they stand arm'd with seely honesty,
With wishing prayers, and neat integritie,
Like Indians'gainst Spanish hosts they bee.

Suspitious boldnesse to this place belongs,
And to'have as many eares as all have tongues;
Tender to know, tough to acknowledge wrongs.

Beleeve mee Sir, in my youths giddiest dayes,
When to be like the Court, was a playes praise,   20
Playes were not so like Courts, as Courts'are like
  playes.

Then let us at these mimicke antiques jeast,
Whose deepest projects, and egregious gests
Are but dull Moralls of a game at Chests.

But now'tis incongruity to smile,
Therefore I end; and bid farewell a while,
At Court; though *From Court*, were the better stile.

                                                      [1597–8]

HENRICO WOTTONI IN
HIBERNIA BELLIGERANTI

Went you to conquer? and have so much lost
Yourself, that what in you was best and most,
Respective friendship, should so quickly dye?
In publique gaine my share'is not such that I
Would lose your love for Ireland: better cheap
I pardon death (who though he do not reap
Yet gleanes hee many of our frends away)
Than that your waking mind should bee a prey
To lethargies. Lett shott, and boggs, and skeines
With bodies deale, as fate bids and restreynes;   10

l.13 seely: useless.
l.24 Chests: chess.

Henrico Wottoni in Hibernia Belligeranti: To Henry Wotton, at War
  in Ireland.

Ere sicknesses attack, yong death is best,
Who payes before his death doth scape arrest.
Lett not your soule (at first with graces fill'd,
And since, and thorough crooked lymbecks, still'd
In many schools and courts, which quicken it,)
It self unto the Irish negligence submit.
I aske not labored letters which should weare
Long papers out: nor letters which should feare
Dishonest carriage: or a seers art:
Nor such as from the brayne come, but the hart.   20

[1599]

TO SIR H[ENRY] W[OTTON]
AT HIS GOING AMBASSADOR
TO VENICE

After those reverend papers, whose soule is
   Our good and great Kings lov'd hand and fear'd
   name,
By which to you he derives much of his,
   And (how he may) makes you almost the same,

A Taper of his Torch, a copie writ
   From his Originall, and a faire beame
Of the same warme, and dazeling Sun, though it
   Must in another Sphere his vertue streame:

After those learned papers which your hand
   Hath stor'd with notes of use and pleasure too,   10
From which rich treasury you may command
   Fit matter whether you will write or doe:

After those loving papers, where friends send
   With glad griefe, to your Sea-ward steps, farewel,
Which thicken on you now, as prayers ascend
   To heaven in troupes at'a good mans passing bell:

l.11 yong death: early death.
l.14 lymbecks: alembics.

Admit this honest paper, and allow
   It such an audience as your selfe would aske;
What you must say at Venice this meanes now,
   And hath for nature, what you have for taske: 20

To sweare much love, not to be chang'd before
   Honour alone will to your fortune fit;
Nor shall I then honour your fortune, more
   Than I have done your honour wanting it.

But'tis an easier load (though both oppresse)
   To want, than governe greatnesse, for wee are
In that, our owne and onely businesse,
   In this, wee must for others vices care;

'Tis therefore well your spirits now are plac'd
   In their last Furnace, in activity;   30
Which fits them (Schooles and Courts and Warres o'rpast)
   To touch and test in any best degree.

For mee, (if there be such a thing as I)
   Fortune (if there be such a thing as shee)
Spies that I beare so well her tyranny,
   That she thinks nothing else so fit for mee;

But though she part us, to heare my oft prayers
   For your increase, God is as neere mee here;
And to send you what I shall begge, his staires
   In length and ease are alike every where.   40

[1604]

TO MRS. M. H. [MAGDALEN HERBERT]

Mad paper stay, and grudge not here to burne
   With all those sonnes whom my braine did create,
At least lye hid with mee, till thou returne
   To rags againe, which is thy native state.

l.26 want: lack.

What though thou have enough unworthinesse
　　To come unto great place as others doe,
That's much; emboldens, pulls, thrusts I confesse,
　　But'tis not all; Thou should'st be wicked too.

And, that thou canst not learne, or not of mee;
　　Yet thou wilt goe? Goe, since thou goest to her　　10
Who lacks but faults to be a Prince, for shee,
　　Truth, whom they dare not pardon, dares preferre.

But when thou com'st to that perplexing eye
　　Which equally claimes *love* and *reverence,*
Thou wilt not long dispute it, thou wilt die;
　　And having little now, have then no sense.

Yet when her warme redeeming hand, which is
　　A miracle; and made such to worke more,
Doth touch thee (saples leafe) thou grow'st by this
　　Her creature; glorify'd more than before.　　20

Then as a mother which delights to heare
　　Her early child mis-speake halfe uttered words,
Or, because majesty doth never feare
　　Ill or bold speech, she Audience affords.

And then, cold speechlesse wretch, thou diest againe,
　　And wisely; what discourse is left for thee?
For, speech of ill, and her, thou most abstaine,
　　And is there any good which is not shee?

Yet maist thou praise her servants, though not her,
　　And wit, and vertue,'and honour her attend,　　30
And since they'are but her cloathes, thou shalt not erre,
　　If thou her shape and beauty'and grace commend.

Who knowes thy destiny? when thou hast done,
　　Perchance her Cabinet may harbour thee,
Whither all noble ambitious wits doe runne,
　　A nest almost as full of Good as shee.

l.12 preferre: promote.

When thou art there, if any, whom wee know,
   Were sav'd before, and did that heaven partake,
When she revolves his papers, marke what show
   Of favour, she alone, to them doth make.   40

Marke, if to get them, she o'r skip the rest,
   Marke, if she read them twice, or kisse the name;
Marke, if she doe the same that they protest,
   Marke, if she marke whether her woman came.

Marke, if slight things be'objected, and o'r blowne,
   Marke, if her oathes against him be not still
Reserv'd, and that shee grieves she's not her owne,
   And chides the doctrine that denies Freewill.

I bid thee not doe this to be my spie;
   Nor to make my selfe her familiar;   50
But so much I doe love her choyce, that I
   Would faine love him that shall be lov'd of her.

                               [c. 1604]

TO SIR HENRY GOODYERE

Who makes the Past, a patterne for next yeare,
   Turnes no new leafe, but still the same things reads,
Seene things, he sees againe, heard things doth heare,
   And makes his life, but like a paire of beads.

A Palace, when'tis that, which it should be,
   Leaves growing, and stands such, or else decayes:
But hee which dwels there, is not so; for hee
   Strives to urge upward, and his fortune raise;

So had your body'her morning, hath her noone,
   And shall not better; her next change is night: 10
But her faire larger guest, to'whom Sun and Moone
   Are sparkes, and short liv'd, claimes another right.

To Sir Henry Goodyere: Goodyere was one of Donne's closest friends.
As the poem indicates, he was something of a spendthrift.

The noble Soule by age growes lustier,
   Her appetite, and her digestion mend,
Wee must not sterve, nor hope to pamper her
   With womens milke, and pappe unto the end.

Provide you manlyer dyet; you have seene
   All libraries, which are Schools, Camps, and Courts;
But aske your Garners if you have not beene
   In harvests, too indulgent to your sports.   20

Would you redeeme it? then your selfe transplant
   A while from hence. Perchance outlandish ground
Beares no more wit, than ours, but yet more scant
   Are those diversions there, which here abound.

To be a stranger hath that benefit,
   Wee can beginnings, but not habits choke.
Goe; whither? Hence; you get, if you forget;
   New faults, till they prescribe in us, are smoake.

Our Soule, whose country'is heaven, and God her
   father,
   Into this world, corruptions sinke, is sent,   30
Yet, so much in her travaile she doth gather,
   That she returnes home, wiser than she went;

It payes you well, if it teach you to spare,
   And make you,'asham'd, to make your hawks praise,
     yours,
Which when herselfe she lessens in the aire,
   You then first say, that high enough she toures.

However, keepe the lively tast you hold
   Of God, love him as now, but feare him more,
And in your afternoones thinke what you told
   And promis'd him, at morning prayer before.   40

Let falshood like a discord anger you,
   Else be not froward. But why doe I touch

l.22 outlandish: foreign.
l.33 spare: save.

Things, of which none is in your practise new,
   And Tables, or fruit-trenchers teach as much;

But thus I make you keepe your promise Sir,
   Riding I had you, though you still staid there,
And in these thoughts, although you never stirre,
   You came with mee to Micham, and are here.

                      [c. 1605–8]

TO MR. ROWLAND WOODWARD

Like one who'in her third widdowhood doth professe
Her selfe a Nunne, tyed to retirednesse,
So'affects my muse now, a chast fallownesse;

Since shee to few, yet to too many'hath showne
How love-song weeds, and Satyrique thornes are
 growne
Where seeds of better Arts, were early sown.

Though to use, and love Poëtrie, to mee,
Betroth'd to no'one Art, be no'adulterie;
Omissions of good, ill, as ill deeds bee.

For though to us it seeme, 'and be light and thinne,   10
Yet in those faithfull scales, where God throwes in
Mens workes, vanity weighs as much as sinne.

If our Soules have stain'd their first white, yet wee
May cloth them with faith, and deare honestie,
Which God Imputes, as native puritie.

There is no Vertue, but Religion:
Wise, valiant, sober, just, are names, which none
Want, which want not Vice-covering discretion.

l.44 Tables: The reference is probably to books of moral counsel.
l.44 fruit-trenchers: fruit-platters. These sometimes had moral maxims
   inscribed on their borders.
l.48 Micham: Donne's residence.

l.18 Want: lack.

Seeke wee then our selves in our selves; for as
Men force the Sunne with much more force to passe,　　20
By gathering his beames with a christall glasse;

So wee, If wee into our selves will turne,
Blowing our sparkes of vertue, may outburne
The straw, which doth about our hearts sojourne.

You know, Physitians, when they would infuse
Into any'oyle, the Soules of Simples, use
Places, where they may lie still warme, to chuse.

So workes retirednesse in us; To rome
Giddily, and be every where, but at home,
Such freedome doth a banishment become.　　30

Wee are but farmers of our selves, yet may,
If we can stocke our selves, and thrive, uplay
Much, much deare treasure for the great rent day.

Manure thy selfe then, to thy selfe be'approv'd,
And with vaine outward things be no more mov'd,
But to know, that I love thee'and would be lov'd.

TO THE COUNTESSE
OF BEDFORD

Madame,
Reason is our Soules left hand, Faith her right,
By these wee reach divinity, that's you;
Their loves, who have the blessings of your light,
Grew from their reason, mine from faire faith grew.

But as, although a squint lefthandednesse
Be'ungracious, yet we cannot want that hand,

l.26 Simples: medicinal plants.
l.31 farmers: in this context, those who cultivate land belonging to others.

ll.5–8 But . . . understand: The stanza expresses in a very complicated
　way Donne's desire to meet the Countess.
l.6 want: do without.

So would I, not to encrease, but to expresse
My faith, as I beleeve, so understand.

Therefore I study you first in your Saints,
Those friends, whom your election glorifies, 10
Then in your deeds, accesses, and restraints,
And what you reade, and what your selfe devize.

But soone, the reasons why you'are lov'd by all,
Grow infinite, and so passe reasons reach,
Then backe againe to'implicite faith I fall,
And rest on what the Catholique voice doth teach;

That you are good: and not one Heretique
Denies it: if he did, yet you are so.
For, rockes, which high top'd and deep rooted sticke,
Waves wash, not undermine, nor overthrow. 20

In every thing there naturally growes
A *Balsamum* to keepe it fresh, and new,
If'twere not injur'd by extrinsique blowes:
Your birth and beauty are this Balme in you.

But you of learning and religion,
And vertue,'and such ingredients, have made
A methridate, whose operation
Keepes off, or cures what can be done or said.

Yet, this is not your physicke, but your food,
A dyet fit for you; for you are here 30
The first good Angell, since the worlds frame stood,
That ever did in womans shape appeare.

l.16 Catholique: universal.
l.22 Balsamum: refers to the natural balm believed by Paracelsus and
    other Renaissance medical authorities to reside in all creatures and to
    act as a preservative and curative; compare Donne's use of the idea
    in his "Nocturnall upon S. Lucies Day."
l.27 methridate: antidote.
l.29 physicke: medicine.

Since you are then Gods masterpeece, and so
His Factor for our loves; do as you doe,
Make your returne home gracious; and bestow
This life on that; so make one life of two.
    For so God helpe mee,'I would not misse you there
    For all the good which you can do me here.

                       [c. 1607–8]

TO THE COUNTESSE
OF BEDFORD

Madame,
You have refin'd mee, and to worthyest things
(Vertue, Art, Beauty, Fortune,) now I see
Rarenesse, or use, not nature value brings;
And such, as they are circumstanc'd, they bee.
    Two ills can ne're perplexe us, sinne to'excuse;
    But of two good things, we may leave and chuse.

Therefore at Court, which is not vertues clime,
(Where a transcendent height, (as, lownesse mee)
Makes her not be, or not show) all my rime
Your vertues challenge, which there rarest bee;   10
    For, as darke texts need notes: there some must bee
    To usher vertue, and say, *This is shee*.

So in the country'is beauty; to this place
You are the season (Madame) you the day,
'Tis but a grave of spices, till your face
Exhale them, and a thick close bud display.
    Widow'd and reclus'd else, her sweets she'enshrines;
    As China, when the Sunne at Brasill dines.

l.34 Factor: agent.

ll.1–4 You . . . bee: The sense of this difficult passage is that observation of the Countess has refined the speaker's perception to such a
point that he recognizes that the "worthyest things" stand out in human experience by virtue of their rareness or utility. Thus, as the
next stanzas make clear, her virtue is most conspicuous at court, where
virtue is seldom found, and her beauty is most conspicuous in the
country.

Out from your chariot, morning breaks at night,
And falsifies both computations so;   20
Since a new world doth rise here from your light,
We your new creatures, by new recknings goe.
  This showes that you from nature lothly stray,
  That suffer not an artificiall day.

In this you'have made the Court the Antipodes,
And will'd your Delegate, the Vulgar Sunne,
To doe profane autumnall offices,
Whilst here to you, wee sacrificers runne;
  And whether Priests, or Organs, you wee'obey,
  We sound your influence, and your Dictates say.   30

Yet to that Deity which dwels in you,
Your vertuous Soule, I now not sacrifice;
These are *Petitions*, and not *Hymnes;* they sue
But that I may survay the edifice.
  In all Religions as much care hath bin
  Of Temples frames, and beauty,'as Rites within.

As all which goe to Rome, doe not thereby
Esteeme religions, and hold fast the best,
But serve discourse, and curiosity,
With that which doth religion but invest,   40
  And shunne th'entangling laborinths of Schooles,
  And make it wit, to thinke the wiser fooles:

So in this pilgrimage I would behold
You as you'are vertues temple, not as shee,
What walls of tender christall her enfold,
What eyes, hands, bosome, her pure Altars bee;
  And after this survay, oppose to all
  Bablers of Chappels, you th'Escuriall.

Yet not as consecrate, but merely'as faire,
On these I cast a lay and country eye.   50

l.41 laborinths . . . Schooles: a reference to the intricate systems of the
  scholastic philosophers.
l.48 Escuriall: The Escorial is the great palace of the kings of Spain; the
  massive complex contains a church, a monastery, and a mausoleum.

Of past and future stories, which are rare
I finde you all record, and prophecie.
  Purge but the booke of Fate, that it admit
  No sad nor guilty legends, you are it.

If good and lovely were not one, of both
You were the transcript, and originall,
The Elements, the Parent, and the Growth,
And every peece of you, is both their All:
  So'intire are all your deeds, and you, that you
  Must do the same thinge still; you cannot two.   60

But these (as nice thinne Schoole divinity
Serves heresie to furder or represse)
Tast of Poëtique rage, or flattery,
And need not, where all hearts one truth professe;
  Oft from new proofes, and new phrase, new doubts
    grow,
  As strange attire aliens the men wee know.

Leaving then busie praise, and all appeale
To higher Courts, senses decree is true,
The Mine, the Magazine, the Commonweale,
The story of beauty,'in Twicknam is, and you.   70
  Who hath seene one, would both; As, who had bin
  In Paradise, would seeke the Cherubin.

                [c. 1607–8]

TO SIR EDWARD HERBERT
AT JULYERS

Man is a lumpe, where all beasts kneaded bee,
  Wisdome makes him an Arke where all agree;
The foole, in whom these beasts do live at jarre,

l.70 Twicknam: the residence of the Countess.

To Sir Edward Herbert at Julyers: Sir Edward Herbert, later Lord
  Herbert of Cherbury, was the eldest son of Magdalen Herbert and
  the brother of George Herbert. He had a distinguished career as poet,
  philosopher, and diplomat. Donne's poem is possibly an answer to
  Herbert's "Satyre I."

Is sport to others, and a Theater;
Nor scapes hee so, but is himselfe their prey,
   All which was man in him, is eate away,
And now his beasts on one another feed,
   Yet couple'in anger, and new monsters breed.
How happy'is hee, which hath due place assign'd
   To'his beasts, and disaforested his minde!   10
Empail'd himselfe to keepe them out, not in;
   Can sow, and dares trust corne, where they have bin;
Can use his horse, goate, wolfe, and every beast,
   And is not Asse himselfe to all the rest.
Else, man not onely is the heard of swine,
   But he's those devills too, which did incline
Them to a headlong rage, and made them worse:
   For man can adde weight to heavens heaviest curse.
As Soules (they say) by our first touch, take in
   The poysonous tincture of Originall sinne,   20
So, to the punishments which God doth fling,
   Our apprehension contributes the sting.
To us, as to his chickins, he doth cast
   Hemlocke, and wee as men, his hemlocke taste;
We do infuse to what he meant for meat,
   Corrosivenesse, or intense cold or heat.
For, God no such specifique poyson hath
   As kills we know not how; his fiercest wrath
Hath no antipathy, but may be good
   At least for physicke, if not for our food.   30
Thus man, that might be'his pleasure, is his rod,
   And is his devill, that might be his God.
Since then our businesse is, to rectifie
   Nature, to what she was, wee'are led awry
By them, who man to us in little show;
   Greater than due, no forme we can bestow
On him; for Man into himselfe can draw
   All; All his faith can swallow,'or reason chaw.
All that is fill'd, and all that which doth fill,
   All the round world, to man is but a pill,   40
In all it workes not, but it is in all

l.11 Empail'd: enclosed.
l.17 Them . . . worse: see Mark 5:11–13.
ll.23–24 as . . . taste: what is harmless food to chickens is poison to
   men.

Poysonous, or purgative, or cordiall,
For, knowledge kindles Calentures in some,
  And is to others icy *Opium*.
As brave as true, is that profession then
  Which you doe use to make; that you know man.
This makes it credible; you have dwelt upon
  All worthy bookes, and now are such an one.
Actions are authors, and of those in you
  Your friends finde every day a mart of new.   50

                              [1610]

TO THE COUNTESSE
OF BEDFORD

T'have written then, when you writ, seem'd to mee
  Worst of spirituall vices, Simony,
And not t'have written then, seemes little lesse
  Than worst of civill vices, thanklessenesse.
In this, my debt I seem'd loath to confesse,
  In that, I seem'd to shunne beholdingnesse.
But 'tis not soe; *nothings*, as I am, may
  Pay all they have, and yet have all to pay.
Such borrow in their payments, and owe more
  By having leave to write so, than before.   10
Yet since rich mines in barren grounds are showne,
  May not I yeeld (not gold) but coale or stone?
Temples were not demolish'd, though prophane:
  Here *Peter Joves*, there *Paul* hath *Dian's* Fane.
So whether my hymnes you admit or chuse,
  In me you'have hallowed a Pagan Muse,
And denizend a stranger, who mistaught
  By blamers of the times they mard, hath sought
Vertues in corners, which now bravely doe
  Shine in the worlds best part, or all It; You.   20
I have beene told, that vertue'in Courtiers hearts
  Suffers an Ostracisme, and departs.
Profit, ease, fitnesse, plenty, bid it goe,

l.43 Calentures: tropical fevers.

l.14 Here . . . Fane: a reference to the transformation of pagan temples
  into Christian churches.

But whither, only knowing you, I know;
Your (or you) vertue two vast uses serves,
  It ransomes one sex, and one Court preserves.
There's nothing but your worth, which being true,
  Is knowne to any other, not to you:
And you can never know it; To admit
  No knowledge of your worth, is some of it.   30
But since to you, your praises discords bee,
  Stoop, others ills to meditate with mee.
Oh! to confesse wee know not what we should,
  Is halfe excuse; wee know not what we would:
Lightnesse depresseth us, emptinesse fills,
  We sweat and faint, yet still goe downe the hills.
As new Philosophy arrests the Sunne,
  And bids the passive earth about it runne,
So wee have dull'd our minde, it hath no ends;
  Onely the bodie's busie, and pretends;   40
As dead low earth ecclipses and controules
  The quick high Moone: so doth the body, Soules.
In none but us, are such mixt engines found,
  As hands of double office: For, the ground
We till with them; and them to heav'n wee raise;
  Who prayer-lesse labours, or, without this, prayes,
Doth but one halfe, that's none; He which said, *Plough*
  And looke not back, to looke up doth allow.
Good seed degenerates, and oft obeyes
  The soyles disease, and into cockle strayes;   50
Let the minds thoughts be but transplanted so,
  Into the body,'and bastardly they grow.
What hate could hurt our bodies like our love?
  Wee (but no forraine tyrants could) remove
These not ingrav'd, but inborne dignities,
  Caskets of soules; Temples, and Palaces:
For, bodies shall from death redeemed bee,
  Soules but preserv'd, not naturally free.

l.37 new Philosophy: the new heliocentric astronomy of Copernicus and Galileo.
l.43 engines: instruments.
l.58 Soules . . . free: The soul is not by its own nature immortal but is preserved by the will of God. Grierson points out that this difficult poem assumes that the intrinsic worth of the body is scarcely less than that of the soul; the body is not by nature degrading, but it is made so by the condition of sin.

As men to'our prisons, new soules to us are sent,
   Which learne vice there, and come in innocent.   60
First seeds of every creature are in us,
   What ere the world hath bad, or pretious,
Mans body can produce, hence hath it beene
   That stones, wormes, frogges, and snakes in man are
    seene:
But who ere saw, though nature can worke soe,
   That pearle, or gold, or corne in man did grow?
We'have added to the world Virginia,'and sent
   Two new starres lately to the firmament;
Why grudge wee us (not heaven) the dignity
   T'increase with ours, those faire soules company.   70
But I must end this letter, though it doe
   Stand on two truths, neither is true to you.
Vertue hath some perversenesse; For she will
   Neither beleeve her good, nor others ill.
Even in you, vertues best paradise,
   Vertue hath some, but wise degrees of vice.
Too many vertues, or too much of one
   Begets in you unjust suspition;
And ignorance of vice, makes vertuelesse,
   Quenching compassion of our wretchednesse.   80
But these are riddles; Some aspersion
   Of vice becomes well some complexion.
Statesmen purge vice with vice, and may corrode
   The bad with bad, a spider with a toad:
For so, ill thralls not them, but they tame ill
   And make her do much good against her will,
But in your Commonwealth, or world in you,
   Vice hath no office, or good worke to doe.
Take then no vitious purge, but be content
   With cordiall vertue, your knowne nourishment.   90
               [After 1609]

l.62 pretious: unusual, prodigious.
l.68 Two . . . starres: Probably a reference to the novae observed in
   1572 and 1604, with perhaps a reference to the recent death of friends
   of the Countess.
l.72 two truths: the wickedness of the world and the virtue of the
   Countess.

TO THE COUNTESSE
OF BEDFORD

ON NEW-YEARES DAY

This twilight of two yeares, not past nor next,
    Some embleme is of mee, or I of this,
Who Meteor-like, of stuffe and forme perplext,
    Whose *what*, and *where*, in disputation is,
    If I should call mee *any thing*, should misse.

I summe the yeares, and mee, and finde mee not
    Debtor to th'old, nor Creditor to th'new,
That cannot say, My thankes I have forgot,
    Nor trust I this with hopes, and yet scarce true
    This bravery is, since these times shew'd mee you.   10

In recompence I would show future times
    What you were, and teach them to'urge towards
    such.
Verse embalmes vertue;'and Tombs, or Thrones of
    rimes,
    Preserve fraile transitory fame, as much
    As spice doth bodies from corrupt aires touch.

Mine are short-liv'd; the tincture of your name
    Creates in them, but dissipates as fast,
New spirits: for, strong agents with the same
    Force that doth warme and cherish, us doe wast;
    Kept hot with strong extracts, no bodies last: 20

So, my verse built of your just praise, might want
    Reason and likelihood, the firmest Base,
And made of miracle, now faith is scant,
    Will vanish soone, and so possesse no place,
    And you, and it, too much grace might disgrace.

When all (as truth commands assent) confesse
    All truth of you, yet they will doubt how I,

l.10 bravery: bravado.

One corne of one low anthills dust, and lesse,
   Should name, know, or expresse a thing so high,
   And not an inch, measure infinity.   30

I cannot tell them, nor my selfe, nor you,
   But leave, lest truth b'endanger'd by my praise,
And turne to God, who knowes I thinke this true,
   And useth oft, when such a heart mis-sayes,
   To make it good, for, such a praiser prayes.

Hee will best teach you, how you should lay out
   His stock of *beauty, learning, favour, blood;*
He will perplex security with doubt,
   And cleare those doubts; hide from you,'and shew
     you good,
   And so increase your appetite and food;   40

Hee will teach you, that good and bad have not
   One latitude in cloysters, and in Court;
Indifferent there the greatest space hath got;
   Some pitty'is not good there, some vaine disport,
   On this side sinne, with that place may comport.

Yet he, as hee bounds seas, will fixe your houres,
   Which pleasure, and delight may not ingresse,
And though what none else lost, be truliest yours,
   Hee will make you, what you did not, possesse,
   By using others, not vice, but weakenesse.   50

He will make you speake truths, and credibly,
   And make you doubt, that others doe not so:
Hee will provide you keyes, and locks, to spie,
   And scape spies, to good ends, and hee will show
   What you may not acknowledge, what not know.

l.28 corne: grain.
l.36 Hee: God.
l.38 security: overconfidence.
l.44 Some . . . there: At court a beautiful woman's pity might be mis-
placed—to sympathize with the protestations of a courtly lover, for
example.

For your owne conscience, he gives innocence,
  But for your fame, a discreet warinesse,
And though to scape, than to revenge offence
  Be better, he showes both, and to represse
  Joy, when your state swells, *sadnesse* when'tis lesse. 60

From need of teares he will defend your soule,
  Or make a rebaptizing of one teare;
Hee cannot, (that's, he will not) dis-inroule
  Your name; and when with active joy we heare
  This private Ghospell, then'tis our New Yeare.

TO THE LADY BEDFORD

You that are she and you, that's double shee,
  In her dead face, halfe of your selfe shall see;
Shee was the other part, for so they doe
  Which build them friendships, become one of two;
So two, that but themselves no third can fit,
  Which were to be so, when they were not yet;
Twinnes, though their birth *Cusco*, and *Musco* take,
  As divers starres one Constellation make,
Pair'd like two eyes, have equall motion, so
  Both but one meanes to see, one way to goe. 10
Had you dy'd first, a carcasse shee had beene;
  And wee your rich Tombe in her face had seene;
She like the Soule is gone, and you here stay,
  Not a live friend; but th'other halfe of clay;
And since you act that part, As men say, here
  Lies such a Prince, when but one part is there,
And do all honour and devotion due
  Unto the whole, so wee all reverence you;
For, such a friendship who would not adore
  In you, who are all what both were before, 20
Not all, as if some perished by this,
  But so, as all in you contracted is.

ll.1–2 You . . . see: The poem was written as a consolation to the Countess of Bedford on the death of a friend. Grierson suggests that the friend was either Lady Markham or Cecilia Boulstred.
l.7 Cusco . . . Musco: Cuzco and Moscow.

As of this all, though many parts decay,
    The pure which elemented them shall stay;
And though diffus'd, and spread in infinite,
    Shall recollect, and in one All unite:
So madame, as her Soule to heaven is fled,
    Her flesh rests in the earth, as in the bed;
Her vertues do, as to their proper spheare,
    Returne to dwell with you, of whom they were;   30
As perfect motions are all circular,
    So they to you, their sea, whence lesse streames are.
Shee was all spices, you all metalls; so
    In you two wee did both rich Indies know;
And as no fire, nor rust can spend or waste
    One dramme of gold, but what was first shall last,
Though it bee forc'd in water, earth, salt, aire,
    Expans'd in infinite, none will impaire;
So, to your selfe you may additions take,
    But nothing can you lesse, or changed make.   40
Seeke not in seeking new, to seeme to doubt,
    That you can match her, or not be without;
But let some faithfull booke in her roome be,
    Yet but of *Judith* no such booke as shee.

                    [c. 1609]

TO THE COUNTESSE OF BEDFORD

Honour is so sublime perfection,
And so refinde; that when God was alone
And creaturelesse at first, himselfe had none;

But as of the elements, these which wee tread,
Produce all things with which wee'are joy'd or fed,
And, those are barren both above our head:

l.31 perfect . . . circular: this ancient idea recurs frequently in Donne's
    work.
l.34 both . . . Indies: the East Indies and the West Indies.
l.44 Judith: Judith in the Old Testament was noted for both her beauty
    and her wisdom.

l.4 elements: the four traditional elements: earth, water, air, and fire.

So from low persons doth all honour flow;
Kings, whom they would have honoured, to us show,
And but *direct* our honour, not *bestow*.

For when from herbs the pure part must be wonne   10
From grosse, by Stilling, this is better done
By despis'd dung, than by the fire or Sunne.

Care not then, Madame,'how low your praysers lye;
In labourers balads oft more piety
God findes, than in *Te Deums* melodie.

And, ordinance rais'd on Towers, so many mile
Send not their voice, nor last so long a while
As fires from th'earths low vaults in *Sicil* Isle.

Should I say I liv'd darker than were true,
Your radiation can all clouds subdue;   20
But one,'tis best light to contemplate you.

You, for whose body God made better clay,
Or tooke Soules stuffe such as shall late decay,
Or such as needs small change at the last day.

This, as an Amber drop enwraps a Bee,
Covering discovers your quicke Soule; that we
May in your through-shine front your hearts thoughts
   see.

You teach (though wee learne not) a thing unknowne
To our late times, the use of specular stone,
Through which all things within without were shown. 30

Of such were Temples; so and of such you are;
Beeing and *seeming* is your equall care,
And *vertues* whole *summe* is but *know* and *dare*.

l.11 Stilling: distillation.
l.18 fires . . . Isle: The reference is to the volcanoes of Sicily.
l.27 through-shine: transparent.
l.29 specular stone: a stone which might be cut into thin, transparent
   sheets and used for glazing. See note to "The Undertaking."

But as our Soules of growth and Soules of sense
Have birthright of our reasons Soule, yet hence
They fly not from that, nor seeke presidence:

Natures first lesson, so, discretion,
Must not grudge zeale a place, nor yet keepe none,
Not banish it selfe, nor religion.

Discretion is a wisemans Soule, and so   40
Religion is a Christians, and you know
How these are one; her *yea*, is not her *no*.

Nor may we hope to sodder still and knit
These two, and dare to breake them; nor must wit
Be colleague to religion, but be it.

In those poor types of God (round circles) so
Religious tipes, the peecelesse centers flow,
And are in all the lines which all waves goe.

If either ever wrought in you alone
Or principally, then religion   50
Wrought your ends, and your wayes discretion.

Goe thither stil, goe the same way you went,
Who so would change, do covet or repent;
Neither can reach you, great and innocent.
                                          [c. 1611–12]

TO THE COUNTESSE
OF HUNTINGDON

Madame,
Man to Gods image, *Eve*, to mans was made,
   Nor finde wee that God breath'd a soule in her,

ll.34–35 But . . . Soule: Renaissance thought conceived of three types of
   soul: the soul of growth, possessed by plants; the soul of sense, by
   animals; the soul of reason, by man. Plants thus possess one soul,
   animals two, man three.
l.46 round circles: Donne's familiar use of the circle as a symbol of
   perfection.

Canons will not Church functions you invade,
  Nor lawes to civill office you preferre.

Who vagrant transitory Comets sees,
  Wonders, because they'are rare; But a new starre
Whose motion with the firmament agrees,
  Is miracle; for, there no new things are;

In woman so perchance milde innocence
  A seldome comet is, but active good   10
A miracle, which reason scapes, and sense;
  For, Art and Nature this in them withstood.

As such a starre, the *Magi* led to view
  The manger-cradled infant, God below:
By vertues beames by fame deriv'd from you,
  May apt soules, and the worst may, vertue know.

If the worlds age, and death be argued well
  By the Sunnes fal, which now towards earth doth
    bend,
Then we might feare that vertue, since she fell
  So low as woman, should be neare her end.   20

But she's not stoop'd, but rais'd; exil'd by men
  She fled to heaven, that's heavenly things, that's you;
She was in all men, thinly scatter'd then,
  But now amass'd, contracted in a few.

She guilded us: But you are gold, and Shee;
  Us she inform'd, but transubstantiates you;
Soft dispositions which ductile bee,
  Elixarlike, she makes not cleane, but new.

l.3 Canons . . . invade: The sense is, "Ecclesiastical law does not wish
you to invade church functions."
l.4 preferre: promote.
ll.6–8 But . . . are: Pre-Copernican astronomy held that no change can
occur in the spheres above that of the moon. The observation of new
stars was a source of concern to Donne and other intellectuals of the
early seventeenth century.
l.18 By . . . fal: the reference may be to autumn. But, as Grierson
points out, Donne may have in mind Copernican astronomy, with its
placing of the sun at the center of the universe.

Though you a wifes and mothers name retaine,
   'Tis not a woman, for all are not soe,   30
But vertue having made you vertue,'is faine
   T'adhere in these names, her and you to show,

Else, being alike pure, wee should neither see;
   As, water being into ayre rarify'd,
Neither appeare, till in one cloud they bee,
   So, for our sakes you do low names abide;

Taught by great constellations, which being fram'd,
   Of the most starres, take low names, *Crab*, and *Bull*,
When single planets by the *Gods* are nam'd,
   You covet not great names, of great things full.   40

So you, as woman, one doth comprehend,
   And in the vaile of kindred others see;
To some ye are reveal'd, as in a friend,
   And as a vertuous Prince farre off, to mee.

To whom, because from you all vertues flow,
   And 'tis not none, to dare contemplate you,
I, which doe so, as your true subject owe
   Some tribute for that, so these lines are due.

If you can thinke these flatteries, they are,
   For then your judgement is below my praise,   50
If they were so, oft, flatteries worke as farre,
   As Counsels, and as farre th'endeavour raise.

So my ill reaching you might there grow good,
   But I remaine a poyson'd fountaine still;
But not your beauty, vertue, knowledge, blood
   Are more above all flattery, than my will.

And if I flatter any,'tis not you
   But my owne judgement, who did long agoe
Pronounce, that all these praises should be true,
   And vertue should your beauty,'and birth outgrow.   60

Now that my prophesies are all fulfill'd,
   Rather than God should not be honour'd too,

And all these gifts confess'd, which hee instill'd,
  Your selfe were bound to say that which I doe.

So I, but your Recorder am in this,
  Or mouth, or Speaker of the universe,
A ministeriall Notary, for'tis
  Not I, but you and fame, that makes this verse;

I was your Prophet in your yonger dayes,
And now your Chaplaine, God in you to praise.   70
               [c. 1614–15]

TO THE COUNTESSE
OF SALISBURY

Faire, great, and good, since seeing you, wee see
What Heaven can doe, and what any Earth can be:
Since now your beauty shines, now when the Sunne
Growne stale, is to so low a value runne,
That his disshevel'd beames and scattered fires
Serve but for Ladies Periwigs and Tyres
In lovers Sonnets: you come to repaire
Gods booke of creatures, teaching what is faire.
Since now, when all is withered, shrunke, and dri'd,
All Vertues ebb'd out to a dead low tyde,   10
All the worlds frame being crumbled into sand,
Where every man thinks by himselfe to stand,
Integritie, friendship, and confidence,
(Ciments of greatnes) being vapor'd hence,
And narrow man being fill'd with little shares,
Court, Citie, Church, are all shops of small-wares,
All having blowne to sparkes their noble fire,
And drawne their sound gold-ingot into wyre;
All trying by a love of littlenesse
To make abridgments, and to draw to lesse,   20
Even that nothing, which at first we were;
Since in these times, your greatnesse doth appeare,
And that we learne by it, that man to get
Towards him that's infinite, must first be great.

l.6 Tyres: attires.

Since in an age so ill, as none is fit
So much as to accuse, much lesse mend it,
(For who can judge, or witnesse of those times
Where all alike are guiltie of the crimes?)
Where he that would be good, is thought by all
A monster, or at best fantasticall: 30
Since now you durst be good, and that I doe
Discerne, by daring to contemplate you,
That there may be degrees of faire, great, good,
Through your light, largenesse, vertue understood:
If in this sacrifice of mine, be showne
Any small sparke of these, call it your owne.
And if things like these, have been said by mee
Of others; call not that Idolatrie.
For had God made man first, and man had seene
The third daies fruits, and flowers, and various greene,   40
He might have said the best that he could say
Of those faire creatures, which were made that day;
And when next day he had admir'd the birth
Of Sun, Moone, Stars, fairer than late-prais'd earth,
Hee might have said the best that he could say,
And not be chid for praising yesterday:
So though some things are not together true,
As, that another is worthiest, and, that you:
Yet, to say so, doth not condemne a man,
If when he spoke them, they were both true then.   50
How faire a proofe of this, in our soule growes?
Wee first have soules of growth, and sense, and those,
When our last soule, our soule immortall came,
Were swallowed into it, and have no name.
Nor doth he injure those soules, which doth cast
The power and praise of both them, on the last;
No more doe I wrong any; I adore
The same things now, which I ador'd before,
The subject chang'd, and measure; the same thing
In a low constable, and in the King   60
I reverence; His power to work on mee:
So did I humbly reverence each degree

ll.52–54 Wee . . . name: This passage summarizes the Renaissance doctrine of the three souls—of growth, of sense, and of reason—of which
plants possess the first only, animals the first and the second, human
beings all three.

Of faire, great, good; but more, now I am come
From having found their *walkes*, to find their *home*.
And as I owe my first soules thankes, that they
For my last soule did fit and mould my clay,
So am I debtor unto them, whose worth,
Enabled me to profit, and take forth
This new great lesson, thus to study you;
Which none, not reading others, first, could doe.   70
Nor lacke I light to read this booke, though I
In a dark Cave, yea in a Grave doe lie;
For as your fellow Angells, so you doe
Illustrate them who come to study you.
The first whom we in Histories doe finde
To have profest all Arts, was one borne blinde:
He lackt those eyes beasts have as well as wee,
Not those, by which Angels are seene and see;
So, though I'am borne without those eyes to live,
Which fortune, who hath none her selfe, doth give,   80
Which are, fit meanes to see bright courts and you,
Yet may I see you thus, as now I doe;
I shall by that, all goodnesse have discern'd,
And though I burne my librarie, be learn'd.
                              [August 1614]

Epithalamions

DONNE'S THREE wedding poems show, in their vivid sensuous imagery, an aspect of the poet's genius which is seldom found in his other work. The earliest, the "Epithalamion Made at Lincolnes Inne," dates from his student years. The second was composed for the marriage of the Princess Elizabeth, daughter of James I, to Frederick, the Elector Palatine (February 14, 1613). The third, consisting of an introductory eclogue and the epithalamion proper, had as its occasion the marriage of Lady Frances Howard and the King's favorite, the Earl of Somerset (December 26, 1613).

EPITHALAMION MADE
AT LINCOLNES INNE

The Sun-beames in the East are spred,
Leave, leave, faire Bride, your solitary bed,
    No more shall you returne to it alone,
It nourseth sadnesse, and your bodies print,
Like to a grave, the yielding downe doth dint;
        You and your other you meet there anon;
        Put forth, put forth that warme balme-breathing
        thigh,

Which when next time you in these sheets wil smother,
    There it must meet another,
            Which never was, but must be, oft, more
            nigh;   10
Come glad from thence, goe gladder than you came,
To day put on perfection, and a womans name.

Daughters of London, you which bee
Our Golden Mines, and furnish'd Treasurie,
    You which are Angels, yet still bring with you
Thousands of Angels on your mariage daies,
Help with your presence and devise to praise
        These rites, which also unto you grow due;
        Conceitedly dresse her, and be assign'd,
By you, fit place for every flower and jewell,   20
    Make her for love fit fewell
        As gay as Flora, and as rich as Inde;
So may shee faire, rich, glad, and in nothing lame,
To day put on perfection, and a womans name.

And you frolique Patricians,
Sonnes of these Senators, wealths deep oceans,
    Ye painted courtiers, barrels of others wits,
Yee country men, who but your beasts love none,
Yee of those fellowships whereof hee's one,
        Of study and play made strange Hermaphrodits,   30
        Here shine; This Bridegroom to the Temple bring.
Loe, in yon path which store of straw'd flowers graceth,
    The sober virgin paceth;
        Except my sight faile, 'tis no other thing;
Weep not nor blush, here is no griefe nor shame,
To day put on perfection, and a womans name.

Thy two-leav'd gates faire Temple unfold,
And these two in thy sacred bosome hold,
    Till, mystically joyn'd, but one they bee;
Then may thy leane and hunger-starved wombe   40
Long time expect their bodies and their tombe,
    Long after their owne parents fatten thee.
    All elder claimes, and all cold barrennesse,

l.16 Thousands . . . Angels: a pun on the name of the coin.

All yeelding to new loves bee far for ever,
    Which might these two dissever,
       All wayes all th'other may each one possesse;
For, the best Bride, best worthy of praise and fame,
Today puts on perfection, and a womans name.

Oh winter dayes bring much delight,
Not for themselves, but for they soon bring night;   50
    Other sweets wait thee than these diverse meats,
Other disports than dancing jollities,
Other love tricks than glancing with the eyes,
    But that the Sun still in our halfe Spheare sweates;
       Hee flies in winter, but he now stands still.
Yet shadowes turne; Noone point he hath attain'd,
    His steeds nill bee restrain'd,
       But gallop lively downe the Westerne hill;
Thou shalt, when he hath runne the worlds half frame,
To night put on a perfection, and a womans name.   60

The amorous evening starre is rose,
Why then should not our amorous starre inclose
    Her selfe in her wish'd bed? Release your strings
Musicians, and dancers take some truce
With these your pleasing labours, for great use
    As much wearinesse as perfection brings;
       You, and not only you, but all toyl'd beasts
Rest duly; at night all their toyles are dispensed;
But in their beds commenced
       Are other labours, and more dainty feasts;   70
She goes a maid, who, lest she turne the same
To night puts on perfection, and a womans name.

Thy virgins girdle now untie,
And in thy nuptiall bed (loves altar) lye
    A pleasing sacrifice; now dispossesse
Thee of these chaines and robes which were put on
T'adorne the day, not thee; for thou, alone,
    Like vertue'and truth, art best in nakednesse;
       This bed is onely to virginitie

l.57 nill: will not.

A grave, but, to a better state, a cradle;   80
Till now thou wast but able
  To be what now thou art; then that by thee
No more be said, *I may bee*, but, *I am*,
To night put on perfection, and a womans name.

Even like a faithfull man content,
That this life for a better should be spent,
  So, shee a mothers rich stile doth preferre,
And at the Bridegroomes wish'd approach doth lye,
Like an appointed lambe, when tenderly
    The priest comes on his knees t'embowell her;   90
      Now sleep or watch with more joy; and O light
Of heaven, to morrow rise thou hot, and early;
This Sun will love so dearely
    Her rest, that long, long we shall want her sight;
Wonders are wrought, for shee which had no maime,
To night puts on perfection, and a womans name.

AN EPITHALAMION, OR
MARIAGE SONG

ON THE LADY ELIZABETH, AND
COUNT PALATINE BEING MARRIED
ON ST. VALENTINES DAY

I

Haile Bishop Valentine, whose day this is,
  All the Aire is thy Diocis,
  And all the chirping Choristers
And other birds are thy Parishioners,
    Thou marryest every yeare
The Lirique Larke, and the grave whispering Dove,
The Sparrow that neglects his life for love,
The household Bird, with the red stomacher,
    Thou mak'st the black bird speed as soone,
As doth the Goldfinch, or the Halcyon;   10

l.7 The . . . love: a reference to the proverbial lechery of the sparrow.
  In popular belief, each sexual act shortened life by one day.

The husband cocke lookes out, and straight is sped,
And meets his wife, which brings her feather-bed.
This day more cheerfully than ever shine,
This day, which might enflame thy self, Old Valentine.

II

Till now, Thou warmd'st with multiplying loves
  Two larkes, two sparrowes, or two Doves,
   All that is nothing unto this,
For thou this day couplest two Phœnixes;
   Thou mak'st a Taper see
What the sunne never saw, and what the Arke   20
(Which was of foules, and beasts, the cage, and park,)
Did not containe, one bed containes, through Thee.
   Two Phœnixes, whose joyned breasts
Are unto one another mutuall nests,
Where motion kindles such fires, as shall give
Yong Phœnixes, and yet the old shall live.
Whose love and courage never shall decline,
But make the whole year through, thy day, O Valen-
 tine.

III

Up then faire Phœnix Bride, frustrate the Sunne,
  Thy selfe from thine affection   30
   Takest warmth enough, and from thine eye
All lesser birds will take their Jollitie.
   Up, up, faire Bride, and call,
Thy starres, from out their severall boxes, take
Thy Rubies, Pearles, and Diamonds forth, and make
Thy selfe a constellation, of them All,
   And by their blazing, signifie,
That a great Princess falls, but doth not die;
Bee thou a new starre, that to us portends
Ends of much wonder; And be Thou those ends.   40
Since thou dost this day in new glory shine,
May all men date Records, from this thy Valentine.

ll.18–20 couplest . . . saw: according to legend, only one of these mythical birds could exist at any one time.

IV

Come forth, come forth, and as one glorious flame
  Meeting Another, growes the same,
  So meet thy Fredericke, and so
To an unseparable union growe.
   Since separation
Falls not on such things as are infinite,
Nor things which are but one, can disunite,
You'are twice inseparable, great, and one;   50
  Goe then to where the Bishop staies,
To make you one, his way, which divers waies
Must be effected; and when all is past,
And that you'are one, by hearts and hands made fast,
You two have one way left, your selves to'entwine,
Besides this Bishops knot, or Bishop Valentine.

V

But oh, what ailes the Sunne, that here he staies,
  Longer to day, than other daies?
  Staies he new light from these to get?
And finding here such store, is loth to set?   60
   And why doe you two walke,
So slowly pac'd in this procession?
Is all your care but to be look'd upon,
And be to others spectacle, and talke?
  The feast, with gluttonous delaies,
Is eaten, and too long their meat they praise,
The masquers come too late, and'I thinke, will stay,
Like Fairies, till the Cock crow them away.
  Alas, did not Antiquity assigne
A night, as well as day, to thee, O Valentine?   70

VI

They did, and night is come; and yet wee see
  Formalities retarding thee.
  What meane these Ladies, which (as though
They were to take a clock in peeces,) goe
  So nicely about the Bride;
A Bride, before a good night could be said,
Should vanish from her cloathes, into her bed,

As Soules from bodies steale, and are not spy'd.
 But now she is laid; What though shee bee?
Yet there are more delayes, For, where is he?   80
He comes, and passes through Spheare after Spheare,
First her sheetes, then her Armes, then any where.
Let not this day, then, but this night be thine,
Thy day was but the eve to this, O Valentine.

VII

Here lyes a shee Sunne, and a hee Moone here,
 She gives the best light to his Spheare,
  Or each is both, and all, and so
They unto one another nothing owe,
  And yet they doe, but are
So just and rich in that coyne which they pay,   90
That neither would, nor needs forbeare nor stay;
Neither desires to be spar'd, nor to spare,
 They quickly pay their debt, and then
Take no acquittances, but pay again;
They pay, they give, they lend, and so let fall
No such occasion to be liberall.
More truth, more courage in these two do shine,
Than all thy turtles have, and sparrows, Valentine.

VIII

And by this act of these two Phenixes
 Nature againe restored is,   100
 For since these two are two no more,
Ther's but one Phenix still, as was before.
 Rest now at last, and wee
As Satyres watch the Sunnes uprise, will stay
Waiting, when your eyes opened, let out day,
Onely desir'd, because your face wee see;
 Others neare you shall whispering speake,
And wagers lay, at which side day will breake,
And win by'observing, then, whose hand it is
That opens first a curtaine, hers or his;   110
This will be tryed to morrow after nine,
Till which houre, wee thy day enlarge, O Valentine.

l.98 turtles: turtledoves.

ECCLOGUE

1613. DECEMBER 26

Allophanes finding Idios in the country in Christmas time, reprehends his absence from court, at the mariage of the Earle of Sommerset, Idios gives an account of his purpose therein, and of his absence thence.

Allophanes.

Unseasonable man, statue of ice,
   What could to countries solitude entice
Thee, in this yeares cold and decrepit time?
   Natures instinct drawes to the warmer clime
Even small birds, who by that courage dare,
   In numerous fleets, saile through their Sea, the aire.
What delicacie can in fields appeare,
   Whil'st Flora'herselfe doth a freeze jerkin weare?
Whil'st windes do all the trees and hedges strip
   Of leafes, to furnish roddes enough to whip   10
Thy madnesse from thee; and all springs by frost
   Have taken cold, and their sweet murmure lost;
If thou thy faults or fortunes would'st lament
   With just solemnity, do it in Lent;
At Court the spring already advanced is,
   The Sunne stayes longer up; and yet not his
The glory is, farre other, other fires.
   First, zeale to Prince and State; then loves desires
Burne in one brest, and like heavens two great lights,
   The first doth governe dayes, the other nights.   20
And then that early light, which did appeare
   Before the Sunne and Moone created were,
The Princes favour is defus'd o'r all,
   From which all Fortunes, Names, and Natures fall;
Then from those wombes of starres, the Brides bright eyes,
   At every glance, a constellation flyes,
And sowes the Court with starres, and doth prevent
   In light and power, the all-ey'd firmament;

l.8 freeze: a pun on *frieze,* a shaggy woolen fabric.

First her eyes kindle other Ladies eyes,
    Then from their beames their jewels lusters rise,   30
And from their jewels torches do take fire,
    And all is warmth, and light, and good desire;
Most other Courts, alas, are like to hell,
    Where in darke plotts, fire without light doth dwell;
Or but like Stoves, for lust and envy get
    Continuall, but artificiall heat;
Here zeale and love growne one, all clouds disgest,
    And make our Court an everlasting East.
And can'st thou be from thence?

Idios.   No, I am there.
As heaven, to men dispos'd, is every where,   40
So are those Courts, whose Princes animate,
    Not onely all their house, but all their State.
Let no man thinke, because he is full, he hath all,
    Kings (as their patterne, God) are liberall
Not onely in fulnesse, but capacitie,
    Enlarging narrow men, to feele and see,
And comprehend the blessings they bestow.
    So, reclus'd hermits often times do know
More of heavens glory, than a worldling can.
    As man is of the world, the heart of man,   50
Is an epitome of Gods great booke
    Of creatures, and man need no farther looke;
So is the Country of Courts, where sweet peace doth,
    As their one common soule, give life to both,
I am not then from Court.

Allophanes.   Dreamer, thou art.
    Think'st thou fantastique that thou hast a part
In the East-Indian fleet, because thou hast
    A little spice, or Amber in thy taste?
Because thou art not frozen, art thou warme?
    Seest thou all good because thou seest no harme?   60
The earth doth in her inward bowels hold
    Stuffe well dispos'd, and which would faine be gold,
But never shall, except it chance to lye,
    So upward, that heaven gild it with his eye;

l.58 Amber: ambergris, formerly much esteemed in cookery.

As, for divine things, faith comes from above,
  So, for best civill use, all tinctures move
From higher powers; From God religion springs,
  Wisdome, and honour from the use of Kings.
Then unbeguile thy selfe, and know with mee,
  That Angels, though on earth employed they bee,   70
Are still in heav'n, so is hee still at home
  That doth, abroad, to honest actions come.
Chide thy selfe then, O foole, which yesterday
  Might'st have read more than all thy books bewray;
Hast thou a history, which doth present
  A Court, where all affections do assent
Unto the Kings, and that, that Kings are just?
  And where it is no levity to trust?
Where there is no ambition, but to'obey,
  Where men need whisper nothing, and yet may;   80
Where the Kings favours are so plac'd, that all
  Finde that the King therein is liberall
To them, in him, because his favours bend
  To vertue, to the which they all pretend?
Thou hast no such; yet here was this, and more,
  An earnest lover, wise then, and before.
Our little Cupid hath sued Livery,
  And is no more in his minority,
Hee is admitted now into that brest
  Where the Kings Counsells and his secrets rest.   90
What hast thou lost, O ignorant man?

Idios.   I knew
  All this, and onely therefore I withdrew.
To know and feele all this, and not to have
  Words to expresse it, makes a man a grave
Of his owne thoughts; I would not therefore stay
  At a great feast, having no grace to say.
And yet I scap'd not here; for being come
  Full of the common joy, I utter'd some;
Reade then this nuptiall song, which was not made
  Either the Court or mens hearts to invade,   100
But since I'am dead, and buried, I could frame
  No Epitaph, which might advance my fame
So much as this poor song, which testifies
  I did unto that day some sacrifice.

EPITHALAMION

I

THE TIME OF THE MARIAGE

Thou art repriv'd old yeare, thou shalt not die,
   Though thou upon thy death bed lye,
     And should'st within five dayes expire,
Yet thou art rescu'd by a mightier fire,
     Than thy old Soule, the Sunne,
When he doth in his largest circle runne.   110
The passage of the West or East would thaw,
And open wide their easie liquid jawe
To all our ships, could a Promethean art
Either unto the Northerne Pole impart
The fire of these inflaming eyes, or of this loving heart.

II

EQUALITY OF PERSONS

But undiscerning Muse, which heart, which eyes.
   In this new couple, dost thou prize,
     When his eye as inflaming is
As hers, and her heart loves as well as his?
     Be tryed by beauty, and then   120
The bridegroome is a maid, and not a man.
If by that manly courage they be tryed,
Which scornes unjust opinion; then the bride
Becomes a man. Should chance or envies Art
Divide these two, whom nature scarce did part?
Since both have both th'enflaming eyes, and both the
 loving heart.

III

RAISING OF THE
BRIDEGROOM

Though it be some divorce to thinke of you
   Singly, so much one are you two,
     Yet let me here contemplate thee,

l.111 passage . . . East: The reference is to the much-sought Northwest
 Passage and Northeast Passage.

First cheerfull Bridegroome, and first let mee see,   130
    How thou prevent'st the Sunne,
And his red foming horses dost outrunne,
How, having laid downe in thy Soveraignes brest
All businesses, from thence to reinvest
Them, when these triumphs cease, thou forward art
To shew to her, who doth the like impart,
The fire of thy inflaming eyes, and of thy loving heart.

I V

RAISING OF THE BRIDE

But now, to Thee, faire Bride, it is some wrong,
    To thinke thou wert in Bed so long,
    Since Soone thou lyest downe first, tis fit   140
Thou in first rising should'st allow for it.
    Pouder thy Radiant haire,
Which if without such ashes thou would'st weare,
Thou, which to all which come to looke upon,
Art meant for Phœbus, would'st be Phaëton.
For our ease, give thine eyes th'unusual part
Of joy, a Teare; so quencht, thou maist impart,
To us that come, thy inflaming eyes, to him, thy loving
  heart.

V

HER APPARRELLING

Thus thou descend'st to our infirmitie,
    Who can the Sun in water see.   150
    Soe dost thou, when in silke and gold,
Thou cloudst thy selfe; since wee which doe behold,
    Are dust, and wormes, 'tis just
Our objects be the fruits of wormes and dust;
Let every Jewell be a glorious starre,
Yet starres are not so pure, as their spheares are.

l.131 prevent'st: anticipatest.
l.145 Phaëton: the son of Phoebus, the sun god, obtained permission to
  drive his father's chariot but lost control of the horses.
l.156 spheanes: the transparent spheres in which the planets and stars
  were thought to be embedded.

And though thou stoope, to'appeare to us in part,
Still in that Picture thou intirely art,
Which thy inflaming eyes have made within his loving
  heart.

VI

GOING TO THE CHAPPELL

Now from your Easts you issue forth, and wee,   160
    As men which through a Cipres see
    The rising sun, doe thinke it two,
Soe, as you goe to Church, doe thinke of you,
    But that vaile being gone,
By the Church rites you are from thenceforth one.
The Church Triumphant made this match before,
And now the Militant doth strive no more;
Then, reverend Priest, who Gods Recorder art,
Doe, from his Dictates, to these two impart
All blessings, which are seene, or thought, by Angels
  eye or heart.   170

VII

THE BENEDICTION

Blest payre of Swans, Oh may you interbring
    Daily new joyes, and never sing;
    Live, till all grounds of wishes faile,
Till honor, yea till wisedome grow so stale,
    That, new great heights to trie,
It must serve your ambition, to die;
Raise heires, and may here, to the worlds end, live
Heires from this King, to take thankes, you, to give,
Nature and grace doe all, and nothing Art.
May never age, or error overthwart   180
With any West, these radiant eyes, with any North,
  this heart.

VIII

FEASTS AND REVELLS

But you are over-blest. Plenty this day
    Injures; it causeth time to stay;
    The tables groane, as though this feast

Would, as the flood, destroy all fowle and beast.
    And were the doctrine new
That the earth mov'd, this day would make it true;
For every part to dance and revell goes.
They tread the ayre, and fal not where they rose.
Though six houres since, the Sunne to bed did part,   190
The masks and banquets will not yet impart
A sunset to these weary eyes, A Center to this heart.

IX

THE BRIDES GOING TO BED

What mean'st thou Bride, this companie to keep?
    To sit up, till thou faine wouldst sleep?
      Thou maist not, when thou art laid, doe so.
Thy selfe must to him a new banquet grow,
    And you must entertaine
And doe all this daies dances o'er againe.
Know that if Sun and Moone together doe
Rise in one point, they doe not set so too;   200
Therefore thou maist, faire Bride, to bed depart,
Thou art not gone, being gone; where e'r thou art,
Thou leav'st in him thy watchfull eyes, in him thy
  loving heart.

X

THE BRIDEGROOMES
COMMING

As he that sees a starre fall, runs apace,
    And findes a gellie in the place,
      So doth the Bridegroome haste as much,
Being told this starre is falne, and findes her such.
    And as friends may looke strange,
By a new fashion, or apparrells change,
Their soules, though long acquainted they had beene,   210
These clothes, their bodies, never yet had seene;
Therefore at first shee modestly might start,
But must forthwith surrender every part,
As freely, as each to each before, gave either eye or
  heart.

ll.204–205 starre . . . place: This was a popular belief of the time.
l.205 gellie: jelly.

XI

THE GOOD-NIGHT

Now, as in Tullias tombe, one lampe burnt cleare,
    Unchang'd for fifteene hundred yeare,
    May these love-lamps we here enshrine,
In warmth, light, lasting, equall the divine.
      Fire ever doth aspire,
And makes all like it selfe, turnes all to fire,   220
But ends in ashes, which these cannot doe,
For none of these is fuell, but fire too.
This is joyes bonfire, then, where loves strong Arts
Make of so noble individuall parts
One fire of foure inflaming eyes, and of two loving
  hearts.

Idios.

As I have brought this song, that I may doe
    A perfect sacrifice, I'll burne it too.

Allophanes.

No Sir. This paper I have justly got,
    For, in burnt incense, the perfume is not
His only that presents it, but of all;   230
    What ever celebrates this Festivall
Is common, since the joy thereof is so.
    Nor may your selfe be Priest: But let me goe,
Backe to the Court, and I will lay'it upon
    Such Altars, as prize your devotion.

ll.215–216 Tullias . . . yeare: A popular story maintained that the tomb
of Tullia, the daughter of Cicero, had been discovered, containing a
lamp which had burned for 1500 years.

Anniversaries and
A Funerall Elegie

TAKEN TOGETHER, Donne's "Funerall Elegie" on Elizabeth Drury and the two "Anniversaries" further lamenting her death constitute his most ambitious, sustained, and scopeful poetic work. They are also among the few poems of Donne published during his lifetime. The fourteen-year-old daughter of Sir Robert Drury, Donne's patron (see Introduction), died in December, 1610. "The First Anniversarie: An Anatomy of the World," followed by "A Funerall Elegie," was published in the course of the next year. "The Second Anniversarie: Of the Progres of the Soule" appeared in 1612. Some lines near the close of "The First Anniversarie" express the poet's intention to write a further anniversary each year for the rest of his life, but that intention was never fulfilled—perhaps fortunately, for it is difficult to see how further extensions could have maintained the intensity, the inventiveness, and the formal balance of the completed work as we have it.

The poems have elicited considerable puzzlement and hostility since their first appearance. Ben Jonson, for example, remarked to Drummond of Hawthornden "that Dones Anniversarie was prophane and full of Blasphemies;

that he told Mr. Donne, if it had been written of the Virgin Marie it had been something." And, in the early years of our century, Donne's great editor and eloquent champion, H. J. C. Grierson found in the poems "much that is both puerile and extravagant"—although he did note the occurrence of "a loftier strain of impassioned reflection and vision." The essential problem, in the twentieth century as in the seventeenth, is resistance to the central conceit on which the "Anniversaries" are founded —that the death of a little girl whom the poet had never seen has caused the death of the world, a world which is, even as he writes, in a state of decomposition. The hyperbole is extreme, even for the overblown taste which distinguishes the funerary verse of the Baroque age. Any defense of the poems—and they have found their defenders —must take as its point of departure the rejoinder which Jonson quotes Donne as making to the charge of blasphemy: "that he described the Idea of a Woman and not as she was."

The statement makes it clear that the poems have as their ultimate subject not the death of an individual girl but rather the death (and transfiguration) of some female principle of vitality, virtue, and creativity, for the evocation of which the death of little Elizabeth serves merely as an occasion. The contention receives support from the full subtitles of the poems. "The First Anniversarie" is subtitled "An Anatomy of the World. Wherein, By Occasion of the Untimely Death of Mistris Elizabeth Drury the Frailty and the Decay of this Whole World Is Represented"; "The Second Anniversarie" is subtitled "Of the Progres of the Soule. Wherein, By Occasion of the Religious Death of Mistris Elizabeth Drury the Incommodities of the Soule in this Life and Her Exaltation in the Next, Are Contemplated."

Of its very nature, the symbolic principle celebrated by Donne is capable of assuming an almost unlimited number of forms. In the admirable introduction to his recent edition of the "Anniversaries," F. Manley draws attention to many of these forms, stressing particularly the symbolic figure of Sophia, or Divine Wisdom in Christian tradition, and mentioning among other things the relevance of C. G. Jung's concept of the *anima*, the image of the soul as experienced in the male unconscious. Other forms emphasized by recent critics include Astraea, the classical Goddess of Justice; Aphrodite Urania, or Heavenly Love; the Virgin Mary; and even the recently deceased Queen Elizabeth I. The conventions employed by Dante, Petrarch, and other Italian poets of the *dolce stil novo*, in terms of which the beloved woman is the spiritual guide, are also influential in Donne's practice.

Manley's edition is of central importance to any serious study of these complex poems. Other important treatments are provided by L. L. Martz, who demonstrates their meditative structure; M. H. Nicolson, who speculates instructively on their true subject; C. M. Coffin and V. H. Harris, who relate the poems to the philosophical and scientific currents of the age; and R. C. Bald, who investigates Donne's relations with the Drurys. Modern scholarship has distinguished itself in making the "Anniversaries" accessible to the modern reader, and it is largely because of this scholarship that we can now see the poems as one of the great achievements of seventeenth-century literature.

THE FIRST ANNIVERSARIE
AN ANATOMY OF THE WORLD

WHEREIN, BY OCCASION OF THE UNTIMELY DEATH OF MISTRIS ELIZABETH DRURY THE FRAILTY AND THE DECAY OF THIS WHOLE WORLD IS REPRESENTED

[handwritten: people will be interested in reading this if they didn't know her]

When that rich soule which to her Heaven is gone,
Whom all they celebrate, who know they have one,
(For who is sure he hath a soule, unlesse

The entrie into the workes.

It see, and Judge, and follow worthinesse,
And by Deedes praise it? He who doth not this,
May lodge an In-mate soule, but tis not his.
When that Queene ended here her progresse time,
And, as t'her standing house, to heaven did climbe,
Where, loth to make the Saints attend her long,
Shee's now a part both of the Quire, and Song,   10
This world, in that great earth-quake languished;
For in a common Bath of teares it bled,
Which drew the strongest vitall spirits out:
But succour'd then with a perplexed doubt,
Whether the world did loose or gaine in this,
(Because since now no other way there is
But goodnes, to see her, whom all would see,
All must endevour to be good as shee,)
This great consumption to a fever turn'd,
And so the world had fits; it joy'd, it mournd.   20
And, as men thinke, that Agues physicke are,
And th'Ague being spent, give over care,
So thou, sicke world, mistak'st thy selfe to bee
Well, when alas, thou'rt in a Letargee.
Her death did wound, and tame thee than, and than
Thou mightst have better spar'd the Sunne, or Man;
That wound was deepe, but 'tis more misery,
That thou hast lost thy sense and memory,
T'was heavy then to heare thy voyce of mone,
But this is worse, that thou art speechlesse growne.   30
Thou hast forgot thy name, thou hadst; thou wast
Nothing but she, and her thou hast o'repast.
For as a child kept from the Font, untill
A Prince, expected long, come to fulfill
The Ceremonies, thou unnam'd hadst laid,
Had not her comming, thee her Palace made:
Her name defin'd thee, gave thee forme and frame,
And thou forgetst to celebrate thy name.
Some moneths she hath beene dead (but being dead,
Measures of times are all determined)   40
But long shee'ath beene away, long, long, yet none

l.6 but . . . his: it belongs to the devil.
l.7 progresse: carries the sense of royal journey.
l.8 standing house: permanent residence of royalty.
l.25 than: then.

Offers to tell us who it is that's gone.
But as in states doubtfull of future heyres,
When sickenes without remedy, empayres
The present Prince, they're loth it should be said,
The Prince doth languish, or the Prince is dead:
So mankind feeling now a generall thaw,
A strong example gone equall to law,
The Cyment which did faithfully compact
And glue all vertues, now resolv'd, and slack'd,   50
Thought it some blasphemy to say sh'was dead;
Or that our weakenes was discovered
In that confession; therefore spoke no more
Then tongues, the soule being gone, the losse deplore.
But though it be too late to succour thee,
Sicke world, yea dead, yea putrified, since shee
Thy'ntrinsique Balme, and thy preservative,
Can never be renew'd, thou never live,
I (since no man can make thee live) will trie,
What we may gaine by thy Anatomy.   60
Her death hath taught us dearely, that thou art
Corrupt and mortall in thy purest part.
Let no man say, the world it selfe being dead,
'Tis labour lost to have discovered
The worlds infirmities, since there is none
Alive to study this dissectione;
For there's a kind of world remaining still,   *What life*
Though shee which did inanimate and fill   *the world*
The world, be gone, yet in this last long night,   *hath still.*
Her Ghost doth walke; that is, a glimmering light,   70
A faint weake love of vertue and of good
Reflects from her, on them which understood
Her worth; And though she have shut in all day,
The twi-light of her memory doth stay;
Which, from the carcasse of the old world, free,
Creates a new world; and new creatures be
Produc'd: The matter and the stuffe of this,
Her vertue, and the forme our practise is.
And though to be thus Elemented, arme
These Creatures, from hom-borne intrinsique harme,   80

l.57 Balme: the vital essence assumed by Paracelsian medicine to exist
   in all created things and to operate as a preservative.
l.60 Anatomy: dissection.

(For all assum'd unto this Dignitee,
So many weedlesse Paradises bee,
Which of themselves produce no venemous sinne,
Except some forraine Serpent bring it in)
Yet, because outward stormes the strongest breake,
And strength it selfe by confidence growes weake,
This new world may be safer, being told

The   The dangers and diseases of the old:
sicknesses For with due temper men do then forgoe,
of the   Or covet things, when they their true worth know.   90
world.   There is no health; Physitians say that we
           At best, enjoy, but a neutralitee.
Impossi- And can there be worse sickenesse, then to know
bility   That we are never well, nor can be so?   *Original*
of health. We are borne ruinous: poore mothers crie,   *Sin*
           That children come not right, nor orderly,
           Except they headlong come, and fall upon
           An ominous precipitation.
           How witty's ruine? how importunate
           Upon mankinde? It labour'd to frustrate   100
           Even Gods purpose; and made woman, sent
           For mans reliefe, cause of his languishment.
           They were to good ends, and they are so still,
           But accessory, and principall in ill.
           For that first mariage was our funerall:
           One woman at one blow, then kill'd us all,
           And singly, one by one, they kill us now.
           We doe delightfully our selves allow
mgr   To that consumption; and profusely blinde,
we have
sex   We kill our selves, to propagate our kinde.   110
more. And yet we doe not that; we are not men:
we die There is not now that mankinde, which was then
           When as the Sunne, and man, did seeme to strive,
Shortnesse (Joynt tenants of the world) who should survive.
of life.   When Stag, and Raven, and the long-liv'd tree,
           Compar'd with man, dy'de in minoritee.
           When, if a slow-pac'd starre had stolne away

l.95 ruinous: tending toward ruin.
ll.106–107 then . . . now: Donne plays with the contemporary colloquial
    meaning of *kill*—to induce sexual climax.
l.110 We . . . kinde: a reference to the popular belief that each sexual
    act shortened life by a day.

From the observers marking, he might stay
Two or three hundred yeares to see't againe,
And then make up his observation plaine;   120
When, as the age was long, the sise was great:
Mans growth confess'd, and recompenc'd the meat:
So spacious and large, that every soule
Did a faire Kingdome, and large Realme controule:
And when the very stature thus erect,
Did that soule a good way towards Heaven direct.
Where is this mankind now? who lives to age,
Fit to be made *Methusalem* his page?
Alas, we scarse live long enough to trie
Whether a new made clocke runne right, or lie.   130
Old Grandsires talke of yesterday with sorrow,
And for our children we reserve to morrow.
So short is life, that every peasant strives,
In a torne house, or field, to have three lives.
And as in lasting, so in length is man
Contracted to an inch, who was a span.   *Smalenesse*
For had a man at first, in Forrests stray'd,   *of stature.*
Or shipwrack'd in the Sea, one would have laid
A wager that an Elephant, or Whale
That met him, would not hastily assaile   140
A thing so equall to him: now alas,
The Fayries, and the Pigmies well may passe
As credible; mankind decayes so soone,
We're scarse our Fathers shadowes cast at noone.
Onely death addes t'our length: nor are we growne
In stature to be men, till we are none.
But this were light, did our lesse volume hold
All the old Text; or had we chang'd to gold
Their silver; or dispos'd into lesse glas,
Spirits of vertue, which then scattred was.   150
But 'tis not so: w'are not retir'd, but dampt;
And as our bodies, so our mindes are cramp't:
'Tis shrinking, not close-weaving, that hath thus,

*l.*122 *meat:* food.
*l.*134 *to . . . lives:* the conventional length of a lease was ninety-nine
years.
*l.*145 *Onely . . . length:* after the body's dissolution the scattered bones
take up more space.
*l.*151 *dampt:* extinguished.

In minde and body both bedwarfed us.
We seeme ambitious, Gods whole worke t'undoe;
Of nothing he made us, and we strive too,
To bring our selves to nothing backe; and we
Do what we can, to do't so soone as hee.
With new diseases on our selves we warre,
And with new phisicke, a worse Engin farre.   160
Thus man, this worlds Vice-Emperor, in whom
All faculties, all graces are at home;
And if in other Creatures they appeare,
They're but mans ministers, and Legats there,
To worke on their rebellions, and reduce
Them to Civility, and to mans use.
This man, whom God did wooe, and loth t'attend
Till man came up, did downe to man descend,
This man, so great, that all that is, is his,
Oh what a trifle, and poore thing he is!   170
If man were any thing, he's nothing now:
Helpe, or at least some time to wast, allow
T'his other wants, yet when he did depart
With her, whom we lament, he lost his hart.
She, of whom th'Auncients seem'd to prophesie,
When they call'd vertues by the name of shee,
She in whom vertue was so much refin'd,
That for Allay unto so pure a minde
Shee tooke the weaker Sex, she that could drive
The poysonous tincture, and the stayne of *Eve*,   180
Out of her thoughts, and deeds; and purifie
All, by a true religious Alchimy;
Shee, shee is dead; shee's dead: when thou knowest this,
Thou knowest how poore a trifling thing man is.
And learn'st thus much by our Anatomee,
The heart being perish'd, no part can be free.
And that except thou feed (not banquet) on
The supernaturall food, Religion,
Thy better Growth growes withered, and scant;

---

l.159 new diseases: primarily syphilis, which made its appearance in
    Europe in the fifteenth century.
l.160 new phisicke: the mineral remedies used by Paracelsian physicians.
l.160 Engin: instrument.
l.180 tincture: a technical term in alchemy.
l.187 banquet: snack.

Be more then man, or thou'rt lesse then an Ant.   190
Then, as mankinde, so is the worlds whole frame
Quite out of joynt, almost created lame:
For, before God had made up all the rest,
Corruption entred, and deprav'd the best:
It seis'd the Angels, and then first of all
The world did in her Cradle take a fall,
And turn'd her braines, and tooke a generall maime
Wronging each joynt of th'universall frame.
The noblest part, man, felt it first; and than
Both beasts and plants, curst in the curse of man.   200   *Decay of*
So did the world from the first houre decay,   *nature in*
The evening was beginning of the day,   *other parts.*
And now the Springs and Sommers which we see,
Like sonnes of women after fifty bee.
And new Philosophy cals all in doubt,   —▷ *Sun becoming*
The Element of fire is quite put out;   *center of universe*
The Sunne is lost, and th'earth, and no mans wit
Can well direct him, where to looke for it.
And freely men confesse, that this world's spent,
When in the Planets, and the Firmament   210
They seeke so many new; they see that this
Is crumbled out againe to his Atomis.
'Tis all in pieces, all cohaerence gone;
All just supply, and all Relation:
Prince, Subject, Father, Sonne, are things forgot,
For every man alone thinkes he hath got
To be a Phoenix, and that there can bee
None of that kinde, of which he is, but hee.
This is the worlds condition now, and now
She that should all parts to reunion bow,   220
She that had all Magnetique force alone,
To draw, and fasten sundred parts in one;

l.205 new Philosophy: the new astronomy of Copernicus and Galileo.
l.206 Element . . . fire: the area of fire which, in the old world-view,
    was located beyond the air.
l.211 new: probably a reference to the observation of new stars by Gali-
    leo, Tycho Brahe, and Kepler.
l.212 Atomis: atoms.
ll.217–218 To . . . hee: the mythical phoenix was unique.
ll.221–222 Magnetique . . . one: a reference to William Gilbert's studies
    of magnetism.

She whom wise nature had invented then
When she observ'd that every sort of men
Did in their voyage in this worlds Sea stray,
And needed a new compasse for their way;
Shee that was best, and first originall
Of all faire copies; and the generall
Steward to Fate; shee whose rich eyes, and brest,
Guilt the West Indies, and perfum'd the East;   230
Whose having breath'd in this world, did bestow
Spice on those Isles, and bad them still smell so,
And that rich Indie which doth gold interre,
Is but as single money, coyn'd from her:
She to whom this world must it selfe refer,
As Suburbs, or the Microcosme of her,
Shee, shee is dead; shee's dead: when thou knowst this,
Thou knowst how lame a cripple this world is.
And learnst thus much by our Anatomy,
That this worlds generall sickenesse doth not lie   240
In any humour, or one certaine part;
But, as thou sawest it rotten at the hart,
Thou seest a Hectique fever hath got hold
Of the whole substance, not to be contrould,
And that thou hast but one way, not t'admit
The worlds infection, to be none of it.
For the worlds subtilst immateriall parts
Feele this consuming wound, and ages darts.
For the worlds beauty is decayd, or gone,
Disformity Beauty, that's colour, and proportion.   250
of parts. We thinke the heavens enjoy their Sphericall
Their round proportion embracing all.
But yet their various and perplexed course,
Observ'd in divers ages doth enforce
Men to finde out so many Eccentrique parts,
Such divers downe-right lines, such overthwarts,
As disproportion that pure forme. It teares
The Firmament in eight and fortie sheeres,
And in those constellations there arise

l.234 single money: small change.
l.241 any humour: The four humours, in the old physiology, were the
    bodily fluids which determined health and temperament.
l.258 sheeres: shares, parts, or, possibly, shires.

New starres, and old do vanish from our eyes: 260
As though heav'n suffred earth-quakes, peace or war,
When new Townes rise, and olde demolish'd are.
They have empayld within a Zodiake
The free-borne Sunne, and keepe twelve signes awake
To watch his steps; the Goat and Crabbe controule,
And fright him backe, who els to eyther Pole,
(Did not these Tropiques fetter him) might runne:
For his course is not round; nor can the Sunne
Perfit a Circle, or maintaine his way
One inche direct; but where he rose to day   270
He comes no more, but with a cousening line,
Steales by that point, and so is Serpentine:
And seeming weary with his reeling thus,
He meanes to sleepe, being now falne nearer us.
So, of the stares which boast that they do runne
In Circle still, none ends where he begunne.
All their proportion's lame, it sinks, it swels.
For of Meridians, and Parallels,
Man hath weav'd out a net, and this net throwne
Upon the Heavens, and now they are his owne.   280
Loth to goe up the hill, or labor thus
To goe to heaven, we make heaven come to us. *telescope*
We spur, we raine the stars, and in their race
They're diversly content t'obey our pace.
But keepes the earth her round proportion still?
Doth not a Tenarif, or higher Hill
Rise so high like a Rocke, that one might thinke
The floating Moone would shipwracke there, and sink?
Seas are so deepe, that Whales being strooke to day,
Perchance to morrow, scarse at middle way   290
Of their wish'd journeys end, the bottom, dye.
And men, to sound depths, so much line untie,
As one might justly thinke, that there would rise

l.260 New starres: a reference to the new stars discovered by Tycho
    Brahe, Kepler, and Galileo.
l.263 empayld: enclosed.
l.265 Goat . . . Crabbe: the zodiacal signs.
l.269 Perfit: perfect.
l.271 cousening: cozening, cheating.
l.286 Tenarif: The peak of Tenerife, in the Canary Islands, was thought
    to be the highest mountain in the world.

At end thereof, one of th'Antipodies:
If under all, a Vault infernall be,
(Which sure is spacious, except that we
Invent another torment, that there must
Millions into a strait hote roome be thrust)
Then solidnes, and roundnes have no place.
Are these but warts, and pock-holes in the face   300
Of th'earth? Thinke so: But yet confesse, in this
The worlds proportion disfigured is,
Disorder in That those two legges whereon it doth relie,
the world. Reward and punishment are bent awrie.
And, Oh, it can no more be questioned,
That beauties best, proportion, is dead,
Since even griefe it selfe, which now alone
Is left us, is without proportion.
Shee by whose lines proportion should bee
Examin'd, measure of all Symmetree,   310
Whom had that Ancient seen, who thought soules made
Of Harmony, he would at next have said
That Harmony was shee, and thence infer,
That soules were but Resultances from her,
And did from her into our bodies go,
As to our eyes, the formes from objects flow:
Shee, who if those great Doctors truely said
That th'Arke to mans proportions was made,
Had beene a type for that, as that might be
A type of her in this, that contrary   320
Both Elements, and Passions liv'd at peace
In her, who caus'd all Civill warre to cease.
Shee, after whom, what forme soe're we see,
Is discord, and rude incongruitee,
Shee, shee is dead, she's dead; when thou knowst this,
Thou knowst how ugly a monster this world is:
And learnst thus much by our Anatomee,
That here is nothing to enamor thee:
And that, not onely faults in inward parts,
Corruptions in our braines, or in our harts,   330
Poysoning the fountaines, whence our actions spring,
Endanger us: but that if every thing
Be not done fitly'nd in proportion,

l.311 Ancient: probably Pythagoras.

To satisfie wise, and good lookers on,
(Since most men be such as most thinke they bee)
They're lothsome too, by this Deformitee.
For good, and well, must in our actions meete:
Wicked is not much worse then indiscreet.
But beauties other second Element,
Colour, and lustre now, is as neere spent. 340
And had the world his just proportion,
Were it a ring still, yet the stone is gone.
As a compassionate Turcoyse which doth tell
By looking pale, the wearer is not well,
As gold fals sicke being stung with Mercury,
All the worlds parts of such complexion bee.
When nature was most busie, the first weeke,
Swadling the new-borne earth, God seemed to like,
That she should sport herselfe sometimes, and play,
To mingle, and vary colours every day. 350
And then, as though she could not make inow,
Himselfe his various Rainbow did allow.
Sight is the noblest sense of any one,
Yet sight hath onely color to feed on,
And color is decayd: summers robe growes
Duskie, and like an oft dyed garment showes.
Our blushing redde, which us'd in cheekes to spred,
Is inward sunke, and onely our soules are redde.
Perchance the world might have recovered,
If she whom we lament had not beene dead: 360
But shee, in whom all white, and redde, and blue
(Beauties ingredients) voluntary grew,
As in an unvext Paradise; from whom
Did all things verdure, and their lustre come,
Whose composition was miraculous,
Being all color, all Diaphanous,
(For Ayre, and Fire but thicke grosse bodies were,
And liveliest stones but drowsie, and pale to her,)
Shee, shee is dead; shee's dead: when thou knowst this,
Thou knowst how wan a Ghost this our world is: 370

l.336 Deformitee: virtue should manifest itself in visible outward actions.
ll.343–344 As . . . well: a popular belief.
l.345 stung: alchemical terminology.
l.351 inow: enough.

And learnst thus much by our Anatomee,
That it should more affright, then pleasure thee.
And that, since all faire color then did sinke,
Tis now but wicked vanity to thinke,
Weaknesse To color vitious deeds with good pretence,
in the Or with bought colors to illude mens sense.
want of Nor in ought more this worlds decay appeares,
correspon- Then that her influence the heav'n forbeares,
dence of Or that the Elements doe not feele this,
heaven and The father, or the mother barren is.   380
earth. The clouds conceive not raine, or doe not powre
In the due birth-time, downe the balmy showre.
Th'Ayre doth not motherly sit on the earth,
To hatch her seasons, and give all things birth.
Spring-times were common cradles, but are toombes;
And false-conceptions fill the generall wombs.
Th'Ayre showes such Meteors, as none can see,
Not onely what they meane, but what they bee.
Earth such new wormes, as would have troubled much,
Th'Egyptian Mages to have made more such.   390
What Artist now dares boast that he can bring
Heaven hither, or constellate any thing,
So as the influence of those starres may bee
Imprisond in an Herbe, or Charme, or Tree,
And doe by touch, all which those starres could do?
The art is lost, and correspondence too.
For heaven gives little, and the earth takes lesse,
And man least knowes their trade, and purposes.
If this commerce twixt heaven and earth were not
Embarr'd, and all this trafique quite forgot,   400
Shee, for whose losse we have lamented thus,
Would worke more fully'and pow'rfully on us.
Since herbes, and roots by dying, lose not all,
But they, yea Ashes too, are medicinall,

l.378 influence: the influence of the stars on earthly things.
l.380 The . . . is: Traditionally, the heavens were conceived of as paternal, the earth as maternal.
l.387 Meteors: The term was applied in Donne's time to any atmospheric phenomena.
l.389 wormes: serpents.
l.390 Mages: magicians.
l.391 Artist: astrologer.

Death could not quench her vertue so, but that
It would be (if not follow'd) wondred at:
And all the world would be one dying Swan,
To sing her funerall prayse, and vanish than.
But as some Serpents poison hurteth not,
Except it be from the live Serpent shot,   410
So doth her vertue need her here, to fit
That unto us; she working more then it.
But she, in whom, to such maturity,
Vertue was growne, past growth, that it must die,
She from whose influence all Impressions came,
But, by Receivers impotencies, lame,
Who, though she could not transubstantiate
All states to gold, yet guilded every state,
So that some Princes have some temperance;
Some Counsaylors some purpose to advance   420
The common profite; and some people have
Some stay, no more then Kings should give, to crave;
Some women have some taciturnity;
Some Nunneries, some graines of chastity.
She that did thus much, and much more could doe,
But that our age was Iron, and rusty too,
Shee, shee is dead; shee's dead: when thou knowst this,
Thou knowest how drie a Cinder this world is.
And learnst thus much by our Anatomy,
That 'tis in vaine to dew, or mollifie   430
It with thy Teares, or Sweat, or Bloud: no thing
Is worth our travaile, griefe, or perishing,
But those rich joyes, which did possesse her hart,
Of which shee's now partaker, and a part.
But as in cutting up a man that's dead,   *Conclusion.*
The body will not last out to have read
On every part, and therefore men direct
Their speech to parts, that are of most effect;
So the worlds carcasse would not last, if I
Were punctuall in this Anatomy.   440

l.408 than: then.
l.422 stay: restraint.
l.426 But . . . too: Recurring in the entire poem are references to the
    ancient idea of the four ages of history—gold, silver, bronze, and iron
    —with the concomitant belief in history as degeneration.
l.440 punctuall: detailed.

Nor smels it well to hearers, if one tell
Them their disease, who faine would think they're wel.
Here therefore be the end: And, blessed maid,
Of whom is meant what ever hath beene said,
Or shall be spoken well by any tongue,
Whose name refines course lines, and makes prose song,
Accept this tribute, and his first yeares rent,
Who till his darke short tapers end be spent,
As oft as thy feast sees this widowed earth,
Will yearely celebrate thy second birth,   450
That is, thy death. For though the soule of man
Be got when man is made, 'tis borne but than
When man doth die. Our body's as the wombe,
And as a mid-wife death directs it home.
And you her creatures, whom she workes upon
And have your last, and best concoction
From her example, and her vertue, if you
In reverence to her, doe thinke it due,
That no one should her prayses thus reherse,
As matter fit for Chronicle, not verse,   460
Vouchsafe to call to minde, that God did make
A last, and lastingst peece, a song. He spake
To *Moses*, to deliver unto all,
That song: because he knew they would let fall,
The Law, the Prophets, and the History,
But keepe the song still in their memory.
Such an opinion (in due measure) made
Me this great Office boldly to invade.
Nor could incomprehensiblenesse deterre
Me, from thus trying to emprison her.   470
Which when I saw that a strict grave could do,
I saw not why verse might not doe so too.
Verse hath a middle nature: heaven keepes soules,
The grave keeps bodies, verse the fame enroules.

wants to remind world of corruption
while perserving Elizabeth's body in it

— no solution

l.446 course: coarse.
l.449 feast: religious holiday.   *anatomy of ills*
l.452 than: then.   *of world*
l.456 concoction: purification.
ll.461–462 that . . . song: see Deuteronomy 32, the song of Moses.

A FUNERALL ELEGIE

Tis lost, to trust a Tombe with such a ghest,
    Or to confine her in a Marble chest.
Alas, what's Marble, Jeat, or Porphiry,
    Priz'd with the Chrysolite of eyther eye,
Or with those Pearles, and Rubies which shee was?
    Joyne the two Indies in one Tombe, 'tis glas;
And so is all to her materials,
    Though every inche were ten escurials.
Yet shee's demolish'd: Can we keepe her then
    In workes of hands, or of the wits of men?   10
Can these memorials, ragges of paper, give
    Life to that name, by which name they must live?
Sickly, alas, short-liv'd, aborted bee
    Those Carkas verses, whose soule is not shee.
And can shee, who no longer would be shee,
    Being such a Tabernacle, stoope to bee
In paper wrap't; Or, when she would not lie
    In such a house, dwell in an Elegie?
But 'tis no matter; we may well allow
    Verse to live so long as the world will now.   20
For her death wounded it. The world containes
    Princes for armes, and Counsailors for braines,
Lawyers for tongues, Divines for hearts, and more,
    The Rich for stomachs, and for backes the Pore;
The Officers for hands, Merchants for feet
    By which remote and distant Countries meet.
But those fine spirits, which doe tune and set
    This Organ, are those peeces which beget
Wonder and love; And these were shee; and shee
    Being spent, the world must needes decrepit bee.   30
For since death will proceed to triumph still,
    He can finde nothing, after her, to kill,
Except the world it selfe, so great as shee.
    Thus brave and confident may Nature bee,
Death cannot give her such another blow,
    Because shee cannot such another show.

l.8 escurials: The Escorial was the great palace of the Spanish kings.
l.27 spirits: the delicate vapors supposed to arise from the blood and
link body and soul. See notes to "The Extasie."

But must we say shee's dead? May't not be said
    That as a sundred Clocke is peece-meale laid,
Not to be lost, but by the makers hand
    Repolish'd, without error then to stand,   40
Or as the Affrique Niger streame enwombs
    It selfe into the earth, and after comes,
(Having first made a naturall bridge, to passe
    For many leagues,) farre greater then it was,
May't not be said, that her grave shall restore
    Her, greater, purer, firmer, then before?
Heaven may say this, and joy in't; but can wee
    Who live, and lacke her, here this vantage see?
What is't to us, alas, if there have beene
    An Angell made a Throne, or Cherubin?   50
We lose by't: And as aged men are glad
    Being tastlesse growne, to joy in joyes they had,
So now the sicke starv'd world must feed upone
    This joy, that we had her, who now is gone.
Rejoyce then nature, and this world, that you
    Fearing the last fires hastning to subdue
Your force and vigor, ere it were neere gone,
    Wisely bestow'd, and layd it all on one.
One, whose cleare body was so pure, and thin,
    Because it neede disguise no thought within.   60
T'was but a through-light scarfe, her minde t'enroule,
    Or exhalation breath'd out from her soule.
One, whom all men who durst no more, admir'd;
    And whom, who ere had worth enough, desir'd;
As when a Temple's built, Saints emulate
    To which of them, it shall be consecrate.
But as when Heav'n lookes on us with new eyes,
    Those new starres ev'ry Artist exercise,

l.41 Affrique Niger: It was formerly believed that the Niger and the
    Nile were parts of the same river and that it ran underground for
    part of its course.
l.50. An . . . Cherubin: Thrones and Cherubim are ranks in the an-
    gelic hierarchy.
l.61 through-light: transparent.
l.68 Artist: astronomer. References to the new stars observed by Renais-
    sance astronomers are obsessive throughout the "Anniversaries" and
    the "Funerall Elegie."

What place they should assigne to them they doubt,
    Argue, and agree not, till those starres go out: 70
So the world studied whose this peece should be,
    Till she can be no bodies else, nor shee:
But like a Lampe of Balsamum, desir'd
    Rather t'adorne, then last, shee soone expir'd;
Cloath'd in her Virgin white integrity;
    For mariage, though it doe not staine, doth dye.
To scape th'infirmities which waite upone
    Woman, shee went away, before sh'was one.
And the worlds busie noyse to overcome,
    Tooke so much death, as serv'd for *opium*.   80
For though she could not, nor could chuse to die,
    Shee'ath yeelded to too long an Extasie.
He which not knowing her sad History,
    Should come to reade the booke of destiny,
How faire and chast, humble and high shee'ad beene,
    Much promis'd, much perform'd, at not fifteene,
And measuring future things, by things before,
    Should turne the leafe to reade, and read no more,
Would thinke that eyther destiny mistooke,
    Or that some leafes were torne out of the booke.   90
But 'tis not so: Fate did but usher her
    To yeares of Reasons use, and then infer
Her destiny to her selfe; which liberty
    She tooke but for thus much, thus much to die.
Her modesty not suffering her to bee
    Fellow-Commissioner with destinee,
Shee did no more but die; if after her
    Any shall live, which dare true good prefer,
Every such person is her delegate,
    T'accomplish that which should have beene her
    fate.   100
They shall make up that booke, and shall have thankes
    Of fate and her, for filling up their blanks.
For future vertuous deeds are Legacies,
    Which from the gift of her example rise.
And 'tis in heav'n part of spirituall mirth,
    To see how well, the good play her, on earth.

l.92 infer: entrust.

THE SECOND ANNIVERSARIE
OF THE PROGRES OF THE SOULE

WHEREIN, BY OCCASION OF THE
RELIGIOUS DEATH OF MISTRIS
ELIZABETH DRURY THE INCOMMODITIES
OF THE SOULE IN THIS LIFE AND
HER EXALTATION IN THE NEXT,
ARE CONTEMPLATED

The   Nothing could make mee sooner to confesse
entrance. That this world had an everlastingnesse,
Then to consider, that a yeare is runne,
Since both this lower worlds, and the Sunnes Sunne,
The Lustre, and the vigor of this All,
Did set; t'were Blasphemy, to say, did fall.
But as a ship which hath strooke saile, doth runne,
By force of that force which before, it wonne,
Or as sometimes in a beheaded man,
Though at those two Red seas, which freely ran,   10
One from the Trunke, another from the Head,
His soule be saild, to her eternall bed,
His eyes will twinckle, and his tongue will roll,
As though he beckned, and cal'd backe his Soul,
He graspes his hands, and he puls up his feet,
And seemes to reach, and to step forth to meet
His soule; when all these motions which we saw,
Are but as Ice, which crackles at a thaw:
Or as a Lute, which in moist weather, rings
Her knell alone, by cracking at her strings.   20
So strugles this dead world, now shee is gone;
For there is motion in corruption.
As some Daies are, at the Creation nam'd,
Before the sunne, the which fram'd Daies, was fram'd,
So after this sunnes set, some show appeares,
And orderly vicisitude of yeares.
Yet a new Deluge, and of Lethe flood,

The Second Anniversarie: Progres means royal journey.
l.2 That . . . everlastingnesse: an idea which was rejected by virtually
    all Renaissance thinkers.
l.3 Then: than.

Hath drown' us all, All have forgot all good,
Forgetting her, the maine Reserve of all;
Yet in this Deluge, grosse and generall,   30
Thou seest mee strive for life; my life shalbe,
To bee hereafter prais'd, for praysing thee,
Immortal Mayd, who though thou wouldst refuse
The name of Mother, be unto my Muse,
A Father since her chast Ambition is,
Yearely to bring forth such a child as this.
These Hymes may worke on future wits, and so
May great Grand-children of thy praises grow.
And so, though not Revive, enbalme, and spice
The world, which else would putrify with vice.   40
For thus, Man may extend thy progeny,
Untill man doe but vanish, and not die.
These Hymns thy issue, may encrease so long,
As till Gods great Venite change the song.
Thirst for that time, O my insatiate soule,
And serve thy thirst, with Gods safe-sealing Bowle.
Bee thirsty still, and drinke still till thou goe;
'Tis th'onely Health, to be Hydropique so.
Forget this rotten world; And unto thee,
Let thine owne times as an old story be,   50
Be not concern'd: study not why, nor whan;
Do not so much, as not beleeve a man.
For though to erre, be worst, to try truths forth,
Is far more busines, then this world is worth.
The World is but a Carkas; thou art fed
By it, but as a worme, that carcas bred;
And why shouldst thou, poore worme, consider more,
When this world will grow better then before,
Then those thy fellow-wormes doe thinke upone
That carkasses last resurrectione?   60
Forget this world, and scarse thinke of it so,
As of old cloaths, cast of a yeare agoe.
To be thus stupid is Alacrity;
Men thus lethargique have best Memory.

A just
disestimation
of this world.

l.37 Hymes: a pun on hims.
l.44 Venite: come; God's final imperative.
l.46 Bowle: the sacrament of the Eucharist.
l.48 Hydropique: dropsical, that is, suffering from an insatiable thirst.
l.62 of: off.

Looke upward; that's towards her, whose happy state
We now lament not, but congratulate.
Shee, to whom all this world was but a stage,
Where all sat harkning how her youthfull age
Should be emploid, because in all, shee did,
Some Figure of the Golden times, was hid.   70
Who could not lacke, what ere this world could give,
Because shee was the forme, that made it live;
Nor could complaine, that this world was unfit,
To be staid in, then when shee was in it;
Shee that first tried indifferent desires
By vertue, and vertue by religious fires,
Shee to whose person Paradise adhear'd,
As Courts to Princes; shee whose eies enspheard
Star-light inough, t'have made the South controll,
(Had shee beene there) the Star-full Northern Pole,   80
Shee, shee is gone; shee is gone; when thou knowest
  this,
What fragmentary rubbidge this world is
Thou knowest, and that it is not worth a thought;
He honors it too much that thinks it nought.

Contem-
pla tion of
our state
in our
deathbed.

Thinke then, My soule, that death is but a Groome,
Which brings a Taper to the outward roome,
Whence thou spiest first a little glimmering light,
And after brings it nearer to thy sight:
For such approches doth Heaven make in death.
Thinke thy selfe laboring now with broken breath,   90
And thinke those broken and soft Notes to bee
Division, and thy happiest Harmonee.
Thinke thee laid on thy death bed, loose and slacke;
And thinke that but unbinding of a packe,
To take one precious thing, thy soule, from thence.
Thinke thy selfe parch'd with fevers violence,
Anger thine Ague more, by calling it
Thy Physicke; chide the slacknesse of the fit.
Thinke that thou hearst thy knell, and thinke no more,
But that, as Bels cal'd thee to Church before,   100
So this, to the Triumphant Church, cals thee.

l.70 Golden times: the Age of Gold.
l.72 forme: in the scholastic sense, as the soul.
l.92 Division: a melodic sequence composed of a number of short notes.
l.98 Physicke: medicine.

Thinke Satans Sergeants round about thee bee,
And thinke that but for Legacies they thrust;
Give one thy Pride, to'another give thy Lust:
Give them those sinnes which they gave thee before,
And trust th'immaculate blood to wash thy score.
Thinke thy frinds weeping round, and thinke that thay
Weepe but because they goe not yet thy way.
Thinke that they close thine eyes, and thinke in this,
That they confesse much in the world, amisse, 110
Who dare not trust a dead mans eye with that,
Which they from God, and Angels cover not.
Thinke that they shroud thee up, and thinke from
  thence
They reinvest thee in white innocence.
Thinke that thy body rots, and (if so lowe,
Thy soule exalted so, thy thoughts can goe,)
Thinke the a Prince, who of themselves create
Wormes which insensibly devoure their state.
Thinke that they bury thee, and thinke that rite
Laies thee to sleepe but a saint Lucies night. 120
Thinke these things cheerefully: and if thou bee
Drowsie or slacke, remember then that shee,
Shee whose Complexion was so even made,
That which of her Ingredients should invade
The other three, no Feare, no Art could guesse:
So far were all remov'd from more or lesse.
But as in Mithridate, or just perfumes,
Where all good things being met, no one presumes
To governe, or to triumph on the rest,
Onely because all were, no part was best. 130
And as, though all doe know, that quantities
Are made of lines, and lines from Points arise,
None can these lines or quantities unjoynt,
And say this is a line, or this a point,

l.102 Sergeants: bailiffs.
l.117 the: thee.
l.120 saint Lucies night: the longest night of the year. See "A Nocturnall upon S. Lucies Day."
l.123 Complexion: temperament.
l.124 Ingredients: the humours, or elements, which determine her temperament.
l.127 Mithridate: antidote.

So though the Elements and Humors were
In her, one could not say, this governes there.
Whose even constitution might have wonne
Any disease to venter on the Sunne,
Rather then her: and make a spirit feare
That he to disuniting subject were.   140
To whose proportions if we would compare
Cubes, th'are unstable; Circles, Angulare;
Shee who was such a Chaine, as Fate emploies
To bring mankind, all Fortunes it enjoies,
So fast, so even wrought, as one would thinke,
No Accident, could threaten any linke,
Shee, shee embrac'd a sicknesse, gave it meat,
The purest Blood, and Breath, that ere it eat.
And hath taught us that though a good man hath
Title to Heaven, and plead it by his Faith,   150
And though he may pretend a conquest, since
Heaven was content to suffer violence,
Yea though he plead a long possession too,
(For they'are in Heaven on Earth, who Heavens
  workes do,)
Though he had right, and power, and Place before,
Yet Death must usher, and unlocke the doore.

Incom- Thinke further on thy selfe, my soule, and thinke;
modities of How thou at first wast made but in a sinke;
the Soule Thinke that it argued some infermitee,
in the That those two soules, which then thou foundst in mee,   160
Body. Thou fedst upon, and drewst into thee, both
My second soule of sence, and first of growth.
Thinke but how poore thou wast, how obnoxious,
Whom a small lump of flesh could poison thus.
This curded milke, this poore unlittered whelpe

l.138 venter: venture.
l.138 Sunne: The sun was by definition incorruptible.
l.147 meat: food.
l.152 Heaven . . . violence: see Matthew 11:12.
l.158 sinke: sewer, cesspool.
ll.160–162 That . . . growth: The passage refers to the ancient doctrine
   of the three souls of created things: the vegetative, possessed by plants
   and animals; the sensitive, possessed by animals; and the rational,
   possessed by human beings, which contained in it the other two.
l.163 obnoxious: exposed to harm.
l.165 unlittered: unborn.

My body, could, beyond escape, or helpe,
Infect thee with originall sinne, and thou
Couldst neither then refuse, nor leave it now.
Thinke that no stubborne sullen Anchorit,
Which fixt to'a Pillar, or a Grave doth sit   170
Bedded and Bath'd in all his Ordures, dwels
So fowly as our soules, in their first-built Cels.
Thinke in how poore a prison thou didst lie
After, enabled but to sucke, and crie.
Thinke, when t'was growne to most, t'was a poore
  Inne,
A Province Pack'd up in two yards of skinne,
And that usurped, or threatned with the rage
Of sicknesses, or their true mother, Age.
But thinke that Death hath now enfranchis'd thee,   *Her liberty*
Thou hast thy'expansion now and libertee;   180   *by death.*
Thinke that a rusty Peece, discharg'd, is flowen
In peeces, and the bullet is his owne,
And freely flies: This to thy soule allow,
Thinke thy sheell broke, thinke thy Soule hatch'd but
  now.
And thinke this slow-pac'd soule, which late did cleave,
To'a body, and went but by the bodies leave,
Twenty, perchance, or thirty mile a day,
Dispatches in a minute all the way,
Twixt Heaven, and Earth: shee staies not in the Ayre,
To looke what Meteors there themselves prepare;   190
Shee carries no desire to know, nor sense,
Whether th'Ayrs middle Region be intense,
For th'Element of fire, shee doth not know,
Whether shee past by such a place or no;
Shee baits not at the Moone, nor cares to trie,
Whether in that new world, men live, and die.
Venus retards her not, to'enquire, how shee
Can, (being one Star) Hesper, and Vesper bee;

l.181 Peece: firearm.
l.190 Meteors: any atmospheric phenomena.
l.192 intense: violent.
l.193 Element . . . fire: presumed to exist above the air.
l.195 baits: pauses.
l.195 trie: observe.
l.198 Hesper . . . Vesper: the morning star and the evening star.

Hee that charm'd Argus eies, sweet Mercury,
Workes not on her, who now is growen all Ey;   200
Who, if shee meete the body of the Sunne,
Goes through, not staying till his course be runne;
Who finds in Mars his Campe, no corps of Guard;
Nor is by Jove, nor by his father bard;
But ere shee can consider how shee went,
At once is at, and through the Firmament.
And as these stars were but so many beades
Strunge on one string, speed undistinguish'd leades
Her through those spheares, as through the beades, a
   string,
Whose quicke succession makes it still one thing: 210
As doth the Pith, which, least our Bodies slacke,
Strings fast the little bones of necke, and backe;
So by the soule doth death string Heaven and Earth,
For when our soule enjoyes this her third birth,
(Creation gave her one, a second, grace,)
Heaven is as neare, and present to her face,
As colours are, and objects, in a roome
Where darknesse was before, when Tapers come.
This must, my soule, thy long-short Progresse bee;
To'advance these thoughts, remember then, that shee   220
Shee, whose faire body no such prison was,
But that a soule might well be pleas'd to passe
An Age in her; shee whose rich beauty lent
Mintage to others beauties, for they went
But for so much, as they were like to her;
Shee, in whose body (if wee dare prefer
This low world, to so high a mark, as shee,)
The Westerne treasure, Esterne spiceree,
Europe, and Afrique, and the unknowen rest
Were easily found, or what in them was best;   230
And when w'have made this large Discoveree,
Of all in her some one part there will bee
Twenty such parts, whose plenty and riches is
Inough to make twenty such worlds as this;
Shee, whom had they knowne, who did first betroth
The Tutelar Angels, and assigned one, both

l.204 his father: Saturn.
l.226 prefer: promote.
l.236 Tutelar: guardian

To Nations, Cities, and to Companies,
To Functions, Offices, and Dignities,
And to each severall man, to him, and him,
They would have given her one for every limme;   240
Shee, of whose soule, if we may say, t'was Gold,
Her body was th'Electrum, and did hold
Many degrees of that; we understood
Her by her sight, her pure and eloquent blood
Spoke in her cheekes, and so distinckly wrought,
That one might almost say, her bodie thought,
Shee, shee, thus richly, and largely hous'd, is gone:
And chides us slow-pac'd snailes, who crawle upon
Our prisons prison, earth, nor thinke us well
Longer, then whil'st we beare our brittle shell.   250
But t'were but little to have chang'd our roome,   *Her ignorance*
If, as we were in this our living Tombe   *in this life*
Oppress'd with ignorance, we still were so.   *and knowl-*
Poore soule in this thy flesh what do'st thou know. *edge in the*
Thou know'st thy selfe so little, as thou know'st not, *next.*
How thou did'st die, nor how thou wast begot.
Thou neither knowst, how thou at first camest in,
Nor how thou took'st the poyson of mans sin.
Nor dost thou, (though thou knowst, that thou art so)
By what way thou art made immortall, know.   260
Thou art to narrow, wretch, to comprehend
Even thy selfe: yea though thou wouldst but bend
To know thy body. Have not all soules thought
For many ages, that our body'is wrought
Of Ayre, and Fire, and other Elements?
And now they thinke of new ingredients.
And one soule thinkes one, and another way
Another thinkes, and ty's an even lay.
Knowst thou but how the stone doth enter in
The bladders Cave, and never breake the skin?   270
Knowst thou how blood, which to the hart doth flow,
Doth from one ventricle to th'other go?
And for the putrid stuffe, which thou dost spit,

---

ll.236–240 and . . . limme: Donne is satirizing the detail of Roman
   Catholic teaching concerning guardian angels.
l.242 Electrum: an alloy of gold and silver.
l.261 to: too.
l.268 ty's: 'tis.

Knowst thou how thy lungs have attracted it?
There are no passages so that there is
(For ought thou knowst) piercing of substances.
And of those many opinions which men raise
Of Nailes and Haires, dost thou know which to praise?
What hope have we to know our selves, when wee
Know not the least things, which for our use bee?   280
We see in Authors, too stiffe to recant,
A hundred controversies of an Ant.
And yet one watches, starves, freeses, and sweats,
To know but Catechismes and Alphabets
Of unconcerning things, matters of fact;
How others on our stage their parts did Act;
What Caesar did, yea, and what Cicero said.
Why grasse is greene, or why our blood is red,
Are mysteries which none have reach'd unto.
In this low forme, poore soule what wilt thou doe?   290
When wilt thou shake off this Pedantery,
Of being taught by sense, and Fantasy?
Thou look'st through spectacles; small things seeme great,
      great,
Below; But up unto the watch-towre get,
And see all things despoyld of fallacies:
Thou shalt not peepe through lattices of eies,
Nor heare through Laberinths of eares, nor learne
By circuit, or collections to discerne.
In Heaven thou straight know'st all, concerning it,
And what concerns it not, shall straight forget.   300
There thou (but in no other schoole) maist bee
Perchance, as learned, and as full, as shee,
Shee who all Libraries had throughly red
At home, in her owne thoughts, and practised
So much good as would make as many more:
Shee whose example they must all implore,
Who would or doe, or thinke well, and confesse
That aie the vertuous Actions they expresse,
Are but a new, and worse edition,
Of her some one thought, or one action: 310

l.283 watches: stays awake.
l.292 Fantasy: that part of the mind which receives and interprets sense
      impressions.
l.308 aie: aye.

Shee, who in th'Art of knowing Heaven, was growen
Here upon Earth, to such perfection,
That shee hath, ever since to Heaven shee came,
(In a far fairer print,) but read the same:
Shee, shee, not satisfied with all this waite,
(For so much knowledge, as would over-fraite
Another, did but Ballast her) is gone,
As well t'enjoy, as get perfection.
And cals us after her, in that shee tooke,
(Taking herselfe) our best, and worthiest booke.   320
Returne not, my soule, from this extasee,   *Of our*
And meditation of what thou shalt bee,   *company in*
To earthly thoughts, till it to thee appeare,   *this life and*
With whom thy conversation must be there.   *in the next.*
With whom wilt thou Converse? what station
Canst thou choose out, free from infection,
That wil nor give thee theirs, nor drinke in thine?
Shalt thou not finde a spungy slack Divine
Drinke and sucke in th'Instructions of Great men,
And for the word of God, vent them agen?   330
Are there not some Courts, (And then, no things bee
So like as Courts) which, in this let us see,
That wits and tongues of Libellars are weake,
Because they doe more ill, then these can speake?
The poyson'is gone through all, poysons affect
Chiefly the cheefest parts, but some effect
In Nailes, and Haires, yea excrements, will show;
So will the poyson of sinne, in the most low.
Up up, my drowsie soule, where thy new eare
Shall in the Angels songs no discord heare;   340
Where thou shalt see the blessed Mother-maid
Joy in not being that, which men have said.
Where shee'is exalted more for being good,
Then for her interest, of mother-hood.
Up to those Patriarckes, which did longer sit
Expecting Christ, then they'have enjoy'd him yet.
Up to those Prophets, which now gladly see
Their Prophecies growen to be Historee.

ll.333–334 *That . . . speake:* It is impossible for even libelers to speak
    sufficient evil of courts.
ll.341–342 *Where . . . said:* a reference to the Roman Catholic doctrine
    that the Virgin Mary was born free from original sin.

Up to th'Apostles, who did bravely runne,
All the Sunnes course, with more light then the Sunne.   350
Up to those Martyrs, who did calmely bleed
Oyle to th'Apostles lamps, dew to their seed.
Up to those Virgins, who thought that almost
They made joyntenants with the Holy Ghost,
If they to any should his Temple give.
Up, up, for in that squadron there doth live
Shee, who hath carried thether, new degrees
(As to their number) to their dignitees.
Shee, who beeing to herselfe a state, enjoyd
All royalties which any state emploid,   360
For shee made wars, and triumph'd; reson still
Did not overthrow, but rectifie her will:
And shee made peace, for no peace is like this,
That beauty and chastity together kisse:
Shee did high justice; for shee crucified
Every first motion of rebellious pride:
And shee gave pardons, and was liberall,
For, onely herselfe except, shee pardond all:
Shee coynd, in this, that her impressions gave
To all our actions all the worth they have: 370
Shee gave protections; the thoughts of her brest
Satans rude Officers could nere arrest.
As these prerogatives being met in one,
Made her a soveraigne state, religion
Made her a Church; and these two made her all.
Shee who was all this All, and could not fall
To worse, by company; (for shee was still
More Antidote, then all the world was ill,)
Shee, shee doth leave it, and by Death, survive
All this, in Heaven; whither who doth not strive   380
The more, because shee'is there, he doth not know
Of   That accidentall joyes in Heaven doe grow.
essentiall   But pause, My soule, and study ere thou fall
joy in this On accidentall joyes, th'essentiall.
life and in Still before Accessories doe abide
the next.   A triall, must the principall be tride.

l.354 joyntenants: joint-tenants.
l.360 royalties: prerogatives.
l.382 accidentall: non-essential. The essential joy of the blessed consists
    in the beatific vision; all other joys are, therefore, accidental.

And what essentiall joy canst thou expect
Here upon earth? what permanent effect
Of transitory causes? Dost thou love
Beauty? (And Beauty worthyest is to move)   390
Poore couse'ned cose'nor, that she, and that thou,
Which did begin to love, are neither now.
You are both fluid, chang'd since yesterday;
Next day repaires, (but ill) last daies decay.
Nor are, (Although the river keep the name)
Yesterdaies waters, and to daies the same.
So flowes her face, and thine eies, neither now
That saint, nor Pilgrime, which your loving vow
Concernd, remaines; but whil'st you thinke you bee
Constant, you'are howrely in inconstancee.   400
Honour may have pretence unto our love,
Because that God did live so long above
Without this Honour, and then lov'd it so,
That he at last made Creatures to bestow
Honor on him; not that he needed it,
But that, to his hands, man might grow more fit.
But since all honors from inferiors flow,
(For they doe give it; Princes doe but show
Whom they would have so honord) and that this
On such opinions, and capacities   410
Is built, as rise, and fall, to more and lesse,
Alas, tis but a casuall happinesse.
Hath ever any man to'himselfe assigned
This or that happinesse, to'arrest his minde,
But that another man, which takes a worse,
Thinks him a foole for having tane that course?
They who did labour Babels tower t'erect,
Might have considerd, that for that effect,
All this whole solid Earth could not allow
Nor furnish forth Materials enow;   420
And that this Center, to raise such a place
Was far to little, to have beene the Base;
No more affoords this world, foundatione

l.391 couse'ned cose'nor: cheated cheater.
l.401 pretence: claim.
l.416 tane: taken.
l.420 enow: enough.
l.421 Center: the earth.

To erect true joye, were all the meanes in one.
But as the Heathen made them severall gods,
Of all Gods Benefits, and all his Rods,
(For as the Wine, and Corne, and Onions are
Gods unto them, so Agues bee, and war)
And as by changing that whole precious Gold
To such small copper coynes, they lost the old,   430
And lost their onely God, who ever must
Be sought alone, and not in such a thrust,
So much mankind true happinesse mistakes;
No Joye enjoyes that man, that many makes.
Then, soule, to thy first pitch worke up againe;
Know that all lines which circles doe containe,
For once that they the center touch, do touch
Twice the circumference; and be thou such.
Double on Heaven, thy thoughts on Earth emploid;
All will not serve; Onely who have enjoyd   440
The sight of God, in fulnesse, can thinke it;
For it is both the object, and the wit.
This is essentiall joye, where neither hee
Can suffer Diminution, nor wee;
Tis such a full, and such a filling good;
Had th'Angels once look'd on him, they had stood.
To fill the place of one of them, or more,
Shee whom we celebrate, is gone before.
Shee, who had Here so much essentiall joye,
As no chance could distract, much lesse destroy;   450
Who with Gods presence was acquainted so,
(Hearing, and speaking to him) as to know
His face, in any naturall Stone, or Tree,
Better then when in Images they bee:
Who kept, by diligent devotion,
Gods Image, in such reparation,
Within her heart, that what decay was growen,
Was her first Parents fault, and not her own:
Who being solicited to any Act,
Still heard God pleading his safe precontract;   460
Who by a faithfull confidence, was here

l.432 thrust: crowd.
l.435 pitch: peak.
l.460 Still: always.

Betrothed to God, and now is married there,
Whose twilights were more cleare, then our mid day,
Who dreamt devoutlier, then most use to pray;
Who being heare fild with grace, yet strove to bee,
Both where more grace, and more capacitee
At once is given: shee to Heaven is gone,
Who made this world in some proportion
A heaven, and here, became unto us all,
Joye, (as our joyes admit) essentiall.   470
But could this low world joyes essentiall touch,   *Of accidentall*
Heavens accidentall joyes would passe them much.   *joyes in both*
How poore and lame, must then our casuall bee?   *places.*
If thy Prince will his subjects to call thee
My Lord, and this doe swell thee, thou art than,
By being a greater, growen to be lesse Man.
When no Physician of Redresse can speake,
A joyfull casuall violence may breake
A dangerous Apostem in thy brest;
And whilst thou joyest in this, the dangerous rest,   480
The bag may rise up, and so strangle thee.
What eie was casuall, may ever bee.
What should the Nature change? Or make the same
Certaine, which was but casuall, when it came?
All casuall joye doth loud and plainly say,
Onely by comming, that it can away.
Onely in Heaven joies strength is never spent;
And accidentall things are permanent.
Joy of a soules arrivall neere decaies;
For that soule ever joyes, and ever staies.   490
Joy that their last great Consummation
Approches in the resurrection;
When earthly bodies more celestiall
Shalbe, then Angels were, for they could fall;
This kind of joy doth every day admit
Degrees of growth, but none of loosing it.
In this fresh joy, tis no small part, that shee,
Shee, in whose goodnesse, he that names degree,
Doth injure her; (Tis losse to be cald best,
There where the stuffe is not such as the rest)   500

l.473 casuall: non-essentiall.
l.479 Apostem: imposthume, abscesse.

Shee, who left such a body, as even shee
Onely in Heaven could learne, how it can bee
Made better; for shee rather was two soules,
Or like to full, on both sides written Rols,
Where eies might read upon the outward skin,
As strong Records for God, as mindes within.
Shee, who by making full perfection grow,
Peeces a Circle, and still keepes it so,
Long'd for, and longing for'it, to heaven is gone,
Where shee receives, and gives addition.   510

Conclusion. Here in a place, where mis-devotion frames
A thousand praiers to saints, whose very names
The ancient Church knew not, Heaven knowes not
  yet,
And where, what lawes of poetry admit,
Lawes of religion, have at least the same,
Immortall Maid, I might invoque thy name.
Could any Saint provoke that appetite,
Thou here shouldst make mee a french convertite.
But thou wouldst not; nor wouldst thou be content,
To take this, for my second yeeres true Rent,   520
Did this Coine beare any other stampe, then his,
That gave thee power to doe, me, to say this.
Since his will is, that to posteritee,
Thou shouldest for life, and death, a patterne bee,
And that the world should notice have of this,
The purpose, and th' Autority is his;
Thou art the Proclamation; and I ame
The Trumpet, at whose voice the people came.

l.511 Here: in France, where Donne was visiting the Drurys. The reference is to the Catholic practice of appealing to the saints for inter-
  cession.
l.518 convertite: a convert to Roman Catholicism.

*Epicedes and Obsequies
upon the Deaths
of Sundry Personages
and Epitaphs*

ᴀᴘᴀʀᴛ ꜰʀᴏᴍ the complex of poems inspired by
the death of Elizabeth Drury, Donne wrote seven funeral
elegies, all but one of which are included in the following
pages. Although they contain occasional striking or felici-
tous passages, all these poems are marked by a frigid ingenuity and a hyperbolic extravagance which, however
much in the style of the age which produced them, have
elicited little positive response from readers of subsequent
generations. With the exception of the problematic "Elegie
on the L. C.," these poems can all be readily dated by the
death dates of their subjects.

Donne's two versions of a witty epitaph on himself are
included in this section.

ELEGIE ON THE L. C. [LORD CHAMBERLAIN] [1596]

Sorrow, who to this house scarce knew the way:
Is, Oh, heire of it, our All is his prey.
This strange chance claimes strange wonder, and to us
Nothing can be so strange, as to weepe thus.
'Tis well his lifes loud speaking workes deserve,
And give praise too, our cold tongues could not serve:
'Tis well, hee kept teares from our eyes before,
That to fit this deepe ill, we might have store.
Oh, if a sweet briar, climbe up by'a tree,
If to a paradise that transplanted bee,   10
Or fell'd, and burnt for holy sacrifice,
Yet, that must wither, which by it did rise,
As wee for him dead: though no familie
Ere rigg'd a soule for heavens discoverie
With whom more Venturers more boldly dare
Venture their states, with him in joy to share.
Wee lose what all friends lov'd, him; he gaines now
But life by death, which worst foes would allow,
If hee could have foes, in whose practise grew
All vertues, whose names subtile Schoolmen knew.   20
What ease, can hope that wee shall see'him, beget,
When wee must die first, and cannot dye yet?
His children are his pictures, Oh they bee
Pictures of him dead, senselesse, cold as he.
Here needs no marble Tombe, since hee is gone,
He, and about him, his, are turn'd to stone.

Elegie on the L. C.: In her edition of the *Elegies and the Songs and Sonets*, Helen Gardner includes this poem with the elegies of the 1590s, on grounds of both style and manuscript evidence. She rejects the argument that it is an elegy on the Lord Chamberlain (or, as was earlier proposed, on the Lord Chancellor), and points out that the phrase "on the L. C." first occurs in the 1635 edition of the poems. Her own contention is that the poem is a consolation addressed *to* L. C. (Lionel Cranfield?) on the death of his father (1595).

ELEGIE ON THE LADY
MARCKHAM [d. 1609]

Man is the World, and death th'Ocean,
   To which God gives the lower parts of man.
This Sea invirons all, and though as yet
   God hath set markes, and bounds, twixt us and it,
Yet doth it rore, and gnaw, and still pretend,
   And breaks our bankes, when ere it takes a friend.
Then our land waters (teares of passion) vent;
   Our waters, then, above our firmament,
(Teares which our Soule doth for her sins let fall);
   Take all a brackish tast, and Funerall,   10
And even these teares, which should wash sin, are sin.
   We, after Gods *Noe,* drowne our world againe.
Nothing but man of all invenom'd things
   Doth worke upon itselfe, with inborne stings.
Teares are false Spectacles, we cannot see
   Through passions mist, what wee are, or what shee.
In her this sea of death hath made no breach,
   But as the tide doth wash the slimie beach,
And leaves embroder'd workes upon the sand,
   So is her flesh refin'd by deaths cold hand.   20
As men of China,'after an ages stay,
   Do take up Porcelane, where they buried Clay;
So at this grave, her limbecke, which refines
   The Diamonds, Rubies, Saphires, Pearles, and Mines,
Of which this flesh was, her soule shall inspire
   Flesh of such stuffe, as God, when his last fire
Annuls this world, to recompence it, shall,
   Make and name then, th'Elixar of this All.
They say, the sea, when it gaines, loseth too;
   If carnall Death (the yonger brother) doe   30
Usurpe the body,'our soule, which subject is
   To th'elder death, by sinne, is freed by this;
They perish both, when they attempt the just;
   For, graves our trophies are, and both deaths' dust.

l.5 pretend: claim.
l.23 limbecke: alembic, apparatus for distillation.

So, unobnoxious now, she'hath buried both;
  For, none to death sinnes, that to sinne is loth,
Nor doe they die, which are not loth to die;
  So hath she this, and that virginity.
Grace was in her extremely diligent,
  That kept her from sinne, yet made her repent. 40
Of what small spots pure white complaines! Alas,
  How little poyson cracks a christall glasse!
She sinn'd, but just enough to let us see
  That God's word must be true, All, sinners be.
Soe much did zeale her conscience rarefie,
  That, extreme truth lack'd little of a lye,
Making omissions, acts; laying the touch
  Of sinne, on things that sometimes may be such.
As *Moses* Cherubines, whose natures doe
  Surpasse all speed, by him are winged too: 50
So would her soule, already'in heaven, seeme then,
  To clyme by teares, the common staires of men.
How fit she was for God, I am content
  To speake, that Death his vaine haste may repent.
How fit for us, how even and how sweet,
  How good in all her titles, and how meet,
To have reform'd this forward heresie,
  That women can no parts of friendship bee;
How Morall, how Divine shall not be told,
  Lest they that heare her vertues, thinke her old: 60
And lest we take Deaths part, and make him glad
  Of such a prey, and to his tryumph adde.

ELEGIE ON MISTRIS
BOULSTRED [d. 1609]

Death I recant, and say, unsaid by mee
  What ere hath slip'd, that might diminish thee.
Spirituall treason, atheisme 'tis, to say,
  That any can thy Summons disobey.
Th'earths face is but thy Table; there are set
  Plants, cattell, men, dishes for Death to eate.

l.35 unobnoxious: unexposed.
l.58 That . . . bee: a commonplace thought in Renaissance writing.

In a rude hunger now hee millions drawes
  Into his bloody, or plaguy, or sterv'd jawes.
Now hee will seeme to spare, and doth more wast,
  Eating the best first, well preserv'd to last.   10
Now wantonly he spoiles, and eates us not,
  But breakes off friends, and lets us peecemeale rot.
Nor will this earth serve him; he sinkes the deepe
  Where harmlesse fish monastique silence keepe,
Who (were Death dead) by Roes of living sand,
  Might spunge that element, and make it land.
He rounds the aire, and breakes the hymnique notes
  In birds (Heavens choristers,) organique throats,
Which (if they did not dye) might seeme to bee
  A tenth ranke in the heavenly hierarchie.   20
O strong and long-liv'd death, how cam'st thou in?
  And how without Creation didst begin?
Thou hast, and shalt see dead, before thou dyest,
  All the foure Monarchies, and Antichrist.
How could I thinke thee nothing, that see now
  In all this All, nothing else is, but thou.
Our births and lives, vices, and vertues, bee
  Wastfull consumptions, and degrees of thee.
For, wee to live, our bellowes weare, and breath,
  Nor are wee mortall, dying, dead, but death.   30
And though thou beest, O mighty bird of prey,
  So much reclaim'd by God, that thou must lay
All that thou kill'st at his feet, yet doth hee
  Reserve but few, and leaves the most to thee.
And of those few, now thou hast overthrowne
  One whom thy blow makes, not ours, nor thine own.
She was more stories high: hopelesse to come
  To her Soule, thou'hast offer'd at her lower roome.
Her Soule and body was a King and Court:
  But thou hast both of Captaine mist and fort.   40
As houses fall not, though the King remove,
  Bodies of Saints rest for their soules above.
Death gets 'twixt soules and bodies such a place
  As sinne insinuates 'twixt just men and grace,

l.20 tenth . . . hierarchie: The reference is to the traditional nine ranks
of angels in the heavenly hierarchy.
l.24 foure Monarchies: traditionally, Babylon, Persia, Greece, and Rome.

Both worke a separation, no divorce.
    Her Soule is gone to usher up her corse,
Which shall be'almost another soule, for there
    Bodies are purer, than best Soules are here.
Because in her, her virtues did outgoe
    Her yeares, would'st thou, O emulous death, do so?   50
And kill her young to thy losse? must the cost
    Of beauty,'and wit, apt to doe harme, be lost?
What though thou found'st her proofe 'gainst sins of
    youth?
    Oh, every age a diverse sinne pursueth.
Thou should'st have stay'd, and taken better hold,
    Shortly, ambitious; covetous, when old,
She might have prov'd: and such devotion
    Might once have stray'd to superstition.
If all her vertues must have growne, yet might
    Abundant virtue'have bred a proud delight.   60
Had she persever'd just, there would have bin
    Some that would sinne, mis-thinking she did sinne.
Such as would call her friendship, love, and faine
    To sociablenesse, a name profane;
Or sinne, by tempting, or, not daring that,
    By wishing, though they never told her what.
Thus might'st thou'have slain more soules, had'st thou
    not crost
    Thy selfe, and to triumph, thine army lost.
Yet though these wayes be lost, thou hast left one,
    Which is, immoderate griefe that she is gone.   70
But we may scape that sinne, yet weepe as much,
    Our teares are due, because we are not such.
Some teares, that knot of friends, her death must cost,
    Because the chaine is broke, though no linke lost.

ELEGIE

DEATH

Language thou art too narrow, and too weake
    To ease us now; great sorrow cannot speake;
If we could sigh out accents, and weepe words,

Elegie: Grierson suggests that Lady Marckham is the subject of this poem,
    but it may possibly have reference to Mistress Boulstred.

Griefe weares, and lessens, that tears breath affords.
Sad hearts, the lesse they seeme the more they are,
  (So guiltiest men stand mutest at the barre)
Not that they know not, feele not their estate,
  But extreme sense hath made them desperate.
Sorrow, to whom we owe all that we bee;
  Tyrant, in the fift and greatest Monarchy,   10
Was't, that she did possesse all hearts before,
  Thou hast kil'd her, to make thy Empire more?
Knew'st thou some would, that knew her not, lament,
  As in a deluge perish th'innocent?
Was't not enough to have that palace wonne,
  But thou must raze it too, that was undone?
Had'st thou staid there, and look'd out at her eyes,
  All had ador'd thee that now from thee flies,
For they let out more light, than they tooke in,
  They told not when, but did the day beginne.   20
She was too Saphirine, and cleare for thee;
  Clay, flint, and jeat now thy fit dwellings be;
Alas, shee was too pure, but not too weake;
  Who e'r saw Christall Ordinance but would break?
And if wee be thy conquest, by her fall
  Th'hast lost thy end, for in her perish all;
Or if we live, we live but to rebell,
  They know her better now, that knew her well.
If we should vapour out, and pine, and die;
  Since, shee first went, that were not miserie.   30
Shee chang'd our world with hers; now she is gone,
  Mirth and prosperity is oppression;
For of all morall vertues she was all,
  The Ethicks speake of vertues Cardinall.
Her soule was Paradise; the Cherubin
  Set to keepe it was grace, that kept out sinne.
Shee had no more than let in death, for wee
  All reape consumption from one fruitfull tree.
God tooke her hence, lest some of us should love
  Her, like that plant, him and his lawes above,   40
And when wee teares, hee mercy shed in this,

---

l.10 Tyrant . . . Monarchy: see "Elegie on Mistris Boulstred," note
to line 24.
l.38 fruitfull tree: the tree of the knowledge of good and evil, in
Genesis.

To raise our mindes to heaven where now she is;
Who if her vertues would have let her stay
  Wee'had had a Saint, have now a holiday.
Her heart was that strange bush, where, sacred fire,
  Religion, did not consume, but'inspire
Such piety, so chast use of Gods day,
  That what we turne to *feast*, she turn'd to *pray*,
And did prefigure here, in devout tast,
  The rest of her high Sabaoth, which shall last.   50
Angels did hand her up, who next God dwell,
  (For she was of that order whence most fell)
Her body left with us, lest some had said,
  Shee could not die, except they saw her dead;
For from lesse vertue, and lesse beautiousnesse,
  The Gentiles fram'd them Gods and Goddesses.
The ravenous earth that now wooes her to be
  Earth too, will be a *Lemnia;* and the tree
That wraps that christall in a wooden Tombe,
  Shall be tooke up spruce, fill'd with diamond;   60
And we her sad glad friends all beare a part
  Of griefe, for all would waste a Stoicks heart.

ELEGIE ON THE UNTIMELY DEATH OF THE INCOMPARABLE PRINCE HENRY [d. 1612]

Look to me, *Faith;* and look to my *Faith,* God:
For, both my *Centres* feel This *Period.*
Of *Waight,* one *Centre;* one of *Greatness* is:
And Reason is That *Centre;* Faith is This.
For into our *Reason* flowe, and there doe end,
All that this naturall World doth comprehend;
Quotidian things, and Equi-distant hence,

l.58 Lemnia: apparently a reference to Lemnian earth, a red clay supposed to be an antidote and preservative.

Elegie on the Untimely Death of the Incomparable Prince Henry: Prince Henry was the eldest son of James I. His death evoked an extraordinary spate of elegiac verse, including an elaborate tribute from Sir Edward Herbert. According to Jonson, Donne wrote this elegy "to match Sir Ed. Herbert in obscurenesse."

Shut-in for Men in one *Circumference:*
But, for th'enormous *Greatnesses,* which are
So disproportion'd and so angulare, 10
As is God's *Essence, Place,* and *Providence,*
Where, How, When, What, Soules do, departed
  hence:
These *Things* (*Eccentrique* else) on Faith do strike;
Yet neither All, nor upon all alike:
For, *Reason,* put t'her best *Extension,*
Almost meetes *Faith,* and makes both *Centres* one:
And nothing ever came so neer to This,
As *Contemplation* of the Prince wee misse.
For, All that *Faith* could credit Mankinde *could,*
Reason still seconded that This Prince *would.* 20
If then, least Movings of the *Centre* make
(More than if whole Hell belcht) the World to shake,
What must This doo, *Centres* distracted so,
That Wee see not what to beleeve or knowe?
Was it not well believ'd, till now, that *Hee,*
Whose *Reputation* was an *Extasie*
On neighbour States; which knew not Why to wake
Till *Hee* discoverd what wayes *Hee* would take:
For *Whom* what *Princes* angled (when they tryed)
Mett a *Torpedo,* and were stupefied: 30
And Others studies, how *Hee* would be bent;
Was His great *Father's* greatest Instrument,
And activ'st spirit to convey and tye
This soule of *Peace* through Christianitie?
Was it not well believ'd, that *Hee* would make
This *general Peace* th'eternall overtake?
And that *His* Times might have stretcht out so far
As to touch Those of which they *Emblems* are?
For, to confirm this just Belief, that Now
The *last Dayes* came, wee saw Heaven did allow 40
That but from *His* aspect and Exercise,
In *Peace*-full times, Rumors of *Warrs* should rise.
But *now* This *Faith* is *Heresie:* wee must
Still stay, and vexe our *Great-Grand-Mother,* Dust.
Oh! Is God prodigall? Hath he spent his store

l.30 Torpedo: the electric ray, known also as *crampfish* or *numbfish.*
l.34 This . . . Christianitie: James I was often praised as a peacemaker.

Of Plagues on us? and only now, when more
Would ease us much, doth he grudge Miserie,
And will not lett's enjoy our *Curse*, to *Dye?*
As, for the Earth throw'n lowest downe of all,
'Twere an *Ambition* to desire to fall: 50
So God, in our *desire* to *dye*, dooth know
Our Plot for *Ease*, in beeing *Wretched* so.
Therefore *Wee live:* though such a Life we have
As but so manie *Mandrakes* on his Grave.

What had *His growth* and *generation* donne?
When what wee are, his *putrefaction*
Sustains in us, Earth, which *Griefs* animate?
Nor hath our World now other *soule* than That.
And could *Grief* gett so high as Heav'n, that *Quire*
Forgetting This, their new Joy, would desire   60
(With grief to see him) *Hee* had staid belowe,
To rectifie Our *Errors* They foreknowe.

Is th'other *Centre*, REASON, faster, then?
Where should wee look for That, now w'are not Men:
For, if our *Reason* be our *Connexion*
Of *Causes*, now to us there can be none.
For, as, if all the *Substances* were spent,
'Twere madnes to enquire of *Accident:*
So is't to looke for *Reason*, HEE being gone,
The only *subject* REASON wrought upon.   70

If *Faith* have such a *chaine*, whose divers Links
Industrious Man discerneth, as he thinks,
When Miracle dooth joine, and so steal-in
A new link Man knowes not where to begin:
At a much deader Fault must *Reason* bee,
Death having broke-off such a Link as *Hee*.
But, now, for us with busie *Proofs* to come
That w'have no *Reason*, would prove we had some:
So would just *Lamentations*. Therefore Wee
May safelier say, that Wee are dead, than *Hee*.   80
So, if our *Griefs* wee doo not well declare,
W'have double Excuse; *Hee* is not *dead*, We are.
Yet would not I dye yet; for though I bee

---

l.54 Mandrakes: Many superstitions are associated with the mandrake
    because of that root's supposed resemblance to the human body.
l.68 Accident: non-essential quality (a scholastic term).

Too narrow, to think HIM, as *Hee* is HEE
(Our *Soule's* best Bayting and Mid-*period*
In her long *journey* of *Considering* GOD)
Yet (no Dishonor) I can reach Him *thus*;
As *Hee* embrac't the *Fires* of *Love* with us.
Oh! May I (*since* I live) but see or hear
That *Shee-Intelligence* which mov'd This *Sphear*,   90
I pardon Fate my Life. Who-e'r thou bee
Which hast the noble *Conscience*, Thou art *Shee*.
I conjure Thee by all the *Charmes Hee* spoke,
By th'Oathes which only you *Two* never broke,
By all the *Soules* you sigh'd; that if you see
These Lines, you wish I knew *Your Historie*:
So, much as *You Two mutual Heavens* were *here*,
I were an *Angel singing* what *You* were.

AN HYMNE TO THE SAINTS, AND
TO MARQUESSE HAMYLTON

TO SIR ROBERT CARR [MARCH 22, 1625]

Sir,

I presume *you rather try what you can doe in me, than
what I can doe in verse; you know my uttermost when it
was best, and even then I did best when I had least truth
for my subjects. In this present case there is so much truth
as it defeats all Poetry. Call therefore this paper by what
name you will, and, if it bee not worthy of him, nor of
you, nor of mee, smother it, and bee that the sacrifice. If
you had commanded mee to have waited on his body to
Scotland and preached there, I would have embraced the
obligation with more alacrity; But, I thanke you that you
would command me that which I was loath to doe, for,
even that hath given a tincture of merit to the obedience of*
Your poore friend and servant in Christ Jesus

J. D.

l.85 Bayting: delay.
l.90 Shee-Intelligence . . . Sphear: The intelligences were the angels
who moved the spheres in which the planets and stars were believed
to be embedded.

Whether that soule which now comes up to you
Fill any former ranke or make a new,
Whether it take a name nam'd there before,
Or be a name it selfe, and *order* more
Than was in heaven till now; (for may not hee
Bee so, if every severall Angell bee
A *kind* alone?) What ever order grow
Greater by him in heaven, wee doe not so.
One of your orders growes by his accesse;
But, by his losse grow all our *orders* lesse;   10
The name of *Father, Master, Friend,* the name
Of *Subject* and of *Prince,* in one are lame;
Faire mirth is dampt, and conversation black,
The *household* widow'd, and the *garter* slack;
The *Chappell* wants an eare, *Councell* a tongue;
Story, a theame; and *Musicke* lacks a song;
Blest *order* that hath him! the losse of him
Gangred all *Orders* here; all lost a limbe.
Never made body such haste to confesse
What a soule was; All former comelinesse   20
Fled, in a minute, when the soule was gone,
And, having lost that beauty, would have none;
So fell our *Monasteries,* in one instant growne
Not to lesse houses, but, to heapes of stone;
So sent this body that faire forme it wore,
Unto the spheare of formes, and doth (before
His soule shall fill up his sepulchrall stone,)
Anticipate a Resurrection;
For, as in his fame, now, his soule is here,
So, in the forme thereof his bodie's there;   30
And if, faire soule, not with first *Innocents*
Thy station be, but with the *Pœnitents,*
(And, who shall dare to aske then when I am
Dy'd scarlet in the blood of that pure Lambe,
Whether that colour, which is scarlet then,
Were black or white before in eyes of men?)
When thou rememb'rest what sins thou didst finde
Amongst those many friends now left behinde,

ll.5–7 Than . . . alone: The idea is derived from Aquinas.
l.18 Gangred: gangrened.
ll.23–24 fell . . . stone: The reference is to the destruction of the English monasteries under Henry VIII.

And seest such sinners as they are, with thee
Got thither by repentance, Let it bee   40
Thy wish to wish all there, to wish them cleane;
Wish *him* a *David*, her a *Magdalen*.

EPITAPH ON HIMSELFE

TO THE COUNTESSE OF BEDFORD

Madame,
  That I might make your Cabinet my tombe,
    And for my fame which I love next my soule,
Next to my soule provide the happiest roome,
    Admit to that place this last funerall Scrowle.
      Others by Wills give Legacies, but I
      Dying, of you doe beg a Legacie.

My fortune and my will this custome breake,
When we are senselesse grown to make stones speak,
Though no stone tell thee what I was, yet thou
In my graves inside see what thou art now: 10
Yet th'art not yet so good; till us death lay
To ripe and mellow there, w'are stubborne clay,
Parents make us earth, and soules dignifie
Us to be glasse, here to grow gold we lie;
Whilst in our soules sinne bred and pampered is,
Our soules become worme-eaten Carkasses.

OMNIBUS

My Fortune and my choice this custome break,
When we are speechlesse grown, to make stones speak,
Though no stone tell thee what I was, yet thou
In my graves inside seest what thou art now:
Yet thou'art not yet so good, till death us lay
To ripe and mellow here, we are stubborne Clay.
Parents make us earth, and soules dignifie
Us to be glasse; here to grow gold we lie.
Whilst in our soules sinne bred and pamper'd is,
Our soules become wormeaten carkases;   10

So we our selves miraculously destroy.
Here bodies with lesse miracle enjoy
Such priviledges, enabled here to scale
Heaven, when the Trumpets ayre shall them exhale.
Heare this, and mend thy selfe, and thou mendst me,
By making me, being dead, doe good to thee,
    And thinke me well compos'd, that I could now
    A last-sicke houre to syllables allow.

Divine Poems

DONNE'S RELIGIOUS poetry can be divided into three major categories: occasional poems, holy sonnets, and hymns. ("The Litanie," a long, ambitious, and fairly early work, stands somewhat apart from these categories.) Throughout his life the poet displayed a strongly religious sensibility: Consideration of such an early poem as "Satyre III," as well as of the compulsive strain of theological and mystical imagery in the *Songs and Sonets* and "Elegie XIX," will reveal the inadequacy of a view, going back at least to Izaak Walton, which sees Donne's life and work as neatly divided into profane and saintly halves. The recent research of H. Gardner and L. L. Martz has further corrected the picture by demonstrating just how many of the *Divine Poems* were written before 1611— not only such occasional pieces as "The Crosse" and "Upon the Annuntiation and Passion," but also the vast majority of the holy sonnets.

In the first edition of Donne's poems (1633), two quite different groups of poems bore the title "Holy Sonnets": a sequence of seven linked sonnets further entitled "La Corona," and a group made up of twelve sonnets more intensely personal in tone. The 1635 edition added four sonnets to the latter group, and three more were first printed from manuscript in the nineteenth century. These nineteen sonnets, printed by H. J. C. Grierson as one con-

tinuous sequence, have long been recognized as consti-
tuting, together with the three late hymns, Donne's finest
achievement in religious poetry. Our understanding of
these poems has been greatly enhanced by H. Gardner's
demonstration that they in fact fall into three coherent
groups: (1) a meditative sequence of twelve sonnets (those
of the 1633 edition), composed probably in 1609, the first
six treating the subjects of death and judgment, the last
six that of divine love; (2) a meditative sequence of four
sonnets (those added in the 1635 edition), composed between 1609 and 1611, and penitential in subject; and (3)
the three unrelated sonnets of the Westmoreland manuscript, composed some time after 1617. Since "La Corona"
can with some confidence be ascribed to 1607 and "The
Litanie" to 1608, it is clear that most of Donne's *Divine
Poems* were written well before his ordination in 1615.

The most valuable critical treatments of the *Divine
Poems* are probably those of H. Gardner and L. L. Martz,
but many modern critics—F. Kermode, J. B. Leishman,
and H. C. White, among others—have had helpful things
to say about them. Both C. Hunt and A. Stein have pro-
vocative readings of the "Hymne to God my God, in my
Sicknesse."

TO THE LADY MAGDALEN
HERBERT: OF ST. MARY
MAGDALEN

Her of your name, whose fair inheritance
   Bethina was, and jointure Magdalo:
An active faith so highly did advance,
   That she once knew, more than the Church did know,

l.2 Bethina . . . Magdalo: Medieval legend associates the place-names
Bethany and Magdalo with the Mary Magdalen of Scripture. As
Gardner points out, the title "Lady Magdalen Herbert" is inaccurate,
Mrs. Herbert never having borne that title. Both Grierson and Gard-
ner think it probable that this poem was sent to Mrs. Herbert with
the seven sonnets which make up "La Corona."

The Resurrection; so much good there is
   Deliver'd of her, that some Fathers be
Loth to believe one Woman could do this;
   But, think these Magdalens were two or three.
Increase their number, Lady, and their fame:
   To their Devotion, add your Innocence;   10
Take so much of th'example, as of the name;
   The latter half; and in some recompence
That they did harbour Christ himself, a Guest,
   Harbour these Hymns, to his dear name addrest.

HOLY SONNETS

LA CORONA

1

Deigne at my hands this crown of prayer and praise,
Weav'd in my low devout melancholie,
Thou which of good, hast, yea art treasury,
All changing unchang'd Antient of dayes;
But doe not, with a vile crowne of fraile bayes,
Reward my muses white sincerity,
But what thy thorny crowne gain'd, that give mee,
A crowne of Glory, which doth flower alwayes;
The ends crowne our workes, but thou crown'st our
  ends,
For, at our end begins our endlesse rest;   10
The first last end, now zealously possest,
With a strong sober thirst, my soule attends.
'Tis time that heart and voice be lifted high,
Salvation to all that will is nigh.

2

ANNUNCIATION

Salvation to all that will is nigh;
That All, which alwayes is All every where,
Which cannot sinne, and yet all sinnes must beare,

La Corona: The "crown of sonnets," made up of seven sonnets linked
  together by line-repetition, was a popular Italian form of the Renaissance.

Which cannot die, yet cannot chuse but die,
Loe, faithfull Virgin, yeelds himselfe to lye
In prison, in thy wombe; and though he there
Can take no sinne, nor thou give, yet he'will weare
Taken from thence, flesh, which deaths force may trie.
Ere by the spheares time was created, thou
Wast in his minde, who is thy Sonne, and Brother;   10
Whom thou conceiv'st, conceiv'd; yea thou art now
Thy Makers maker, and thy Fathers mother;
Thou'hast light in darke; and shutst in little roome,
Immensity cloystered in thy deare wombe.

3
NATIVITIE

Immensity cloystered in thy deare wombe,
Now leaves his welbelov'd imprisonment,
There he hath made himselfe to his intent
Weake enough, now into our world to come;
But Oh, for thee, for him, hath th' Inne no roome?
Yet lay him in this stall, and from the Orient,
Starres, and wisemen will travell to prevent
Th'effect of *Herods* jealous generall doome.
Seest thou, my Soule, with thy faiths eyes, how he
Which fils all place, yet none holds him, doth lye?   10
Was not his pity towards thee wondrous high,
That would have need to be pittied by thee?
Kisse him, and with him into Egypt goe,
With his kinde mother, who partakes thy woe.

4
TEMPLE

With his kinde mother who partakes thy woe,
Joseph turne backe; see where your child doth sit,
Blowing, yea blowing out those sparks of wit,
Which himselfe on the Doctors did bestow;
The Word but lately could not speake, and loe
It sodenly speakes wonders, whence comes it,
That all which was, and all which should be writ,
A shallow seeming child, should deeply know?

l.7 prevent: anticipate.

His Godhead was not soule to his manhood,
Nor had time mellowed him to this ripenesse, 10
But as for one which hath a long taske, 'tis good,
With the Sunne to beginne his businesse,
He in his ages morning thus began
By miracles exceeding power of man.

5

CRUCIFYING

By miracles exceeding power of man,
Hee faith in some, envie in some begat,
For, what weake spirits admire, ambitious, hate;
In both affections many to him ran,
But Oh! the worst are most, they will and can,
Alas, and do, unto the immaculate,
Whose creature Fate is, now prescribe a Fate,
Measuring selfe-lifes infinity to'a span,
Nay to an inch. Loe, where condemned hee
Beares his owne crosse, with paine, yet by and by 10
When it beares him, he must beare more and die.
Now thou art lifted up, draw mee to thee,
And at thy death giving such liberall dole,
Moyst, with one drop of thy blood, my dry soule.

6

RESURRECTION

Moyst with one drop of thy blood, my dry soule
Shall (though she now be in extreme degree
Too stony hard, and yet too fleshly,) bee
Freed by that drop, from being starv'd, hard, or foule,
And life, by this death abled, shall controule
Death, whom thy death slue; nor shall to mee
Feare of first or last death, bring miserie,
If in thy little booke my name thou enroule,
Flesh in that long sleep is not putrified,
But made that there, of which, and for which 'twas; 10
Nor can by other meanes be glorified.

l.4 starv'd: withered.
l.5 abled: made able.
l.6 slue: slew.

May then sinnes sleep, and deaths soone from me passe,
That wak't from both, I againe risen may
Salute the last, and everlasting day.

7

ASCENTION

Salute the last, and everlasting day,
Joy at the uprising of this Sunne, and Sonne,
Yee whose just teares, or tribulation
Have purely washt, or burnt your drossie clay;
Behold the Highest, parting hence away,
Lightens the darke clouds, which hee treads upon,
Nor doth hee by ascending, show alone,
But first hee, and hee first enters the way.
O strong Ramme, which hast batter'd heaven for mee,
Mild Lambe, which with thy blood, hast mark'd the
   path;   10
Bright Torch, which shin'st, that I the way may see,
Oh, with thy owne blood quench thy owne just wrath,
And if thy holy Spirit, my Muse did raise,
Deigne at my hands this crown of prayer and praise.

THE CROSSE

Since Christ embrac'd the Crosse it selfe, dare I
His image, th'image of his Crosse deny?
Would I have profit by the sacrifice,
And dare the chosen Altar to despise?
It bore all other sinnes, but is it fit
That it should beare the sinne of scorning it?
Who from the picture would avert his eye,
How would he flye his paines, who there did dye?
From mee, no Pulpit, nor misgrounded law,
Nor scandall taken, shall this Crosse withdraw,   10
It shall not, for it cannot; for, the losse

ll.7–8 Nor . . . way: Christ re-enters Heaven at the head of the host
of the saved.

l.10 this . . . withdraw: These lines refer disapprovingly to the Puritan
opposition to the use of the cross as a devotional adjunct.

Of this Crosse, were to mee another Crosse;
Better were worse, for, no affliction,
No Crosse is so extreme, as to have none.
Who can blot out the Crosse, which th'instrument
Of God, dew'd on mee in the Sacrament?
Who can deny mee power, and liberty
To stretch mine armes, and mine owne Crosse to be?
Swimme, and at every stroake, thou art thy Crosse;
The Mast and yard make one, where seas do tosse;   20
Looke downe, thou spiest out Crosses in small things;
Looke up, thou seest birds rais'd on crossed wings;
All the Globes frame, and spheares, is nothing else
But the Meridians crossing Parallels.
Material Crosses then, good physicke bee,
But yet spirituall have chiefe dignity.
These for extracted chimique medicine serve,
And cure much better, and as well preserve;
Then are you your own physicke, or need none,
When Still'd, or purg'd by tribulation.   30
For when that Crosse ungrudg'd, unto you stickes,
Then are you to your selfe, a Crucifixe.
As perchance, Carvers do not faces make,
But that away, which hid them there, do take.
Let Crosses, soe, take what hid Christ in thee,
And be his image, or not his, but hee.
But, as oft Alchimists doe coyners prove,
So may a selfe-dispising, get selfe-love;
And then as worst surfets, or best meates bee,
Soe is pride, issued from humility,   40
For, 'tis no child, but monster; therefore Crosse
Your joy in crosses, else, 'tis double losse,
And crosse thy senses, else, both they, and thou
Must perish soone, and to destruction bowe.
For if the'eye seeke good objects, and will take
No crosse from bad, wee cannot scape a snake.
So with harsh, hard, sowre, stinking, crosse the rest,
Make them indifferent all; call nothing best.

l.25 physicke: medicine.
l.27 extracted . . . medicine: The reference is to Paracelsian medicine,
  which, in contrast to traditional Galenic medicine, was based on the
  concept of purging disease through antagonistic remedies.

But most the eye needs crossing, that can rome,
And move; To th'other th'objects must come home.   50
And crosse thy heart: for that in man alone
Points downewards, and hath palpitation.
Crosse those dejections, when it downeward tends,
And when it to forbidden heights pretends.
And as the braine through bony walls doth vent
By sutures, which a Crosses forme present,
So when thy braine workes, ere thou utter it,
Crosse and correct concupiscence of witt.
Be covetous of Crosses, let none fall.
Crosse no man else, but crosse thy selfe in all.   60
Then doth the Crosse of Christ worke fruitfully
Within our hearts, when wee love harmlessly
That Crosses pictures much, and with more care
That Crosses children, which our Crosses are.

RESURRECTION, IMPERFECT

Sleep sleep old Sun, thou canst not have repast
As yet, the wound thou took'st on friday last;
Sleepe then, and rest; The world may beare thy stay,
A better Sun rose before thee to day,
Who, not content to'enlighten all that dwell
On the earths face, as thou, enlightned hell,
And made the darke fires languish in that vale,
As, at thy presence here, our fires grow pale.
Whose body having walk'd on earth, and now
Hasting to Heaven, would, that he might allow   10
Himselfe unto all stations, and fill all,
For these three daies become a minerall;
Hee was all gold when he lay downe, but rose
All tincture, and doth not alone dispose
Leaden and iron wills to good, but is
Of power to make even sinfull flesh like his.

Resurrection, Imperfect: unfinished.
l.1 repast: recovered from.
ll.12–14 For . . . tincture: The conception on which this passage is
    based is alchemical: buried substances become minerals, buried gold
    becomes the tincture, or essential gold capable of working transforma-
    tions.

Had one of those, whose credulous pietie
Thought, that a Soule one might discerne and see
Goe from a body,'at this sepulcher been,
And, issuing from the sheet, this body seen, 20
He would have justly thought this body a soule,
If not of any man, yet of the whole.

Desunt cætera

UPON THE ANNUNTIATION
AND PASSION

FALLING UPON ONE DAY.
1608 [MARCH 25, 1608/9]

Tamely, fraile body,'abstaine to day; to day
My soule eates twice, Christ hither and away.
She sees him man, so like God made in this,
That of them both a circle embleme is,
Whose first and last concurre; this doubtfull day
Of feast or fast, Christ came, and went away.
Shee sees him nothing twice at once, who'is all;
Shee sees a Cedar plant it selfe, and fall,
Her Maker put to making, and the head
Of life, at once, not yet alive, yet dead. 10
She sees at once the virgin mother stay
Reclus'd at home, Publique at Golgotha;
Sad and rejoyc'd shee's seen at once, and seen
At almost fiftie, and at scarce fifteene.
At once a Sonne is promis'd her, and gone,
Gabriell gives Christ to her, He her to John;
Not fully a mother, Shee's in Orbitie,
At once receiver and the legacie.
All this, and all betweene, this day hath showne,
Th'Abridgement of Christs story, which makes one 20
(As in plaine Maps, the furthest West is East)
Of the'Angels *Ave*,'and *Consummatum est*.
How well the Church, Gods Court of faculties
Deales, in some times, and seldome joyning these!

Desunt cætera: The rest is missing.

l.17 Orbitie: bereavement
l.21 plaine: flat.

As by the selfe-fix'd Pole wee never doe
Direct our course, but the next starre thereto,
Which showes where the'other is, and which we say
(Because it strayes not farre) doth never stray;
So God by his Church, neerest to him, wee know
And stand firme, if wee by her motion goe;   30
His Spirit, as his fiery Pillar doth
Leade, and his Church, as cloud; to one end both.
This Church, by letting these daies joyne, hath shown
Death and conception in mankinde is one;
Or'twas in him the same humility,
That he would be a man, and leave to be:
Or as creation he hath made, as God,
With the last judgement, but one period,
His imitating Spouse would joyne in one
Manhoods extremes: He shall come, he is gone: 40
Or as though one blood drop, which thence did fall,
Accepted, would have serv'd, he yet shed all;
So though the least of his paines, deeds, or words,
Would busie a life, she all this day affords;
This treasure then, in grosse, my Soule uplay,
And in my life retaile it every day.

THE LITANIE

I

THE FATHER

Father of Heaven, and him, by whom
It, and us for it, and all else, for us
    Thou madest, and govern'st ever, come
And re-create mee, now growne ruinous:
        My heart is by dejection, clay,
        And by selfe-murder, red.
From this red earth, O Father, purge away
All vicious tinctures, that new fashioned
I may rise up from death, before I'm dead.

l.38 one period: period of time.

ll.5–7 My . . . earth: Donne is playing with ideas from Renaissance
  physiology: the four bodily humours correspond to the four elements,
  the melancholy humour corresponding to earth.
l.8 tinctures: impurities.

II
THE SONNE

O Sonne of God, who seeing two things,   10
Sinne, and death crept in, which were never made,
  By bearing one, tryed'st with what stings
The other could thine heritage invade;
     O be thou nail'd unto my heart,
     And crucified againe,
Part not from it, though it from thee would part,
But let it be, by applying so thy paine,
Drown'd in thy blood, and in thy passion slaine.

III
THE HOLY GHOST

O Holy Ghost, whose temple I
Am, but of mudde walls, and condensed dust,   20
  And being sacrilegiously
Halfe wasted with youths fires, of pride and lust,
     Must with new stormes be weatherbeat;
     Double in my heart thy flame,
Which let devout sad teares intend; and let
(Though this glasse lanthorne, flesh, do suffer maime)
Fire, Sacrifice, Priest, Altar be the same.

IV
THE TRINITY

O Blessed glorious Trinity,
Bones to Philosophy, but milke to faith,
  Which, as wise serpents, diversly   30
Most slipperinesse, yet most entanglings hath,
     As you distinguish'd undistinct
     By power, love, knowledge bee,
Give mee a such selfe different instinct
Of these; let all mee elemented bee,
Of power, to love, to know, you unnumbred three.

l.25 intend: intensify.
l.29 Bones . . . Philosophy: incomprehensible to reason.
l.35 elemented: composed.

V

THE VIRGIN MARY

For that faire blessed Mother-maid,
Whose flesh redeem'd us; That she-Cherubin,
  Which unlock'd Paradise, and made
One claime for innocence, and disseiz'd sinne,   40
     Whose wombe was a strange heav'n for there
     God cloath'd himselfe, and grew,
Our zealous thankes wee poure. As her deeds were
Our helpes, so are her prayers; nor can she sue
In vaine, who hath such titles unto you.

VI

THE ANGELS

And since this life our nonage is,
And wee in Wardship to thine Angels be,
  Native in heavens faire Palaces,
Where we shall be but denizen'd by thee,
     As th'earth conceiving by the Sunne,   50
     Yeelds faire diversitie,
Yet never knowes which course that light doth run,
So let mee study, that mine actions bee
Worthy their sight, though blinde in how they see.

VII

THE PATRIARCHES

And let thy Patriarches Desire
(Those great Grandfathers of thy Church, which saw
  More in the cloud, than wee in fire,
Whom Nature clear'd more, than us Grace and Law,
     And now in Heaven still pray, that wee
     May use our new helpes right,)   60
Be satisfy'd, and fructifie in mee;
Let not my minde be blinder by more light
Nor Faith, by Reason added, lose her sight.

l.49 denizen'd: admitted to residence.

VIII

THE PROPHETS

Thy Eagle-sighted Prophets too,
Which were thy Churches Organs, and did sound
   That harmony, which made of two
One law, and did unite, but not confound;
      Those heavenly Poëts which did see
      Thy will, and it expresse
In rythmique feet, in common pray for mee,   70
That I by them excuse not my excesse
In seeking secrets, or Poëtiquenesse.

IX

THE APOSTLES

And thy illustrious Zodiacke
Of twelve Apostles, which ingirt this All,
   (From whom whosoever do not take
Their light, to darke pits, throw downe, and fall,)
      As through their prayers, thou'hast let mee know
      That their bookes are divine;
May they pray still, and be heard, that I goe
Th'old broad way in applying; O decline   80
Mee, when my comment would make thy word mine.

X

THE MARTYRS

And since thou so desirously
Did'st long to die, that long before thou could'st,
   And long since thou no more couldst dye,
Thou in thy scatter'd mystique body wouldst
      In Abel dye, and ever since
      In thine; let their blood come
To begge for us, a discreet patience
Of death, or of worse life: for Oh, to some
Not to be Martyrs, is a martyrdome.   90

l.66 harmony: The reference is to the harmony of the Old and New
   Testaments.
l.80 decline: cast down.

XI

THE CONFESSORS

Therefore with thee triumpheth there
A Virgin Squadron of white Confessors,
   Whose bloods betroth'd, not marryed were,
Tender'd, not taken by those Ravishers:
      They know, and pray, that wee may know,
      In every Christian
Hourly tempestuous persecutions grow;
Tentations martyr us alive; A man
Is to himselfe a Dioclesian.

XII

THE VIRGINS

The cold white snowie Nunnery,   100
Which, as thy mother, their high Abbesse, sent
   Their bodies backe againe to thee,
As thou hadst lent them, cleane and innocent,
      Though they have not obtain'd of thee,
      That or thy Church, or I,
Should keep, as they, our first integrity;
Divorce thou sinne in us, or bid it die,
And call chast widowhead Virginitie.

XIII

THE DOCTORS

Thy sacred Academie above
Of Doctors, whose paines have unclasp'd, and taught   110
   Both bookes of life to us (for love
To know thy Scriptures tells us, we are wrote
      In thy other booke) pray for us there
      That what they have misdone
Or mis-said, wee to that may not adhere;
Their zeale may be our sinne. Lord let us runne
Meane waies, and call them stars, but not the Sunne.

l.109 Academie: accented on the third syllable.
l.111 Both . . . us: God's two books are the Bible and the list of the
   elect.

XIV

And whil'st this universall Quire,
That Church in triumph, this in warfare here,
   Warm'd with one all-partaking fire   120
Of love, that none be lost, which cost thee deare,
     Prayes ceaslesly,'and thou hearken too,
     (Since to be gratious
Our taske is treble, to pray, beare, and doe)
Heare this prayer Lord: O Lord deliver us
From trusting in those prayers, though powr'd out thus.

XV

From being anxious, or secure,
Dead clods of sadnesse, or light squibs of mirth,
   From thinking, that great courts immure
All, or no happinesse, or that this earth   130
     Is only for our prison fram'd,
     Or that thou art covetous
To them thou lovest, or that they are maim'd
From reaching this worlds sweet, who seek thee thus,
With all their might, Good Lord deliver us.

XVI

From needing danger, to bee good,
From owing thee yesterdaies teares to day,
   From trusting so much to thy blood,
That in that hope, wee wound our soule away,
     From bribing thee with Almes, to excuse   140
     Some sinne more burdenous,
From light affecting, in religion, newes,
From thinking us all soule, neglecting thus
Our mutuall duties, Lord deliver us.

XVII

From tempting Satan to tempt us,
By our connivence, or slack companie,
   From measuring ill by vitious,

l.126 powr'd: poured.
l.127 secure: overconfident.
l.128 squibs: firecrackers.
l.142 newes: innovations.

Neglecting to choake sins spawne, Vanitie,
    From indiscreet humilitie,
      Which might be scandalous,   150
And cast reproach on Christianitie,
From being spies, or to spies pervious,
From thirst, or scorne of fame, deliver us.

XVIII

    Deliver us for thy descent
Into the Virgin, whose wombe was a place
    Of middle kind; and thou being sent
To'ungratious us, staid'st at her full of grace;
      And through thy poore birth, where first thou
        Glorifiedst Povertie,
And yet soone after riches didst allow,   160
By accepting Kings gifts in the Epiphanie,
Deliver, and make us, to both waies free.

XIX

    And through that bitter agonie,
Which is still the agonie of pious wits,
    Disputing what distorted thee,
And interrupted evennesse, with fits;
      And through thy free confession
        Though thereby they were then
Made blind, so that thou might'st from them have gone,
Good Lord deliver us, and teach us when   170
Wee may not, and we may blinde unjust men.

XX

    Through thy submitting all, to blowes
Thy face, thy clothes to spoile; thy fame to scorne,
    All waies, which rage, or Justice knowes,
And by which thou could'st shew, that thou wast born
      And through thy gallant humblenesse
        Which thou in death did'st shew,

l.152 pervious: accessible.
l.164 pious wits: intellects, i.e., theologians.
l.167 free confession: Christ's admission of his identity when accosted
   by his persecutors. See John 18: 4–6.

Dying before thy soule they could expresse,
Deliver us from death, by dying so,
To this world, ere this world doe bid us goe.   180

XXI

When senses, which thy souldiers are,
Wee arme against thee, and they fight for sinne,
   When want, sent but to tame, doth warre
And worke despaire a breach to enter in,
      When plenty, Gods image, and seale
      Makes us Idolatrous,
And love it, not him, whom it should reveale,
When wee are mov'd to seeme religious
Only to vent wit, Lord deliver us.

XXII

In Churches, when the'infirmitie   190
Of him which speakes, diminishes the Word,
   When Magistrates doe mis-apply
To us, as we judge, lay or ghostly sword,
      When plague, which is thine Angell, raignes,
      Or wars, thy Champions, swaie,
When Heresie, thy second deluge, gaines;
In th'houre of death, the'Eve of last judgement day,
Deliver us from the sinister way.

XXIII

Heare us, O heare us Lord; to thee
A sinner is more musique, when he prayes,   200
   Than spheares, or Angels praises bee,
In Panegyrique Allelujaes;
      Heare us, for till thou heare us, Lord
      We know not what to say;
Thine eare to'our sighes, teares, thoughts gives voice
   and word.
O Thou who Satan heard'st in Jobs sicke day,
Heare thy selfe now, for thou in us dost pray.

l.178 expresse: press out.
l.184 And . . . in: to make a breach through which despair may enter.
l.193 ghostly: spiritual. The contrast is between secular and ecclesiastical
   power.

XXIV

That wee may change to evennesse
This intermitting aguish Pietie;
  That snatching cramps of wickednesse   210
And Apoplexies of fast sin, may die;
    That musique of thy promises,
    Not threats in Thunder may
Awaken us to our just offices;
What in thy booke, thou dost, or creatures say,
That we may heare, Lord heare us, when wee pray.

XXV

That our eares sicknesse wee may cure,
And rectifie those Labyrinths aright,
  That wee, by harkning, not procure
Our praise, nor others dispraise so invite,   220
    That wee get not a slipperinesse,
    And senslesly decline,
From hearing bold wits jeast at Kings excesse,
To'admit the like of majestie divine,
That we may locke our eares, Lord open thine.

XXVI

That living law, the Magistrate,
Which to give us, and make us physicke, doth
  Our vices often aggravate,
That Preachers taxing sinne, before her growth,
    That Satan, and invenom'd men   230
    Which well, if we starve, dine,
When they doe most accuse us, may see then
Us, to amendment, heare them; thee decline:
That we may open our eares, Lord lock thine.

XXVII

That learning, thine Ambassador,
From thine allegeance wee never tempt,
  That beauty, paradises flower
For physicke made, from poyson be exempt,

l.211 fast: firm.
l.220 Our . . . invite: May we not listen to either flattery of ourselves
or slander of others.

That wit, borne apt high good to doe,
    By dwelling lazily   240
On Natures nothing, be not nothing too,
That our affections kill us not, nor dye,
Heare us, weake ecchoes, O thou eare, and cry.

XXVIII

Sonne of God heare us, and since thou
By taking our blood, owest it us againe,
    Gaine to thy self, or us allow;
And let not both us and thy selfe be slaine;
        O Lambe of God, which took'st our sinne
        Which could not stick to thee,
O let it not returne to us againe,   250
But Patient and Physition being free,
As sinne is nothing, let it no where be.

TO E. OF D. [THE EARL
OF DORSET?] WITH SIX
HOLY SONNETS

See Sir, how as the Suns hot Masculine flame
    Begets strange creatures on Niles durty slime,
    In me, your fatherly yet lusty Ryme
(For, these songs are their fruits) have wrought the
    same;

l.243 Heare . . . cry: cf. stanza XXIII.

l.252 As . . . be: In scholastic philosophy, sin, like evil in general, has
no positive existence. It is to be defined as the absence of a positive
element.

To E. of D. with Six Holy Sonnets: Both Grierson and Gardner identify
"E. of D." as the Earl of Dorset. For some account of Gardner's division of the *Holy Sonnets* and her contentions as to the particular
six poems accompanying this verse letter, see the introduction to this
section.

l.2 Begets . . . slime: It was popularly believed, from ancient times on,
that the reptiles of Egypt were produced by the action of the sun on
the mud of the Nile.

But though the ingendring force from whence they
  came
   Bee strong enough, and nature doe admit
   Seaven to be borne at once, I send as yet
But six; they say, the seaventh hath still some maime.
   I choose your judgement, which the same degree
   Doth with her sister, your invention, hold,   10
As fire these drossie Rymes to purifie,
   Or as Elixar, to change them to gold;
You are that Alchimist which alwaies had
Wit, whose one spark could make good things of bad.

HOLY SONNETS: DIVINE
MEDITATIONS (FIRST SEQUENCE)

I [II]

As due by many titles I resigne
My selfe to thee, O God, first I was made
By thee, and for thee, and when I was decay'd
Thy blood bought that, the which before was thine;
I am thy sonne, made with thy selfe to shine,
Thy servant, whose paines thou hast still repaid,
Thy sheepe, thine Image, and, till I betray'd
My selfe, a temple of thy Spirit divine;
Why doth the devill then usurpe on mee?
Why doth he steale, nay ravish that's thy right?   10
Except thou rise and for thine owne worke fight,
O I shall soone despaire, when I doe see
That thou lov'st mankind well, yet wilt'not chuse me,
And Satan hates mee, yet is loth to lose mee.

Holy Sonnets: Divine Meditations (First Sequence): Donne's nineteen
  Holy Sonnets are presented in the order suggested by Helen Gardner
  in her edition of the *Divine Poems*. Her suggested division of the
  poems into one sequence of twelve related sonnets, one sequence
  of four related sonnets, and three autonomous sonnets is also
  observed. The numbering found in Grierson's edition is, however,
  preserved in brackets, as critical works usually cite the poems under
  those numbers.

II [IV]

Oh my blacke Soule! now thou art summoned
By sicknesse, deaths herald, and champion;
Thou art like a pilgrim, which abroad hath done
Treason, and durst not turne to whence hee is fled,
Or like a thiefe, which till deaths doome be read,
Wisheth himselfe delivered from prison;
But damn'd and hal'd to execution,
Wisheth that still he might be imprisoned.
Yet grace, if thou repent, thou canst not lacke;
But who shall give thee that grace to beginne?   10
Oh make thy selfe with holy mourning blacke,
And red with blushing, as thou art with sinne;
Or wash thee in Christs blood, which hath this might
That being red, it dyes red soules to white.

III [VI]

This is my playes last scene, here heavens appoint
My pilgrimages last mile; and my race
Idly, yet quickly runne, hath this last pace,
My spans last inch, my minutes latest point,
And gluttonous death, will instantly unjoynt
My body, and soule, and I shall sleepe a space,
But my'ever-waking part shall see that face,
Whose feare already shakes my every joynt:
Then, as my soule, to'heaven her first seate, takes flight,
And earth-borne body, in the earth shall dwell,   10
So, fall my sinnes, that all may have their right,
To where they are bred, and would presse me, to hell.
Impute me righteous, thus purg'd of evill,
For thus I leave the world, the flesh, the devill.

IV [VII]

At the round earths imagin'd corners, blow
Your trumpets, Angells, and arise, arise

l.7 damn'd: condemned.

From death, you numberlesse infinities
Of soules, and to your scattred bodies goe,
All whom the flood did, and fire shall o'erthrow,
All whom warre, dearth, age, agues, tyrannies,
Despaire, law, chance, hath slaine, and you whose eyes,
Shall behold God, and never tast deaths woe.
But let them sleepe, Lord, and mee mourne a space,
For, if above all these, my sinnes abound,   10
'Tis late to aske abundance of thy grace,
When wee are there; here on this lowly ground,
Teach mee how to repent; for that's as good
As if thou'hadst seal'd my pardon, with thy blood.

VII [IX]

If poysonous mineralls, and if that tree,
Whose fruit threw death on else immortall us,
If lecherous goats, if serpents envious
Cannot be damn'd; Alas; why should I bee?
Why should intent or reason, borne in mee,
Make sinnes, else equall, in mee more heinous?
And mercy being easie, and glorious
To God; in his sterne wrath, why threatens hee?
But who am I, that dare dispute with thee
O God? Oh! of thine onely worthy blood,   10
And my teares, make a heavenly Lethean flood,
And drowne in it my sinnes blacke memorie;
That thou remember them, some claime as debt,
I thinke it mercy, if thou wilt forget.

VI [X]

Death be not proud, though some have called thee
Mighty and dreadfull, for, thou art not soe,
For, those, whom thou think'st, thou dost overthrow,
Die not, poore death, nor yet canst thou kill mee.
From rest and sleepe, which but thy pictures bee,
Much pleasure, then from thee, much more must flow,
And soonest our best men with thee doe goe,

Rest of their bones, and soules deliverie.
Thou art slave to Fate, Chance, kings, and desperate
 men,
And dost with poyson, warre, and sicknesse dwell,   10
And poppie, or charmes can make us sleepe as well,
And better than thy stroake; why swell'st thou then?
One short sleepe past, wee wake eternally,
And death shall be no more; death, thou shalt die.

VII [XI]

Spit in my face you Jewes, and pierce my side,
Buffet, and scoffe, scourge, and crucifie mee,
For I have sinn'd, and sinn'd, and onely hee,
Who could do no iniquitie, hath dyed:
But by my death can not be satisfied
My sinnes, which passe the Jewes impiety:
They kill'd once an inglorious man, but I
Crucifie him daily, being now glorified.
Oh let mee then, his strange love still admire:
Kings pardon, but he bore our punishment.   10
And *Jacob* came cloth'd in vile harsh attire
But to supplant, and with gainfull intent:
God cloth'd himselfe in vile mans flesh, that so
Hee might be weake enough to suffer woe.

VIII [XII]

Why are wee by all creatures waited on?
Why doe the prodigall elements supply
Life and food to mee, being more pure than I,
Simple, and further from corruption?
Why brook'st thou, ignorant horse, subjection?
Why dost thou bull, and bore so seelily

l.8 deliverie: liberation.

l.5 But . . . satisfied: atoned for.
ll.11–12 And . . . intent: see Genesis 27.

ll.2–4 Why . . . corruption: The elements, unlike man, are not composed of a mixture.
l.6 bore: boar.
l.6 seelily: sillily.

Dissemble weaknesse, and by'one mans stroke die,
Whose whole kinde, you might swallow and feed upon?
Weaker I am, woe is mee, and worse than you,
You have not sinn'd, nor need be timorous.　　　　　10
But wonder at a greater wonder, for to us
Created nature doth these things subdue,
But their Creator, whom sin, nor nature tyed,
For us, his Creatures, and his foes, hath dyed.

IX　[XIII]

What if this present were the worlds last night?
Marke in my heart, O Soule, where thou dost dwell,
The picture of Christ crucified, and tell
Whether that countenance can thee affright,
Teares in his eyes quench the amazing light,
Blood fills his frownes, which from his pierc'd head fell.
And can that tongue adjudge thee unto hell,
Which pray'd forgivenesse for his foes fierce spight?
No, no; but as in my idolatrie
I said to all my profane mistresses,　　　　　10
Beauty, of pitty, foulnesse onely is
A signe of rigour: so I say to thee,
To wicked spirits are horrid shapes assign'd,
This beauteous forme assures a pitious minde.

X　[XIV]

Batter my heart, three person'd God; for, you
As yet but knocke, breathe, shine, and seeke to mend;
That I may rise, and stand, o'erthrow mee,'and bend
Your force, to breake, blowe, burn and make me new.
I, like an usurpt towne, to'another due,
Labour to'admit you, but Oh, to no end,
Reason your viceroy in mee, mee should defend,
But is captiv'd, and proves weake or untrue.
Yet dearely'I love you,'and would be loved faine,

l.5 amazing: terrifying.
l.11 foulnesse: ugliness.

But am betroth'd unto your enemie: 10
Divorce mee,'untie, or breake that knot againe,
Take mee to you, imprison mee, for I
Except you'enthrall mee, never shall be free,
Nor ever chast, except you ravish mee.

XI [XV]

Wilt thou love God, as he thee? then digest,
My Soule, this wholsome meditation,
How God the Spirit, by Angels waited on
In heaven, doth make his Temple in thy brest.
The Father having begot a Sonne most blest,
And still begetting, (for he ne'r begonne)
Hath deign'd to chuse thee by adoption,
Coheire to'his glory,'and Sabbaths endlesse rest;
And as a robb'd man, which by search doth finde
His stolne stuffe sold, must lose or buy'it againe: 10
The Sonne of glory came downe, and was slaine,
Us whom he'had made, and Satan stolne, to unbinde.
'Twas much, that man was made like God before,
But, that God should be made like man, much more.

XII [XVI]

Father, part of his double interest
Unto thy kingdome, thy Sonne gives to mee,
His joynture in the knottie Trinitie
Hee keepes, and gives to me his deaths conquest.
This Lambe, whose death, with life the world hath blest,
Was from the worlds beginning slaine, and he
Hath made two Wills, which with the Legacie
Of his and thy kingdome, doe thy Sonnes invest.

*l.*6 *And . . . begonne:* The begetting of Christ is an eternal process
  since God exists outside time.
*l.*12 *Us . . . stolne:* us whom Satan had stolen.

*l.*1 *double interest:* double claim.
*l.*3 *joynture:* joint possession.
*l.*7 *two Wills:* The reference is to the Old and the New Testaments.
*l.*8 *invest:* give possession of.

Yet such are thy laws, that men argue yet
Whether a man those statutes can fulfill;   10
None doth; but all-healing grace and spirit
Revive againe what law and letter kill.
Thy lawes abridgement, and thy last command
Is all but love; Oh let this last Will stand!

New Testament – let that take precendence

HOLY SONNETS: DIVINE
MEDITATIONS (SECOND SEQUENCE)

1 [I]

Thou hast made me, And shall thy worke decay?
Repaire me now, for now mine end doth haste,
I runne to death, and death meets me as fast,
And all my pleasures are like yesterday;
I dare not move my dimme eyes any way,
Despaire behind, and death before doth cast
Such terrour, and my feeble flesh doth waste
By sinne in it, which it t'wards hell doth weigh;
Onely thou art above, and when towards thee
By thy leave I can looke, I rise againe;   10
But our old subtle foe so tempteth me,
That not one houre my selfe I can sustaine;
Thy Grace may wing me to prevent his art,
And thou like Adamant draw mine iron heart.

II [v]

I am a little world made cunningly
Of Elements, and an Angelike spright,
But black sinne hath betraid to endlesse night

l.14 Is . . . love: is nothing but love.

l.13 prevent: frustrate.
l.14 Adamant: a magnetic stone.

l.2 Elements: the four humours, of which man was believed to be composed.
l.2 spright: spirit.

My worlds both parts, and (oh) both parts must die.
You which beyond that heaven which was most high
Have found new sphears, and of new lands can write,
Powre new seas in mine eyes, that so I might
Drowne my world with my weeping earnestly,
Or wash it if it must be drown'd no more:
But oh it must be burnt! alas the fire   10
Of lust and envie have burnt it heretofore,
And made it fouler; Let their flames retire,
And burne me ô Lord, with a fiery zeale
Of thee and thy house, which doth in eating heale.

III   [III]

O might those sighes and teares returne againe
Into my breast and eyes, which I have spent,
That I might in this holy discontent
Mourne with some fruit, as I have mourn'd in vaine;
In mine Idolatry what showres of raine
Mine eyes did waste? what griefs my heart did rent?
That sufferance was my sinne; now I repent;
'Cause I did suffer I must suffer paine.
Th'hydroptique drunkard, and night-scouting thiefe,
The itchy Lecher, and selfe tickling proud   10
Have the remembrance of past joyes, for reliefe
Of comming ills. To (poore) me is allow'd
No ease; for, long, yet vehement griefe hath beene
Th'effect and cause, the punishment and sinne.

IV   [VIII]

If faithfull soules be alike glorifi'd
As Angels, then my fathers soul doth see,

l.6 found . . . write: a reference to the new astronomers.
l.14 Of . . . heale: see Psalm 69:9.

l.5 Idolatry: of profane love.
l.6 rent: rend.
l.9 hydroptique: dropsical, hence, always thirsty.
l.9 night-scouting: night-prowling.

And adds this even to full felicitie,
That valiantly I hels wide mouth o'rstride:
But if our mindes to these soules be descry'd
By circumstances, and by signes that be
Apparent in us, not immediately,
How shall my mindes white truth by them be try'd?
They see idolatrous lovers weepe and mourne,
And vile blasphemous Conjurers to call   10
On Jesus name, and Pharisaicall
Dissemblers feigne devotion. Then turne
O pensive soule, to God, for he knowes best
Thy true griefe, for he put it in my breast.

ADDITIONAL HOLY SONNETS
(FROM THE WESTMORELAND MS.)

1 [XVII]

Since she whom I lov'd hath payd her last debt
To Nature, and to hers, and my good is dead,
And her Soule early into heaven ravished,
Wholly on heavenly things my mind is sett.
Here the admyring her my mind did whett
To seeke thee God; so streames do shew their head;
But though I have found thee, and thou my thirst hast
     fed,
A holy thirsty dropsy melts mee yett.
But why should I begg more Love, when as thou
Dost wooe my soule for hers; offring all thine: 10
And dost not only feare least I allow
My Love to Saints and Angels things divine,

ll.1–4 If . . . o'rstride: The central question in this poem is whether
   the souls of the blessed have, like angels, intuitive knowledge, or
   whether, like the living, they are obliged to reason from appearances.

1: This poem was written some time after the death of Donne's wife,
   Anne, on August 15, 1617.

l.10 Dost . . . thine: Gardner is almost certainly right in proposing that
   the punctuation of this line be emended, inserting a comma after
   "soule" and removing the semicolon after "hers." The sense of the
   passage is that God offers His love in place of that of the beloved.

Gods (old Testament) — God is petty

But in thy tender jealosy dost doubt
Least the World, Fleshe, yea Devill putt thee out.

these things might become more important
nothing can comfort him

love of God should be enough but its not

II [XVIII]

true Church

Show me deare Christ, thy Spouse, so bright and clear.
What! is it She, which on the other shore
Goes richly painted? or which rob'd and tore
Laments and mournes in Germany and here?
Sleepes she a thousand, then peepes up one yeare?
Is she selfe truth and errs? now new, now outwore?
Doth she, and did she, and shall she evermore
On one, on seaven, or on no hill appeare?
Dwells she with us, or like adventuring knights
First travaile we to seeke and then make Love?   10
Betray kind husband thy spouse to our sights,
And let myne amorous soule court thy mild Dove,   *symbol of Christ?*
Who is most trew, and pleasing to thee, then
When she'is embrac'd and open to most men.

III [XIX]

Oh, to vex me, contraryes meet in one:
Inconstancy unnaturally hath begott
A constant habit; that when I would not
I change in vowes, and in devotione.
As humorous is my contritione
As my prophane Love, and as soone forgott:
As ridlingly distemper'd, cold and hott,
As praying, as mute; as infinite, as none.

l.1 Spouse: The true Church.
ll.2–3 which . . . painted: the Catholic Church.
ll.3–4 which . . . here: the Protestant churches.
l.6 selfe truth: truth itself.
l.8 On . . . appeare: The Temple of Solomon was erected on Mt. Moriah; the Roman Catholic Church is evoked metaphorically by the seven hills of Rome; the Church of Calvinist Geneva is evoked by "no hill."

l.5 humorous: capricious.

I durst not view heaven yesterday; and to day
In prayers, and flattering speaches I court God: 10
To morrow I quake with true feare of his rod.
So my devout fitts come and go away
Like a fantastique Ague: save that here
Those are my best dayes, when I shake with feare.

GOODFRIDAY, *1613*. RIDING
WESTWARD

[handwritten: business trip / riding his horse / going one way physically / another way mentally]

Let mans Soule be a Spheare, and then, in this,
The intelligence that moves, devotion is,
And as the other Spheares, by being growne
Subject to forraigne motions, lose their owne,
And being by others hurried every day,
Scarce in a yeare their naturall forme obey:
Pleasure or businesse, so, our Soules admit
For their first mover, and are whirld by it.
Hence is't, that I am carryed towards the West
This day, when my Soules forme bends towards the
    East.   10
There I should see a Sunne, by rising set,
And by that setting endlesse day beget;
But that Christ on this Crosse, did rise and fall,
Sinne had eternally benighted all.
Yet dare I'almost be glad, I do not see
That spectacle of too much weight for mee.
Who sees Gods face, that is selfe life, must dye;
What a death were it then to see God dye?
It made his owne Lieutenant Nature shrinke,
It made his footstoole crack, and the Sunne winke.   20
Could I behold those hands which span the Poles,
And tune all spheares at once, peirc'd with those holes?
Could I behold that endlesse height which is

ll.1–2 Let . . . is: In Renaissance thought, each of the spheres in which
the various planets are embedded is guided by an angel, called an intelligence. See "The Extasie," lines 51–52 and note.
l.4 forraigne motions: the motions of the other spheres.
l.6 forme: moving principle.
l.20 footstoole: the earth

Zenith to us, and our Antipodes,
Humbled below us? or that blood which is
The seat of all our Soules, if not of his,
Made durt of dust, or that flesh which was worne
By God, for his apparell, rag'd, and torne?
If on these things I durst not looke, durst I
Upon his miserable mother cast mine eye,   30
Who was Gods partner here, and furnish'd thus
Halfe of that Sacrifice, which ransom'd us?
Though these things, as I ride, be from mine eye,
They'are present yet unto my memory,
For that looks towards them; and thou look'st towards
    mee,
O Saviour, as thou hang'st upon the tree;
I turne my backe to thee, but to receive ——— *to be whipped beaten*
Corrections, till thy mercies bid thee leave.
O thinke mee worth thine anger, punish mee,
Burne off my rusts, and my deformity,
Restore thine Image, so much, by thy grace,   40
That thou may'st know mee, and I'll turne my face.

once you have beaten me enough I will feel worthy punishment of catholic martyrs that he wasn't subject to

UPON THE TRANSLATION
OF THE PSALMES

BY SIR PHILIP SYDNEY, AND
THE COUNTESSE OF PEMBROKE
HIS SISTER

Eternall God, (for whom who ever dare
Seeke new expressions, doe the Circle square,
And thrust into strait corners of poore wit
Thee, who art cornerlesse and infinite)
I would but blesse thy Name, not name thee now;
(And thy gifts are as infinite as thou:)
Fixe we our prayses therefore on this one,
That, as thy blessed Spirit fell upon
These Psalmes first Author in a cloven tongue;

ll.25–26 or . . . his: The blood was conceived of by some authorities
as the seat of the soul. The blood of Christ, whether or not it may be
conceived of as the seat of His soul, is the seat of all human souls.
l.38 leave: stop.

(For 'twas a double power by which he sung   10
The highest matter in the noblest forme;)
So thou hast cleft that spirit, to performe
That worke againe, and shed it, here, upon
Two, by their bloods, and by thy Spirit one;
A Brother and a Sister, made by thee
The Organ, where thou art the Harmony.
Two that make one *John Baptists* holy voyce,
And who that Psalme, *Now let the Iles rejoyce*,
Have both translated, and apply'd it too,
But told us what, and taught us how to doe.   20
They shew us Ilanders our joy, our King,
They tell us *why*, and teach us *how* to sing;
Make all this All, three Quires, heaven, earth, and
  sphears;
The first, Heaven, hath a song, but no man heares,
The Spheares have Musick, but they have no tongue,
Their harmony is rather danc'd than sung;
But our third Quire, to which the first gives eare,
(For, Angels learne by what the Church does here)
This Quire hath all. The Organist is hee
Who hath tun'd God and Man, the Organ we: 30
The songs are these, which heavens high holy Muse
Whisper'd to *David, David* to the Jewes:
And *Davids* Successors, in holy zeale,
In formes of joy and art doe re-reveale
To us so sweetly and sincerely too,
That I must not rejoyce as I would doe
When I behold that these Psalmes are become
So well attyr'd abroad, so ill at home,
So well in Chambers, in thy Church so ill,
As I can scarce call that reform'd untill   40
This be reform'd; Would a whole State present
A lesser gift than some one man hath sent?
And shall our Church, unto our Spouse and King
More hoarse, more harsh than any other, sing?
For *that* we pray, we praise thy name for *this*.
Which, by this *Moses* and this *Miriam*, is

*l.*20 *But . . . doe:* see Psalm 97.
*ll.*37–38 *When . . . home:* a reference to the excellence of some Con-
   tinental versions of the Psalms.
*l.*46 *this . . . Miriam:* see Exodus 15:20–21.

Already done; and as those Psalmes we call
(Though some have other Authors) *Davids* all:
So though some have, some may some Psalmes trans-
  late,
We thy Sydnean Psalmes shall celebrate,   50
And, till we come th'Extemporall song to sing,
(Learn'd the first hower, that we see the King,
Who hath translated those translators) may
These their sweet learned labours, all the way
Be as our tuning, that, when hence we part,
We may fall in with them, and sing our part.

TO MR. TILMAN AFTER HE
HAD TAKEN ORDERS

Thou, whose diviner soule hath caus'd thee now
To put thy hand unto the holy Plough,
Making Lay-scornings of the Ministry,
Not an impediment, but victory;
What bringst thou home with thee? how is thy mind
Affected since the vintage? Dost thou finde
New thoughts and stirrings in thee? and as Steele
Toucht with a Loadstone, dost new motions feele?
Or, as a Ship after much paine and care,
For Iron and Cloth brings home rich Indian ware,   10
Hast thou thus traffiqu'd, but with farre more gaine
Of noble goods, and with lesse time and paine?
Thou art the same materials, as before,
Onely the stampe is changed; but no more.
And as new crowned Kings alter the face,
But not the monies substance; so hath grace
Chang'd onely Gods old Image by Creation,
To Christs new stampe, at this thy Coronation;
Or, as we paint Angels with wings, because
They beare Gods message, and proclaime his lawes,   20
Since thou must doe the like, and so must move,

l.52 hower: hour.

ll.1–4 Thou . . . victory: as in lines 25–36 below, Donne refers to the
   contempt in which some members of the gentry held the clerical profession.

Art thou new feather'd with cœlestiall love?
Deare, tell me where thy purchase lies, and shew
What thy advantage is above, below.
But if thy gainings doe surmount expression,
Why doth the foolish world scorne that profession,
Whose joyes passe speech? Why do they think unfit
That Gentry should joyne families with it?
As if their day were onely to be spent
In dressing, Mistressing and complement;   30
Alas poore joyes, but poorer men, whose trust
Seemes richly placed in refined dust;
(For, such are cloathes and beauty, which though gay,
Are, at the best, but of sublimed clay.)
Let then the world thy calling disrespect,
But goe thou on, and pitty their neglect.
What function is so noble, as to bee
Embassadour to God and destinie?
To open life, to give kingdomes to more
Than Kings give dignities; to keepe heavens doore?   40
Maries prerogative was to beare Christ, so
'Tis preachers to convey him, for they doe
As Angels out of clouds, from Pulpits speake;
And blesse the poore beneath, the lame, the weake.
If then th'Astronomers, whereas they spie
A new-found Starre, their Opticks magnifie,
How brave are those, who with their Engine, can
Bring man to heaven, and heaven againe to man?
These are thy titles and preheminences,
In whom must meet Gods graces, mens offences,   50
And so the heavens which beget all things here,
And the earth our mother, which these things doth
  beare,
Both these in thee, are in thy Calling knit,
And make thee now a blest Hermaphrodite.

l.46 Opticks: telescopes.
l.47 Engine: instrument.

A HYMNE TO CHRIST,

AT THE AUTHORS LAST GOING
INTO GERMANY

In what torne ship soever I embarke,
That ship shall be my embleme of thy Arke;
What sea soever swallow mee, that flood
Shall be to mee an embleme of thy blood;
Though thou with clouds of anger do disguise
Thy face; yet through that maske I know those eyes,
    Which, though they turne away sometimes,
       They never will despise.

I sacrifice this Iland unto thee,
And all whom I lov'd there, and who lov'd mee;   10
When I have put our seas twixt them and mee,
Put thou thy sea betwixt my sinnes and thee.
As the trees sap doth seeke the root below
In winter, in my winter now I goe,
    Where none but thee, th'Eternall root
       Of true Love I may know.

Nor thou nor thy religion dost controule,
The amorousnesse of an harmonious Soule,
But thou would'st have that love thy selfe: As thou
Art jealous, Lord, so I am jealous now,   20
Thou lov'st not, till from loving more, thou free
My soule: Who ever gives, takes libertie:
    O, if thou car'st not whom I love
       Alas, thou lov'st not mee.

Seale then this bill of my Divorce to All,
On whom those fainter beames of love did fall;
Marry those loves, which in youth scattered bee
On Fame, Wit, Hopes (false mistresses) to thee.
Churches are best for Prayer, that have least light:

A Hymne to Christ, at the Authors Last Going into Germany: In May,
   1619, Donne, as chaplain, accompanied Lord Doncaster on a diplo-
   matic mission to Germany.
l.12 sea: the blood of Christ.

To see God only, I goe out of sight:
   And to scape stormy dayes, I chuse
     An Everlasting night.

A HYMNE TO GOD
THE FATHER

I

Wilt thou forgive that sinne where I begunne,
   Which is my sin, though it were done before?
Wilt thou forgive those sinnes, through which I runne,
   And do run still: though still I do deplore?
     When thou hast done, thou hast not done,
       For, I have more.

II

Wilt thou forgive that sinne by which I'have wonne
   Others to sinne? and, made my sinne their doore?
Wilt thou forgive that sinne which I did shunne
   A yeare, or two: but wallowed in, a score?   10
     When thou hast done, thou hast not done,
       For I have more.

III

I have a sinne of feare, that when I have spunne
   My last thred, I shall perish on the shore;
Sweare by thy selfe, that at my death thy sonne
   Shall shine as he shines now, and heretofore;
     And, having done that, Thou haste done,
       I feare no more.

A Hymne to God the Father: This poem was probably written after
Donne's serious illness of 1623, the same illness which evoked his
prose *Devotions upon Emergent Occasions.*
l.2 Which . . . before: a reference to original sin.
l.5 done: Throughout the poem Donne puns on his name.
ll.7-8 Wilt . . . doore: a reference to the profane poetry of his earlier
years.
l.15 sonne: another occurrence of a pun frequently found in Donne's
work.

HYMNE TO GOD MY GOD, *familiar idea*
IN MY SICKNESSE

Since I am comming to that Holy roome,
  Where, with thy Quire of Saints for evermore,
I shall be made thy Musique; As I come *much more complex than Wotton*
  I tune the Instrument here at the dore,
  And what I must doe then, thinke here before.

Whilst my Physitians by their love are growne
  Cosmographers, and I their Mapp, who lie
Flat on this bed, that by them may be showne
  That this is my South-west discoverie
  Per fretum febris, by these streights to die,   10

I joy, that in these straits, I see my West;
  For, though theire currants yeeld returne to none,
What shall my West hurt me? As West and East
  In all flatt Maps (and I am one) are one,
  So death doth touch the Resurrection.

Is the Pacifique Sea my home? Or are
  The Easterne riches? Is *Jerusalem*?
Anyan, and *Magellan*, and *Gibraltare*,
  All streights, and none but streights, are wayes to
    them,
  Whether where *Japhet* dwelt, or *Cham*, or *Sem*.   20

We thinke that *Paradise* and *Calvarie*,
  Christs Crosse, and *Adams* tree, stood in one place;

Hymne to God my God, in my Sicknesse: According to Walton, Donne
wrote this poem on his deathbed, in 1631. It is, however, possible that,
like the preceding poem, it was written after the illness of 1623.
l.10 Per fretum febris: through the strait of fever. The word *fretum*
means both *strait* and *raging;* there is a further pun on *strait* as meaning *difficulty.*
ll.13–14 As . . . one: the edges of a flat map of the world correspond
with each other.
l.18 Anyan: Bering Strait.
l.20 Japhet . . . Sem: the three sons of Noah, whose offspring were
said to have populated Europe, Africa, and Asia after the Flood.

Looke Lord, and finde both *Adams* met in me;
   As the first *Adams* sweat surrounds my face,
   May the last *Adams* blood my soule embrace.

So, in his purple wrapp'd receive mee Lord,
   By these his thornes give me his other Crowne;
And as to others soules I preach'd thy word,
   Be this my Text, my Sermon to mine owne,
    Therefore that he may raise the Lord throws down.   30

ll.21–25 We . . . embrace: What seems implied in these lines is a belief
   which is not traditionally encountered. Gardner points out that *place*
   in this context may mean simply *region.* But see "Metempsychosis,"
   p. 134.
l.25 Adams: Christ's.

Paradoxes
and Problemes

THE SLIGHT, witty prose exercises which were first
published posthumously under the title *Juvenilia: or Certaine Paradoxes and Problemes* (1633) are the earliest of
Donne's extant prose works, with the exception of some
of his letters. Probably composed between 1598 and 1602,
they were designed for the delectation of Donne's intimate
friends, and as a result have nothing of the somber, public
eloquence which distinguishes his greater and better-
known achievements in prose. Nevertheless, in their un-
flagging wit as in their cultivation of an immediate, in-
formal, and asymmetrical style, they are typical both of
their author and of the age which produced him. Beneath
the high spirits of the *Paradoxes and Problemes* one sometimes detects the note of melancholy so recurrent in
Donne.

In their form — the intellectual, quasi-legal, quasi-phil-
osophical defense of outrageous propositions — as in their
tone — impudence heightened by cynicism — these exercises inevitably remind the reader of such evaporations as
"The Indifferent," "Communitie," and "Confined Love,"
as well as of some of the *Elegies*. Similarly, the *Paradoxes
and Problemes* reflect both Donne's exposure to a legal-
istic and rhetorical Renaissance education and his sensi-
tivity to the currents of fashionable naturalism and skepti-
cism prevalent around 1600.

Relatively little attention has been paid to these essentially trivial pieces. E. M. Simpson gives some account of them.

PARADOXES

I

A DEFENCE OF WOMENS INCONSTANCY

That Women are *Inconstant*, I with any man confess, but that *Inconstancy* is a bad quality, I against any man will maintain: For every thing as it is one better than another, so is it fuller of *change;* The *Heavens* themselves continually turn, the *Stars* move, the *Moon* changeth; *Fire* whirleth, *Aire* flyeth, *Water* ebbs and flowes, the face of the *Earth* altereth her looks, *time* staies not; the Colour that is most light, will take most dyes: so in Men, they that have the most reason are the most alterable in their designes, and the darkest or most ignorant, do seldomest change; therefore Women changing more than Men, have also more *Reason.* They cannot be immutable like stocks, like stones, like the Earths dull Center; Gold that lyeth still, rusteth; Water, corrupteth; Aire that moveth not, poysoneth; then why should that which is the perfection of other things, be imputed to Women as greatest imperfection? Because thereby they deceive Men. Are not your wits pleased with those jests, which cozen[1] your expectation? You can call it pleasure to be beguil'd in troubles, and in the most excellent toy in the world, you call it Treachery: I would you had your *Mistresses* so constant, that they would never change, no not so much as their *smocks*, then should you see what sluttish vertue, *Constancy* were. *Inconstancy* is a most commendable and cleanly quality, and Women in this quality are far more absolute than the Heavens, than the Stars, Moon, or any thing beneath it; for long observation hath pickt certainty

1. *cozen:* cheat.

out of their mutability. The Learned are so well acquainted with the Stars, Signes and Planets, that they make them but Characters, to read the meaning of the Heaven in his own forehead. Every simple fellow can bespeak the change of the *Moon* a great while beforehand: but I would fain have the learnedst man so skilfull, as to tell when the simplest Woman meaneth to vary. Learning affords no rules to know, much less knowledge to rule the minde of a Woman: For as *Philosophy* teacheth us, that *Light things do always tend upwards*, and *heavy things decline downward;* Experience teacheth us otherwise, that the disposition of a *Light* Woman, is to fall down, the nature of women being contrary to all Art and Nature. Women are like *Flies*, which feed among us at our Table, or *Fleas* sucking our very blood, who leave not our most retired places free from their familiarity, yet for all their fellowship will they never be tamed nor commanded by us. Women are like the *Sun*, which is violently carried one way, yet hath a proper course contrary:[2] so though they, by the mastery of some over-ruling churlish husbands, are forced to his Byas, yet have they a motion of their own, which their husbands never know of: It is the nature of nice and fastidious mindes to know things only to be weary of them: Women by their slye *changeableness*, and pleasing doubleness, prevent even the mislike of those, for they can never be so well known, but that there is still more unknown. Every woman is a *Science;* for he that plods upon a woman all his life long, shall at length finde himself short of the knowledge of her: they are born to take down the pride of wit, and ambition of wisdom, making *fools* wise in the adventuring to win them, *wisemen* fools in conceit[3] of losing their labours; *witty* men stark mad, being confounded with their uncertainties. *Philosophers* write against them for spight, not desert, that having attained to some knowledge in all other things, in them only they know nothing, but are meerly ignorant: *Active* and *Experienced* men rail against them, because they love in

2. *Sun . . . contrary:* In traditional astronomy the sphere of the sun, like those of the other planets, is conceived of as pursuing its own proper motion while at the same time being influenced by the contrary motion of other spheres.
3. *conceit:* imagination.

their liveless and decrepit age, when all goodness leaves them. These envious *Libellers* ballad against them, because having nothing in themselves able to deserve their love, they maliciously discommend all they cannot obtain, thinking to make men believe they know much, because they are able to dispraise much, and rage against *Inconstancy*, when they were never admitted into so much favour as to be forsaken. In mine opinion such men are happie that women are *Inconstant*, for so may they chance to be beloved of some excellent woman (when it comes to their turn) out of their *Inconstancy* and mutability, though not out of their own desert. And what reason is there to clog any woman with one man, be he never so singular? Women had rather, and it is far better and more Judicial to enjoy all the vertues in several men, than but some of them in one, for otherwise they lose their taste, like divers sorts of meat minced together in one dish: and to have all excellencies in one man (if it were possible) is *Confusion* and *Diversity*. Now who can deny, but such as are obstinately bent to undervalue their worth, are those that have not soul enough to comprehend their excellency, Women being the most excellent Creatures, in that Man is able to subject all things else, and to grow wise in every thing, but still persists a fool in Woman? The greatest *Scholler*, if he once take a wife, is found so unlearned, that he must begin his *Horn-book*,[4] and all is by *Inconstancy*. To conclude therefore; this name of *Inconstancy*, which hath so much been poysoned with slanders, ought to be changed into *variety*, for the which the world is so delightfull, *and a Woman for that the most delightful thing in this world.*

II

THAT WOMEN OUGHT TO PAINT

Foulness is *Lothsome:* can that be so which helps it? who forbids his beloved to gird in her waste? to mend by shoo-

---

4. *Horn-book:* primer, with a pun on the horns reputed to grow from the head of a cuckold.

ing her uneven lameness? to burnish her teeth? or to perfume her breath? yet that the *Face* be more precisely regarded, it concerns more: For as open confessing sinners
are always punished, but the wary and concealing offend-
ers without witness do it also without punishment; so the
secret parts needs the less respect; but of the *Face*, discovered to all Examinations and surveys, there is not too
nice a Jealousie. Nor doth it only draw the busie Eyes,
but it is subject to the divinest touch of all, to *kissing*, the
strange and mystical union of souls. If she should prostitute her self to a more unworthy man than thy self, how
earnestly and justly wouldst thou exclaim, that for want
of this easier and ready way of repairing, to betray her
body to ruine and deformity (the tyrannous *Ravishers*,
and sodain *Deflourers* of all women) what a hainous adultery is it! What thou lovest in her *face* is *colour*, and
painting gives that, but thou hatest it, not because it is,
but because thou knowest it. Fool, whom Ignorance makes
happy, the Stars, the Sun, the Skye whom thou admirest,
alas, have no colour, but are fair, because they seem to be
coloured: If this seeming will not satisfie thee in her, thou
hast good assurance of her *colour*, when thou seest her *lay*
it on. If her *face* be *painted* on a Board or Wall, thou wilt
love it, and the Board, and the Wall: Canst thou loath it
then when it speaks, smiles, and kisses, because it is
painted? Are we not more delighted with seeing Birds,
Fruits, and Beasts *painted* than we are with Naturals? And
do we not with pleasure behold the *painted* shape of Monsters and Devils, whom true, we durst not regard? We
repair the ruines of our houses, but first cold tempests
warn us of it, and bites us through it; we mend the wrack
and stains of our Apparell, but first our eyes, and other
bodies are offended; but by this providence of Women,
this is prevented. If in *Kissing* or *breathing* upon her, the
painting fall off, thou art angry; wilt thou be so, if it stick
on? Thou didst love her; if thou beginnest to hate her,
then 'tis because she is not *painted*. If thou wilt say now,
thou didst hate her before, thou didst hate her and love
her together. Be constant in something, and love her who
shews her great *love* to thee, in taking this pains to seem
lovely to thee.

IV

THAT GOOD IS MORE COMMON
THAN EVIL

I have not been so pittifully tired with any *vanity*, as with silly *Old Mens* exclaiming against these times, and extolling their own: Alas! they betray themselves, for if the *times* be *changed*, their manners have changed them. But their senses are to *pleasures*, as *sick mens* tastes are to *Liquors;* for indeed no *new thing* is done in the *world*, all things are what, and as they were, and *Good* is as ever it was, more plenteous, and must of necessity be *more common than Evil*, because it hath this for *nature* and *perfection* to be *common*. It makes *Love* to all *Natures*, all, all affect it. So that in the *Worlds* early *Infancy*, there was a time when nothing was *Evill*, but if this World shall suffer *dotage*, in the extreamest *Crookednesse* thereof, there shall be no time when nothing shall be *good*. It dares appear and spread, and glister in the *World*, but *Evill* buries it self in night and darkness, and is chastised and suppressed when *Good* is cherished and rewarded. And as *Imbroderers*, *Lapidaries*, and other *Artisans*, can by all things adorn their works; for by adding better things, the better they shew in [*Lustre*] and in *Eminency;* so *Good* doth not only prostrate her *Amiablenesse* to all, but refuses no end, no not of her utter contrary *Evill*, that she may be the more *common* to us. For *Evill Manners* are *Parents* of *good Lawes;* and in every *Evill* there is an *excellency*, which (in common speech) we call *good*. For the fashions of *habits*, for our moving in *gestures*, for phrases in our *speech*, we say they are *good* as long as they were used, that is, as long as they were *common;* and we eat, we walk, only when it is, or seems *good* to do so. All *fair*, all *profitable*, all *vertuous*, is, *good*, and these three things I think embrace all things, but their utter *contraries;* of which also *fair* may be *rich* and *vertuous; poor*, may be *vertuous* and *fair; vitious*, may be *fair* and *rich;* so that *Good* hath this good means to be *common*, that some subjects she can possess entirely; and in subjects poysoned with *Evill*, she can humbly stoop to accompany the *Evill*. And of *Indifferent* things many things are become perfectly good by being *Common*, as *Customs* by use are made binding *Lawes*. But I remember nothing that is therefore *ill*, because it is *Common*, but *Women*, of whom also: *They that are most Common, are the best of that Occupation they profess.*

VI

THAT IT IS POSSIBLE TO FINDE SOME VERTUE IN SOME WOMEN

I am not of that seard [5] *Impudence* that I dare defend *Women*, or pronounce them good; yet we see *Physitians* allow some *vertue* in every *poyson*. Alas! why should we except *Women?* since certainly, they are good for *Physicke* [6] at least, so as some *wine* is good for a *feaver*. And though they be the *Occasioners* of many sins, they are also the *Punishers* and *Revengers* of the same sins: For I have seldom seen one which consumes his *substance* and *body* upon them, escape *diseases*, or *beggery;* and this is their *Justice*. And if *suum cuique dare*, [7] be the fulfilling of all *Civil Justice*, they are *most just;* for they deny that which is theirs to no man.

Tanquam non liceat nulla puella negat. [8]

And who may doubt of great wisdome in them, that doth but observe with how much labour and cunning our *Justicers* and other *dispensers* of the *Laws* studie to imbrace them: and how zealously our *Preachers* dehort [9] men from them, only by urging their *subtilties* and *policies*, and *wisdom*, which are in them? Or who can deny them a good measure of *Fortitude*, if he consider how *valiant men* they have overthrown, and being themselves over-

5. *seard:* unfeeling.
6. *Physicke:* medicine.
7. *suum cuique dare:* to give to each his own.
8. *Tanquam . . . negat:* No girl will deny it as long as it's forbidden.
9. *dehort:* discourage.

thrown, how much and how patiently they *bear?* And though they be most *intemperate*, I care not, for I undertook to furnish them with *some vertue*, not with *all. Necessity*, which makes even bad things good, prevails also for them, for we must say of them, as of some sharp pinching *Laws:* If men were free from *infirmities*, they were needless. These or none must serve for *reasons*, and it is my great happiness that *Examples* prove not *Rules*, for to confirm this *Opinion*, the World yields not *one Example*.

VIII

THAT NATURE IS OUR WORST GUIDE

Shall she be *guide* to all *Creatures*, which is her self one? Of if she also have a *guide*, shall any *Creature* have a better guide than we? The affections of *lust* and *anger*, yea even to *erre* is natural, shall we follow these? Can she be a good *guide* to us, which hath *corrupted* not us only but her self? was not the first *Man*, by the desire of *knowledge*, corrupted even in the *whitest integrity* of *Nature?* And did not *Nature*, (if *Nature* did any thing) infuse into him this desire of *knowledge*, and so this *Corruption* in him, into us? If by *Nature* we shall understand our *essence*, our *definition* [*our reasonableness*], then this being alike common to all (the *Idiot* and the *Wizard* being equally *reasonable*) why should not all men having equally all one *nature*, follow one course? Or if we shall understand our *inclinations;* alas! how unable a guide is that which follows the *temperature* of our slimie *bodies!* For we cannot say that we derive our *inclinations*, our *mindes*, or *soules* from our *Parents* by any way: to say that it is *all from all*, is *errour* in *reason*, for then with the first nothing remains; or is a *part from all*, is *errour* in *experience*, for then this *part* equally imparted to many children, would like *Gavellkind lands*,[10] in few generations become nothing: or to say it by *communication*, is *errour* in *Divinity*, for to communicate the *ability* of communicating *whole essence* with any

10. *Gavell-kind lands:* land to be equally divided among all heirs.

but God, is utterly *blasphemy*. And if thou hit thy *Fathers*
nature and *inclination*, he also had his *Fathers*, and so
climbing up, all comes of one man, and have one *nature*,
all shall imbrace one course; but that cannot be, therefore
our *Complexions* and whole *Bodies*, we inherit from *Par-*
ents; our *inclinations* and minds follow that: For our *mind*
is heavy in our *bodies afflictions*, and rejoyceth in our
bodies pleasure: how then shall this *nature* governe us, that
is governed by the worst part of us? *Nature though oft*
chased away, it will return; 'tis true, but those *good mo-*
tions and *inspirations* which be our guides must be *wooed*,
courted, and *welcomed*, or else they abandon us. And that
old *Axiome, nihil invita, &c.* must not be said thou *shalt*,
but thou *wilt* doe nothing against *Nature;* so *unwilling* he
notes us to curbe our *naturall appetites*. Wee call our
bastards alwayes our *naturall issue*, and we define a *Foole*
by nothing so ordinary, as by the name of *naturall*. And
that poore knowledge whereby we conceive what *rain* is,
what *wind*, what *thunder*, we call *Metaphysicke, super-*
naturall; such *small* things, such *no* things do we allow to
our pliant *Natures*, apprehension. Lastly, by following her,
we lose the pleasant, and lawfull *Commodities* of this *life*,
for we shall drinke water and eate rootes, and those not
sweet and delicate, as now by Mans *art* and *industry* they
are made: we shall lose all the necessities of *societies, lawes,*
arts, and *sciences*, which are all the workemanship of
Man: yea we shall lack the last *best refuge* of misery,
death, because *no death is naturall:* for if yee will not dare
to call all *death violent* (though I see not why *sicknesses*
be not *violences*) yet *causes* of all *deaths* proceed of the
defect of that which *nature* made perfect, and would preserve, and therefore all against *nature*.

X

THAT A WISE MAN IS KNOWN BY MUCH LAUGHING

Ride, si sapis, ô puella ride; If thou beest *wise*, laugh: for
since the *powers* of *discourse*, and *Reason*, and *laughter*,
be equally *proper* unto Man only, why shall not he be

only most *wise*, which hath most use of *laughing*, as well as he which hath most of *reasoning* and *discoursing?* I always did, and shall understand that *Adage;*

Per risum multum possi cognoscere stultum,[11]

That by much *laughing* thou maist know there is a *fool*, not, that the *laughers* are *fools*, but that among them there is some *fool*, at whom *wise men* laugh: which moved *Erasmus* to put this as his first *Argument* in the mouth of his *Folly*, that *she made Beholders laugh:* for *fools* are the most laughed at, and laugh the least themselves of any. And *Nature* saw this *faculty* to be so necessary in man, that she hath been content that by *more causes* we should be importuned to *laugh*, than to the *exercise* of any other *power;* for things in themselves utterly *contrary*, beget this effect; for we *laugh* both at *witty* and *absurd* things: At both which sorts I have seen men *laugh so long*, and *so earnestly*, that at last they have *wept* that they could laugh no more. And therefore the *Poet* having described the *quietnesse* of a *wise retired man*, saith in one, what we have said before in many lines; *Quid facit Canius tuus? ridet.*[12] We have received that even the *extremity* of *laughing*, yea of *weeping* also, hath been accounted *wisdom:* and that *Democritus* and *Heraclitus*, the *lovers* of these *Extreams*, have been called *lovers of Wisdom.* Now among our *wise men*, I doubt not but many would be found, who would laugh at *Heraclitus* weeping, none which weep at *Democritus* laughing. At the hearing of *Comedies* or other *witty* reports, I have noted some, which not understanding *jests*, &c. have yet chosen this as the best means to seem *wise* and *understanding*, to *laugh* when their *Companions laugh;* and I have presumed them *ignorant*, whom I have seen *unmoved.* A *fool* if he come into a *Princes Court*, and see a *gay* man leaning at the wall, so *glistering*, and so *painted* in many *colours* that he is hardly discerned from one of the *Pictures* in the *Arras*[13] hanging,

11. *Per . . . stultum:* This quotation, like the one at the beginning of the paradox, is followed immediately by Donne's translation.
12. *Quid . . . ridet:* What does your Canius do? He laughs.
13. *Arras:* tapestry.

his *body* like an *Ironbound chest*, girt in and thick *ribb'd* with *broad gold laces*, may (and commonly doth) envy him. But alas! shall a *wise man*, which may not only not *envy*, but not *pitty* this *Monster*, do nothing? Yes, let him *laugh*. And if one of these *hot cholerick firebrands*, which nourish themselves by *quarrelling*, and kindling others, spit upon a *fool* one *sparke* of *disgrace*, he, like a *thatcht house* quickly burning, may be *angry*; but the *wise man*, as *cold* as the *Salamander*,[14] may not only not be *angry* with him, but not be *sorry* for him; therefore let him *laugh*: so he shall be known a Man, because he can *laugh*, a *wise Man* that he knows at *what* to *laugh*, and a *valiant Man* that he *dares* laugh: for he that *laughs* is just·ly reputed more *wise*, than at whom it is *laughed*. And hence I think proceeds that which in these later *formal* times I have much noted; that now when our *superstitious civilitie* of *manners* is become a mutuall *tickling flattery* of one another, almost every man affecteth an *humour* of *jesting*, and is content to be *deject*, and to *deform* himself, yea become *fool* to no other *end* that I can spie, but to give his *wise Companion* occasion to *laugh*; and to shew themselves in *promptness* of *laughing* is so great in *wise men*, that I think all *wise men*, if any *wise men* do read this *Paradox*, will *laugh* both at it and me.

XI

THAT THE GIFTS OF THE BODY ARE BETTER THAN THOSE OF THE MINDE

I say again, that the *body* makes the *minde*, not that it created it a *minde*, but *forms* it a *good* or a *bad minde*; and this *minde* may be confounded with *soul* without any violence or injustice to *Reason* or *Philosophy*: then the *soul* it seems is enabled by our *Body*, not this by it.[15] My *Body* licenseth my *soul* to *see* the worlds *beauties* through

14. *Salamander*: reputed to be able to live in fire.
15. *soul . . . it*: The body is not enabled by the soul.

mine *eyes:* to *hear* pleasant things through mine *ears;* and affords it apt *Organs* for the conveiance of all perceivable *delight.* But alas! my *soul* cannot make any *part,* that is not of it self disposed to *see* or *hear,* though without doubt she be as able and as willing to see *behinde as before.* Now if my *soule* would say, that she enables any part to taste these *pleasures,* but is her selfe only delighted with those rich *sweetnesses* which her *inward eyes* and *senses* apprehend, shee should dissemble; for I see her often solaced with *beauties,* which shee sees through mine *eyes,* and with *musicke* which through mine *eares* she heares. This *perfection* then my *body* hath, that it can impart to my *minde* all his *pleasures;* and my *mind* hath still many, that she can neither teach my *indisposed* part her *faculties,* nor to the best *espoused* parts shew it *beauty* of *Angels,* of *Musicke,* of *Spheres,* whereof she boasts the *contemplation.* Are *Chastity, Temperance,* and *Fortitude* gifts of the *minde?* I appeale to *Physitians* whether the *cause* of these be not in the *body; health* is the gift of the *body,* and *patience* in sicknesse the gift of the *minde:* then who will say that *patience* is as good a *happinesse,* as *health,* when wee must be extremely *miserable* to purchase this *happinesse.* And for nourishing of *civill societies* and *mutuall love* amongst men, which is our *chief end* while we are men; I say, this *beauty, presence,* and *proportion* of the *body,* hath a more *masculine* force in begetting this *love,* than the *vertues* of the *minde:* for it strikes us *suddenly,* and possesseth us *immoderately;* when to know those *vertues* requires some *Judgement* in him which shall discerne, a *long time* and *conversation* between them. And even at last how much of our *faith* and *beleefe* shall we be driven to bestow, to assure our selves that these *vertues* are not *counterfeited:* for it is the same to *be,* and *seem vertuous,* because that he that hath *no vertue,* can *dissemble* none, but he which hath a *little,* may *gild* and *enamell,* yea and transforme much *vice* into *vertue:* For allow a man to be *discreet* and *flexible* to *complaints,* which are great *vertuous* gifts of the *minde,* this *discretion* will be to him the *soule* and *Elixir*[16] of all *vertues,* so that touched with this, even *pride* shall be made *humility;* and *Cowardice,* honourable and wise *val-*

16. *Elixir:* the panacea sought by the alchemists.

our. But in things seen there is not this danger, for the *body* which thou lovest and esteemest *faire*, is *faire*: certainly if it be not *faire* in *perfection*, yet it is *faire* in the same *degree* that thy *Judgment* is good. And in a *faire body*, I do seldom suspect a *disproportioned minde*, and as seldome hope for a *good*, in a *deformed*. When I see a *goodly house*, I assure my selfe of a *worthy possessour*, from a *ruinous weather-beaten building* I turn away, because it seems either stuffed with *varlets* as a *Prison*, or handled by an *unworthy* and *negligent tenant*, that so suffers the *wast* thereof. And truly the gifts of *Fortune*, which are *riches*, are only *handmaids*, yea *Pandars* of the *bodies pleasure;* with their service we nourish *health*, and preserve *dainty*, and wee buy *delights;* so that *vertue* which must be loved for *it selfe*, and respects no further *end*, is indeed *nothing:* And *riches*, whose *end* is the *good* of the *body*, cannot be so *perfectly good*, as the *end* whereto it levels.

XII

THAT VIRGINITY IS
A VERTUE

I call not that *Virginity a vertue*, which resideth onely in the *Bodies integrity;* much lesse if it be with a purpose of perpetuall keeping it: for then it is a most inhumane vice —But I call that *Virginity a vertue* which is willing and desirous to yeeld it selfe upon honest and lawfull terms, when just reason requireth; and until then, is kept with a modest chastity of Body and Mind. Some perchance will say that *Virginity* is in us by *Nature*, and therefore no *vertue*. True, as it is in us by *Nature*, it is neither a *Vertue* nor *Vice*, and is onely in the body: (as in Infants, Children, and such as are incapable of parting from it) But that *Virginity* which is in Man or Woman of perfect age, is not in them by *Nature: Nature* is the greatest enemy to it, and with most subtile allurements seeks the overthrow of it, continually beating against it with her *Engines*,[17] and giving such forcible assaults to it, that it is a strong and more than ordinary *vertue* to hold out till marriage. *Ethick*

17. *Engines*: instruments, weapons.

Philosophy saith, *That no Vertue is corrupted, or is taken away by that which is good:* Hereupon some may say, that *Virginity* is therfore, no *vertue*, being taken away by marriage. *Virginity* is no otherwise taken away by marriage, than is the light of the starres by a greater light (the light of the Sun:) or as a lesse Title is taken away by a greater (an Esquire by being created an Earle:) yet *Virginity* is a *vertue*, and hath her Throne in the middle: The extreams are, in *Excesse*, to violate it before marriage; in *Defect*, not to marry. In ripe years as soon as reason perswades and opportunity admits, These extreams are equally removed from the mean: The excesse proceeds from *Lust*, the defect from *Peevishnesse*, *Pride* and *Stupidity*. There is an old Proverb, That, *they that dy maids, must lead Apes in Hell*. An Ape is a ridiculous and an unprofitable Beast, whose flesh is not good for meat, nor its back for burden, nor is it commodious to keep an house: and perchance for the unprofitablenesse of this Beast did this proverb come up: For surely nothing is more unprofitable in the Commonwealth of *Nature*, than they that dy old maids, because they refuse to be used to that end for which they were only made. The Ape bringeth forth her young, for the most part by twins; that which she loves best, she killeth by pressing it too hard: so foolish maids soothing themselves with a false conceit[18] of *vertue*, in fond obstinacie, live and die maids; and so not onely kill in themselves the *vertue* of *Virginity*, and of a *Vertue* make it a *Vice*, but they also accuse their parents in condemning marriage. If this application hold not touch, yet there may be an excellent one gathered from an Apes tender love to Conies in keeping them from the Weasel and Ferret. From this similitude of an Ape and an old Maid did the foresaid proverb first arise. But alas, there are some old Maids that are *Virgins* much against their wills, and fain would change their *Virgin-life* for a *Married:* such if they never have had any offer of fit Husbands, are in some sort excusable, and their willingnesse, their desire to marry, and their forbearance from all dishonest, and unlawfull copulation, may be a kind of inclination to *vertue*, although not *Vertue* it selfe. This *Vertue* of *Virginity* (though it be small and fruitlesse) it is an extraor-

18. *conceit:* imagination.

dinary, and no common *Vertue*. All other *Vertues* lodge in
the *Will* (it is the *Will* that makes them vertues.) But it
is the unwillingnesse to keep it, the desire to forsake it,
that makes this a *vertue*. As in the naturall generation and
formation made of the seed in the womb of a woman, the
body is joynted and organized about the 28 day, and so it
begins to be no more an *Embrion*, but capable as a matter
prepared to its form to receive the soule, which faileth
not to insinuate and innest it selfe into the body about the
fortieth day; about the third month it hath motion and
sense: Even so *Virginity* is an *Embrion*, an unfashioned
lump, till it attain to a certain time, which is about twelve
years of age in women, fourteen in men, and then it be-
ginneth to have the soule of *Love* infused into it, and to
become a *vertue:* There is also a certain limited time when
it ceaseth to be a *vertue*, which in men is about fourty, in
women about thirty years of age: yea, the losse of so
much time makes their *Virginity* a *Vice*, were not their
endeavour wholly bent, and their desires altogether fixt
upon marriage: In Harvest time do we not account it a
great vice of sloath and negligence in a Husband-man, to
overslip a week or ten dayes after his fruits are fully ripe;
May we not much more account it a more heynous vice,
for a *Virgin* to let her Fruit (*in potentia*) consume and rot
to nothing, and to let the *vertue* of her *Virginity* degenerate into *Vice*, (for *Virginity* ever kept is ever lost.)
Avarice is the greatest deadly sin next Pride: it takes more
pleasure in hoording Treasure than in making use of it,
and will neither let the possessor nor others take benefit
by it during the Misers life; yet it remains intire, and
when the Miser dies must come to som body. *Virginity*
ever kept, is a vice far worse than Avarice, it will neither
let the possessor nor others take benefit by it, nor can it
be bequeathed to any: with long keeping it decayes and
withers, and becomes corrupt and nothing worth. Thus
seeing that *Virginity* becomes a vice in defect, by exceeding a limited time; I counsell all female *Virgins* to make
choyce of some *Paracelsian*[19] for their Physitian, to pre-

19. *Paracelsian:* a follower of Paracelsus (1493–1541), alchemist and
physician, whose advocacy of chemical remedies and a radical conception of the nature of healing had a considerable effect on the
thought of the later Renaissance.

vent the death of that *Vertue:* The *Paracelsians* (curing like by like) say, That if the lives of living Creatures could be taken down, they would make us immortall. By this Rule, female *Virgins* by a discreet marriage should swallow down into their *Virginity* another *Virginity*, and devour such a life and spirit into their womb, that it might make them, as it were, immortall here on earth, besides their perfect immortality in heaven: And that *Vertue* which otherwise would putrifie and corrupt, shall then be compleat; and shall be recorded in Heaven, and enrolled here on Earth; and the name of *Virgin* shal be exchanged for a farre more honorable name, *A Wife.*

PROBLEMES

II

WHY PURITANS MAKE LONG SERMONS?

It needs not for *perspicuousness*, for God knows they are plain enough: nor do all of them use *Sem-brief-Accents*,[1] for some of them have *Crotchets*[2] enough. It may be they intend not to rise like *glorious Tapers* and *Torches*, but like *Thin-wretched-sick-watching-Candles*, which *languish* and are in a Divine *Consumption* from the first minute, yea in their *snuff*, and *stink*, when others are in their more profitable *glory*. I have thought sometimes, that out of conscience, they allow *long measure* to *course*[3] *ware*. And sometimes, that *usurping* in that *place* a *liberty* to *speak freely* of *Kings*, they would *reigne* as long as they could. But now I think they do it out of a *zealous* imagination, that, *It is their duty to Preach on till their Auditory wake.*

1. *Sem-brief*: semibreve—whole note, the longest note in music.
2. *Crotchets*: quarter note, with a pun on crotchet as eccentric belief.
3. *course*: coarse; extra quantity for inferior quality.

V

WHY DOE YOUNG LAY-MEN SO MUCH STUDIE DIVINITY? [4]

Is it because others tending busily *Churches preferment*[5] neglect *studie?* Or had the *Church* of *Rome* shut up all our wayes, till the *Lutherans* broke downe their *uttermost stubborne dores,* and the *Calvinists* picked their *inwardest* and *subtlest lockes?* Surely the *Divell* cannot bee such a *Foole* to hope that hee shall make this study *contemptible,* by making it *common.* Nor that as the *Dwellers* by the river *Origus* are said (by drawing infinite *ditches* to sprinckle their *barren Countrey*) to have exhausted and intercepted their *maine channell,* and so lost their more profitable course to the *Sea;* so wee, by providing every *ones selfe, divinity* enough for his *owne use,* should neglect our *Teachers* and *Fathers.* Hee cannot hope for better *heresies* than he hath had, nor was his *Kingdome* ever so much advanced by *debating Religion* (though with some *aspersions* of *Error*) as by a *Dull* and *stupid security,*[6] in which many *grosse things* are swallowed. Possible out of such an *Ambition* as we have now, to speake *plainely* and *fellow-like* with *Lords* and *Kings,* wee thinke also to acquaint our selves with *Gods secrets:* Or perchance when wee study it by *mingling humane* respects, *It is not Divinity.*

4. *Divinity:* theology.
5. *preferment:* advancement.
6. *security:* overconfidence.

VI

WHY HATH THE COMMON OPINION AFFORDED WOMEN SOULES?

It is agreed that we have not so much from them as any *part* of either our *mortal soules* of *sense* or *growth*,[7] and we deny *soules* to others equall to them in all but in *speech* for which they are beholding to their *bodily instruments:* For perchance an *Oxes* heart, or a *Goates*, or a *Foxes*, or a *Serpents* would speake just so, if it were in the *breast*, and could move that *tongue* and *jawes*. Have they so many *advantages* and *means* to hurt us (for, ever their *loving* destroyed us[8]) that we dare not *displease* them, but give them what they will? And so when some call them *Angels*, some *Goddesses*, and the [*Peputian*] *Hereticks* made them *Bishops*, we descend so much with the stream, to allow them *Soules?* Or do we somewhat (in this dignifying of them) flatter *Princes* and *great Personages* that are so much governed by them? Or do we in that *easiness* and *prodigality*, wherein we daily lose our own *souls* to we care not whom, so labour to perswade our selves, that sith a *woman* hath a *soul*, a *soul* is no great matter? Or do we lend them *souls* but for use,[9] since they for our sakes, give their *souls* again, and their *bodies* to boot? Or perchance because the *Devil* (who is all *soul*) doth most *mischief*, and for convenience and proportion, because they would come *nearer* him, we allow them some souls: and so as the *Romans* naturalized some *Provinces* in revenge, and made them *Romans*, only for the *burthen* of the *Common-wealth;* so we have given *women* souls only to make them capable of *Damnation?*

7. *mortal . . . growth:* Renaissance thinkers posited the existence of three souls: of growth, of sense, and of reason, the third being immortal. Plants were held to possess only the first soul, animals the first and second, human beings all three.

8. *loving . . . us:* a reference to the popular belief that each sexual act diminished life by a day.

9. *use:* usury.

VIII

WHY VENUS-STARRE ONELY DOTH CAST A SHADOW?

Is it because it is *neerer* the *earth?* But they whose *profession* it is to see that nothing be done in *heaven* without their *consent* (as *Re-[Kepler]* saies in himselfe of *Astrologers*) have bid *Mercury* to bee *neerer*. Is it because the *workes* of *Venus* want *shadowing, covering,* and *disguising?* But those of *Mercury*[10] needs it more; for *Eloquence,* his *Occupation,* is all *shadow* and *colours;*[11] let our *life* be a *sea,* and then our *reason* and *Even passions* are *wind* enough to carry us whether we should go, but *Eloquence* is a *storme* and *tempest* that miscarries: and who doubts that *Eloquence* which must perswade *people* to take a *yoke* of *soveraignty* (and then beg and make lawes to tye them *faster,* and then give money to the *Invention,* repaire and strengthen it) needs more *shadowes* and *colouring,* than to perswade any Man or Woman to that which is *naturall.* And *Venus markets* are so *naturall,* that when we solicite the best way (which is by *marriage*) our perswasions worke not so much to *draw* a woman *to us,* as against her *Nature* to draw her *from all other* besides. And so when we goe against *Nature,* and from *Venus-worke* (for *marriage* is *chastity*) we need *shadowes* and *colours,* but not else. In *Seneca's* time it was a course, an *unromane* and a *contemptible* thing even in a *Matrone,* not to have had a *love* beside her *husband,* which though the *Law* required not at their hands, yet they did it *zealously* out of the counsell of *Custome* and *fashion,* which was *venery* of *Supererogation:*

Et te spectator plusquam delectat Adulter, saith *Martial:* And *Horace,* because many *lights* would not shew him enough, created many *images* of the same *Object* by *wainscoting* his *chamber* with *looking-glasses:* so that *Venus flyes not light,* so much as *Mercury,* who creeping into our *understanding,* our *darknesse* would bee defeated, if hee

10. *Mercury:* a deity associated with oratory.
11. *shadow . . . colours:* figures of rhetoric.

were perceived. Then either this *shaddow* confesseth that
same darke *Melancholy Repentance*, which accompanies;
or that so *violent fires*, needes some *shadowy* refreshing,
and *Intermission:* Or else *light* signifying both *day* and
youth, and *shadow* both *night* and *Age*, shee pronounceth
by this that shee professeth both all *persons* and *times*.

IX

WHY IS VENUS-STAR MULTINOMINOUS, CALLED BOTH HESPERUS [12] AND VESPER? [13]

The *Moone* hath as many *names*, but not as she is a *starre*,
but as she hath divers *governments;* but *Venus* is *multi-
nominous* to give example to her *prostitute disciples*, who
so often, either to *renew* or *refresh* them selves towards
lovers, or to *disguise* themselves from *Magistrates*, are to
take *new names.* It may be she takes *new names* after her
many *functions*, for as she is *Supreme* Monarch of all *Love*
at large (which is *lust*) so is she joyned in Commission
with all *Mythologicks*, with *Juno*, *Diana*, and all others
for *Marriage.* It may be because of the divers *names* to her
self, for her *Affections* have more *names* than any *vice;*
*scilicet: Pollution, Fornication, Adultery, Lay-Incest,
Church-Incest, Rape, Sodomy, Mastupration, Masturba-
tion,* and a thousand others. Perchance her divers *names*
shewed her appliableness to divers men, for *Neptune* dis-
tilled and wet her in *Love*, the *Sunne* warms and melts her,
Mercury perswaded and swore her, *Jupiters* authority
secured, and *Vulcan* hammer'd her. As *Hesperus* she presents you with her *bonum utile*,[14] because it is *wholesomest*
in the *Morning:* As *Vesper* with her *bonum delectabile*,[15]
because it is *pleasantest* in the *Evening.* And because *industrious* men rise and endure with the *Sunne* in their
civill businesses, this *starre* cals them up a little before,

12. *Hesperus:* the morning star.
13. *Vesper:* the evening star.
14. *bonum utile:* useful good.
15. *bonum delectabile:* delightful good.

and remembers them again a little after for her business; for certainly,

Venit Hesperus, ite capellae:[16]

was spoken to *lovers* in the persons of *Goats.*

XI

WHY DOTH THE POXE[17] SOE MUCH AFFECT TO UNDERMINE THE NOSE?

Paracelsus perchance saith true, That every Disease hath his Exaltation in some part certaine. But why this in the Nose? Is there so much mercy in this desease, that it provides that one should not smell his own stinck? Or hath it but the common fortune, that being begot and bred in obscurest and secretest places, because therefore his serpentine crawling and insinuation should not be suspected, nor seen, he comes soonest into great place, and is more able to destroy the worthiest member, than a Disease better born? Perchance as mice defeat Elephants by knawing their *Proboscis*, which is their Nose, this wretched Indian Vermine practiseth to doe the same upon us. Or as the ancient furious Custome and Connivency of some Lawes, that one might cut off their Nose whome he deprehended in Adulterie, was but a Tipe[18] of this; And that now more charitable lawes having taken away all Revenge from particular hands, this common Magistrate and Executioner is come to doe the same Office invisibly? Or by withdrawing this conspicuous part, the Nose, it warnes us from all adventuring upon that Coast; for it is as good a marke to take in a flag, as to hang one out. Possibly heate, which is more potent and active than cold, thought her selfe injured, and the Harmony of the world out of tune,

16. *Venit . . . capellae:* Hesperus comes; go, my she-goats (Virgil, *Eclogue X*). The goat was symbolic of lust.
17. *Poxe:* syphilis.
18. *Tipe:* a typological prefiguration.

when cold was able to shew the high-way to Noses in *Muscovia*, except she found the meanes to doe the same in other Countries. Or because by the consent of all, there is an Analogy, Proportion and affection between the Nose and that part where this disease is first contracted, and therefore *Heliogabalus* chose not his Minions in the Bath but by the Nose; And *Albertus* had a knavish meaning when he prefered great Noses; And the licentious Poet[19] was *Naso Poeta*. I think this reason is nearest truth, That the Nose is most compassionate with this part: Except this be nearer, that it is reasonable that this Disease in particular should affect the most eminent and perspicuous part, which in general doth affect to take hold of the most eminent and conspicuous men.

XVI

WHY ARE COURTIERS SOONER ATHEISTS THAN MEN OF OTHER CONDITIONS?

Is it because as *Physitians* contemplating Nature, and finding many abstruse things subject to the search of Reason, think therfore that all is so; so they (seeing mens destinies, mad[e] at Court, neck[s] [put] out and [in] joynt there, *War, Peace, Life* and *Death* derived from thence) climb no higher? Or doth a familiarity with greatness, and daily conversation and acquaintance with it breed a contempt of all greatness? Or because that they see that opinion or need of one another, and fear makes the degrees of servants, Lords and Kings, do they think that God likewise for such Reason hath been mans Creator? Perchance it is because they see Vice prosper best there, and, burthened with sinne, doe they not, for their ease, endeavour to put off the feare and Knowledge of God, as facinorous[20] men deny Magistracy? Or are the most Atheists in that place, because it is the foole that said in his heart, There is no God.

19. *Poet:* Ovid (Publius Ovidius Naso. *Naso: nose*).
20. *facinorous:* wicked.

Devotions upon Emergent Occasions

I_N 1621 Donne was appointed Dean of St. Paul's Cathedral. In 1623 he suffered a nearly fatal illness, the psychological impact of which evoked from him not only the "Hymne to God the Father" and, possibly, the "Hymne to God my God, in my Sicknesse," but also the *Devotions upon Emergent Occasions*, which ranks with the finest of his sermons as a masterpiece of Baroque prose. It consists of a series of twenty-three devotions, each subdivided into a meditation, an expostulation, and a prayer. The following pages contain all the meditations, together with one complete sequence, the nineteenth. The *Devotions* traces the course of Donne's illness from its onset to its cure, drawing from each phase a wealth of metaphorical applications, social and political as well as religious. In method the work relies heavily on the practice of formal meditation, which also influenced Donne's poetry (see L. L. Martz, *The Poetry of Meditation*), and it constitutes one of the last great and sustained expressions of the Renaissance doctrine of universal analogy.

Published in 1624, the *Devotions* enjoyed wide popularity and has remained among the most admired of Donne's prose writings. The standard authorities on Donne's prose discuss the work (see E. M. Simpson and J.

Webber for example); it is treated also in J. Sparrow's modern edition and I. Husain's study of Donne's theology.

THE EPISTLE DEDICATORIE TO THE MOST EXCELLENT PRINCE "PRINCE" CHARLES

Most Excellent Prince,

I have had three Births; *One,* Naturall, *when I came into the* World; *One,* Supernatural, *when I entred into the* Ministery; *and now, a* preter-naturall Birth, *in returning to* Life, *from this* Sicknes. *In my* second Birth, *your* Highnesse Royall Father *vouchsafed mee his Hand, not onely to sustaine mee in it, but to lead mee to it. In this last* Birth, *I my selfe am borne a* Father: *This* Child *of mine, this* Booke, *comes into the world, from mee, and with me. And therefore, I presume (as I did the* Father *to the* Father) *to present the* Sonne *to the* Sonne; *This* Image *of my* Humiliation, *to the lively* Image *of his* Majesty *your* Highnesse. *It might bee enough, that* God *hath seene my* Devotions: *But* Examples *of* Good Kings *are* Commandments; *And* Ezechiah *with the* Meditations *of his* Sicknesse, *after his* Sicknesse. *Besides, as I have liv'd to see* (*not as a* Witnesse *onely, but as a* Partaker) *the happinesses of a part of your* Royal Fathers *time, so shall I live* (in my way) *to see the happinesses of the times of your* Highnesse *too, if this* Child *of mine, inanimated by your gracious* Acceptation, *may so long preserve alive the* Memory of

> Your Highnesse
> Humblest and
> Devotedst
>
> John Donne

| Insultus Morbi Primus; | *The first alteration, The first grudging of the sicknesse.* |

I. MEDITATION

Variable, and therfore miserable condition of Man; this minute I was well, and am ill, this minute. I am surpriz'd with a sodaine change, and alteration to worse, and can impute it to no cause, nor call it by any name. We study *Health*, and we deliberate upon our *meats*,[1] and *drink*, and *ayre*, and *exercises*, and we hew, and wee polish every stone, that goes to that building; and so our *Health* is a long and a regular work; But in a minute a Canon batters all, overthrowes all, demolishes all; a *Sicknes* unprevented for all our diligence, unsuspected for all our curiositie; nay, undeserved, if we consider only *disorder*, summons us, seizes us, possesses us, destroyes us in an instant. O miserable condition of Man, which was not imprinted by *God*, who as hee is *immortall* himselfe, had put a *coale*, a *beame* of *Immortalitie* into us, which we might have blowen into a *flame*, but blew it out, by our first sinne; wee beggard our selves by hearkning after false riches, and infatuated our selves by hearkning after false knowledge. So that now, we doe not onely die, but die upon the Rack, die by the torment of sicknesse; nor that onely, but are pre-afflicted, super-afflicted with these jelousies and suspitions, and apprehensions of *Sicknes*, before we can cal it a sicknes; we are not sure we are ill; one hand askes the other by the pulse, and our eye asks our urine, how we do. O multiplied misery! we die, and cannot enjoy death, because wee die in this torment of sicknes; we are tormented with sicknes, and cannot stay till the torment come, but preapprehensions and presages, prophecy those torments, which induce that *death* before either come; and our dissolution is conceived in these *first changes*, *quickned* in the *sicknes* it selfe and *borne* in *death*, which beares date from these first changes. Is this the honour which Man hath by being a *litle world*,[2] That he hath these *earthquakes* in him selfe, sodaine shakings; these *lightnings*, sodaine flashes; these *thunders*, sodaine noises; these *Eclypses*, sodain offuscations, and darknings of his senses; these *Blazing stars*, sodaine fiery exhalations; these *Rivers of blood*, sodaine red waters? Is he a *world* to himselfe onely therefore, that he hath inough in himself, not only to destroy, and execute himselfe, but to presage that execution upon himselfe; to

1. *meats*: foods.
2. *litle world*: the ancient conception of man as a microcosm, or little world, a conception typical of the analogical thinking characteristic of the Renaissance.

assist the sicknes, to antidate the sicknes, to make the sicknes the more irremediable, by sad apprehensions, and as
if he would make a fire the more vehement, by sprinkling
water upon the coales, so to wrap a hote fever in cold
Melancholy, least the fever alone should not destroy fast
enough, without this contribution nor perfit[3] the work
(which is *destruction*) except we joynd an artificiall
sicknes, of our owne *melancholy*, to our natural, our unnaturall fever. O perplex'd discomposition, O ridling distemper, O miserable condition of Man!

Actio Laesa.   *The strength, and the function*
                           of the Senses, and other faculties
                           change and faile.

II. MEDITATION

The *Heavens* are not the less constant, because they move
continually, because they move continually one and the
same way. The *Earth* is not the more constant, because it
lyes stil continually, because continually it changes, and
melts in al parts thereof. *Man*, who is the noblest part of
the *Earth*, melts so away, as if he were a *statue*, not of
Earth, but of *Snowe*. We see his owne *Envie* melts
him, he growes leane with that; he will say, anothers
beautie melts him; but he feeles that a *Fever* doth not
melt him like *snow*, but powr him out like *lead*, like *iron*,
like *brasse* melted in a furnace: It doth not only *melt* him,
but *calcine* him, reduce him to *Atomes*, and to *ashes;* not
to *water*, but to *lime*. And how quickly? Sooner than
thou canst receive an answer, sooner than thou canst conceive the question; *Earth* is the *center* of my *Bodie*,
Heaven is the *center* of my *Soule;* these two are the
naturall places of those two; but those goe not to these
two in an equall pace: My *body* falls downe without push-
ing, my *Soule* does not go up without pulling: *Ascension*
is my *Soules* pace and measure, but *precipitation* my *bodies:* And, even *Angells*, whose home is *Heaven*, and who
are winged too, yet had a *Ladder* to goe to *Heaven*, by

3. *perfit:* perfect.

steps.[1] The *Sunne* who goes so many miles in a minut, the *Starres* of the *Firmament*, which go so very many more, goe not so fast, as my *body* to the *earth*. In the same instant that I feele the first attempt of the disease, I feele the victory; In the twinckling of an eye, I can scarse see, instantly the tast is insipid, and fatuous; instantly the appetite is dull and desirelesse: instantly the knees are sinking and strengthlesse; and in an instant, sleepe, which is the *picture*, the *copie* of *death*, is taken away, that the *Originall*, *Death* it selfe may succeed, and that so I might have death to the life. It was part of *Adams* punishment, *In the sweat of thy browes thou shalt eate thy bread:* it is multiplied to me, I have earned bread in the sweat of my browes, in the labor of my calling, and I have it; and I sweat againe, and againe, from the brow, to the sole of the foot, but I eat no bread, I tast no sustenance: Miserable distribution of *Mankind*, where one halfe lackes meat, and the other stomacke.

Decubitus sequitur tandem.   *The Patient takes his bed.*

III. MEDITATION

Wee attribute but one priviledge and advantage to Mans body, above other moving creatures, that he is not as others, groveling, but of an erect, of an upright form, naturally built, and disposed to the contemplation of *Heaven*. Indeed it is a thankfull forme, and recompences that *soule*, which gives it, with carrying that soule so many foot higher, towards *heaven*. Other creatures look to the *earth;* and even that is no unfit object, no unfit contemplation for *Man;* for thither hee must come; but because, *Man* is not to stay there, as other creatures are, *Man* in his naturall forme, is carried to the contemplation of that place, which is his *home*, *Heaven*. This is *Mans* prerogative; but what state hath he in this *dignitie?* A fever can fillip him downe, a fever can depose him; a fever can bring that head, which yesterday caried a *crown* of gold, five foot towards a *crown* of glory, as low as his own foot,

1. *even . . . steps:* see Genesis 28:10–15.

today. When *God* came to breath into *Man* the breath of life, he found him flat upon the ground; when he comes to withdraw that breath from him againe, hee prepares him to it, by laying him flat upon his bed. Scarse any prison so close, that affords not the prisoner two, or three steps. The *Anchorites* that barqu'd themselves up in hollowe trees, and immur'd themselves in hollow walls; that perverse man, that barrell'd himselfe in a Tubb, all could stand, or sit, and enjoy some change of posture. A sicke bed, is a grave; and all that the patient saies there, is but a varying of his owne *Epitaph.* Every nights bed is a *Type* of the *grave:* At night wee tell our servants at what houre wee will rise; here we cannot tell our selves, at what day, what week, what moneth. Here the head lies as low as the foot; the *Head* of the people, as lowe as they, whome those feete trod upon; And that hande that signed Pardons, is too weake to begge his owne, if he might have it for lifting up that hand: Strange fetters to the feete, strange Manacles to the hands, when the feete, and handes are bound so much the faster, by how much the coards are slacker; So much the lesse able to doe their Offices, by how much more the Sinewes and Ligaments are the looser. In the *Grave* I may speak through the stones, in the voice of my friends, and in the accents of those wordes, which their love may afford my memory; Here I am mine owne *Ghost,* and rather affright my beholders, than instruct them; they conceive the worst of me now, and yet feare worse; they give me for dead now, and yet wonder how I doe, when they wake at midnight, and aske how I doe to morrow. Miserable and, (though common to all) inhuman *posture,* where I must practise my lying in the *grave,* by lying still, and not practise my *Resurrection,* by rising any more.

Medicusque vocatur.   *The Phisician is sent for.*

IV. MEDITATION

It is too little to call *Man* a *little World;* Except *God,* Man is a *diminutive* to nothing. Man consistes of more pieces, more parts, than the world; than the world doeth, nay than the world is. And if those pieces were extended, and stretched out in Man, as they are in the world, Man would bee the *Gyant*, and the Worlde the *Dwarfe*, the World but the *Map*, and the Man the *World*. If all the *Veines* in our bodies, were extended to *Rivers*, and all the *Sinewes*, to *Vaines of Mines*, and all the *Muscles*, that lye upon one another, to *Hilles*, and all the *Bones* to *Quarries* of stones, and all the other pieces, to the proportion of those which correspond to them in the world, the *Aire* would be too litle for this *Orbe* of Man to move in, the firmament would bee but enough for this *Starre;* for, as the whole world hath nothing, to which something in man doth not answere, so hath man many pieces, of which the whole world hath no representation. Inlarge this Meditation upon this *great world, Man*, so farr, as to consider the immensitie of the creatures this world produces; our *creatures* are our *thoughts, creatures* that are borne *Gyants;* that reach from *East* to *West*, from *Earth* to *Heaven*, that doe not onely bestride all the *Sea*, and *Land*, but span the *Sunn and Firmament* at once; My thoughts reach all, comprehend all. Inexplicable mistery; I their *Creator* am in a close prison, in a sicke bed, any where, and any one of my *Creatures*, my *thoughts*, is with the *Sunne*, and beyond the *Sunne*, overtakes the *Sunne*, and overgoes the *Sunne* in one pace, one steppe, everywhere. And then as the other *world* produces *Serpents*, and *Vipers*, malignant, and venimous creatures, and *Wormes*, and *Caterpillars*, that endeavour to devoure that world which produces them, and *Monsters* compiled [1] and complicated of divers parents, and kinds, so this world, our selves, produces all these in us, in producing *diseases*, and *sicknesses*, of all those sorts; venimous, and infectious diseases, feeding and consuming diseases, and manifold and entangled diseases, made up of many several ones. And can the other world name so many *venimous*, so many consuming, so many monstrous creatures, as we can diseases, of all these kindes? O miserable abundance, O beggarly riches! how much doe wee lacke of having *remedies* for everie disease, when as yet we have not *names* for them? But wee have a *Hercules* against these *Gyants*, these *Monsters;* that is, the *Phisician;* hee musters

1. *compiled:* composed.

up al the forces of the other world,[2] to succour this; all Nature to relieve Man. We *have* the *Phisician*, but we *are not* the *Phisician*. Heere we shrinke in our proportion, sink in our dignitie, in respect of verie meane creatures, who are *Phisicians* to themselves. The *Hart* that is pursued and wounded, they say, knowes an Herbe, which being eaten, throwes off the arrow: A strange kind of *vomit*. The *dog* that pursues it, though hee bee subject to sicknes, even *proverbially*, knowes his *grasse* that recovers him. And it may be true, that the *Drugger*[3] is as neere to *Man*, as to other *creatures*, it may be that obvious and present *Simples*,[4] easie to be had, would cure him; but the *Apothecary* is not so neere him, nor the *Phisician* so neere him, as they two are to other creatures; Man hath not that *innate instinct*, to apply these naturall medicines to his present danger, as those inferiour creatures have; he is not his owne *Apothecary*, his owne *Phisician*, as they are. Call back therefore thy Meditation again, and bring it downe; whats become of mans great extent and proportion, when himselfe shrinkes himselfe, and consumes himselfe to a handfull of dust? whats become of his soaring thoughts, his compassing thoughts, when himselfe brings himselfe to the ignorance, to the thoughtlessnesse of the *Grave?* His *diseases* are his owne, but the *Phisician* is not; hee hath them at home, but hee must send for the *Phisician*.

Solus adest.   *The Phisician comes.*

V. MEDITATION

As *Sicknes* is the greatest misery, so the greatest misery of sicknes, is *solitude;* when the infectiousnes of the disease deterrs them who should assist, from comming; even the *Phisician* dares scarse come. *Solitude* is a torment which is not threatned in *hell* it selfe. Meere *vacuitie*, the first *Agent, God*, the first *instrument* of *God, Nature*, will not admit; Nothing can be utterly *emptie*, but so neere a de-

2. *other world:* the macrocosm, or great world.
3. *Drugger:* druggist.
4. *Simples:* herbs.

gree towards *Vacuitie*, as *Solitude*, to bee but one, they love not. When I am dead, and my body might infect, they have a remedy, they may bury me; but when I am but sick, and might infect, they have no remedy, but their absence, and my solitude. It is an *excuse* to them that are *great*, and pretend, and yet are loth to come; it is an *inhibition* to those who would truly come, because they may be made instruments, and pestiducts,[1] to the infection of others, by their comming. And it is an *Outlawry*, an *Excommunication* upon the *Patient*, and seperats him from all offices not onely of *Civilitie*, but of *working Charitie*. A long sicknesse will weary friends at last, but a pestilentiall sicknes averts them from the beginning. *God* himself would admit a *figure* of *Society*, as there is a plurality of persons in *God*, though there bee but one *God*; and all his externall actions testifie a love of *Societie*, and communion. In *Heaven* there are *Orders* of *Angels*, and *Armies* of *Martyrs*, and *in that house, many mansions; in Earth*, *Families*, *Cities*, *Churches*, *Colleges*, all *plurall things*; and lest either of these should not be company enough alone, there is an association of both, a *Communion of Saints*, which makes the *Militant*, and *Triumphant Church*,[2] one Parish; So that *Christ*, was not out of his *Dioces*, when hee was upon the *Earth*, nor out of his *Temple*, when he was in our flesh. *God*, who sawe that all that hee made, was good, came not so neer seeing a *defect* in any of his works, as when he saw that it was not good, for man to bee *alone*, therefore *hee made him a helper*; and one that should helpe him so, as to increase the *number*, and give him *her owne*, and *more societie*. *Angels* who do not propagate, nor multiply, were made at the first in an abundant number; and so were starres: But for the things of this world, their blessing was, *Encrease*; for I think, I need not aske leave to think, that there is no *Phenix*;[3] nothing singular, nothing alone: Men that inhere upon[4] *Nature* only, are so far from thinking, that there is

1. *pestiducts:* carriers of infection.
2. *Militant . . . Church:* The Church Militant is composed of the faithful on earth; the Church Triumphant of the souls of the faithful in heaven.
3. *Phenix:* the mythical Arabian bird, said to be unique.
4. *inhere upon:* belong to.

anything *singular* in this world, as that they will scarce thinke, that this world it selfe is *singular*, but that every *Planet*, and every *Starre*, is another *world* like this; They finde reason to conceive, not onely a *pluralitie* in every *Species* in the world, but a *pluralitie of worlds;* so that the abhorrers of *Solitude*, are not solitary; for *God*, and *Nature*, and *Reason* concurre against it. Now a man may counterfeyt the *Plague* in a *vowe*, and mistake a *Disease* for *Religion;* by such a retiring, and recluding[5] of himselfe from all men, as to doe good to no man, to converse with no man. *God* hath two *Testaments*, two *Wils;* but this is a *Scedule*, and not of his, a *Codicill*, and not of his, not in the *body* of his *Testaments*, but *interlin'd*, and *postscrib'd* by others, that the way to the *Communion of Saints*, should be by such a *solitude*, as excludes all doing of good here. That is a *disease* of the *mind;* as the height of an infectious disease of the body, is *solitude*, to be left alone: for this makes an infectious bed, equall, nay worse than a *grave*, that thogh in both I be equally alone, in my bed I *know* it, and *feele* it, and shall not in my *grave:* and this too, that in my bedd, my soule is still in an infectious body, and shall not in my grave bee so.

Metuit.   *The Phisician is afraid.*

VI. MEDITATION

I observe the *Phisician*, with the same diligence, as hee the *disease;* I see hee *feares*, and I feare with him: I overtake him, I overrun him in his feare, and I go the faster, because he makes his pace slow; I feare the more, because he disguises his fear, and I see it with the more sharpnesse, because hee would not have me see it. He knowes that his *feare* shall not disorder the practise, and exercise of his *Art*, but he knows that my *fear* may disorder the effect, and working of his practise. As the ill affections of the *spleene*, complicate, and mingle themselves with every infirmitie of the body, so doth *feare* insinuat it self in every *action* or *passion* of the *mind;* and as the *wind* in the body

5. *recluding:* separation.

will counterfet any disease, and seem the *stone* and seem the *Gout*, so feare will counterfet any disease of the *Mind;* It shall seeme *love*, a love of having, and it is but a *fear*, a jealous, and suspitious feare of loosing; It shall seem *valor* in despising, and undervaluing danger, and it is but *feare*, in an overvaluing of *opinion*, and *estimation*, and a feare of loosing that. A man that is not afraid of a *Lion* is afraid of a *Cat;* not afraid of *starving*, and yet is afraid of some *joynt of meat* at the table, presented to feed him; not afraid of the sound of *Drummes*, and *Trumpets*, and *Shot*, and those, which they seeke to drowne, the last cries of men, and is afraid of some particular *harmonious instrument;* so much afraid, as that with any of these the *enemy* might drive this man, otherwise valiant enough, out of the field. I know not, what fear is, nor I know not what it is that I fear now; I feare not the hastening of my *death*, and yet I do fear the increase of the *disease;* I should belie *Nature*, if I should deny that I feared this, and if I should say that I feared *death*, I should belye *God;* My weaknesse is from *Nature*, who hath but her *Measure*, my strength is from *God*, who possesses, and distributes infinitely. As then every cold ayre, is not a *dampe*,[1] every *shivering* is not a *stupefaction*, so every *feare*, is not a *fearefulnes*, every *declination* is not a running away, every debating is not a resolving, every wish, that it were not thus, is not a murmuring, nor a dejection though it bee thus; but as my *Phisicians* fear puts not him from his *practise*, neither doth mine put me, from receiving from *God*, and *Man*, and *my selfe*, *spirituall* and *civill*, and *morall* assistances, and consolations.

Socios sibi jungier instat. *The Phisician desires to have others joyned with him.*

VII. MEDITATION

There is *more feare*, therefore *more cause*. If the *Phisician* desire help, the burden grows great: There is a growth of the *Disease* then: But there must bee an *Autumne* to; But

1. *dampe:* noxious vapor.

whether an *Autumne* of the *disease* or *mee*, it is not my part to choose: but if it bee of *mee*, it is of *both*; My disease cannot *survive mee*, I may *overlive* it. Howsoever, his desiring of others, argues his *candor*, and his *ingenuitie*; if the danger be *great*, he *justifies* his proceedings, and he *disguises* nothing, that calls in *witnesses*; And if the danger bee not *great*, hee is not *ambitious*, that is so readie to divide the thankes, and the honour of that work, which he begun alone, with others. It diminishes not the dignitie of a *Monarch*, that hee derive part of his care upon others; *God* hath not made many *Suns*, but he hath made many *bodies*, that *receive*, and *give* light. The *Romanes* began with *one King*; they came to *two Consuls*; they returned in extremities, to *one Dictator*: whether in *one*, or *many*, the *Soveraigntie* is the same, in all *States*, and the danger is not the more, and the providence is the more, where there are more *Phisicians*; as the State is the happier, where businesses are carried by more counsels, than can bee in one breast, how large soever. *Diseases* themselves hold *Consultations*, and conspire how they may multiply, and joyn with one another, and *exalt* one anothers force, so; and shal we not call *Phisicians*, to *consultations? Death* is in an olde mans dore, he appeares, and tels him so, and *death* is at a young mans *backe*, and saies nothing; *Age* is a *sicknesse*, and *Youth* is an *ambush*; and we need so many *Phisicians*, as may make up a *Watch*, and spie every inconvenience. There is scarce any thing, that hath not killed some body; a *haire*, a *feather* hath done it; Nay, that which is our best *Antidote* against it, hath donn it; the best *Cordiall* hath bene *deadly poyson*; Men have dyed of *Joy*, and allmost forbidden their friends to weepe for them, when they have seen them dye laughing. Even that Tiran *Dyonisius* (I thinke the same, that suffered so much after) who could not die of that sorrow, of that high fal, from a *King* to a *wretched private man*, dyed of so poore a *Joy*, as to be declard by the *people* at a *Theater*, that hee was a good *Poet*. We say often that a *Man may live of a litle*; but, alas, of how much lesse may a Man dye! And therfore the more assistants, the better; who comes to a day of hearing, in a cause of any importance, with one *Advocate?* In our *Funerals*, we our selves have no interest; there wee cannot *advise*, we cannot *direct*: And though some *Nations,* (the *Egiptians* in particular) built themselves better *tombs,* than *houses,* because they were to dwell *longer* in them; yet, amongst our selves, the greatest *Man of Stile,* whom we have had, *The Conqueror,* was left, as soone as his soule left him, not only without persons to assist at his *grave,* but without a *grave.* Who will keepe us then, we know not; As long as we can, let us admit as much *helpe* as wee can; Another, and another *Phisician,* is not another, and another *Indication,* and *Symptom* of *death,* but another, and another *Assistant,* and *Proctor* of *life:* Nor doe they so much feed the imagination with apprehension of *danger,* as the understanding with *comfort;* Let not one bring *Learning,* another *Diligence,* another *Religion,* but every one bring all, and, as many Ingredients enter into a Receit,[1] so may many men make the Receit. But why doe I exercise my Meditation so long upon this, of having plentifull helpe in time of need? Is not my Meditation rather to be enclined another way, to condole, and commiserate their distresse, who have *none?* How many are sicker (perchance) than I, and laid on their wofull straw at home (if that corner be a home) and have no more hope of helpe, though they die, than of preferment,[2] though they live? Nor doe no more expect to see a *Phisician* then, than to be an *Officer* after; of whome, the first that takes knowledge, is the *Sexten* that buries them; who buries them in *oblivion* too? For they doe but fill up the number of the dead in the Bill,[3] but we shall never heare their *Names,* till wee reade them in the Booke of life, with our owne. How many are sicker (perchance) than I, and thrown into *Hospitals,* where, (as a fish left upon the Sand, must stay the tide) they must stay the *Phisicians* houre of visiting, and then can bee but *visited?* How many are sicker (perchaunce) than all we, and have not this *Hospitall* to cover them, not this straw, to lie in, to die in, but have their *Grave-stone* under them, and breathe out their soules in the eares, and in the eies of passengers, harder than their bed, the flint of the street? That taste of no part of our *Phisick,* but a sparing *dyet;* to whom ordinary porridge would bee *Julip*

1. *Receit:* recipe.
2. *preferment:* advancement.
3. *Bill:* the weekly list of deaths from the Plague.

enough, the refuse of our servants, *Bezar*[4] enough, and the off-scouring of our Kitchen tables, *Cordiall* enough. O my *soule*, when thou art not enough awake, to blesse thy *God* enough for his plentifull mercy, in affoording thee many *Helpers*, remember how many lacke them, and helpe them to them, or to those other things, which they lacke as much as them.

Et Rex ipse	*The King sends his*
suum mittit.	*owne Phisician.*

VIII. MEDITATION

Stil when we return to that *Meditation*, that *Man* is a *World*, we find new *discoveries*. Let him be a *world*, and him self will be the *land*, and *misery* the *sea*. His misery (for misery is his, his own; of the happinesses of this world hee is but *Tenant*, but of misery the *Free-holder*; of happines he is but the *farmer*, but the *usufructuary*, but of misery, the *Lord*, the *proprietary*) his misery, as the *sea*, swells above all the hilles, and reaches to the remotest parts of this *earth*, *Man*; who of himselfe is but *dust*, and coagulated and kneaded into earth, by *teares*; his *matter* is *earth*, his *forme*, *misery*. In this *world*, that is *Mankinde*, the highest ground, the eminentest *hils*, are *Kings*; and have they line, and lead enough to fadome this *sea*, and say, My misery is but this deepe? Scarce any misery equal to *sicknesse*; and they are subject to that equally, with their lowest subject. A glasse is not the lesse brittle, because a *Kings* face is represented in it; nor a King the lesse brittle, because *God* is represented in him. They have *Phisicians* continually about them, and therfore *sicknesses*, or the worst of sicknesses, continuall feare of it. Are they *gods*? He that calld them so, cannot flatter. They are *Gods*, but *sicke gods*; and *God* is presented to us under many human affections, as far as *infirmities*; *God* is called *Angry*, and *Sorry*, and *Weary*, and *Heavy*; but never a *sicke God*: for then hee might *die* like men, as our *gods* do. The

---

4. *Bezar*: a precious remedy, reputedly able to split rocks apart and to open the eyes of nestlings.

worst that they could say in reproch, and scorne of the *gods* of the *Heathen*, was, that perchance they were *asleepe;* but *Gods* that are so sicke, as that they cannot sleepe, are in an infirmer condition. A *God*, and need a *Phisician?* A *Jupiter* and need an *Æsculapius?* that must have *Rheubarbe* to purge his *choller*, lest he be too angry, and *Agarick* to purge his *flegme*, lest he be too drowsie; that as *Tertullian* saies of the *Ægyptian gods, plants* and *herbes, That God was beholden to Man, for growing in his garden,* so wee must say of these *gods, Their eternity,* (*an eternity* of three score and ten yeares) is in the *Apothecaryes* shop, and not in the *Metaphoricall Deity.* But their *Deitye* is better expressed in their *humility* than in their *heighth:* when abounding and overflowing, as *God,* in means of doing good, they descend, as *God,* to a communication of their abundances with men, according to their necessities, then they are *Gods.* No man is well, that understands not, that values not his being well; that hath not a cheerefulnesse, and a joy in it; and whosoever hath this *Joy*, hath a desire to communicate, to propagate that, which occasions his happinesse, and his *Joy*, to others; for every man loves witnesses of his happinesse; and the best witnesses, are experimentall witnesses; they who have tasted of that in themselves, which makes us happie: It consummates therefore, it perfits the happinesse of *Kings,* to confer, to transfer, honor, and riches, and (as they can) health, upon those that need them.

Medicamina scribunt.	*Upon their Consultation,* *they prescribe.*

IX. MEDITATION

They have seene me, and heard mee, arraign'd mee in these fetters, and receiv'd the *evidence;* I have cut up mine *Anatomy*, dissected my selfe, and they are gon to *read* upon me. O how manifold, and perplexed a thing, nay, how wanton and various a thing is *ruine* and *destruction!* God presented to *David* three kinds, *War, Famine,* and *Pestilence; Satan* left out these, and brought in, *fires from heaven,* and *windes from the wildernes.* [As] if there were no *ruine* but *sicknes,* wee see, the Masters of that *Art,* can scarce *number,* nor *name* all sicknesses; every thing that *disorders* a faculty, and the function of that is a sick-nesse: The names wil not serve them which are given from the *place affected,* the *Plurisie* is so; nor from the *effect* which it works, the *falling sicknes* is so; they cannot have names enow, from *what it does,* nor *where it is,* but they must extort names from what *it is like,* what it *resembles,* and but in some one thing, or els they would lack names; for the *Wolf,* and the *Canker,* and the *Polypus* are so; and that question, *whether there be more names or things,* is as perplexed in sicknesses, as in any thing else; except it be easily resolvd upon that side, that there are more *sicknesses* than *names.* If *ruine* were reduc'd to that one way, that Man could perish noway but by *sicknes,* yet his danger were infinit; and if *sicknes* were reduc'd to that one way, that there were no *sicknes* but a *fever,* yet the way were infinite still; for it would overlode, and oppress any naturall, disorder and discompose any artificiall [1] *Memory,* to deliver the *names* of severall *fevers;* how intricate a worke then have they, who are gone to *consult,* which of these *sicknesses* mine is, and then which of these *fevers,* and then what it would do, and then how it may be countermind. But even in *ill,* it is a degree of *good,* when the *evil* wil admit *consultation.* In many *diseases,* that which is but an *accident,* but a *symptom* of the main *disease,* is so violent, that the *Phisician* must attend the cure of that, though hee pretermit (so far as to intermit) the cure of the *disease* it self. Is it not so in *States* too? somtimes the insolency of those that are *great,* put[s] the people into *commotions;* the great disease, and the greatest danger to the *Head,* is the *insolency of the great ones;* and yet, they execute *Martial law,* they come to present ex-ecutions upon the *people,* whose commotion was indeed but a *symptom,* but an *accident* of the maine *disease;* but this *symptom,* grown so violent, would allow no time for a *consultation.* Is it not so in the accidents of the *diseases* of our *mind* too? Is it not evidently so in our *affections,*

1. *artificiall:* artful.

in our *passions?* If a *cholerick*[2] man be ready to strike, must I goe about to purge his *choler*, or to breake the blow? But where there is room for *consultation*, things are not desperate. They *consult;* so there is nothing *rashly, inconsideratly* done; and then they *prescribe*, they *write*, so there is nothing *covertly, disguisedly, unavowedly* done. In *bodily diseases* it is not alwaies so; sometimes, as soon as the *Phisicians* foote is in the *chamber*, his *knife* is in the patients *arme;* the disease would not allow a *minutes* forbearing of *blood*, nor *prescribing* of other remedies. In States and matter of government it is so too; they are somtimes surprizd with such *accidents*, as that the *Magistrat* asks not what may be done by *law*, but does that, which must *necessarily* be don in that case. But it is a degree of *good*, in *evill*, a degree that carries hope and comfort in it, when we may have recourse to that which is *written*, and that the proceedings may be apert, and ingenuous, and candid, and avowable, for that gives satisfaction, and acquiescence. They who have received my *Anatomy* of my selfe, *consult*, and end their *consultation* in *prescribing*, and in prescribing *Phisick;* proper and convenient remedy: for if they should come in again, and chide mee, for some disorder, that had occasion'd, and inducd, or that had hastned and exalted this *sicknes*, or if they should begin to write now rules for my *dyet*, and *exercise* when I were well, this were to *antidate*, or to *postdate* their *Consultation*, not to give *Phisicke*. It were rather a vexation, than a reliefe, to tell a condemnd prisoner, you might have liv'd if you had done this; and if you can get pardon, you shal do wel, to take this, or this course hereafter. I am glad they know (I have hid nothing from them) glad they consult, (they hide nothing from one another) glad they write (they hide nothing from the world) glad that they write and prescribe *Phisick*, that there are *remedies* for the present case.

2. *cholerick:* suffering from an excess of the humour called choler; hence, wrathful.

Lentè et Serpenti
satagunt occurrere
Morbo.

*They find the Disease to steale
on insensibly, and endeavour to
meet with it so.*

X. MEDITATION

This is *Natures nest of Boxes;* The Heavens containe the
Earth, the *Earth, Cities, Cities, Man.* And all these are
Concentrique; the common *center* to them all, is *decay,
ruine;* only that is *Eccentrique,* which was never made;
only that place, or garment rather, which we can *imagine,* but not *demonstrate,* That light, which is the very
emanation of the light of *God,* in which the *Saints* shall
dwell, with which the *Saints* shall be appareld, only that
bends not to this *Center,* to *Ruine;* that which was not
made of *Nothing,* is not threatned with this annihilation.
All other things are; even *Angels,* even our *soules;* they
move upon the same *poles,* they bend to the same *Center;*
and if they were not made immortall by *preservation,*
their *Nature* could not keep them from sinking to this
center, Annihilation. In all these (the *frame of the heavens,*
the *States upon earth,* and *Men in them,* comprehend all).
Those are the greatest mischifs, which are least discerned;
the most insensible in their *wayes* come to bee the most
sensible in their *ends.* The *Heavens* have had their *Dropsie,*
they drownd the world, and they shall have their *Fever,*
and burn the world. Of the *dropsie,* the flood, the world
had a foreknowledge 120 yeares before it came; and so
some made provision against it, and were saved; the *fever*
shall break out in an instant, and consume all; The *dropsie*
did no harm to the *heavens,* from whence it fell, it did not
put out those *lights,* it did not quench those *heates;* but the
fever, the fire shall burne the *furnace* it selfe, annihilate
those *heavens,* that breath it out; Though the *Dog-Starre*
have a pestilent breath, an infectious exhalation, yet because we know when it wil rise, we clothe our selves,
and wee diet our selves, and we shadow our selves to a
sufficient prevention; but *Comets* and *blazing starres,*[1]
whose effects, or significations no man can interrupt or

1. *blazing starres:* regarded as omens of disaster.

frustrat, no man foresaw: no *Almanack* tells us, when a *blazing starre* will break out, the matter is carried up in secret; no *Astrologer* tels us when the effects will be accomplished, for thats a secret of a higher spheare, than the other; and that which is most *secret*, is most *dangerous*. It is so also here in the *societies* of men, in *States*, and *Commonwealths*. Twentie *rebellious drums* make not so dangerous a noise, as a few *whisperers*, and secret plotters in corners. The *Canon* doth not so much hurt against a wal, as a *Myne* under the wall; nor a thousand enemies that threaten, so much as a few that take an *oath* to say *nothing*. *God* knew many heavy sins of the people, in the wildernes and after, but still he charges them with that one, with *Murmuring, murmuring* in their *hearts*, secret disobediences, secret repugnances against his declar'd wil; and these are the most deadly, the most pernicious. And it is so too, with the *diseases* of the *body;* and that is my case. The *pulse*, the *urine*, the *sweat*, all have sworn to say nothing, to give no *Indication*, of any dangerous *sicknesse*. My forces are not enfeebled, I find no decay in my strength; my provisions are not cut off, I find no abhorring in mine appetite; my counsels are not corrupted or infatuated, I find no false apprehensions, to work upon mine understanding; and yet they see, that invisibly, and I feele, that insensibly the *disease* prevailes. The *disease* hath established a *Kingdome*, an *Empire* in mee, and will have certaine *Arcana Imperii, secrets of State*, by which it will proceed, and not be bound to *declare* them. But yet against those secret conspiracies in the State, the *Magistrate* hath the *rack;* and against the insensible diseases, *Phisicians* have their *examiners;* and those these employ now.

Nobilibusque trahunt, a cincto
Corde, venenum, Succis et
Gemmis, et quæ generosa,
Ministrant Ars, et Natura,
instillant.

*They use Cordials, to
keep the venim and Ma-
lignitie of the disease
from the Heart.*

XI. MEDITATION

Whence can wee take a better argument, a clearer demonstration, that all the *Greatnes* of this world, is built upon
opinion of others, and hath in itself no *reall being*, nor
power of subsistence, than from the *heart of man?* It is
always in *action*, and *motion*, still busie, still pretending
to doe all, to furnish all the powers, and faculties with all
that they have; But if an enemy dare rise up against it, it
is the soonest endangered, the soonest defeated of any
part. The *Braine* will hold out longer than it, and the *Liver*
longer than that; They will endure a *Seige;* but an unnatural heat, a rebellious heat, will blow up the *heart*, like
a *Myne*, in a *minute.* But howsoever, since the *Heart* hath
the *birthright* and *Primogeniture*, and that it is *Natures
eldest Sonne* in us, the part which is first borne to life in
man, and that the other parts, as *younger brethren*, and
servants in this family, have a dependance upon it, it is
reason that the principall care bee had of it, though it
bee not the strongest part; as the *eldest* is oftentimes not
the strongest of the family. And since the *Braine*, and
Liver, and *Heart*, hold not a *Triumvirate* in *Man*, a *Soveraigntie* equally shed upon them all, for his *well-being*,
as the foure *Elements* doe, for his very *being*, but the
Heart alone is in the *Principalitie*, and in the *Throne*, as
King, the rest as *Subjects*, though in eminent *Place* and
Office, must contribute to that, as *Children* to their *Parents*, as all persons to all kinds of *Superiours*, though oftentimes, those *Parents*, or those *Superiours*, bee not of
stronger parts, than them selves, that serve and obey them
that are weaker; Neither doth this Obligation fall upon us,
by second *Dictates* of *Nature*, by *Consequences* and *Conclusions* arising out of *Nature*, or deriv'd from *Nature*, by
Discourse, (as many things binde us even by the Law of

Nature, and yet not by the *primarie* Law of *Nature;* as all Lawes of *Proprietie* in that which we possesse, are of the Law of *Nature,* which law is, *To give every one his owne,* and yet in the *primarie* law of Nature there was no *Proprietie,* no *Meum* and *Tuum,*[1] but an universall *Communitie* over all; So the Obedience of *Superiours,* is of the law of *Nature,* and yet in the *primarie* law of *Nature,* there was no *Superioritie,* no *Magistracie;*) but this contribution of assistance of all to the *Soveraigne,* of all parts to the *Heart,* is from the very *first dictates of Nature;* which is, in the first place, to have care of our owne *Preservation,* to look first to ourselves; for therefore doth the *Phisician* intermit the present care of *Braine,* or *Liver,* because there is a possibilitie that they may subsist, though there bee not a present and a particular care had of them, but there is no possibilitie that they can subsist, if the *Heart* perish: and so, when wee seem to begin with others, in such assistances, indeed wee doe beginne with ourselves, and wee ourselves are principally in our contemplation; and so all these officious, and mutual assistances are but *complements* towards others, and our true end is *ourselves.* And this is the reward of the paines of *Kings;* sometimes they neede the power of law, to be obey'd; and when they seeme to be obey'd *voluntarily,* they who doe it, doe it for their owne sakes. O how little a thing is all the *greatnes of man,* and through how false glasses doth he make shift to *multiply it,* and *magnifie* it to himselfe! And yet this is also another misery of this *King of man,* the *Heart,* which is also applyable to the *Kings of this world, great men,* that the venime and poyson of every pestilentiall disease directs itself to the *Heart,* affects that (pernicious affection,) and the *malignity* of ill men, is also directed upon the *greatest,* and the *best;* and not only *greatnesse,* but *goodnesse* looses the vigour of beeing an *Antidote,* or *Cordiall* against it. And as the noblest, and most generous *Cordialls* that *Nature* or *Art* afford, or can prepare, if they be often taken, and made *familiar,* become no *Cordialls,* nor have any extraordinary operation, so the greatest *Cordiall* of the *Heart,* patience, if it bee much exercis'd, exalts the *venim* and the *malignity* of the *Enemy,* and the

1. *Meum and Tuum:* mine and yours.

more we suffer, the more wee are insulted upon. When
God had made this *Earth* of *nothing*, it was but a little
helpe, that he had, to make other things of this *Earth:*
nothing can be neerer nothing, than this *Earth;* and yet
how little of this *Earth* is the *greatest Man!* Hee thinkes
he treads upon the *Earth*, that all is under his feete, and
the *Braine* that thinkes so, is but *Earth;* his highest Region,
the flesh that covers that, is but *earth;* and even the toppe
of that, that, wherein so many *Absolons* take so much
pride, is but a bush growing upon that *Turfe of Earth.*
How litle of the world is the *Earth!* And yet that is all
that *Man hath*, or *is.* How little of a *Man* is the *Heart*, and
yet it is all, by which he *is;* and this continually subject,
not only to forraine poysons, conveyed by others, but to
intestine poysons, bred in ourselves by pestilentiall sicknesses. O who, if before hee had a beeing, he could have
sense of this miserie, would buy a being here upon these
conditions?

Spirante Columbâ
Suppositâ pedibus, Revocantur
ad ima vapores.

*They apply Pidgeons, to
draw the vapors from the
Head.*

XII. MEDITATION

What will not kill a man if a *vapor* will? How great an
Elephant, how small a *Mouse* destroys! To dye by a *bullet*
is the *Souldiers dayly bread;* but few men dye by *haile-
shot:* A man is more worth, than to bee sold for *single
money;* a *life* to be valued above a *trifle.* If this were a
violent shaking of the Ayre by *Thunder*, or by *Canon*,
in that case the *Ayre* is condensed above the thicknesse
of *water*, of *water* baked into *Ice*, almost *petrified*, almost
made stone, and no wonder that kills; but that that which
is but a *vapor*, and a *vapor* not forced, but breathed, should
kill, that our *Nourse* should overlay us, and *Ayre* that
nourishes us, should destroy us, but that it is a *halfe Atheisme* to murmure against *Nature*, who is *Gods immediate
commissioner*, who would not think himselfe miserable
to bee put into the hands of *Nature*, who does not only set
him up for a *marke* for others to shoote at, but delights

herselfe to blow him up like a glasse, till shee see him breake, even with her owne breath? nay, if this infectious *vapor* were sought for, or travail'd to, as *Plinie* hunted after the *vapor* of *Ætna*, and dared and challenged *Death*, in the forme of a vapor, to doe his worst, and felt the worst, he dyed; or if this *vapor* were met withall in an *ambush*, and we surprised with it, out of a long shutt *Well*, or out of a new opened *Myne*, who would lament, who would accuse, when we had nothing to accuse, none to lament against but *Fortune*, who is lesse than a *vapor:* But when our selves are the *Well*, that breaths out this exhalation, the *Oven* that spits out this fiery smoke, the *Myne* that spues out this suffocating, and strangling *dampe*, who can ever after this, aggravate his sorrow, by this *Circumstance*, That it was his *Neighbor*, his *familiar Friend*, his *Brother*, that destroyed him, and destroyed him with a whispering, and a calumniating breath, when wee our selves doe it to our selves by the same meanes, kill our selves with our owne *vapors?* Or if these occasions of this selfe-destruction, had any contribution from our owne *Wils*, any assistance from our owne *intentions*, nay from our own *errors*, we might divide the rebuke, and chide our selves as much as them. *Fevers* upon wilful distempers of drinke, and surfets, *Consumptions* upon intemperances, and licentiousnes, *Madnes* upon misplacing, or overbending our naturall faculties, proceed from our selves, and so, as that our selves are in the plot, and wee are not onely *passive*, but *active* too, to our owne destruction; But what have I done, either to *breed*, or to *breath* these *vapors?* They tell me it is my *Melancholy;* Did I infuse, did I drinke in *Melancholly* into my selfe? It is my *thoughtfulnesse;* was I not made to *thinke?* It is my *study;* doth not my *Calling*[1] call for that? I have don nothing, wilfully, perversly toward it, yet must suffer in it, die by it; There are too many *Examples* of men, that have bin their own *executioners*, and that have made hard shift to bee so; some have alwayes had *poyson* about them, in a *hollow ring* upon their finger, and some in their *Pen* that they used to write with: some have beat out their *braines* at the wal of their prison, and some have eate the *fire* out of their chimneys: and one is said to have come

1. *Calling:* the ministry.

neerer our case than so, to have strangled himself, though his hands were bound, by crushing his throat between his knees; But I doe nothing upon my selfe, and yet am mine owne *Executioner*. And we have heard of *death* upon small occasions, and by scornefull *instruments*: a *pinne*, a *combe*, a *haire*, pulled, hath gangred,[2] and killd; But when I have said, a *vapour*, if I were asked again, what is a *vapour*, I could not tell, it is so insensible a thing; so neere *nothing* is that that reduces us to *nothing*. But extend this *vapour*, rarefie it; from so narow a roome, as our *Naturall bodies*, to any *Politike body*, to a *State*. That which is *fume* in us, is in a State, *Rumor*, and these *vapours* in us, which wee consider here pestilent and infectious fumes, are in a State *infectious rumors*, detracting and dishonourable *Calumnies*, *Libels*. The *Heart* in that *body* is the *King;* and the *Braine*, his *Councell;* and the whole *Magistracie*, that ties all together, is the *Sinewes*, which proceed from thence; and the *life* of all is *Honour*, and just *respect*, and due *reverence;* and therfore, when these *vapors*, these venimous *rumors*, are directed against these *Noble parts*, the whole body suffers. But yet for all their priviledges, they are not priviledged from our *misery;* that as the *vapours* most pernitious to us, arise in our owne bodies, so do the most dishonorable *rumours*, and those that wound a *State* most, arise at home. What ill *ayre*, that I could have met in the street, what *Channell*,[3] what *Shambles*, what *Dunghill*, what *vault*, could have hurt mee so much, as these homebredd *vapours?* What *Fugitive*, what *Almesman of any forraine State*, can doe so much harme as a *Detracter*, a *Libeller*, a scornefull *Jester* at home? For, as they that write of *poysons*, and of creatures naturally disposed to the ruine of Man, do as well mention the *Flea*, as the *Viper*, because the *Flea*, though hee kill none, hee does all the harme hee can; so even these libellous and licentious *Jesters* utter the venim they have, though sometimes *vertue*, and alwaies *power*, be a good *Pigeon* to draw this *vapor* from the *Head*, and from doing any deadly harme there.

2. *gangred:* gangrened.
3. *Channell:* sewer.

Ingeniumque malum, nu-
 meroso stigmate, fassus
Pellitur ad pectus, Mor-
 bique Suburbia, Morbus.

The Sicknes declares the infection and malignity thereof by spots.

XIII. MEDITATION

Wee say, that the world is made of *sea,* and *land,* as though they were equall; but we know that ther is more *sea* in the *Western,* than in the *Eastern Hemisphere:* We say that the *Firmament* is full of *starres,* as though it were equally full; but we know, that there are more *stars* under the *Northerne,* than under the *Southern Pole.* We say, the *Elements* of man are *misery,* and *happinesse,* as though he had an equal proportion of both, and the dayes of man vicissitudinary, as though he had as many *good* daies, as *ill,* and that he liv'd under a perpetuall *Equinoctiall night,* and *day* equall, good and ill fortune in the same measure. But it is far from that; hee *drinkes misery,* and he *tastes happinesse;* he *mowes misery,* and he *gleanes happinesse;* he *journies in misery,* he does but *walke in happinesse;* and which is worst, his misery is *positive,* and *dogmaticall,* his happinesse is but *disputable,* and *problematicall;* All men call *Misery, Misery,* but *Happinesse* changes the name, by the taste of man. In this *accident* that befalls mee now, that this sicknesse declares itself by *Spots,* to be a malignant, and pestilentiall disease, if there be a *comfort* in the declaration, that therby the *Phisicians* see more cleerely what to doe, there may bee as much *discomfort* in this, That the malignitie may bee so great, as that all that they can doe, shall doe *nothing;* That an enemy *declares* himselfe, then, when he is able to subsist, and to pursue, and to atchive his ends, is no great comfort. In intestine Conspiracies, *voluntary Confessions* doe more good, than Confessions upon the *Rack;* in these Infections, when *Nature* her selfe confesses, and cries out by these outward declarations, which she is able to put forth of her selfe, they minister *comfort;* but when all is by strength of *Cordials,* it is but a *Confession upon the Racke,* by which though

wee come to knowe the malice of that man, yet wee doe
not knowe whether there bee not as much malice in his
heart then, as before his confession; we are sure of his
Treason, but not of his *Repentance;* sure of *him,* but not of
his *Complices.* It is a faint comfort to know the worst,
when the worst is *remedilesse;* and a weaker than that, to
know *much ill,* and not to know, that that is the worst.
A woman is comforted with the birth of her *Son,* her
body is eased of a burthen; but if shee could *prophetically*
read his *History,* how *ill a man,* perchance how *ill a sonne,*
he would prove, shee should receive a greater burthen into
her *Mind.* Scarce any purchase that is not clogged with
secret *encumbrances;* scarce any *happines* that hath not in
it so much of the *nature* of false and base money, as that
the *Allay*[1] is more than the *Metall.* Nay, is it not so, (at
least much towards it) even in the exercise of *Vertues?* I
must bee poore, and want, before I can exercise the vertue
of *Gratitude;* miserable, and in torment, before I can exercise the vertue of *patience;* How deepe do we dig, and for
how coarse gold? And what other *Touchstone* have we
of our *gold,* but *comparison?* Whether we be as happy,
as others, or as ourselves at other times; O poore stepp
toward being well, when these *spots* do only tell us, that
we are worse, than we were sure of before.

Idque notant Criticis, Me-	*The Phisicians observe*
dici evenisse Diebus.	*these accidents to have*
	fallen upon the criticall
	dayes.

XIV. MEDITATION

I would not make *Man* worse than hee is, Nor his Condition more miserable than it is. But could I though I would?
As a man cannot *flatter God,* nor over prayse him, so a
man cannot *injure* Man, nor undervalue him. Thus much
must necessarily be presented to his remembrance, that
those *false Happinesses,* which he hath in this World,
have their *times,* and their *seasons,* and their *critical dayes,*

1. *Allay:* alloy.

and they are *Judged,* and *Denominated* according to the times, when they befall us. What poore *Elements* are our *happinesses* made of, if *Tyme, Tyme* which wee can scarce consider to be *any thing,* be an esssential part of our happines! All things are done in some *place;* but if we consider *Place* to be no more, but the next hollow *Superficies* of the *Ayre, Alas,* how thinne, and fluid a thing is *Ayre,* and how thinne a *filme* is a *Superficies,* and a *Superficies* of *Ayre!* All things are done in *time* too; but if we consider *Tyme* to be but the *Measure of Motion,* and howsoever it may seeme to have three *stations, past, present,* and *future,* yet the *first* and *last* of these *are* not (one is not, now, and the other is not yet) and that which you call *present,* is not *now* the same that it was, when you began to call it so in this *Line,* (before you sound that word, *present,* or that *Monosyllable, now,* the present, and the *Now* is past), if this *Imaginary halfe-nothing, Tyme,* be of the Essence of our *Happinesses,* how can they be thought *durable? Tyme* is not so; How can they bee thought to be? *Tyme* is not so; not so, considered in any of the *parts* thereof. If we consider *Eternity,* into that, *Tyme* never entred; *Eternity* is not an everlasting flux of *Tyme;* but *Tyme* is a short *parenthesis* in a longe *period;* and *Eternity* had been the same, as it is, though time had never beene; If we consider, not *Eternity,* but *Perpetuity,* not that which had no *Tyme* to beginne in, but which shall outlive *Tyme* and be, when *Tyme shall bee no more,* what *A Minute* is the life of the Durablest *Creature,* compared to that! And what a Minute is Mans life in respect of the *Sunnes,* or of a Tree! and yet how little of our *life* is *Occasion, opportunity* to receyve good in; and how litle of that *occasion,* doe wee apprehend, and lay hold of! How busie and perplexed a *Cobweb,* is the *Happinesse* of Man here, that must bee made up with a *Watchfulnesse,* to lay hold upon *Occasion,* which is but a little peece of that, which is *Nothing, Tyme!* And yet the best things are *Nothing* without that. *Honors, Pleasures, Possessions,* presented to us, out of time, in our decrepit, and distasted, and unapprehensive *Age,* loose their *Office,* and loose their *Name;* They are not *Honors* to us, that shall never appeare, nor come abroad into the Eyes of the people, to receive *Honor,* from them who give it: Nor *pleasures* to us, who have lost our sense to taste them; nor

possessions to us, who are departing from the possession
of them. Youth is their *Criticall Day;* that *Judges* them,
that *Denominates* them, that *inanimates,* and *informes*
them, and makes them *Honors,* and *Pleasures,* and *Possessions;* and when they come in an unapprehensive *Age,*
they come as a *Cordial* when the bell rings out,[1] as a
Pardon, when the Head is off. We rejoyce in the Comfort
of *fire,* but does any man cleave to it at *Midsomer;* Wee
are glad of the freshnesse, and coolenes of a *Vault,* but
does any man keepe his *Christmas* there; or are the pleasures of the *Spring* acceptable in *Autumne?* If happinesse
be in the *season,* or in the *Clymate,* how much happier
then are *Birdes* than *Men,* who can change the *Climate,*
and accompanie, and enjoy the same season ever.

Intereà insomnes noctes Ego   *I sleepe not day*
   duco, Diesque.   *nor night.*

XV. MEDITATION

Naturall men have conceived a twofold use of *sleepe;* That
it is a *refreshing* of the body in this life; That it is a *pre-
paring* of the *soule* for the next; That it is a *feast,* and it is
the *grace* at that *feast;* That it is our *recreation,* and cheeres
us, and it is our *Catechisme* and instructs us; wee lie downe
in a hope, that wee shall rise the stronger; and we lie
downe in a knowledge, that wee may rise no more. *Sleepe*
is an *Opiate* which gives us *rest,* but such an *Opiate,* as
perchance, being under it, we shall wake no more. But
though naturall men, who have induced secondary and
figurative considerations, have found out this second, this
emblematicall use of *sleepe,* that it should be a *representation of death, God,* who wrought and perfected his worke,
before *Nature* began, (for *Nature* was but his *Apprentice,*
to learne in the first *seven daies,* and now is his *foreman,*
and works next under him) *God,* I say, intended *sleepe*
onely for the *refreshing* of man by bodily rest, and not
for a *figure of death,* for he intended not *death* it selfe then.

1. *when . . . out:* when it tolls for one's death.

But *Man* having induced *death* upon himselfe, *God* hath taken *Mans Creature, death,* into his hand, and mended it; and whereas it hath in itselfe a fearefull forme and aspect, so that Man is afraid of his own *Creature, God* presents it to him, in a *familiar,* in an *assiduous,*[1] in an *agreeable* and *acceptable* forme, in *sleepe,* that so when hee awakes from *sleepe,* and saies to himselfe, shall I bee no otherwise when I am dead, than I was even now, when I was asleep, hee may bee ashamed of his waking *dreames,* and of his *Melancholique* fancying out a horrid and an affrightfull figure of that *death* which is so like sleepe. As then wee need *sleepe* to live out our *threescore and ten yeeres,* so we need *death,* to live that *life* which we cannot *out-live.* And as *death* being our *enemie, God* allowes us to defend ourselves against it (for wee *victuall* ourselves against *death, twice* every day, as often as we *eat*) so *God* having so sweetned *death* unto us as hee hath in *sleepe,* wee put ourselves into our *enemies* hands *once* every day; so farre, as *sleepe* is *death;* and *sleepe* is as much *death,* as *meat* is *life.* This then is the *misery* of my *sicknesse,* That death as it is produced from mee, and is mine owne *Creature,* is now before mine *Eyes,* but in that forme, in which *God* hath mollified it to us, and made it acceptable, in *sleepe,* I cannot see it: how many *prisoners,* who have even hollowed themselves their *graves* upon that *Earth,* on which they have lien long under heavie fetters, yet at this *houre* are *asleepe,* though they bee yet working upon their owne *graves* by their owne *waight!* Hee that hath seene his *friend* die to *day,* or knowes hee shall see it to *morrow,* yet will sinke into a sleepe betweene. I cannot; and oh, if I be entring now into *Eternitie,* where there shall bee no more distinction of *houres,* why is it al my businesse now *to tell Clocks?*[2] why is none of the heavinesse of my *heart,* dispensed into mine *Eye-lids,* that they might fall as my heart doth? And why, since I have lost my delight in all objects, cannot I discontinue the facultie of seeing them, by closing mine *eyes* in *sleepe?* But why rather being entring into that presence, where I shall

1. *assiduous:* desirous of pleasing.
2. *to . . . Clocks:* to count the striking of the hours.

wake continually and never sleepe more, doe I not interpret my continuall waking here, to bee a *parasceve*,[3] and a *preparation* to that?

Et properare meum clamant, è Turre propinqua, Obstreperæ Campanæ aliorum in funere, funus.	*From the Bells of the Church adjoyning, I am daily remembred of my buriall in the funeralls of others.*

XVI. MEDITATION

We have a *Convenient Author*, who writ a *Discourse of Bells*, when hee was prisoner in *Turky*. How would hee have enlarged himselfe if he had beene my *fellow-prisoner* in this *sicke bed*, so neere to that *Steeple*, which never ceases, no more than the *harmony of the spheres*, but is more heard. When the *Turkes* took *Constantinople*, they melted the *Bells* into *Ordnance;* I have heard both *Bells* and *Ordnance*, but never been so much affected with those, as with these *Bells*. I have *lien* near a *Steeple*, in which there are said to be more than *thirty Bels;* And neere another, where there is one so bigge, as that the *Clapper* is said to weigh more than *six hundred pound*, yet never so affected as here. Here the *Bells* can scarse solemnise the funerall of any person, but that I knew him, or knew that he was my *Neighbour:* we dwelt in houses neere to one another before, but now hee is gone into that house, into which I must follow him. There is a way of correcting the *Children* of great persons, that other *Children* are corrected in their *behalfe*, and in their names, and this workes upon them, who indeed had more deserved it. And when these *Bells* tell me, that now one, and now another is buried, must not I acknowledge, that they have the *correction* due to me, and paid the *debt* that I owe? There is a story of a *Bell* in a *Monastery* which, when any of the house was sicke to death, rung alwaies *voluntarily*, and they knew the inevitablenesse of the danger by that. It rung once, when no man was sicke; but the next day one of the house, fell

3. *parasceve:* preparation.

from the *steeple*, and died, and the *Bell* held the reputation
of a *Prophet* still. If these *Bells* that warne to a *Funerall*
now, were appropriated to none, may not I, by the houre
of the *Funerall*, supply? How many men that stand at an
execution, if they would aske, for what dies that man,
should heare their owne faults condemned, and see themselves executed, by *Atturney?* We scarce heare of any
man *preferred*,[1] but wee thinke of our selves, that wee
might very well have beene that *Man;* Why might not I
have beene that *Man*, that is carried to his *grave* now?
Could I fit my selfe, to *stand*, or *sit* in any mans *place*,
and not to lie in any mans *grave?* I may lacke much of the
good parts of the meanest, but I lacke nothing of the
mortality of the weakest; They may have acquired better
abilities than I, but I was borne to as many *infirmities* as
they. To be an *Incumbent* by lying down in a *grave*, to be
a *Doctor* by teaching *Mortification* by *Example*, by *dying*,
though I may have *seniors*, others may be *elder* than I,
yet I have proceeded apace in a good *University*, and gone
a great way in a little time, by the furtherance of a vehement *Fever;* and whomsoever these *Bells* bring to the
ground to day, if hee and I had beene compared yesterday,
perchance I should have been thought likelier to come to
this preferment, then, than he. *God* hath kept the power
of *death* in his owne hands, lest any man should *bribe
death.* If man knew the *gaine of death*, the *ease of death*,
he would solicite, he would provoke *death* to assist him,
by any hand, which he might use. But as when men see
many of their owne professions preferd, it ministers a
hope that that may light upon them; so when these hourely
Bells tell me of so many *funerals* of men like me, it presents,
if not a *desire* that it may, yet a *comfort* whensoever mine
shall come.

1. *preferred:* promoted.

Nunc lento sonitu dicunt,	*Now, this Bell tolling softly*
Morieris.	*for another, saies to me,*
	Thou must die.

XVII. MEDITATION

Perchance hee for whom this *Bell* tolls, may be so ill, as that he knowes not it tolls for him; And perchance I may thinke my selfe so much better than I am, as that they who are about mee, and see my state, may have caused it to toll for mee, and I know not that. The *Church* is *Catholike, universall,* so are all her *Actions; All* that she does, belongs to *all.* When she *baptizes a child,* that action concernes mee; for that child is thereby connected to that *Head* which is my *Head* too, and engraffed into that *body,* whereof I am a *member.* And when she *buries* a *Man,* that action concernes me: All *mankinde* is of one *Author,* and is one *volume;* when one Man dies, one *Chapter* is not *torne* out of the *booke,* but *translated* into a better *language;* and every *Chapter* must be so *translated;* God emploies several *translators;* some peeces are translated by *age,* some by *sicknesse,* some by *warre,* some by *justice;* but *Gods* hand is in every *translation;* and his hand shall binde up all our scattered leaves againe, for that *Librarie* where every *booke* shall lie open to one another: As therefore the *Bell* that rings to a *Sermon,* calls not upon the *Preacher* onely, but upon the *Congregation* to come; so this *Bell* calls us all: but how much more mee, who am brought so neere the *doore* by this *sicknesse.* There was a *contention* as farre as a *suite,* (in which both *pietie* and *dignitie, religion,* and *estimation,*[1] were mingled) which of the religious *Orders* should ring to *praiers* first in the *Morning;* and it was *determined,* that *they should ring first that rose earliest.* If we understand aright the *dignitie* of this *Bell* that tolls for our *evening prayer,* wee would bee glad to make it ours, by rising early, in that *application,* that it might bee ours, as wel as his, whose indeed it is. The *Bell* doth toll for him that *thinkes* it doth; and though it *intermit* againe, yet from that *minute* that that occasion

1. *estimation:* prestige.

wrought upon him, hee is united to *God*. Who casts not up his *Eye* to the *Sunne* when it rises? but who takes off his *Eye* from a *Comet* when that breakes out? Who bends not his *eare* to any *bell*, which upon any occasion rings? but who can remove it from that *bell*, which is passing a *peece of himselfe* out of this *world*? No man is an *Iland*, intire of it selfe; every man is a peece of the *Continent*, a part of the *maine*; if a *Clod* bee washed away by the *Sea*, *Europe* is the lesse, as well as if a *Promontorie* were, as well as if a *Mannor* of thy *friends* or of *thine owne* were; any mans *death* diminishes *me*, because I am involved in *Mankinde*; And therefore never send to know for whom the *bell* tolls; It tolls for *thee*. Neither can we call this a *begging* of *Miserie* or a *borrowing* of *Miserie*, as though we were not miserable enough of our selves, but must fetch in more from the next house, in taking upon us the *Miserie* of our *Neighbours*. Truly it were an excusable *covetous-nesse* if wee did; for *affliction* is a *treasure*, and scarce any man hath *enough* of it. No man hath *affliction* enough that is not matured, and ripened by it, and made fit for *God* by that *affliction*. If a man carry *treasure* in *bullion*, or in a *wedge* of *gold*, and have none coined into *currant Monies*, his *treasure* will not defray him as he travells. *Tribulation* is *Treasure* in the *nature* of it, but it is not *currant money* in the *use* of it, except wee get nearer and nearer our *home*, *Heaven*, by it. Another man may be sicke too, and sick to *death*, and this *affliction* may lie in his *bowels*, as *gold* in a *Mine*, and be of no use to him; but this *bell*, that tells me of his *affliction*, digs out, and applies that *gold* to *mee*; if by this consideration of anothers danger, I take mine owne into contemplation, and so secure my selfe, by making my recourse to my *God*, who is our onely securitie.

At inde	*The Bell rings out, and tells*
Mortuus es, Sonitu celeri,	*me in him, that I am dead.*
pulsuque agitato.	

XVIII. MEDITATION

The *Bell* rings out; the *pulse* thereof is changed; the *tolling* was a *faint,* and *intermitting pulse,* upon one side; this *stronger,* and argues *more* and *better life.* His *soule* is gone out; and as a Man, who had a lease of 1000. *yeeres* after the expiration of a short one, or an inheritance after the *life* of a man in a *consumption,* he is now entred into the possession of his *better estate.* His *soule* is gone; *whither?* Who saw it *come in,* or who saw it *goe out? No body;* yet every body is sure, he *had one,* and *hath none.* If I will aske meere[1] *Philosophers,* what the *soule* is, I shall finde amongst them, that will tell me, it is nothing, but the *temperament* and *harmony,* and *just and equall composition of the Elements in the body,* which produces all those *faculties* which we ascribe to the *soule;* and so, in it selfe is *nothing,* no *seperable substance,* that overlives the *body.* They see the *soule* is nothing else in other *Creatures,* and they affect an *impious humilitie,* to think *as low* of Man. But if my *soule* were no more than the soul of a *beast,* I could not thinke so; that *soule* that can *reflect* upon it selfe, *consider* it selfe, is *more* than so. If I will aske, not meere *Philosophers,* but *mixt men, Philosophicall Divines, how* the *soule,* being a *separate substance,* enters into *Man,* I shall finde some that will tell me, that it is by *generation,* and *procreation* from *parents,* because they thinke it hard, to charge the *soule* with the guiltiness of *originall* sinne, if the *soule* were infused into a *body,* in which it must necessarily grow *foule,* and contract *originall sinne,* whether it *will* or *no;* and I shall finde some that will tell mee, that it is by *immediate infusion from God,* because they think it hard, to *maintaine* an *immortality* in such a *soule,* as should be begotten, and derived with the *body* from *mortall parents.* If I will aske, not a *few men,* but almost *whole bodies, whole Churches,* what becomes of

1. *meere:* simple, unmodified.

the *soules* of the *righteous,* at the *departing* thereof from the *body,* I shall bee told by some, *That they attend an expiation, a purification in a place of torment;* By some, that *they attend the fruition of the sight of God, in a place of rest; but yet, but of expectation;* By some, *that they passe to an immediate possession of the presence of God.* S. *Augustine* studied the *nature* of the *soule,* as much as anything, but the *salvation of the soule;* and he sent an expresse *Messenger* to Saint *Hierome,*[2] to consult of some things concerning the *soule:* But he satisfies himselfe with this: *Let the departure of my soule to salvation be evident to my faith, and I care the lesse, how darke the entrance of my soule, into my body, bee to my reason.* It is the *going out,* more than the *comming in,* that concernes us. This *soule,* this Bell tells me, is *gone out; Whither?* Who shall tell mee that? I know not *who it is;* much less *what he was;* The condition of the man, and the course of his life, which should tell mee *whither* hee is gone, I know not. I was not there in his *sicknesse,* nor at his *death;* I saw not his *way,* nor his *end,* nor can aske them, who did, thereby to *conclude,* or *argue,* whither he is gone. But yet I have one neerer mee than all these; mine owne *Charity;* I aske that; and that tels me, *He is gone to everlasting rest,* and *joy,* and *glory:* I owe him a good *opinion;* it is but *thankfull charity* in mee, because I received *benefit* and *instruction* from him when his *Bell* told: and I, being made the fitter to *pray,* by that disposition, wherein I was assisted by his occasion, did *pray* for him; and I *pray* not without *faith;* so I doe *charitably,* so I do *faithfully* beleeve, that that *soule* is gone to everlasting *rest,* and *joy,* and *glory.* But for the *body,* how poore a wretched thing is *that?* wee cannot expresse it *so fast,* as it growes *worse* and *worse.* That *body* which scarce *three minutes* since was such a *house,* as that that *soule,* which made but one step from thence to *Heaven,* was scarse thorowly content, to leave that for *Heaven:* that *body* hath lost the *name* of a *dwelling house,* because none dwells in it, and is making haste to lose the name of a *body,* and dissolve to *putrefaction.* Who would not bee affected, to see a cleere and sweet *River* in the *Morning,* grow a *ken-*

2. *Saint Hierome:* St. Jerome.

nell [3] of muddy land water by *noone*, and condemned to the saltnesse of the *Sea* by *night?* And how lame a *picture*, how faint a *representation* is that, of the precipitation of mans body to *dissolution! Now* all the parts built up, and knit by a lovely *soule*, *now* but a *statue* of *clay*, and *now*, these limbs melted off, as if that *clay* were but *snow;* and now, the whole *house* is but a *handfull* of *sand*, so much *dust*, and but a *pecke* of *rubbidge*,[4] so much *bone*. If *he*, who, as this *Bell* tells mee, is gone now, were some *excellent Artificer*, who comes to him for a *clocke*, or for a *garment* now? or for *counsaile*, if hee were a *Lawyer?* If a *Magistrate*, for *Justice?* Man, before hee hath his *immortall soule*, hath a *soule* of *sense*, and a *soule* of *vegitation* before that: [5] This *immortall soule* did not forbid other *soules*, to be in us before, but when this *soule* departs, it carries all with it; no more *vegetation*, no more *sense:* such a *Mother in law* is the *Earth*, in respect of our *naturall mother;* in her *wombe* we *grew;* and when she was delivered of us, wee were planted in some *place*, in some *calling* in the *world;* In the wombe of the *earth*, wee *diminish*, and when shee is *deliverd* of us, our *grave opened* for another, wee are not *transplanted*, but *transported*, our *dust* blowne away with *prophane dust*, with *every wind*.

3. *kennell:* gutter.
4. *rubbidge:* rubbish.
5. *immortall . . . that:* The reference is to the supposed three souls—vegetative, sensitive, and rational—of which plants possess the first, animals the first and second, human beings all three.

Oceano tandem emenso, as-
picienda resurgit
Terra; vident, justis, me-
dici, jam cocta mederi se
posse, indiciis.

*At last, the Physitians, after
a long and stormie voyage,
see land; They have so good
signes of the concoction[1] of
the disease, as that they may
safely proceed to purge.*

XIX. MEDITATION

All this while the *Physitians* themselves have beene *patients*, patiently attending when they should see any *land*
in this *Sea*, any *earth*, any *cloud*, any *indication* of *concoction* in these waters. Any *disorder* of mine, any *preter-
mission* of theirs, exalts the disease, accelerates the rages
of it; no *diligence* accelerates the *concoction*, the *ma-
turitie* of the *disease;* they must stay till the *season* of the
sicknesse come, and till it be ripened of it selfe, and then
they may put to their hand, to *gather* it before it *fall* off,
but they cannot hasten the *ripening*. Why should wee
looke for it in a *disease*, which is the *disorder*, the *discord*,
the *irregularitie*, the *commotion*, and *rebellion* of the *body?*
It were scarce a *disease*, if it could bee *ordered*, and made
obedient to our *times*. Why should wee looke for that in
disorder, in a *disease*, when we cannot have it in *Nature*,
who is so *regular*, and so *pregnant*, so forward to bring
her *worke* to perfection, and to light? Yet we cannot
awake the *July-flowers* in *January*, nor retard the *flowers*
of the *spring* to *autumne*. We cannot bid the *fruits* come
in *May*, nor the *leaves* to sticke on in *December*. A *woman*
that is weake cannot put off her *ninth moneth* to a *tenth*,
for her *deliverie*, and say shee will stay till shee bee
stronger; nor a *Queene* cannot hasten it to a *seventh*,
that shee may bee ready for some other pleasure. *Nature*
(if we looke for *durable* and *vigorous* effects) will not
admit *preventions*, nor *anticipations*, nor *obligations* upon
her; for they are *precontracts*, and she will bee left to
her *libertie*. *Nature* would not be spurred, nor forced to
mend her pace; nor power, the *power of man;* greatnesse
loves not that kinde of *violence* neither. There are of

1. *concoction:* maturation.

them that will *give*, that will *do justice*, that will *pardon*, but they have their owne *seasons* for al these, and he that knowes not *them*, shall *starve* before that gift come, and *ruine*, before the Justice, and *dye* before the pardon save him: some *tree* beares no fruit, except much *dung* be laid about it; and *Justice* comes not from some, till they bee richly manured: some *trees* require much *visiting*, much *watring*, much *labour;* and some men give not their *fruits* but upon *importunitie;* some *trees* require *incision*, and *pruning*, and *lopping;* some men must bee *intimidated* and *syndicated* with *Commissions*, before they will deliver the fruits of *Justice;* some *trees* require the *early* and the *often* accesse of the *Sunne;* some men *open* not, but upon the *favours* and *letters* of *Court mediation;* some *trees* must bee *housd* and kept within *doores;* some men locke up, not onely their liberalitie, but their *Justice*, and their *compassion*, till the sollicitation of a *wife*, or a *sonne*, or a *friend*, or a *servant* turne the *key*. *Reward* is the *season* of one man, and *importunitie* of another; *feare* the *season* of one man, and *favour* of another; *friendship* the *season* of one man, and *naturall affection* of another; and hee that knowes not their *seasons*, nor cannot *stay* them, must lose the *fruits;* As *Nature* will not, so *power* and *greatnesse* will not bee put to change their *seasons;* and shall wee looke for this *Indulgence* in a *disease*, or thinke to shake it off before it bee *ripe?* All this while, therefore, we are but upon a *defensive warre*, and that is but a *doubtfull state;* especially where they who are *besieged* doe know the *best* of their *defenses*, and doe not know the *worst* of their *enemies power;* when they cannot mend their *works within*, and the *enemie* can increase his *numbers without*. O how many farre more miserable, and farre more worthy to be lesse miserable than I, are besieged with this *sicknesse*, and lacke their *Sentinels*, their *Physitians* to *watch*, and lacke their *munition*, their *cordials* to *defend*, and perish before the *enemies* weaknesse might invite them to *sally*, before the *disease* shew any *declination*, or admit any way of *working* upon it selfe! In me the *siege* is so farre slackned, as that we may come to *fight*, and so die in the *field*, if I *die*, and not in a *prison*.

XIX. EXPOSTULATION

My *God*, my *God*, Thou art a *direct God*, may I not say a *literall God*, a *God* that wouldest bee understood *literally*, and according to the *plaine sense* of all that thou saiest? But thou art also (*Lord* I intend it to thy *glory*, and let no *prophane misinterpreter* abuse it to thy *diminution*) thou art a *figurative*, a *metaphoricall God too*: A *God* in whose words there is such a height of *figures*, such *voyages*, such *peregrinations* to fetch remote and precious *metaphors*, such *extentions*, such *spreadings*, such *Curtaines* of *Allegories*, such *third Heavens* of *Hyperboles*, so *harmonious eloquutions*, so *retired* and so *reserved expressions*, so *commanding perswasions*, so *perswading commandments*, such *sinewes* even in thy *milke*, and such *things* in thy *words*, as all *prophane Authors*, seeme of the seed of the *Serpent*, that *creepes*, thou art the *Dove*, that flies. O, what words but thine, can expresse the inexpressible *texture*, and *composition* of thy *word;* in which, to one man, that *argument* that binds his faith to beleeve that to bee the Word of *God*, is *the reverent simplicity* of the Word, and to another, the *majesty* of the Word; and in which two men, equally pious, may meet, and one wonder, that all should not understand it, and the other, as much, that any man should. So, *Lord*, thou givest us the same *earth*, to labour on and to lie in; a *house*, and a *grave*, of the same *earth;* so Lord, thou givest us the same *Word* for our *satisfaction*, and for our *Inquisition*, for our *instruction*, and for our *Admiration* too; for there are places, that thy servants *Hierom* and *Augustine* would scarce beleeve (when they grew warm by mutual letters) of one another, that they understood them, and yet both *Hierome* and *Augustine* call upon persons, whom they knew to bee farre weaker, than they thought one another (*old women and young maids*) to read thy *Scriptures*, without confining them, to these or those places. Neither art thou thus a *figurative*, a *metaphoricall God* in thy *word* only, but in thy *workes* too. The *stile* of thy *works*, the *phrase* of thine *actions*, is *metaphoricall*. The *institution* of thy whole *worship* in the *old Law*, was a continuall

Allegory; types and *figures* overspread all; and *figures* flowed into *figures*, and powred themselves out into *farther figures; Circumcision* carried a *figure* of *Baptisme,* and *Baptisme* carries a *figure* of that *purity,* which we shall have in *perfection* in the *new Jerusalem.* Neither didst thou *speake* and *worke* in this *language,* onely in the time of thy *Prophets;* but since thou spokest in thy *Son,* it is so too. How often, how much more often doth thy *Sonne* call himselfe a *way,* and a *light,* and a *gate,* and a *Vine,* and *bread,* than the *Sonne of God,* or of *Man?* How much oftener doth he exhibit a *Metaphoricall Christ,* than a *reall,* a *literall?* This hath occasioned thine ancient *servants,* whose delight it was to write after thy *Copie,* to proceede the same way in their *expositions* of the *Scriptures,* and in their composing both of *publike liturgies,* and of *private prayers* to thee, to make their accesses to thee in such a kind of *language,* as thou was pleased to speake to them, in a *figurative,* in a *Metaphoricall language;* in which manner I am bold to call the comfort which I receive now in this *sicknesse,* in the *indication* of the *concoction* and *maturity* thereof, in certaine *clouds,* and *recidences,*[1] which the *Physitians* observe, a discovering of *land* from *Sea,* after a long, and tempestuous *voyage.* But wherefore, O my *God,* hast thou presented to us the *afflictions* and *calamities* of this life, in the name of *waters?* so often in the name of *waters,* and *deepe waters,* and *Seas of waters?* must we looke to bee *drowned?* are they *bottomlesse,* are they *boundles?* Thats not the *dialect* of thy *language;* thou hast given a *Remedy* against the deepest *water,* by *water;* against the *inundation* of sinne, by *Baptisme;* and the first *life,* that thou gavest to any *Creatures,* was in *waters;* therefore thou dost not threaten us, with an *irremediable-nesse,* when our *affliction* is a *Sea.* It is so, if we consider *our selves;* so thou callest *Gennezareth,* which was but a Lake, and not *salt,* a *Sea;* so thou callest the *Mediterranean Sea,* still the *great Sea,* because the *inhabitants* saw no other *Sea;* they that dwelt there, thought a *Lake,* a *Sea,* and the others thought a *little Sea,* the *greatest,* and wee that know not the *afflictions* of others, call our owne the *heaviest.* But, O my *God,* that is *truly great,* that over-

---

1. *recidences:* relapses.

flowes the *channell;* that is *really* a *great affliction,* which is above my *strength,* but thou, O *God,* art my *strength,* and then what can bee above it? *Mountaines shake with the swelling of thy Sea, secular mountaines,* men *strong in power, spirituall mountaines,* men *strong in grace,* are shaked with *afflictions;* but *thou laiest up thy sea in store-houses;* even thy *corrections* are of thy *treasure,* and thou wilt not waste thy *corrections;* when they have done their *service,* to humble thy *patient,* thou wilt call them in againe, for *thou givest the Sea thy decree, that the waters should not passe thy Commandement.* All our *waters* shal run into *Jordan,* and *thy servants passed Jordan dry foot;* they shall run into the red Sea (the Sea of thy *Sons bloud*) and the red Sea, that red Sea, drownes none of *thine.* But, *they that saile in the Sea, tell of the danger thereof;* I that am yet in this affliction, owe the *glory* of *speaking* of it; But, as the *Wise man* bids me, I say, I may *speak much, and come short; wherefore in sum thou art all.* Since thou art so, O my *God,* and *affliction* is a *Sea,* too *deepe* for us, what is our *refuge?* thine *Arke,* thy *ship.* In all other *Seas,* in all other *afflictions,* those *meanes* which thou hast or-dained; In this *Sea,* in *Sicknesse,* thy *Ship* is thy *Physitian. Thou hast made a way in the Sea, and a safe path in the waters, shewing that thou canst save from all dangers; yea, though a man went to Sea without art;* yet where I finde all that, I finde this added, *Neverthelesse thou wouldest not, that the worke of thy wisdome should be idle.* Thou canst save without *meanes;* but thou hast told no man that thou *wilt:* Thou hast told every man, that thou *wilt not.* When the *Centurion* beleeved the *Master* of the *ship* more than Saint *Paul,* they were all opened to a great danger; this was a *preferring* of thy *meanes,* before thee, the *Au-thor* of the *meanes;* but, my *God,* though thou beest *every where,* I have no promise of *appearing* to me, but in thy *ship:* Thy blessed *Sonne preached out of a ship:* The *meanes* is preaching, he did that; and the *Ship* was a *type* of the *Church;* hee did it there. *Thou gavest S. Paul the lives of all of them, that saild with him;* If they had not beene in the *Ship* with him, the gift had not extended to them. *As soone as thy Son was come out of the ship, immediately there met him out of the tombes, a man with an uncleane spirit, and no man could hold him, no not with chaines.* Thy *Sonne* needed no use of *meanes;* yet there wee apprehend the *danger* to us; if we leave the *ship,* the *meanes;* in this case, the *Physitian.* But as they are *Ships* to us in those *Seas,* so is there a *Ship* to them too, in which they are to stay. Give mee leave, O my *God,* to assist my selfe with such a *construction* of these words of thy servant *Paul,* to the *Centurion,* when the *Mariners* would have left the *Ship, Except these abide in the Ship, you cannot be safe;* Except they who are our *Ships,* the *Physitians,* abide in that which is theirs, and our *ship,* the *truth,* and the *sincere* and *religious worship of thee,* and thy *Gospell,* we cannot promise our selves, so good *safety;* for though we have our *ship,* the *Physitian,* he hath not his *ship, Religion;* And meanes are not meanes, but in their *concatenation,* as they *depend,* and are *chained* together. *The ships are great,* saies thy *Apostle, but a helme turns them;* the *men* are *learned,* but their *Religion* turnes their *labours* to good: And therefore it was a heavy *curse, when the third part of the ships perished:* It is a heavy case, where either *all Religion,* or *true Religion* should forsake many of these *ships,* whom thou hast sent to convey us over these *Seas.* But, O my *God,* my *God,* since *I have my ship,* and *they theirs,* I have *them,* and they have *thee,* why are we yet no neerer land? As soone as thy *Sonnes disciple* had taken him into the *ship, immediatly the ship was at the land, whither they went.* Why have not *they* and *I* this dispatch? Every thing is *immediatly* done, which is done when *thou* wouldst have it done. Thy purpose *terminates* every action, and what was *done* before that, is *undone* yet. Shall that slacken my *hope?* Thy *Prophet* from *thee,* hath forbid it. *It is good that a man should both hope, and quietly wait for the salvation* of the Lord. Thou puttest off many *judgements,* till the *last* day, and many passe this life without any; and shall not I endure the putting off thy *mercy* for a day? and yet, O my *God,* thou puttest me not to that; for, the *assurance* of *future mercy,* is *present mercy.* But what is my *assurance* now? What is my *seale?* It is but a *cloud;* that which my *Physitians* call a *cloud,* is *that,* which gives them their *Indication.* But a *cloud?* Thy *great Seale* to all the world, the *Rainebow,* that secured the *world* for ever, from *drowning,* was but a *reflexion upon a cloud.* A *cloud* it selfe was a *pillar* which guided the *church*, and *the glory of God*, not only *was*, but *appeared in a cloud*. Let me returne, O my *God*, to the consideration of thy *servant Eliahs* proceeding, in a time of *desperate drought;* he bids them look towards the *Sea;* They looke, and see *nothing.* He bids them *againe* and *againe*, *seven times:* and at the *seventh time*, they saw a little *cloud* rising out of the *Sea;* and presently they had their desire of *raine. Seven dayes,* O my *God*, have we looked for this *cloud*, and now we have it; none of thy *Indications* are *frivolous;* thou makest thy *signes*, *seales;* and thy *seales, effects;* and thy *effects, consolation,* and *restitution,* wheresoever thou maiest receive *glory* by that way.

XIX. PRAYER

O Eternall and most gracious *God*, who though thou passedst over infinite millions of generations, before thou camest to a *Creation* of this *world*, yet when thou beganst, didst never intermit that *worke*, but continuedst *day* to *day*, till thou hadst perfited all the *worke*, and deposed it in the hands and rest of a *Sabbath*, though thou have beene pleased to *glorifie* thy selfe in a long exercise of my *patience*, with an *expectation* of thy *declaration* of thy selfe in this my *sicknesse*, yet since thou hast now of thy goodnesse afforded that, which affords us some hope, if that bee still *the way* of thy *glory*, proceed in *that way*, and perfit *that worke*, and establish me in a *Sabbath*, and *rest* in *thee*, by this thy *seale* of *bodily restitution.* Thy *Priests* came up to thee, by *steps* in the *Temple;* Thy *Angels* came *downe* to *Iaacob*, by *steps* upon the *ladder;* we finde no *staire*, by which thou *thy selfe* camest to *Adam* in *Paradise*, nor to *Sodome* in thine *anger;* for *thou*, and *thou onely* art able to doe all at once. But, O *Lord*, I am not *wearie* of thy *pace*, nor *wearie* of mine owne *patience.* I provoke thee not with a *praier*, not with a *wish*, not with a *hope*, to more haste than consists with thy *purpose*, nor looke that any other thing should have entred into thy *purpose*, but thy *glory.* To *heare* thy steps comming *towards* mee is the same comfort, as to see thy face present with mee; whether thou doe the worke of a *thousand yeeres* in a *day*, or extend the *worke of a day* to a *thousand yeeres*, as long as *thou workest*, it is *light*, and *comfort*. *Heaven* it selfe is but an *extention* of the same *joy;* and an *extention* of this *mercie*, to proceed at thy *leisure*, in the way of *restitution*, is a *manifestation of heaven* to me here upon *earth*. From that *people*, to whom thou appearedst in *signes* and in *Types*, the *Jewes*, thou art departed, because they trusted in *them;* but from thy *Church*, to whom thou hast appeared in *thy selfe*, in thy *Sonne*, thou wilt never depart; because we cannot trust *too much* in *him*. Though thou have afforded me these *signes* of *restitution*, yet if I *confide* in *them*, and beginne to say, all was but a *naturall accident*, and *nature* begins to *discharge* her selfe, and shee will *perfit* the whole *worke*, my *hope* shall vanish because it is not in *thee*. If thou shouldest take thy *hand* utterly from me, and have nothing to doe with me, *nature* alone were able to *destroy* me; but if thou withdraw thy *helping hand*, alas how frivolous are the helps of *Nature*, how impotent the assistances of *Art*? [1] As therefore the *morning dew*, is a *pawne* of the *evening fatnesse*, so, O *Lord*, let *this daies* comfort be the *earnest* of to *morrowes*, so far as may *conforme* me entirely to thee, to what *end*, and by what *way* soever thy *mercie* have appointed mee.

Id agunt.   *Upon these Indications of digested*
                     matter, they proceed to purge.

XX. MEDITATION

Though *counsel* seeme rather to consist of *spirituall parts*, than *action*, yet *action* is the *spirit* and the *soule* of *counsell*. *Counsels* are not alwaies determined in *Resolutions;* wee cannot alwaies say, *this was concluded;* actions are alwaies determined in *effects;* wee can say *this was done*. Then have *Lawes* their *reverence*, and their *majestie*, when we see the *Judge* upon the *Bench* executing them. Then have *counsels of warre* their *impressions*, and their *operations*, when we see the *seale* of an *Armie* set to them. It

1. *Art:* skill.

was an ancient way of celebrating the *memorie* of such as deserved well of the *State*, to afford them that kinde of *statuarie representation*, which was then called *Hermes;* which was, *the head and shoulders of a man, standing upon a Cube,* but those *shoulders* without *armes* and *hands.* All together it figured a *constant supporter of the State,* by his *counsell:* But in this *Hieroglyphique,* which they made without *hands,* they passe their consideration no farther, but that the *Counsellor* should bee without *hands,* so farre as *not to reach out his hand to forraigne tentations*[1] *of bribes, in matters of Counsell,* and that it was not necessary, that the *head* should employ *his owne hand;* that *the same men* should serve in the *execution,* which assisted in the *Counsell;* but that there should not belong *hands* to every *head, action* to every *counsell,* was never intended, so much as in *figure,* and *representation.* For, as *Matrimonie* is scarce to bee called *Matrimonie,* where there is a *resolution* against the *fruits of matrimonie,* against the having of *Children,* so *counsels* are not *counsels,* but *illusions,* where there is from the beginning no purpose to execute the determinations of those *counsels.* The *arts* and *sciences* are most properly referred to the *head;* that is their proper *Element* and *Spheare;* but yet the *art* of *proving, Logique,* and the *art* of *perswading, Rhetorique,* are deduced to the *hand,* and *that* expressed by a *hand* contracted into a *fist,* and *this* by a *hand* enlarged, and expanded; and evermore the *power of man,* and the *power of God* himselfe is expressed so, *All things are in his hand;* neither is *God* so often presented to us, by names that carry our consideration upon *counsell,* as upon *execution* of *counsell;* he is oftner called the *Lord of Hosts,* than by all other *names,* that may be referred to the other signification. Hereby therefore wee take into our *meditation,* the slipperie condition of *man,* whose *happinesse,* in any kinde, the defect of *any one thing,* conducing to that *happinesse,* may *ruine;* but it must have *all the peeces* to make it up. Without *counsell,* I had not got thus farre; without *action* and *practise,* I should goe no farther towards *health.* But what is the present necessary *action?* purging: A *withdrawing,* a violating of *Nature,* a farther

1. *tentations:* temptations.

weakening: O deare price, and *O strange* way of *addition*, to doe it by *subtraction;* of *restoring* Nature, to *violate* Nature; of *providing strength*, by *increasing weaknesse!* Was I not *sicke* before? And is it a *question* of *comfort* to be asked now, Did *your Physicke make you sicke?* Was that it that my *Physicke* promised, to make me *sicke?* This is another *step*, upon which we may stand, and see farther into the *miserie of man*, the *time*, the *season* of his *Miserie:* It must bee done *now: O over-cunning, over-watchfull, over-diligent*, and *over-sociable misery of man*, that seldome comes alone, but then when it may accompanie other *miseries*, and so put one another into the higher *exaltation*, and better *heart!* I am ground even to an *attenuation*, and must proceed to *evacuation*, all waies to exinanition[2] and annihilation.

Atque annuit Ille, Qui, per eos, clamat, Linquas jam, Lazare, lectum.

God prospers their practise, and he, by them, calls Lazarus *out of his tombe, mee out of my bed.*

XXI. MEDITATION

If man had beene left *alone* in this *world*, at first, shall I thinke, that he would not have *fallen?* If there had beene no *Woman*, would not man have served, to have beene his own *Tempter?* When I see him now, subject to infinite weaknesses, fall into *infinite sinne*, without any *forraine tentations*, shall I thinke, hee would have had *none*, if hee had beene *alone? God* saw that Man needed a *Helper*, if hee should bee well; but to make *Woman* ill, the *Devill* saw, that there needed no *third.* When *God*, and *wee* were *alone*, in *Adam*, that was not enough; when the *Devill* and wee were *alone*, in *Eve*, it was enough. O what a *Giant* is *Man*, when he fights against himselfe, and what a *Dwarfe* when hee *needs*, or *exercises* his owne assistance for himselfe! I cannot *rise* out of my bed, till the *Physitian enable* mee, nay I cannot tel, that I am able to rise, till *hee tell* me so. I *doe* nothing, I *know* nothing of

2. *exinanition:* emptiness.

my selfe: how *little*, and how *impotent* a *peece* of the *world*, is any *Man* alone! and how much lesse a *peece* of *himselfe* is *that Man!* So *little*, as that when it falls out, (as it falls out in some cases) that more *misery*, and more *oppression*, would be an *ease* to a *man*, he cannot give himselfe that *miserable addition*, of *more misery;* a *man* that is *pressed to death*, and might be eased by more *weights*, cannot lay those more *weights* upon himselfe: Hee can sinne *alone*, and suffer *alone*, but not *repent*, not bee *absolved*, without *another*. Another tels mee, *I may rise;* and *I doe* so. But is every *raising* a *preferment?* or is every present *preferment* a *station?* I am readier to fall to the *Earth*, now I am up, than I was when I *lay* in the bed: O *perverse way*, *irregular motion* of *Man;* even *rising* it selfe is the way to *Ruine.* How many *men* are raised,[1] and then doe not *fill* the place they are raised to? No *corner* of any place can bee *empty;* there can be no *vacuity;* If that *Man* doe not fill the place, *other men* will; complaints of his *insufficiency* will *fill* it; Nay, such an *abhorring* is there in *Nature*, of *vacuity*, that if there be but an *imagination* of not *filling*, in any *man*, that which is but *imagination* neither, will *fill* it, that is, *rumor* and *voice*, and it will be *given out*, (upon no ground, but *Imagination*, and no man knowes *whose imagination*) that hee is *corrupt* in his place, or *insufficient* in his place, and another prepared to *succeed* him in his place. A man *rises*, sometimes, and *stands* not, because hee doth not, or is not beleeved to *fill* his place; and sometimes he *stands* not, because hee *overfills* his place: Hee may bring so much *vertue*, so much *Justice*, so much *integrity* to the place, as shall *spoile* the place, *burthen* the place; his *integrity* may bee a *Libell* upon his *Predecessor*, and cast an *infamy* upon him, and a *burthen* upon his *successor*, to proceede by *example*, and to bring the place itselfe to an *under-value*, and the *market* to an *uncertainty*. I am *up*, and I seeme to *stand*, and I go *round;* and I am a new *Argument* of the *new Philosophie*,[2] That the *Earth* moves round; why may I not beleeve, that the *whole earth* moves in a *round motion*, though that seeme to mee to *stand*, when as I seeme to

1. *raised:* promoted.
2. *new Philosophie:* the new astronomy of Copernicus and Galileo.

stand to my *Company*, and yet am *carried*, in a giddy, and *circular motion*, as I *stand?* Man hath no *center* but *misery; there* and onely *there*, hee is *fixt*, and sure to finde him-selfe. How little soever hee bee *raised*, he *moves*, and moves in a *circle*, giddily; and as in the *Heavens*, there are but a few *Circles*, that goe about the whole world, but many *Epicircles*, and other lesser *Circles*, but yet *Circles*, so of those men, which are *raised*, and put into *Circles*, few of them move from *place* to *place*, and passe through many and beneficiall places, but fall into little *Circles*, and, within a step or two, are at their *end*, and not so well, as they were in the *Center*, from which they were *raised*. Every thing serves to *exemplifie*, to *illustrate* mans *misery*. But I need goe no farther, than *my selfe:* for a long time, I was not able to *rise;* At last, I must bee *raised* by others; and now I am *up*, I am ready to sinke *lower* than before.

Sit morbi fomes tibi cura;	*The Physitians consider the root and occasion, the embers, and coales, and fuell of the disease, and seeke to purge or correct that.*

XXII. MEDITATION

How *ruinous* a *farme* hath *man* taken, in taking *himselfe!* How ready is the *house* every day to fall downe, and how is all the *ground* overspread with *weeds, all the* body with *diseases!* where not onely every *turfe*, but every *stone*, beares *weeds;* not onely every *muscle* of the *flesh*, but every *bone* of the *body*, hath some *infirmitie;* every little *flint* upon the *face* of this *soile*, hath some *infectious weede*, every *tooth* in our *head*, such a paine as a *constant man* is afraid of, and yet *ashamed* of that *feare*, of that sense of the paine. How *deare*, and how *often* a *rent* doth Man pay for this *farme!* hee paies *twice a day*, in *double meales*, and how little time he hath to *raise his rent!* How many *holy daies* to call him from his labour! Every day is *halfe-holy day*, halfe spent in *sleepe*. What *reparations*, and *subsidies*, and *contributions* he is put to, besides his *rent!* What *medicines*, besides his *diet!* and what *Inmates* he is *faine* to take in, besides his owne *familie*, what *infectious diseases*, from *other men! Adam* might have had *Paradise* for *dressing* and *keeping* it; and *then* his rent was not *improved* to such a *labour*, as would have made his *brow sweat;* and yet he gave it over; how farre greater a *rent* doe wee pay for this farme, this *body*, who pay *our selves*, who pay the *farme it selfe*, and cannot *live* upon it! Neither is our *labour* at an end, when wee have cut downe some *weed*, as soone as it sprung up, corrected some *violent* and dangerous *accident* of a *disease*, which would have destroied *speedily;* nor when wee have pulled up that *weed*, from the very *root*, recovered *entirely* and *soundly*, from that *particular disease;* but the whole *ground* is of an *ill nature*, the whole soile *ill disposed;* there are inclinations, there is a propensenesse[1] to *diseases* in the *body*, out of which without any other *disorder*, *diseases* will grow, and so wee are put to a continuall labour upon this *farme*, to a continuall studie of the whole *complexion* and *constitution* of our *body*. In the *distempers* and *diseases* of *soiles*, *sourenesse*, *drinesse*, *weeping*, any kinde of *barrennesse*, the *remedy* and the *physicke*, is, for a great part, sometimes in *themselves;* sometime[s] the very *situation* releeves them; the *hanger* of a *hill*, will purge and vent his owne *malignant moisture;* and the burning of the upper *turfe* of some ground (as *health* from *cauterizing*) puts a *new* and a *vigorous youth* into that *soile*, and there rises a kinde of *Phœnix* out of the *ashes*, a *fruitfulnesse* out of that which was *barren* before, and *by that*, which is the barrennest of all, *ashes*. And where the *ground* cannot give it selfe *Physicke*, yet it receives *Physicke* from other grounds, from other soiles, which are not the worse, for having contributed that helpe to them, from *Marle* in other *hils*, or from *slimie sand* in other *shoares: grounds* help *themselves*, or hurt not other *grounds*, from whence they receive *helpe*. But I have taken a *farme* at this *hard rent*, and upon those *heavie covenants*, that it can afford it selfe no *helpe;* (no part of my *body*, if it were cut off, would *cure* another part; in some cases it might *preserve* a sound part, but in no case *recover* an infected) and, if my *body* may have any *Physicke*, any *Medicine* from an-

---

1. *propensenesse:* propensity.

other *body*, one *Man* from the flesh of another *Man* (as by Mummy,[2] or any such *composition*,) it must bee from a man that is dead, and not, as in other *soiles*, which are never the worse for contributing their *Marle*, or their fat slime to my *ground*. There is nothing in the same *man*, to helpe *man*, nothing in *mankind* to help *one another* (in this sort, by way of *Physicke*) but that hee who *ministers* the *helpe*, is in as ill case, as he that *receives* it would have beene, if he had not had it; for hee from whose *body* the *Physicke* comes, is *dead*. When therefore I tooke this *farme*, undertooke this body, I undertooke to *draine*, not a *marish*,[3] but a *moat*, where there was, not water *mingled* to offend, but all was *water*; I undertooke to *perfume dung*, where no one part, but all was equally *unsavory*; I undertooke to make such a thing *wholsome*, as was not *poison* by any manifest quality, *intense heat*, or *cold*, but *poison* in the *whole substance*, and in the *specifique forme* of it. To cure the *sharpe accidents* of *diseases*, is a great *worke*; to cure the *disease it selfe* is a greater; but to cure the *body*, the *root*, the *occasion* of *diseases*, is a worke reserved for the great *Phisitian*, which he doth never any other way, but by *glorifying* these *bodies* in the next world.

Metusque, relabi.   *They warne mee of the fearefull danger of relapsing.*

XXIII. MEDITATION

It is not in *mans body*, as it is in the *Citie*, that when the *Bell*[1] hath rung, to cover your *fire*, and rake up the *embers*, you may lie downe and sleepe without feare. Though you have by *physicke* and *diet*, raked up the *embers* of your *disease*, stil there is a feare of a *relapse*; and the *greater* danger is in that. Even in *pleasures*, and in

2. *Mummy:* Ground-up mummy's flesh was esteemed as a remedy in the Renaissance.
3. *marish:* marsh.

1. *Bell:* the curfew.

paines, there is a *propriety,*[2] a *Meum* and *Tuum;*[3] and a
man is most affected with that *pleasure* which is *his, his*
by forme, enjoying and experience, and most intimidated
with those *paines* which are *his, his* by a wofull sense of
them, in former afflictions. A *covetous* person, who hath
preoccupated all his senses, filled all his capacities, with
the *delight* of *gathering,* wonders how any man can have
any *taste* of *any pleasure* in *any opennesse,* or *liberalitie;*
So also in *bodily paines,* in a fit of the *stone,* the Patient
wonders why any man should call the *Gout* a *paine:* And
hee that hath felt neither, but the *tooth-ach,* is as much
afraid of a fit of that, as either of the other, of either of
the other. *Diseases,* which we never *felt* in our selves,
come but to a *compassion* of others that have endured
them; Nay, *compassion* it selfe comes to no great *degree,*
if wee have not felt in some *proportion,* in *our selves,* that
which wee lament and condole in another. But when wee
have had those torments in their *exaltation, our selves,*
wee tremble at a relapse. When wee must *pant* through
all those *fierie heats,* and *saile* thorow all those *overflowing sweats,* when wee must *watch* through all those long
nights, and *mourne* through all those long *daies, (daies*
and *nights,* so *long,* as that *Nature* her selfe shall seeme
to be *perverted,* and to have put the *longest day,* and the
longest night, which should bee *six moneths* asunder, into
one *naturall, unnaturall day*) when wee must stand at the
same *barre,* expect the returne of *Physitians* from their
consultations, and not bee sure of the same *verdict,* in any
good *Indications,* when we must goe the same *way* over
againe, and not see the same *issue,* this is a *state,* a *condition,* a *calamitie,* in respect of which, any other *sicknesse,* were a *convalescence,* and any *greater, lesse.* It
addes to the *affliction,* that *relapses* are, (and for the most
part justly) imputed to *our selves,* as occasioned by some
disorder in us; and so we are not onely *passive,* but *active,*
in our owne *ruine;* we doe not onely stand under a *falling
house,* but *pull* it downe upon us; and wee are not onely
executed, (that implies *guiltinesse*) but wee are *executioners,* (that implies *dishonor*) and *executioners of our*

2. *propriety:* property.
3. *Meum and Tuum:* mine and yours.

selves, (and that implies *impietie.*) And wee fall from that *comfort* which wee might have in our first *sicknesse,* from that *meditation, Alas, how generally miserable is Man, and how subject to diseases,* (for in that it is some degree of *comfort,* that wee are but in the state *common* to all) we fall, I say, to this *discomfort,* and *selfe accusing,* and *selfe condemning; Alas, how unprovident, and in that, how unthankfull to God and his instruments am I, in making so ill use of so great benefits, in destroying so soone, so long a worke, in relapsing, by my disorder, to that from which they had delivered mee;* and so my *meditation* is fearefully transferred from the *body* to the *minde,* and from the consideration of the *sicknesse* to that sinne, that *sinful carelessnes,* by which I have occasioned my *relapse.* And amongst the many *weights* that aggravate a *relapse,* this also is one, that a *relapse* proceeds with a more violent dispatch, and more *irremediably,* because it finds the *Countrie weakned,* and *depopulated* before. Upon a *sicknesse,* which as yet appeares not, wee can scarce fix a *feare,* because wee know not what to feare; but as *feare* is the *busiest,* and *irksomest affection,*[4] so is a *relapse* (which is still [5] *ready to come*) into that, which is but newly gone, the *nearest object,* the *most immediate* exercise of that *affection* of *feare.*

4. *affection:* emotion.
5. *still:* always.

Sermons

DONNE IS perhaps the greatest preacher of the great age of English preaching. Of his more than 160 sermons, a few were published individually (some of them during his lifetime), but the majority were contained in the large folio collections of 1640, 1649, and 1660. Taken as a whole, they constitute an extraordinary body of Baroque prose, marked by the qualities of dramatic immediacy and imaginative extravagance characteristic of the literature of the age. Donne, as we might expect from his poetry, makes striking use of the device of the *concetto predicabile*, or "preachable conceit," which had spread during the seventeenth century from Italy to other European countries.

Donne's pulpit style frequently crystallizes into seemingly self-contained passages of fervent eloquence. As a result, brief excerpts from his sermons are frequently printed out of context. This edition, however, represents Donne's work in this genre by reprinting three sermons in full, since Donne the preacher is most faithfully mirrored in the unified, whole works of art which are his sermons. The following pages contain a sermon written shortly before Donne's appointment as Dean of St. Paul's Cathedral, one written shortly thereafter, and "Deaths Duell," his last sermon, which occasioned Izaak Walton's observation "that Dr. Donne had preach't his own Funerall Sermon."

All three sermons are typical of Donne the clergyman in their avoidance of polemical points of dogma in order to concentrate on the essentials of Christian faith. They are typical of Donne the man in their obsessive concern with death and with the promised resurrection which he believed would abrogate that death. At once universally Christian and intensely personal, the *Sermons* reflect the temperament of the author almost as completely as do his poems.

The definitive edition of the *Sermons* by G. R. Potter and E. M. Simpson is of primary importance to the student of these works. Also of considerable utility are E. M. Simpson's *A Study of the Prose Works of John Donne* and the works of J. Webber, I. Husain, and W. F. Mitchell.

PREACHED AT LINCOLNS INNE

VOLUME III: NUMBER 3 [1]

JOB 19.26. *AND THOUGH, AFTER MY SKIN, WORMES DESTROY THIS BODY, YET IN MY FLESH SHALL I SEE GOD.*

Amongst those *Articles*, in which our Church hath explain'd, and declar'd her faith, this is the *eight* Article, that the three Creeds, (that of the councell of *Nice*, that of *Athanasius*, and that which is commonly known by the name of the *Apostles Creed*) ought throughly to be received, and embrac'd. The meaning of the Church is not, that onely that should be beleev'd in which those *three Creeds agree*; (for, the *Nicen Creed* mentions no Article after that of the *holy Ghost*, not the Catholique Church, not the Communion of Saints, not the Resurrection of the flesh; *Athanasius* his Creed does mention the Resurrection, but not the Catholique Church, nor the communion of

---

1. *Number 3:* The numbering of the sermons included in this edition is that of the definitive edition, edited by G. R. Potter and E. M. Simpson. This sermon appeared originally as No. 14 in *Fifty Sermons* (London, 1649).

Saints,) but that *all* should be beleev'd, which is in any of them, all which is summ'd up in the Apostles Creed. Now, the reason expressed in that Article of our Church, why all this is to be beleeved, is; *Because all this may be prov'd by most certaine warrants of holy Scriptures*. The Article does not insist upon particular places of Scripture; not so much as point to them. But, they who have enlarged the Articles, by way of explanation, have done that. And when they come to cite those places of Scripture, which prove the Article of the Resurrection, I observe that amongst those places they forbeare this text; so that it may seem, that in their opinion, this Scripture doth not concerne the *Resurrection*. It will not therefore be impertinent, to make it a first part of this exercise, whether this Scripture be to be understood of the Resurrection, or no; And then, to make the particular handling of the words, a second part. In the first, we shall see, that the *Jews* always had, and have still, a persuasion of the Resurrection. We shall look after, by *what light* they saw that; whether by the light of *naturall reason;* And, if not by that, by what light given in other places of Scripture; and then, we shall shut up this inquisition with a unanime consent, (so unanime, as I can remember but *one* that denies it, and he but faintly) that in this text, the doctrine of the resurrection is established. In the second part, the doctrine it selfe comprised in the words of the text, (*And though after my skin, wormes destroy this body, yet in my flesh shall I see God*) we shall see first, that the *Saints* of God themselves, are not priviledged from the common corruption and dissolution of the body; After that curse upon the Serpent, *super pectus gradieris*, upon thy belly shalt thou goe, we shall as soon see a Serpent goe upright, and not craule, as, after that Judgment, *In pulverem reverteris*, to dust thou shalt returne, see a man, that shall not see death, and corruption in death. Corruption upon our *skin*, says the text, (our outward beauty;) corruption upon our *body*, (our whole strength, and constitution.) And, this corruption, not a green palenesse, not a yellow jaundise, not a blue lividnesse, not a black morpheu[2] upon our skin, not a bony leannesse, not a sweaty faintnesse,

Gen. 3.14

[Gen. 3.19]

---

2. *morpheu:* a scurfy eruption of the skin.

not an ungratious decrepitnesse upon our body, but a destruction, a destruction to both, *After my skin my body
shall be destroyed.* Though not destroyed by being resolved to ashes in the fire, (perchance I shall not be
burnt) not destroyed by being washed to slime, in the sea,
(perchance I shall not be drowned) but destroyed con-
temptibly, by those whom I breed, and feed, by wormes;
(*After my skin wormes shall destroy my body.*) And thus
farre our case is equall; one event to the good and bad;
wormes shall destroy all in them all. And farther then
this, their case is equall too, for, they shall both rise
againe from this destruction. But in this lies the future
glory, in this lies the present comfort of the Saints of God,
that, *after all this,* (so that this is not my last act, to dye,
nor my last scene, to lie in the grave, nor my last *exit,*
to goe-out of the grave) *after,* says *Job;* And indefinitely,
After, I know not how soone, nor how late, I presse not
into Gods secrets for that; but, *after all this, Ego,* I, I that
speak now, and shall not speak then, silenced in the grave,
I that see now, and shall not see then, *ego videbo,* I shall
see, (I shall have a new *faculty*) *videbo Deum,* I shall see
God (I shall have a new *object*) and, *In carne,* I shall see
him in the *flesh,* (I shall have a new *organ,* and a new
medium) and, *In carne mea,* that flesh shall be *my flesh,*
(I shall have a new propriety in that flesh) this flesh which
I have now, is not *mine,* but the wormes; but that flesh
shall be so mine, as I shall never *devest it more,* but *In my
flesh I shall see God for ever.*

1 Part

*Judæi
credunt*

Numb.
16.32

[Isa.]
26.19

14

In the first part then, which is an inquiry, whether this
text concerne the Resurrection, or no, we take knowledge
of a *Crediderunt,* and of a *Credunt* in the *Jews,* that the
Jews did beleeve a Resurrection, and that they doe beleeve
it still. That they doe so now, appears out of the doctrine
of their *Talmud,* where we find, that *onely the Jews* shall
rise againe, but all the Gentiles shall perish, body and soule
together, as *Korah, Dathan,* and *Abiram* were swallowed
all at once, body, and soule into hell. And to this purpose,
(for the first part thereof, that the *Jews* shall rise) they
abuse that place of *Esay, Thy dead men shall live; awake
and sing, yee that dwell in the dust.* And, for the second
part, that the Gentiles shall not rise, they apply the words
of the same Prophet before, *They are dead, they shall not*

live, they are deceased, they shall not rise. The *Jews* onely,
say they shall rise; but, *not all they;* but onely the *righteous*
amongst them. And, to that purpose, they abuse that place
of the Prophet *Zachary, two parts shall be cut off, and* 13.8
*dye, but the third shall be left therein, and I will bring
that third part, through the fire, and will refine them, as
silver is refined, and try them, as gold is tried.* The *Jews*
onely of all men, the good *Jews* onely of all *Jews,* and of
these good *Jews,* onely they who were buried in the land
of promise shall have this present, and immediate resurrection; And to that purpose they force that place in
Genesis where *Jacob,* upon his deathbed, advised his sonne 47.29
Joseph, to bury him in *Canaan,* and not in *Egypt,* and to
that purpose, they detort also, that place of *Jeremy,* where 20.6
the Prophet lays that curse upon *Pashur, That he should
dye in Babylon, and be buried there.* For, though the *Jews*
doe not absolutely say, that all that are buried out of
Canaan, shall be without a resurrection, yet, they say, that
even those good and righteous *Jews,* which are not buried
in that great Churchyard, the land of promise, must, at
the day of judgment, be brought through the hollow parts
of the earth, into the land of promise at that time, and
onely in that place, receive their resurrection, wheresoever they were buried. But yet, though none but *Jews,*
none but righteous *Jews,* none but righteous *Jews* in that
place, must be partakers of the Resurrection, yet still a
Resurrection there is in their doctrine.

It is so now; it was so always. We see, in that time, *Crediderunt*
when *Christ* walked upon the earth, when he came to the
raising of *Lazarus,* and said to his sister *Martha, Thy* John 11.23
brother shall rise againe, she replies to Christ, *Alas, I know
he shall rise againe, at the Resurrection of the last day,* I
make no doubt of that, we all know that. So also, when
Christ put forth that parable, that in placing of benefits, Luke 14.14
we should rather choose such persons, as were able to
make no recompense, he gives that reason, *Thou shalt be
recompensed at the resurrection of the just.* The Resurrection was a vulgar[3] doctrine, well knowne to the *Jews*
then, and always. For, even *Herod,* when Christ preached
and did miracles, was apt to say, *John Baptist is risen from* Mar. 6.14

3. *vulgar:* common.

the dead; And when it is said of those two great *Apostles,* (the loving, and the beloved Apostle, *Peter,* and *John*) that as yet they knew not the Scripture, that *Christ must rise from the dead,* this argues no more, but that as *Peters* compassion before Christs death, made him disswade Christ from going up to *Jerusalem,* to suffer, so their extreme passion after Christs death, made them the lesse attentively to consider those particular Scriptures, which spoke of the Resurrection. For, the *Jews* in generall, (much more, they) had always an apprehension, and an acknowledgment of the Resurrection of the dead. By what light they saw this, and how they came to this knowledge, is our next consideration.

Had they this by the common notions of other men, out of naturall *Reason? Melancthon,*[4] (who is no bold, nor rash, nor dangerous expressor of himselfe) says well, *Articulus resurrectionis propria Ecclesiæ vox;* It is the Christian Church, that hath delivered to us the article of the resurrection. Nature says it not, Philosophy says it not; it is the language and the Idiotisme[5] of the Church of God, that the resurrection is to be beleeved as an article of faith. For, though articles of faith be not *facta Ecclesiæ,* they are *dicta Ecclesiæ,* though the Church doe not *make* articles, yet she *declares* them. In the Creation, the way was, *Dixit & facta sunt,* God spake, and so things were made; In the Gospell, the way is, *Fecit, & dicta sunt,* God makes articles of faith, and the Church utters them, presents them. That's *manifestè verum,* evidently, undeniably true, that Nature, and Philosophy say nothing of articles of faith. But, even in Nature, and in Philosophy, there is some preparation *A priore,* and much illustration *A posteriore,* of the Resurrection. For, first, we know by naturall reason, that it is no such thing, as God cannot doe; It implies no contradiction in it selfe, as that new article of *Transubstantiation*[6] does; It implies no defectivenesse in God, as that new article, *The necessity of a perpetuall*

---

4. *Melancthon:* Philip Melanchthon (1497–1560), Reformation theologian.

5. *Idiotisme:* idiom.

6. *Transubstantiation:* the Catholic doctrine of the real presence of God in the sacrament of the Eucharist.

John 20.9

Mat. 16.22

An ex ratione

Vicar[7] *upon earth,* does. For, things contradictory in themselves, (which necessarily imply a falshood) things arguing
a defectivenesse in God, (which implies necessarily a dero-
gation, to his nature, to his naturall goodnesse, to that
which we may justly call even *the God of God,* that
which makes him God to us, *his mercy*) such things God
himselfe cannot doe, not things which make him an un-
mercifull, a cruell, a precondemning God. But, excepting
onely such things, God, who is that, *Quod cum dicitur,*
non potest dici, whom if you name you cannot give him
halfe his name; for, if you call him God, he hath not his
Christen name, for he is Christ as well as God, a Saviour,
as well as a Creator; *Quod cum æstimatur, non potest*
æstimari, If you value God, weigh God, you cannot give
him halfe his weight; for, you can put nothing into the
balance, to weigh him withall, but all this world; and,
there is no single sand in the sea, no single dust upon the
earth, no single atome in the ayre, that is not likelyer to
weigh down all the world, then all the world is to counter-
pose God; *What is the whole world to a soule?* says
Christ; but what are all the soules of the world, to God?
What is man, that God should be mindefull of him, that
God should ever thinke of him, and not forget that there
is such a thing, such a nothing? *Quod cum definitur, ipsa*
definitione crescit, says the same Father; If you limit God
with any definition, hee growes larger by that definition;
for even by that definition you discerne presently that he
is something else then that definition comprehends: That
God, *Quem omnia nesciunt, & metuendo sciunt,* whom no
man knows perfectly, yet every man knows so well, as
to stand in feare of him, this incomprehensible God, I say,
that works, and who shall let[8] *it? can* raise our bodies
again from the dead, because, to doe so, implies no dero-
gation to himselfe, no contradiction to his word.

Our reason tells us, he *can* doe it; doth our reason tell us
much of his *will,* that he will doe it? Our reason tells us,
that he will doe, whatsoever is most convenient for the
Creature, whom, because he hath made him, he loves, and
for his owne glory. Now this dignity afforded to the dead

Greg.
Nazianz.

Mar. 8.36

Psal. 8.4

Idem

Esay 43.13

An velit

7. *Vicar:* the Pope.
8. *let:* prevent.

body of man, cannot be conceived, but, as a great addition
to him. Nor can it be such a diminution to God, to take
man into heaven, as it was for God to descend, and to
take mans nature upon him, upon Earth. A King does not
diminish himselfe so much, by taking an inferior person
into his bosome at Court, as he should doe by going to
live with that person, in the Countrey, or City; and this
God did, in the incarnation of his Sonne. It cannot be
thought inconvenient, it cannot be thought hard. Our
reason tells us, that in all Gods works, in all his materiall
works, still his latter works are easier than his former. The
Creation, which was the first, and was a meer[9] production
out of nothing, was the hardest of all. The *specification*
of Creatures, and the disposing of them, into their severall
kinds, the making of that which was made something of
nothing before, a particular thing, a beast, a fowle, a fish,
a plant, a man, a Sun or Moon, was not so hard, as the
first production out of nothing. And then, the *conservation* of all these, in that order in which they are first
created, and then distinguished, the Administration of
these creatures by a constant working of second causes,
which naturally produce their effects, is not so hard as
that. And so, accordingly, and in that proportion, the last
worke is easiest of all; Distinction and specification easier
then creation, conservation and administration easier then
that distinction, and restitution by resurrection, easiest of
Tertull.　all. *Tertullian* hath expressed it well, *Plus est fecisse quam
refecisse, & dedisse quam reddidisse;* It is a harder worke
to make, then to mend, and, to give thee that which was
mine, then to restore thee that which was thine. *Et in-
stitutio carnis quàm destitutio;* It is a lesse matter to recover a sicke man, then to make a whole man. Does this
Just. Mart.　trouble thee, says *Justin Martyr*, (and *Athenagoras* pro-
Athenago.　ceeds in the same way of argumentation too, in his
Apology) does this trouble thee, *Quòd homo à piscibus,
& piscis ab homine comeditur*, that one man is devoured
by a fish, and then another man that eats the flesh of that
fish, eats, and becomes the other man? *Id nec hominem
resolvit in piscem, nec piscem in hominem*, that first man
did not become that fish that eate him, nor that fish be-

9. *meer:* simple.

come that second man, that eate it; *sed utriusque resolutio fit in elementa,* both that man, and that fish are resolved into their owne elements, of which they were made at first. Howsoever it be, if thine imagination could carry thee so low, as to thinke, not onely that thou wert become some other thing, a fish, or a dogge that had fed upon thee, and so, thou couldst not have thine owne body, but therewithall must have his body too, but that thou wert infinitely farther gone, that thou wert annihilated, become nothing, canst thou chuse but thinke God as perfect now, at least as he was at first, and can hee not as easily make thee up againe of nothing, as he made thee of nothing at first? *Recogita quid fueris, antequam esses;* Thinke over thy selfe; what wast thou before thou wast any thing? *Meminisses utique, si fuisses;* If thou hadst been any thing then, surely thou wouldst remember it now. *Qui non eras, factus es; Cum iterum non eris, fies;* Thou that wast once nothing, wast made this that thou art now; and when thou shalt be nothing againe, thou shalt be made better then thou art yet. And, *Redde rationem quâ factus es, & ego reddam rationem quâ fies;* Doe thou tell me, how thou wast made then, and I will tell thee how thou shalt be made hereafter. And yet as *Solomon* sends us to creatures, and to creatures of a low rank and station, to Ants and Spiders, for instruction, so Saint *Gregory* sends us to creatures, to learne the Resurrection. *Lux quotidie moritur, & quotidie resurgit;* That glorious creature, that first creature, the light, dyes every day, and every day hath a resurrection; *In arbustis folia resurrectione erumpunt;* from the Cedar of *Libanus,* to the Hyssop upon the wall, every leafe dyes every yeare, and every yeare hath a Resurrection. *Ubi in brevitate seminis, tam immensa arbor latuit?* (as he pursues that meditation.) If thou hadst seen the bodies of men rise out of the grave, at Christs Resurrection, could that be a stranger thing to thee, then, (if thou hadst never seen, nor heard, nor imagined it before) to see an Oake that spreads so farre, rise out of an Akorne? Or if Churchyards did vent themselves every spring, and that there were such a Resurrection of bodies every yeare, when thou hadst seen as many Resurrections as years, the Resurrection would be no stranger to thee, then the spring is. And thus, this, and many other good and reverend men,

Tertull.

[Prov. 6.6
30.25, 28]
Greg.

and so the *holy Ghost* himselfe sends us to *Reason,* and to
the *Creature,* for the doctrine of the Resurrection; *Saint*
Paul allowes him not the reason of a man, that proceeds
not so; *Thou fool,* says he, *that which thou sowest, is not*
quickned except it dye; but then it is. It is truly harder to
conceive a translation of the body into heaven, then a
Resurrection of the body from the earth. *Num in homini-*
bus terra degenerat, quæ omnia regenerare consuevit? Doe
all kinds of earth regenerate, and shall onely the Church-
yard degenerate? Is there a yearely Resurrection of every
other thing, and never of men? *Omnia pereundo servantur,*
All other things are preserved, and continued by dying;
Tu homo solus ad hoc morieris, ut pereas? And canst thou,
O man, suspect of thy selfe, that the end of thy dying is
an end of thee? Fall as low as thou canst, corrupt and
putrefie as desperately as thou canst, *sis nihil,* thinke thy
selfe nothing; *Ejus est nihilum ipsum cujus est totum,* even
that nothing is as much in his power, as the world which
he made of nothing; And, as he called thee when thou
wast not, as if thou hadst been, so will he call thee againe,
when thou art ignorant of that being which thou hast in
the grave, and give thee againe thy former, and glorifie it
with a better being.

The *Jews* then, if they had no other helpes, might have,
(as naturall men may) preparations *à Priore,* and illustra-
tions *à Posteriore,* for the doctrine of the Resurrection.
The *Jews* had seen resuscitations from the dead in particular persons, and they had seen miraculous cures done by
their Prophets. And *Gregory Nyssen* says well, that those
miraculous cures which Christ wrought, with a *Tolle*
grabatum,[10] and an *Esto sanus,*[11] and no more, they were
præludia resurrectionis, halfe-resurrections, prologues, and
inducements to the doctrine of the resurrection, which
shall be transacted with a *Surgite mortui,*[12] and no more.
So these naturall helps in the consideration of the creature, are *præludia resurrectionis,* they are halfe-resurrections, and these naturall resurrections carry us halfe way
to the miraculous resurrection. But certainely, the *Jews,*

Marginal notes: 1 Cor. 15.36; Ambr.; Tertull.; Idem; *An ex Scripturis*; Greg. Nyss.

10. *Tolle grabatum:* take up thy bed.
11. *Esto sanus:* be whole.
12. *Surgite mortui:* arise from the dead.

who had that, which the Gentiles wanted,[13] *The Scriptures*, had from them, a generall, though not an explicite knowledge of the resurrection. That they had it, we see by that practise of *Judas the Maccabee*, in gathering a contribution to send to *Jerusalem*, which is therefore commended, because he was therein mindefull of the Resurrection. Neither doth Christ find any that opposed the doctrine of the Resurrection, but those, who though they were tolerated in the State, because they were otherwise great persons, were absolute *Heretiques*, even amongst the *Jews*, *The Sadduces*. And *Saint Paul*, when, finding himselfe to bee oppressed in Judgement, hee used his Christian wisedome, and to draw a strong party to himselfe, protested himselfe to bee of the sect of the *Pharisees*, and that, as they, and all the rest, in generall, did, he maintained the Resurrection, he knew it would seem a strange injury, and an oppression, to be called in question for that, that they all beleeved; Though therefore our Saviour Christ, who disputed then, onely against the Sadduces, argued for the doctrine of the Resurrection, onely from that place of the Scripture, which those Sadduces acknowledged to be Scripture, (for they denied all but the *bookes of Moses*) and so insisted upon those words, *I am the God of Abraham, the God of Isaac, and the God of Jacob,* yet certainely the *Jews* had established that doctrine, upon other places too, though to the Sadduces who accepted *Moses* onely, *Moses* were the best evidence. It is evident enough in that particular place of *Daniel, Many of them that sleep in the dust of the earth, shall awake, some to everlasting life, and some to shame, and everlasting contempt.* And in *Daniel*, that word *many*, must not be restrained[14] to lesse then all; *Daniel* intends by that many, that how many soever they are, they shall all arise; as Saint *Paul* does, when he says, By one mans disobedience, *many* were made sinners; that is, *All;* for, death passed over *all men; for all* have sinned. And Christ doth but paraphrase that place of *Daniel*, who says, *Multi,* many, when he says, *Omnes,* all; *All that are in the grave shall heare his voyce and shall come forth;* They that have done good, unto the resur-

2 Macab.
12.43

Act. 23.6

Luke 20.3
Exod. 3.6

12.2

Rom. 5.19
12

John 5.28

---

13. *wanted:* lacked.
14. *restrained:* restricted.

rection of life, and they that have done evill to the resurrection of damnation. This then being thus far settled, that the *Jews understood* the resurrection, and more then that, they *beleeved* it, and therefore, as they had light in nature, they had assurance in Scripture, come we now, to that which was our last purpose in this first part, whether in *this* text, in these words of *Job*, (*though after my skin, wormes destroy my body*) there be any such light of the Resurrection given.

An ex hâc Scriptura

It is true, that in the new Testament, where the doctrine of the resurrection is more evidently, more liquidly delivered, then in the old, (though it be delivered in the old too) there is no place cited out of the book of *Job*, for the resurrection; and so, this is not. But it is no marvaile; both upon that reason which we noted before, that they who were to be convinced, were such as received onely the *books* of *Moses*, and therefore all citations from this booke of *Job*, or any other had been impertinently and frivolously employed, and, because in the new Testament, there is but one place of this booke of *Job* cited at all. To

1 [Cor.] 3.19

the *Corinthians* the Apostle makes use of those words in *Job*, *God taketh the wise in their owne craft;* And more then this one place, is not, (I thinke) cited out of this

[Job] 5.13

booke of *Job* in the new Testament. But, the authority of *Job* is established in another place; *you have heard of the*

[Jas.] 5.11

patience of Job, and you have seen the end of the Lord, says Saint *James.* As you have seen this, so you have heard that; seen and heard one way, out of the Scripture; you have hard [15] that out of the booke of *Job*, you have seen this out of the Gospell. And further then this, there is no naming of *Jobs* person, or his booke in the new Testa-

Præfat. in Job

ment. Saint *Hierome* confesses, that both the Greeke, and Latine Copies of this booke, were so defective in his time, that seven or eight hundred verses of the originall were wanting in the booke. And, for the originall it selfe, he says, *Obliquus totus liber fertur, & lubricus,* it is an uncertaine and slippery book. But this is onely for the sense of some places of the book; And that made the authority of this book, to be longer suspended in the Church, and oftener called into question by particular men, then any other

---

15. *hard*: heard.

book of the Bible. But, in those who have, for many ages, received this book for Canonicall, there is an unanime acknowledgement, (at least, tacitely) that this peece of it, this text, (*When, after my skin, wormes shall destroy my body, yet in my flesh I shall see God*) does establish the Resurrection.

Divide the expositors into three branches; (for, so, the world will needs divide them) The first, the Roman Church will call theirs; though they have no other title to them, but that they received the same translation that they doe. And all they use this text for the resurrection. *Verba viri in gentilitate positi erubescamus;* It is a shame for us, who have the word of God it selfe, (which *Job* had not) and have had such a commentary, such an exposition upon al the former word of God, as the reall, and actuall, and visible resurrection of Christ himselfe, *Erubescamus verba viri in gentilitate positi,* let us be ashamed and confounded, if *Job,* a person that lived not within the light of the covenant, saw the resurrection more clearly, and professed it more constantly then we doe. And, as this *Gregory* of *Rome,* so *Gregory Nyssen* understood *Job* too. For, he considers *Jobs* case thus; God promised *Job twofold* of all that he had lost; And in his sheep and camels, and oxen, and asses, which were utterly destroyed, and brought to nothing, God performes it punctually, he had all in a double proportion. But *Job* had seven sonnes, and three daughters before, and God gives him but seven sonnes, and three daughters againe; And yet *Job* had *twofold* of these too; for, *Postnati cum prioribus numerantur, quia omnes deo vivunt;* Those which were gone, and those which were new given, lived all one life, because they lived all in God; *Nec quicquam aliud est mors, nisi vitiositatis expiatio;* Death is nothing else, but a devesting of those defects, which made us lesse fit for God. And therefore, agreeably to this purpose, says Saint *Cyprian, Scimus non amitti, sed præmitti;* thy dead are not lost, but lent. *Non recedere, sed præcedere;* They are not gone into any other wombe, then we shall follow them into; *nec acquirendæ atræ vestes, pro iis qui albis induuntur,* neither should we put on *blacks,* for them that are clothed in white, nor mourne for them, that are entred into their Masters joy. We can enlarge our selfes no farther

Partes

Greg.

Greg.
Nyss.
42.10

13

Cyprian

in this consideration of the first branch of expositors, but that all the *ancients* tooke occasion from this text to argue for the resurrection.

Lutheran
Calvinist

Take into your Consideration the other two branches of moderne expositors, (whom others sometimes contume-liously, and themselves sometimes perversly have call'd *Lutherans* and *Calvinists*) and you may know, that in the first ranke, *Osiander*, and with him, all his [followers] interpret these words so; And in the other ranke, *Tre-mellius*, and *Pellicanus*, heretofore, *Polanus* lately, and *Piscator*, for the present; All these, and all the Translators into the vulgar tongues of all our neighbours of Europe, do all establish the doctrine of the Resurrection by these

Calvin
words, this place of *Job*. And therefore, though one, (and truly for any thing I know, but one) though one, to whom we all owe much, for the interpretation of the Scriptures, do think that *Job* intends no other resurrection in this place, but that, when he shall be reduc'd to the miserablest estate that can bee in this life, still he will look upon God, and trust in him for his restitution, and reparation in this life; let us with the whole Christian Church, embrace and magnifie this Holy and Heroicall Spirit of *Job*; *Scio*, says he; I know it, (which is more in him, then the *Credo* is in us, more to *know* it then, in that state, then to *believe* it now, after it hath been so evidently declar'd, not onely to be a certain truth, but to be an article of faith) *Scio Redemptorem*, says he; I know not onely a Creator, but a Redeemer; And, *Redemptorem meum*, My Redeemer, which implies a confidence, and a personall application of that Redemption to himself. *Scio vivere*, says he; I know that he lives; I know that hee begunne not in his Incarna-tion, I know he ended not in his death, but it always was, and is now, and shall for ever be true, *Vivit*, that he lives still. And then, *Scio venturum*, says he too; I know hee shall stand at the last day to Judge me and all the world; And after that, and *after my skinne and body is destroyed by worms, yet in my flesh I shall see God*. And so have you as much as we proposed for our first part; That the Jews do now, that they always did believe a Resurrection; That as naturall men, and by naturall reason they might know it, both in the possibility of the thing, and in the purpose of God, that they had better helpes then naturall reason, for

they had divers places of their Scripture, and that this place of Scripture, which is our text, hath evermore been received for a proof of the Resurrection. Proceed we now, to those particulars which constitute our second part, such instructions concerning the Resurrection, as arise out of the words, *Though after my skinne, worms destroy my body, yet in my flesh I shall see God.*

In this second part, the first thing that was propos'd, was, That the Saints of God, are not priviledg'd from this, which fell upon *Job,* This Death, this dissolution after death. Upon the *Morte morieris,* that double death, interminated by God upon *Adam,* there is a *Non obstante; Revertere,* turn to God, and thou shalt not dy the death, not the second death. But upon that part of the sentence, *In pulverem revertêris, To dust thou shalt return,* there is no *Non obstante;* though thou turn to God, thou must turn into the grave; for, hee that redeem'd thee from the other death, redeem'd not himself from this. Carry this consideration to the last minute of the world, when we that remain shall bee caught up in the clouds, yet even that last fire may be our fever, those clouds our winding sheets, that rapture our dissolution; and so, with *Saint Augustine,* most of the ancients, most of the latter men think, that there shall be a sudden dissolution of body and soul, which is death, and a sudden re-uniting of both, which is resurrection, in that instant; *Quis Homo,* is *Davids* question; *What man is he that liveth and shall not see death?* Let us adde, *Quis Deorum?* What god is he amongst the Gentiles, that hath not seen death? Which of their three hundred *Jupiters,* which of their thousands of other gods, have not seen death? *Mortibus moriuntur;* we may adde to that double death in Gods mouth, another death; The gods of the Gentiles have dyed *thrice;* In body, in soul, and in fame; for, though they have been glorified with a Deification, not one of all those old gods, is, at this day, worship, in any part of the world, but all those temporary, and transitory Gods, are worn out, and dead in all senses. Those gods, who were but men, fall under *Davids* question, *Quis Homo?* And that man who was truly God, fals under it too, Christ Jesus; He saw death, though he saw not the death of this text, *Corruption.* And, if we consider the effusion of his precious blood, the contusion of his sacred

margin: 2 Part
Sancti non eximuntur

1 Thes. 4.17

Psal. 89.48

flesh, the extension of those sinews, and ligaments which tyed heaven, and earth together, in a reconciliation, the departing of that Intelligence from that sphear, of that high Priest from that Temple, of that Dove from that Arke, of that soul from that body, that dissolution (which, as an ordinary man he should have had in the grave, but that the decree of God, declar'd in the infallibility of the manifold prophesies, preserv'd him from it) had been but a slumber, in respect of these tortures, which he did suffer; The *Godhead* staid with him in the grave, and so he did not corrupt, but, though our souls be gone up to God, our bodies shall.

In pella *Corruption in the skin,* says *Job;* In the outward beauty, These be the Records of velim, these be the parchmins,[16] the endictments, and the evidences that shall condemn many of us, at the last day, our *own skins;* we have the book of God, the Law, written in our own hearts; we have the image of God imprinted in our own souls; wee have the character, and seal of God stamped in us, in our baptism; and, all this is bound up in this velim, in this parchmin, in this skin of ours, and we neglect book, and image, and character, and seal, and all for the covering. It is not a clear case, if we consider the originall words

2 Reg properly, That *Jesabel* [17] *did paint;* and yet all translators,
9.30 and expositors have taken a just occasion, out of the ambiguity of those words, to cry down that abomination of painting. It is not a clear case, if we consider the propriety

2 Sam. of the words, That *Absolon was hanged by the hair of the*
18.9 *head;* and yet the Fathers and others have made use of that indifferency, and verisimilitude, to explode that abomination, of cherishing and curling haire, to the enveagling, and ensnaring, and entangling of others; *Judicium*

Hieron. *patietur æternum,* says *Saint Hierome,* Thou art guilty of a murder, though no body die; *Quia vinum attulisti, si fuisset qui bibisset;* Thou hast poyson'd a cup, if any would drink, thou hast prepar'd a tentation, if any would

Tertul. swallow it. *Tertullian* thought he had done enough, when he had writ his book *De Habitu muliebri,* against the excesse of women in clothes, but he was fain to adde another

16. *parchmins:* parchments.
17. *Jesabel:* Jezebel.

with more vehemence, *De cultu fœminarum*, that went
beyond their clothes to their skin. And he concludes,
Illud ambitionis crimen, there's vain-glory in their excesse
of clothes, but, *Hoc prostitutionis*, there's prostitution in
drawing the eye to the skin. *Pliny* says, that when their
thin silke stuffes were first invented at Rome, *Excogitatum
ad fœminas denudandas;* It was but an invention that
women might go naked in clothes, for their skins might bee
seen through those clothes, those thinne stuffes: Our
women are not so carefull, but they expose their nakednesse professedly, and paint it, to cast bird-lime for the
passengers eye. Beloved, good dyet makes the best Complexion, and a good Conscience is a continuall feast; A
cheerfull heart makes the best blood, and peace with God
is the true cheerfulnesse of heart. Thy Saviour neglected
his skin so much, as that at last, hee scarse had any; all
was torn with the whips, and scourges; and thy skin shall
come to that absolute corruption, as that, though a hundred years after thou art buryed, one may find thy bones,
and say, this was a *tall* man, this was a *strong* man, yet we
shall soon be past saying, upon any relique of thy skinne,
This was a *fair*[18] man; Corruption seises the skinne, all
outward beauty quickly, and so it does the body, the
whole frame and constitution, which is another consideration; *After my skinne, my Body.*

If *the whole body were an eye, or an ear, where were
the body,* says Saint *Paul;* but, when of the whole body
there is neither eye nor ear, nor any member left, where
is the body? And what should an eye do there, where
there is nothing to be seen but loathsomnesse; or a nose
there, where there is nothing to be smelt, but putrefaction;
or an ear, where in the grave they doe not praise God?
Doth not that body that boasted but yesterday of that
priviledge above all creatures, that it onely could goe
upright, lie to day as flat upon the earth as the body of a
horse, or of a dogge? And doth it not to morrow lose his
other priviledge, of looking up to heaven? Is it not farther
remov'd from the eye of heaven, the Sunne, then any
dogge, or horse, by being cover'd with the earth, which
they are not? Painters have presented to us with some

In corpore
1 Cor.
12.17

18. *fair:* beautiful.

horrour, the *sceleton,* the frame of the bones of a mans body; but the state of a body, in the dissolution of the grave, no pencil can present to us. Between that excremen-tall jelly that thy body is made of at first, and that jelly which thy body dissolves to at last; there is not so noy-some, so putrid a thing in nature. This skinne, (this out-ward beauty) this body, (this whole constitution) must be destroy'd, says *Job,* in the next place.

Destroyed The word is well chosen, by which all this is expressed, in this text, *Nakaph,* which is a word of as heavy a signifi-cation, to expresse an utter abolition, and annihilation, as perchance can be found in all the Scriptures. *Tremellius* hath mollifyed it in his translation; there it is but *Confo-dere,* to pierce. And yet it is such a piercing, such a sap-ping, such an undermining, such a demolishing of a fort or Castle, as may justly remove us from any high valua-tion, or any great confidence, in that skinne, and in that body, upon which this *Confoderint* must fall. But, in the great Bible it is *Contriverint,* Thy *skinne,* and thy *body* shall be *ground* away, trod away upon the ground. Aske where that iron is that is ground off of a knife, or axe; Aske that marble that is worn off of the threshold in the Church-porch by continuall treading, and with that iron, and with that marble, thou mayst finde thy Fathers skinne, and body; *Contrita sunt,* The knife, the marble, the skinne, the body are ground away, trod away, they are destroy'd, who knows the revolutions of dust? Dust upon the Kings high-way, and dust upon the Kings grave, are both, or neither, Dust Royall, and may change places; who knows the revolutions of dust? Even in the dead body of Christ Jesus himself, one dram of the decree of his Father, one sheet, one sentence of the prediction of the Prophets preserv'd his body from corruption, and incineration, more then all *Josephs* new tombs, and fine linnen, and great proportion of spices could have done. O, who can expresse this inexpressible mystery? The soul of Christ Jesus, which took no harm by him, contracted no Originall sin, in coming to him, was guilty of no more sin, when it went out, then when it came from the breath and bosome of God; yet this soul left this body in death. And the Divinity, the Godhead, incomparably better then that soul, which soul was incomparably better then all the

Saints, and Angels in heaven, that Divinity, that God-head did not forsake the body, though it were dead. If we might compare things infinite in themselves, it was nothing so much, that God did assume mans nature, as that God did still cleave to that man, then when he was no man, in the separation of body and soul, in the grave. But fall we from incomprehensible mysteries; for, there is morti-fication enough, (and mortification is vivification, and ædification) in this obvious consideration; *skinne and body*, beauty and substance must be destroy'd; And, *Destroyed by wormes*, which is another descent in this humiliation, and exinanition of man, in death; *After my skinne, wormes shall destroy this body*.

I will not insist long upon this, because it is not in the Originall; In the Originall there is no mention of *wormes*. But because in other places of *Job* there is, (*They shal lye down alike in the dust, and the* worms *shall cover them*) (*The* womb *shal forget them, and the* worm *shal feed sweetly on them*) and because the word *Destroying* is presented in that form and number, *Contriverint*, when *they* shall destroy, *they* and no other persons, no other creatures named; both our later translations, (for indeed, our first translation hath no mention of *wormes*) and so very many others, even *Tremellius* that adheres most to the letter of the Hebrew, have filled up this place, with that addition, *Destroyed by worms*. It makes the destruc-tion the more contemptible; Thou that wouldest not admit the beames of the Sunne upon thy skinne, and yet hast ad-mitted the pollutions of sinne; Thou that wouldst not admit the breath of the ayre upon thy skinne, and yet hast admitted the spirit of lust, and unchast solicitations to breath upon thee, in execrable oathes, and blasphemies, to vicious purposes; Thou, whose body hath (as farre as it can) putrefyed and corrupted even the body of thy Saviour, in an unworthy receiving thereof, in this *skinne*, in this *body*, must be the food of worms, the prey of destroying worms. After a low birth thou mayst passe an honourable life, after a sentence of an ignominious death, thou mayst have an honourable end; But, in the grave canst thou make these worms silke worms? They were bold and early worms that eat up *Herod* before he dyed; They are bold and everlasting worms, which after

Vermes

21.26

24.20

Acts 12.23

thy skinne and body is destroyed, shall remain as long as
God remains, in an eternall gnawing of thy conscience;
long, long after the destroying of skinne and body, by
bodily worms.

Post   Thus farre then to the *destroying of skinne and body by
worms,* all men are equall; Thus farre all's *Common law,*
and no *Prerogative,*[19] so is it also in the next step too; The
Resurrection is common to all: The Prerogative lies not
in the Rising, but in the rising to the fruition of the sight
of God; in which consideration, the first beam of comfort
is the *Postquam, After all this,* destruction before by worms;
ruinous misery before; but there is something else to be
done upon me after. God leaves no state without comfort.
God leaves some inhabitants of the earth, under longer
nights then others, but none under an everlasting night;
and, those, whom he leaves under those long nights, he
recompenses with as long days, after. I were miserable, if
there were not an *Antequam* in my behalfe; if before I had
done well or ill actually in this world, God had not
wrapped me up, in his *good purpose* upon me. And I
were miserable againe, if there were not a *Postquam* in my
behalfe; If, after my sinne had cast me into the grave,
there were not a lowd trumpet to call me up, and a gracious countenance to looke upon me, when I were risen.
Nay, let my life have been as religious, as the infirmities
1 Cor.   of this life can admit, yet, *If in this life onely we have
15.19   hope in Christ, we are, of all men, most miserable.* For, for
the worldly things of this life, first, the children of God
have them in the least proportions of any; and, besides
that, those children of God, which have them in larger
proportion, do yet make the least use of them, of any
others, because the children of the world, are not so
tender conscienced, nor so much afraid, lest those worldly
things should become snares, and occasions of tentation to
them, if they open themselves to a full enjoying thereof,
as the children of God are. And therefore, after my wanting of many worldly things, (after a penurious life) and,
after my not daring to use those things that I have, so
freely as others doe, after that holy and conscientious
forbearing of those things that other men afford them-

19. *Prerogative:* privilege.

selves, after my leaving all these absolutely behind me here, and my skin and body in destruction in the grave, After all, there remaines something else for me. *After;* but *how long after?* That's next.

When Christ was in the body of that flesh, which we are in, now, (sinne onely excepted) he said, in that state that he was in then, *Of that day and houre, no man knoweth, not the Angels, not the Sonne.* Then, in that state, he excludes himselfe. And when Christ was risen againe, in an uncorruptible body, he said, even to his nearest followers, *Non est vestrum,* it is not for you, to know times, and seasons. Before in his state of mortality, *seipsum annumeravit ignorantibus,* he pretended to know no more of this, then they that knew nothing. After, when he had invested immortality, *per sui exceptionem,* (says that Father) he excepts none but himselfe; all the rest, even the *Apostles,* were left ignorant thereof. For this *non est vestrum,* (it is not for you) is part of the last sentence that ever Christ spake to them. If it be a convenient answer to say, Christ knew it not, as man, how bold is that man that will pretend to know it? And, if it be a convenient interpretation of Christs words, that he knew it not, that is, knew it not so, as that he might tell it them, how indiscreet are they, who, though they may seem to know it, will publish it? For, thereby they fill other men with scruples, and vexations, and they open themselves to scorne and reproach, when their predictions prove false, as Saint *Augustine* observed in his time, and every age hath given examples since, of confident men that have failed in these conjectures. It is a poore pretence to say, this intimation, this impression of a certaine time, prepares men with better dispositions. For, they have so often been found false, that it rather weakens the credit of the thing it selfe. In the old world they knew exactly the time of the destruction of the world; that there should be an hundred and twenty years, before the flood came; And yet, upon how few, did that prediction, though from the mouth of God himselfe, work to repentance? *Noah* found grace in Gods eyes; but it was not because he mended his life upon that prediction, but he was gratious in Gods sight before. At the day of our death, we write *Pridie resurrectionis,* the day before the resurrection; It is *Vigilia resurrectionis;*

Quando?

Mar. 13.32

Acts 1.7
Basil

Gen. 6.3

Our Easter Eve. *Adveniat regnum tuum*, possesse my soule of thy kingdome then: And, *Fiat voluntas tua*, my body shall arise after, but how soon after, or how late after, thy will bee done then, by thy selfe, and thy will bee knowne, till then, to thy selfe.

Ego   We passe on. As in *Massa damnata*, the whole lump of mankind is under the condemnation of *Adams* sinne, and yet the good purpose of God severs some men from that condemnation, so, at the resurrection, all shall rise; but not all to glory. But, amongst them, that doe, *Ego*, says *Job*, I shall. I, as I am the same man, made up of the same body, and the same soule. Shall I imagine a difficulty in my body, because I have lost an Arme in the East, and a leg in the West? because I have left some bloud in the North, and some bones in the South? Doe but remember, with what ease you have sate in the chaire, casting an account, and made a shilling on one hand, a pound on the other, or five shillings below, ten above, because all these lay easily within your reach. Consider how much lesse, all this earth is to him, that sits in heaven, and spans all this world, and reunites in an instant armes, and legs, bloud, and bones, in what corners so ever they be scattered. The greater work may seem to be in reducing the soul; That that soule which sped so ill in that body, last time it came to it, as that it contracted *Originall sinne* then, and was put to the slavery to serve that body, and to serve it in the ways of sinne, not for an Apprentiship of seven, but seventy years after, that that soul after it hath once got loose by death, and liv'd God knows how many thousands of years, free from that body, that abus'd it so before, and in the sight and fruition of that God, where it was in no danger, should willingly, nay desirously, ambitiously seek this scattered body, this Eastern, and Western, and Northern, and Southern body, this is the most inconsiderable considera- tion; and yet, *Ego*, I, I the same body, and the same soul, shall be recompact again, and be identically, numerically, individually the same man. The same integrity of body, and soul, and the same integrity in the Organs of my body, and in the faculties of my soul too; I shall be all there, my body, and my soul, and all my body, and all my soul. I am not all here, I am here now preaching upon this text, and I am at home in my Library considering whether *S*.

Gregory, or *S. Hierome*, have said best of this text, before. I am here speaking to you, and yet I consider by the way, in the same instant, what it is likely you will say to one another, when I have done. You are not all here neither; you are here now, hearing me, and yet you are thinking that you have heard a better Sermon somewhere else, of this text before; you are here, and yet you think you could have heard some other doctrine of downright *Predestination*, and *Reprobation* roundly delivered somewhere else with more edification to you; you are here, and you remember your selves that now yee think of it, this had been the fittest time, now, when every body else is at Church, to have made such and such a private visit; and because you would bee there, you are there. I cannot say, you cannot say so perfectly, so entirely now, as at the Resurrection, *Ego*, I am here; I, body and soul; I, soul and faculties; as Christ sayd to *Peter*, *Noli timere, Ego sum, Fear nothing, it is I;* so I say to my selfe, *Noli timere;* My soul, why art thou so sad, my body, why dost thou languish? *Ego*, I, body and soul, soul and faculties, shall say to Christ Jesus, *Ego sum*, Lord, it is I, and hee shall not say, *Nescio te, I know thee not*, but avow me, and place me at his right hand. *Ego sum, I am the man that hath seen affliction, by the rod of his wrath; Ego sum*, and I the same man, shall receive the crown of glory which shall not fade. [Mat. 14.27]

Lam. 3.1
1 Pet. 5.4

Ego, I, the same person; *Ego videbo*, I shall see; I have had no looking-glasse in my grave, to see how my body looks in the dissolution; I know not how. I have had no houre-glasse in my grave to see how my time passes; I know not when: for, when my eylids are closed in my death-bed, *the Angel hath said to me, That time shall be no more;* Till I see eternity, the ancient of days, I shall see no more; but then I shall. Now, why is *Job* gladder of the use of this sense of seeing, then of any of the other? He is not; He is glad of seeing, but not of the sense, but of the Object. It is true that is said in the School,[20] *Vicinius se habent potentiæ sensitivæ ad animam quàm corpus;* Our sensitive faculties have more relation to the soul, then to the body; but yet to some purpose, and in some measure, *Videbo*

Apoc. 10.6
Dan. 7.9

Aquin. sup.
q. 82 ar. 4

20. *School:* among the scholastic philosophers

all the senses shall be in our glorifyed bodies, *In actu*, or *in potentiâ*, say they; so as that wee shall use them, or so as that we might. But this sight that *Job* speaks of, is onely the fruition of the presence of God, in which consists eternall blessednesse. Here, in this world, we see God *per speculum*, says the Apostle, by reflection, upon a glasse; we see a creature; and from that there arises an assurance that there is a Creator; we see him *in ænigmate*, says he; which is not ill rendred in the margin, in a *Riddle;* we see him in the Church, but men have made it a riddle, which is the Church; we see him in the Sacrament, but men have made it a riddle, by what light, and at what window: Doe I see him at the window of bread and wine; Is he in that; or doe I see him by the window of faith; and is he onely in that? still it is in a riddle. Doe I see him *à Priore*, (I see that I am elected, and therefore I cannot sinne to death?) Or doe I see him *à Posteriore*, (because I see my selfe carefull not to sin to death, therefore I am elected?) I shall see all problematicall things come to be dogmaticall, I shall see all these rocks in Divinity, come to bee smooth alleys; I shall see Prophesies untyed, Riddles dissolved, controversies reconciled; but I shall never see that, till I come to this sight which follows in our text, *Videbo Deum, I shall see God.*

1 Cor. 13.12

Deum

No man ever saw God and liv'd; and yet, I shall not live till I see God; and when I have seen him I shall never dye. What have I ever seen in this world, that hath been truly the same thing that it seemed to me? I have seen marble buildings, and a chip, a crust, a plaster, a face of marble hath pilld off, and I see brick-bowels within. I have seen beauty, and a strong breath from another, tels me, that that complexion is from without, not from a sound constitution within. I have seen the state of Princes, and all that is but ceremony; and, I would be loath to put a *Master of ceremonies* to define *ceremony*, and tell me what it is, and to include so various a thing as ceremony, in so constant a thing, as a Definition. I see a great Officer, and I see a man of mine own profession, of great revenues, and I see not the interest of the money, that was paid for it, I see not the pensions, nor the Annuities, that are charged upon that Office, or that Church. As he that fears God, fears nothing else, so, he that sees God, sees every thing else: when we shall see God, *Sicuti est*, as he is, we shall see all things *Sicuti sunt*, as they are; for that's their Essence, as they conduce to his glory. We shall be no more deluded with outward appearances: for, when this sight, which we intend [21] here comes, there will be no delusory thing to be seen. All that we have made as though we saw, in this world, will be vanished, and I shall see nothing but God, and what is in him; and him I shall see *In carne, in the flesh*, which is another degree of Exaltation in mine Exinanition.[22]

I shall see him, *In carne suâ, in his flesh*: And this was one branch in *Saint Augustines* great wish, That he might have seen Rome in her state, That he might have heard S. *Paul* preach, That he might have seen Christ in the flesh: *Saint Augustine* hath seen Christ in the flesh one thousand two hundred yeares; in Christs glorifyed flesh; but, it is with the eyes of his understanding, and in his soul. Our flesh, even in the Resurrection, cannot be a spectacle, a perspective glasse[23] to our soul. We shall see the Humanity of Christ with our bodily eyes, then glorifyed; but, that flesh, though glorifyed, cannot make us see God better, nor clearer, then the soul alone hath done, all the time, from our death, to our resurrection. But as an indulgent Father, or as a tender mother, when they go to see the King in any Solemnity, or any other thing of observation, and curiosity, delights to carry their child, which is flesh of their flesh, and bone of their bone, with them, and though the child cannot comprehend it as well as they, they are as glad that the child sees it, as that they see it themselves; such a gladnesse shall my soul have, that this flesh, (which she will no longer call her prison, nor her tempter, but her friend, her companion, her wife) that this flesh, that is, I, in the re-union, and redintegration of both parts, shall see God; for then, one principall clause in her rejoycing, and acclamation, shall be, that this flesh is her flesh; *In carne meâ, in my flesh I shall see God*.

It was the flesh of every wanton object here, that would allure it in the petulancy of mine eye. It was the flesh of every Satyricall Libeller, and defamer, and calumniator of

margin: 1 John 3.2

margin: In carne

margin: In carne

margin: Mea

21. *intend*: consider.
22. *Exinanition*: emptiness.
23. *glasse*: telescope.

other men, that would call upon it, and tickle mine ear
with aspersions and slanders of persons in authority. And
in the grave, it is the flesh of the worm; the possession
is transfer'd to him. But, in heaven, it is *Caro mea, My
flesh,* my souls flesh, my Saviours flesh. As my meat is
assimilated to my flesh, and made one flesh with it; as my
2 Pet. 1.4 soul is assimilated to my God, and *made partaker of the
1 Cor. 6.17 divine nature,* and *Idem Spiritus,* the same Spirit with it;
so, there my flesh shall be assimilated to the flesh of my
Athanas. Saviour, and made the same flesh with him too. *Verbum
caro factum, ut caro resurgeret;* Therefore the Word was
made flesh, therefore God was made man, that that union
might exalt the flesh of man to the right hand of God.
That's spoken of the flesh of Christ; and then to facilitate
Cyril the passage for us, *Reformat ad immortalitatem suam par-
ticipes sui;* those who are worthy receivers of his flesh
Rom. 8.11 here, are the same flesh with him; And, *God shall quicken
your mortall bodies, by his Spirit that dwelleth in you.*
But this is not in consummation, in full accomplishment,
till this resurrection, when it shall be *Caro mea,* my flesh,
so, as that nothing can draw it from the allegiance of my
God; and *Caro mea, My flesh,* so, as that nothing can devest me of it. Here a bullet will aske a man, where's your
arme; and a Wolf wil ask a woman, where's your breast?
A sentence in the Star-chamber[24] will aske him, where's
your ear, and a months close prison will aske him, where's
your flesh? a fever will aske him, where's your Red, and
a morphew will aske him, where's your white? But when
after all this, when *after my skinne worms shall destroy
my body, I shall see God,* I shall see him in my flesh, which
shall be mine as inseparably, (in the *effect,* though not in
the *manner*) as the *Hypostaticall union* of God, and man,
in Christ, makes our nature and the Godhead one person
in him. My flesh shall no more be none of mine, then Christ
shall not be man, as well as God.

24. *Star-chamber:* refers to the secret tribunal of Stuart England, the
   sentences of which included the pillory and loss of ears.

PREACHED AT WHITE-HALL,
MARCH 8. *1621* [*1621/2*]

VOLUME IV: NUMBER 1[1]

I COR. 15.26. *THE LAST ENEMIE THAT SHALL
BE DESTROYED, IS DEATH.*

This is a Text of the Resurrection, and it is not Easter
yet; but it is Easter Eve; All Lent, is but the Vigill, the Eve
of Easter: to so long a Festivall as never shall end, the
Resurrection, wee may well begin the Eve betimes. Forty
yeares long was God grieved for that Generation which he   [Psa.
loved; let us be content to humble our selves forty daies,   95.10]
to be fitter for that glory which we expect. In the Booke
of God there are many *Songs;* there is but one *Lamenta-
tion:* And that one Song of *Solomon,* nay some one of
Davids hundred and fiftie Psalmes, is longer then the whole
booke of Lamentations. Make way to an everlasting
Easter by a short Lent, to an undeterminable glory, by
a temporary humiliation. You must weepe these teares,
teares of contrition, teares of mortification, before God
will wipe all teares from your eyes; You must dye this
death, this death of the righteous, the death to sin, before
this *last enemy, Death,* shalbe destroyed in you, and you
made partakers of everlasting life in soule and body too.

Our division shall be but a short, and our whole exercise   *Divisio*
but a larger paraphrase upon the words. The words imply
first, That the Kingdome of Christ, which must be perfected, must be accomplished, (because all things must
be subdued unto him) is not yet perfected, not accomplished yet. Why? what lacks it? It lacks the bodies of
Men, which yet lie under the dominion of another. When
we shall also see by that Metaphor which the Holy Ghost
chooseth to expresse that in, which is that there is *Hostis,*
and so *Militia,* an enemie, and a warre, and therefore that
Kingdome is not perfected, that he places perfect happinesse, and perfect glory, in perfect peace. But then how

1. *Number 1:* This sermon was originally published as No. 15 in
LXXX Sermons (London, 1640).

far is any State consisting of many men, how far the state, and condition of any one man in particular, from this perfect peace? How truly a warfare is this life, if the Kingdome of Heaven it selfe, have not this peace in perfection? And it hath it not, *Quia hostis,* because there is an enemy: though that enemy shall not overthrow it, yet because it plots, and workes, and machinates, and would overthrow it, this is a defect in that peace.

Who then is this enemy? An enemy that may thus far thinke himselfe equall to God, that as no man ever saw God, and lived; so no man ever saw this enemy and lived, for it is Death; And in this may thinke himselfe in number superiour to God, that many men live who shall never see God; But *Quis homo,* is *Davids* question, which was never answered, *Is there any man that lives, and shall not see death?* An enemie that is so well victualled against man, as that he cannot want as long as there are men, for he feeds upon man himselfe. And so well armed against Man, as that he cannot want Munition, while there are men, for he fights with our weapons, our owne faculties, nay our calamities, yea our owne pleasures are our death. And therefore he is *Novissimus hostis,* saith the Text, *The last enemy.*

We have other Enemies; Satan about us, sin within us; but the power of both those, this enemie shall destroy; but when they are destroyed, he shall retaine a hostile, and triumphant dominion over us. But *Usque quo Domine?* How long O Lord? for ever? No, *Abolebitur:* wee see this Enemy all the way, and all the way we feele him; but we shall see him destroyed; *Abolebitur.* But how? or when? At, and by the resurrection of our bodies: for as upon my expiration, my transmigration from hence, as soone as my soule enters into Heaven, I shall be able to say to the Angels, I am of the same stuffe as you, spirit, and spirit, and therefore let me stand with you, and looke upon the face of your God, and my God; so at the Resurrection of this body, I shall be able to say to the Angel of the great Councell, the Son of God, Christ Jesus himselfe, I am of the same stuffe as you, Body and body, Flesh and flesh, and therefore let me sit downe with you, at the right hand of the Father in an everlasting security from this

[Exod. 33.20]

[Psa. 89.48]

[Rev. 6.10]

[Isa. 9.6 Sept.]

last enemie, who is now destroyed, death. And in these seven steps we shall passe apace, and yet cleerely through this paraphrase.

We begin with this; That the Kingdome of Heaven hath not all that it must have to a consummate perfection, till it have bodies too. In those infinite millions of millions of generations, in which the holy, blessed, and glorious Trinity enjoyed themselves one another, and no more, they thought not their glory so perfect, but that it might receive an addition from creatures; and therefore they made a world, a materiall world, a corporeall world, they would have bodies. In that noble part of that world which *Moses* cals the Firmament, that great expansion from Gods chaire to his footstoole,[2] from Heaven to earth, there was a defect, which God did not supply that day, nor the next, but the fourth day, he did; for that day he made those bodies, those great, and lightsome bodies, the Sunne, and Moone, and Starres, and placed them in the Firmament. So also the Heaven of Heavens, the Presence Chamber of God himselfe, expects the presence of our bodies. *Vestig.* 1 *Quia desunt Corpora*

[Gen. 1.6-8]

[Gen. 1.14-16]

No State upon earth, can subsist without those bodies, Men of their owne. For men that are supplied from others, may either in necessity, or in indignation, be withdrawne, and so that State which stood upon forraine legs, sinks. Let the head be gold, and the armes silver, and the belly brasse, if the feete be clay, Men that may slip, and molder away, all is but an Image, all is but a dreame of an Image: for forraine helps are rather crutches then legs. There must be bodies, Men, and able bodies, able men; Men that eate the good things of the land, their owne figges and olives; Men not macerated with extortions: They are glorified bodies that make up the kingdome of Heaven; bodies that partake of the good of the State, that make up the State. Bodies, able bodies, and lastly, bodies inanimated with one soule: one vegetative soule, head and members must grow together, one sensitive soule, all must be sensible and compassionate of one anothers miserie; and especially one Immortall soule, one supreame soule, Dan. 2.32

---

2. *footstoole:* God's footstool is a traditional epithet for nature. See "Goodfriday, 1613."

one Religion.[3] For as God hath made us under good Princes, a great example of all that, Abundance of Men, Men that live like men, men united in one Religion, so wee need not goe farre for an example of a slippery, and uncertaine being, where they must stand upon other Mens men, and must over-load all men with exactions, and have admitted distractions and distortions, and convulsions, and earthquakes in the multiplicity of Religions.

The Kingdome of Heaven must have bodies; Kingdomes of the earth must have them; and if upon the earth thou beest in the way to Heaven, thou must have a body too, a body of thine owne, a body in thy possession: for thy body hath thee, and not thou it, if thy body tyrannize over thee. If thou canst not withdraw thine eye from an object of tentation,[4] or withhold thy hand from subscribing against thy conscience, nor turne thine eare from a popular, and seditious Libell, what hast thou towards a man? Thou hast no soule, nay thou hast no body: There is a body, but thou hast it not, it is not thine, it is not in thy power. Thy body will rebell against thee even in a sin: It will not performe a sin, when, and where thou wouldst have it. Much more will it rebell against any good worke, till thou have imprinted *Stigmata Jesu, The Markes of the Lord Jesus,* which were but exemplar in him, but are essentiall, and necessary to thee, abstinencies, and such discreete disciplines, and mortifications, as may subdue that body to thee, and make it thine: for till then it is but thine enemy, and maintaines a warre against thee; and war, and enemie is the Metaphore which the holy Ghost hath taken here to expresse a want, a kind of imperfectnesse even in Heaven it selfe. *Bellum Symbolum mali.* As peace is of all goodnesse, so warre is an embleme, a Hieroglyphique, of all misery; And that is our second step in this paraphrase.

If the feete of them that preach peace, be beautifull, (And, *O how beautifull are the feete of them that preach peace?* The Prophet *Isaiah* askes the question, 52.7. And

Gal. 6.17

Vestig. 2
Pax &
bellum

3. *one . . . Religion:* Donne makes use of the concept of the three souls—vegetative, sensitive, and rational—of which plants were believed to possess only the first, animals the first two, and human beings all three.

4. *tentation:* temptation.

the Prophet *Nahum* askes it, 1.15. and the Apostle S. *Paul*
askes it, *Rom.* 10.15. They all aske it, but none answers it)
who shall answer us, if we aske, How beautifull is his face,
who is the Author of this peace, when we shall see that
in the glory of Heaven, the Center of all true peace? It
was the inheritance of Christ Jesus upon the earth, he had
it at his birth, he brought it with him, *Glory be to God on*   Luke 2.14
high, peace upon earth. It was his purchase upon earth,
He made peace (indeed he bought peace) *through the*   Colos.
blood of his Crosse. It was his Testament, when he went   1.20
from earth; *Peace I leave with you, my peace I give unto*   John
you. Divide with him in that blessed Inheritance, partake   14.27
with him in that blessed Purchase, enrich thy selfe with
that blessed Legacy, his Peace.

Let the whole world be in thy consideration as one
house; and then consider in that, in the peacefull harmony
of creatures, in the peacefull succession, and connexion of
causes, and effects, the peace of Nature. Let this Kingdome, where God hath blessed thee with a being, be the
Gallery, the best roome of that house, and consider in
the two walls of that Gallery, the Church and the State,
the peace of a royall, and a religious Wisedome; Let thine
owne family be a Cabinet in this Gallery, and finde in all
the boxes thereof, in the severall duties of Wife, and
Children, and servants, the peace of vertue, and of the
father and mother of all vertues, active discretion, passive
obedience; and then lastly, let thine owne bosome be the
secret box, and reserve in this Cabinet, and find there the
peace of conscience, and truelie thou hast the best Jewell
in the best Cabinet, and that in the best Gallery of the
best house that can be had, peace with the Creature,[5] peace
in the Church, peace in the State, peace in thy house, peace
in thy heart, is a faire Modell, and a lovely designe even
of the heavenly Jerusalem which is *Visio pacis*,[6] where
there is no object but peace.

And therefore the holy Ghost to intimate to us, that
happy perfectnesse, which wee shall have at last, and not
till then, chooses the Metaphor of an enemy, and enmity,
to avert us from looking for true peace from any thing

5. *Creature:* created nature.
6. *Visio pacis:* vision of peace.

that presents it selfe in the way. Neither truly could the holy Ghost imprint more horror by any word, then that which intimates war, as the word *enemy* does. It is but a little way that the Poet hath got in the description of war, *Jam seges est*, that now, that place is ploughed where the great City stood: for it is not so great a depopulation to translate a City from Merchants to husbandmen, from shops to ploughes, as it is from many Husbandmen to one Shepheard, and yet that hath beene often done. And all that, at most, is but a depopulation, it is not a devastation, that Troy was ploughed. But, when the Prophet *Isaiah* comes to the devastation, to the extermination of a war, he expresses it first thus; *Where there were a thousand Vineyards at a cheape rate, all the land [shall] become briars and thornes:* That is much; but there is more, *The earth shall be removed out of her place; that Land, that Nation, shall no more be called that Nation, nor that Land:* But, yet more then that too; Not onely, not that people, but no other shall ever inhabit it. *It shall never be inhabited from generation to generation, neither shall Shepheards be there;* Not onely no Merchant, nor Husbandman, but no depopulator: *none but Owles, and Ostriches, and Satyres,* Indeed God knowes what, *Ochim,* and *Ziim,* words which truly we cannot translate.

Esay 7.23

Esay 13.13

Esay 13.20–21

In a word, the horror of War is best discerned in the company he keeps, in his associates. And when the Prophet *Gad* brought *War* into the presence of *David,* there came with him *Famine,* and *Pestilence.* And when Famine entred, we see the effects; It brought Mothers to eat their Children of a span long; that is, as some Expositors take it, to take medicines to procure abortions, to cast their Children, that they might have Children to eate. And when War's other companion, the Pestilence entred, we see the effects of that too: In lesse then half the time that it was threatned for, it devoured three-score and ten thousand of *Davids* men; and yet for all the vehemence, the violence, the impetuousnesse of this Pestilence, *David* chose this Pestilence rather then a War. *Militia* and *Malitia,* are words of so neare a sound, as that the vulgat Edition takes them as one. For where the Prophet speaking of the miseries that Hierusalem had suffered, sayes, *Finita militia ejus,* Let her *warfare* be at an end, they

2 Sam. 24.13 [Lam. 2.20]

Esay 40.2

reade, *Finita malitia ejus,* Let her *misery* be at an end;
War and Misery is all one thing. But is there any of this
in heaven? Even the Saints in heaven lack something of
the consummation of their happinesse, *Quia hostis,* because
they have an enemy. And that is our third and next step.

Now there is noe warre in heaven. There was warre in
heaven, sayes St. *John, Michael* and his Angels fought
against the devill and his Angels; though that war ended
in victory, yet (taking that war, as divers Expositors doe,
for the fall of Angels) that Kingdome lost so many inhabitants, as that all the soules of all that shall be saved,
shall but fill up the places of them that fell, and so make
that Kingdome but as well as it was before that war: So
ill effects accompany even the most victorious war. There
is no war in heaven, yet all is not well, because there is
an enemy; for that enemy would kindle a war again, but
that he remembers how ill he sped last time he did so.
It is not an enemy that invades neither, but only detaines:
he detaines the bodies of the Saints which are in heaven,
and therefore is an enemy to the Kingdome of Christ; He
that detaines the soules of men in Superstition, that detaines the hearts and allegeance of Subjects in an hæsitation,
a vacillation, an irresolution, where they shall fix them,
whether upon their Soveraign, or a forraigne power, he is
in the notion, and acceptation of enemy in this Text; an
enemy, though no hostile act be done. It is not a war, it is
but an enemy; not an invading, but a detaining enemy;
and then this enemy is but one enemy, and yet he troubles,
and retards the consummation of that Kingdome.

Antichrist alone is enemy enough; but never carry this
consideration beyond thy self. As long as there remaines
in thee one sin, or the sinfull gain of that one sin, so long
there is one enemy, and where there is one enemy, there
is no peace. Gardners that husband their ground to the
best advantage, sow all their seeds in such order, one under another, that their Garden is alwayes full of that
which is then in season. If thou sin with that providence,
with that seasonablenesse, that all thy spring, thy youth
be spent in wantonnesse, all thy Summer, thy middle-age
in ambition, and the wayes of preferment, and thy Autumne, thy Winter in indevotion and covetousnesse,
though thou have no farther taste of licentiousnesse, in thy

Apoc. 12.7
Vest. 3
Quia
Hostis

middle-age, thou hast thy satiety in that sin, nor of ambition in thy last yeares, thou hast accumulated titles of honour, yet all the way thou hast had one enemy, and therefore never any perfect peace. But who is this one enemy in this Text? As long as we put it off, and as loath as we are to look this enemy in the face, yet we must, *Mors* though it be Death. And this is *Vestigium quartum,* The fourth and next step in this paraphrase.

Jer. 18.2 *Surge & descende in domum figuli,* sayes the Prophet *Jeremy,* that is, say the Expositors, to the consideration of thy Mortality. It is *Surge, descende, Arise and go down:* A descent with an ascension: Our grave is upward, and our heart is upon *Jacobs* Ladder, in the way, and nearer to heaven. Our daily Funerals are some Emblemes of that; for though we be laid down in the earth after, yet we are lifted up upon mens shoulders before. We rise in the descent to death, and so we do in the descent to the contemplation of it. In all the Potters house, is there one vessell made of better stuffe then clay? There is his matter. And of all formes, a Circle is the perfectest,[7] and art thou loath to make up that Circle, with returning to the earth again?

Thou must, though thou be loath. *Fortasse,* sayes S. *Augustine,* That word of contingency, of casualty, Perchance, *In omnibus ferme rebus, præterquam in morte locum habet:* It hath roome in all humane actions excepting death. He makes his example thus: such a man is married; where he would, or at least where he must, where his parents, or his Gardian will have him; shall he have Children? *Fortasse,* sayes he, They are a yong couple, perchance they shall: And shall those Children be sons? *Fortasse,* they are of a strong constitution, perchance they shall: And shall those sons live to be men? *Fortasse,* they are from healthy parents, perchance they shall: And when they have lived to be men, shall they be good men? Such as good men may be glad they may live? *Fortasse,* still; They are of vertuous parents, it may be they shall: But when they are come to that *Morientur,* shall those good men die? here, sayes that Father, the *Fortasse* vanishes; here it is *omnino, certè, sine dubitatione;* infallibly, inevi-

---

7. *Circle . . . perfectest:* a generally. received notion in Renaissance thought.

tably, irrecoverably they must die. Doth not man die even
in his birth? The breaking of prison is death, and what
is our birth, but a breaking of prison? Assoon as we were
clothed by God, our very apparell was an Embleme of
death. In the skins of dead beasts, he covered the skins of
dying men. Assoon as God set us on work, our very occupation was an Embleme of death; It was to digge the
earth; not to digge pitfals for other men, but graves for
our selves. Hath any man here forgot to day, that yesterday is dead? And the Bell tolls for to day, and will ring
out anon; and for as much of every one of us, as apper-
taines to this day. *Quotidiè morimur, & tamen nos esse
æternos putamus,* sayes S. *Hierome;* We die every day, and
we die all the day long; and because we are not absolutely
dead, we call that an eternity, an eternity of dying: And
is there comfort in that state? why, that is the state of
hell it self, Eternall dying, and not dead.

But for this there is enough said, by the Morall man[8];
(that we may respite divine proofes, for divine points anon,
for our severall Resurrections) for this death is meerly
naturall, and it is enough that the morall man sayes, *Mors
lex, tributum, officium mortalium.* First it is *lex,* you were   Seneca
born under that law, upon that condition to die: so it is
a rebellious thing not to be content to die, it opposes the
Law. Then it is *Tributum,* an imposition which nature the
Queen of this world layes upon us, and which she will
take, when and where she list; here a yong man, there an
old man, here a happy, there a miserable man; And so it
is a seditious thing not to be content to die, it opposes
the prerogative. And lastly, it is *Officium,* men are to have
their turnes, to take their time, and then to give way by
death to successors; and so it is *Incivile, inofficiosum,* not
to be content to die, it opposes the frame and form of
government. It comes equally to us all, and makes us all
equall when it comes. The ashes of an Oak in the Chim-
ney, are no Epitaph of that Oak, to tell me how high or
how large that was; It tels me not what flocks it sheltered
while it stood, nor what men it hurt when it fell. The
dust of great persons graves is speechlesse too, it sayes
nothing, it distinguishes nothing: As soon the dust of a

8. *Morall man:* Seneca.

wretch whom thou wouldest not, as of a Prince whom thou couldest not look upon, will trouble thine eyes, if the winde blow it thither; and when a whirle-winde hath blowne the dust of the Church-yard into the Church, and the man sweeps out the dust of the Church into the Church-yard, who will undertake to sift those dusts again, and to pronounce, This is the Patrician, this is the noble flowre, and this the yeomanly, this the Plebeian bran? So is the death of *Jesabel* (*Jesabel* was a Queen) ex-

2 Kings 9   pressed; *They shall not say, this is Jesabel;* not only not wonder that it is, nor pity that it should be, but they shall not say, they shall not know, This is *Jesabel*. It comes to all, to all alike; but not alike welcome to all. To die too willingly, out of impatience to wish, or out of violence to hasten death, or to die too unwillingly, to murmure at Gods purpose revealed by age, or by sicknesse, are equall distempers; and to harbour a disobedient loathnesse all the way, or to entertain it at last, argues but an irreligious ignorance; An ignorance, that death is in nature but *Expiratio*, a breathing out, and we do that every minute; An ignorance that God himself took a day to rest in, and a good mans grave is his Sabbath; An ignorance that *Abel* the best of those whom we can compare with him, was the first that dyed. Howsoever, whensoever, all times are

August.   Gods times: *Vocantur boni ne diutius vexentur à noxiis, mali ne diutiùs bonos persequantur,* God cals the good to take them from their dangers, and God takes the bad to take them from their triumph. And therefore neither grudge that thou goest, nor that worse stay, for God can make his profit of both; *Aut ideo vivit ut corrigatur, aut ideo ut per illum bonus exerceatur;* God reprieves him to mend him, or to make another better by his exercise; and not to exult in the misery of another, but to glorifie God

Gregor.   in the ways of his justice, let him know, *Quantumcunque serò, subitò ex hac vita tollitur, qui finem prævidere nescivit:* How long soever he live, how long soever he lie sick, that man dies a sudden death, who never thought of it. If we consider death in S. *Pauls Statutum est, It is decreed that all men must die,* there death is indifferent;

[Phil. 1.21]   If we consider it in his *Mori lucrum, that it is an advantage to die,* there death is good; and so much the vulgat Edition seemes to intimate, when (*Deut.* 30.19.) whereas

we reade, I have set before you life and death, that reades
it, *Vitam & bonum*, Life, and that which is good. If then
death be at the worst indifferent, and to the good, good,
how is it *Hostis*, an enemy to the Kingdome of Christ? **Hostis**
for that also is *Vestigium quintum*, the fift and next step
in this paraphrase.

First God did not make death, saies the Wiseman,[9] And **Sap. 1.13**
therefore S. *Augustine* makes a reasonable prayer to God,
*Ne permittas Domine quod non fecisti, dominari Creaturæ
quam fecisti;* Suffer not O Lord, death, whom thou didst
not make, to have dominion over me whom thou didst.
Whence then came death? The same Wiseman hath
shewed us the father, Through envy of the devill, came **Sap. 2 ult.**
death into the world; and a wiser then he, the holy Ghost
himselfe hath shewed us the Mother, *By sin came death* **Rom. 5.12**
into the world. But yet if God have naturalized death,
taken death into the number of his servants, and made
Death his Commissioner to punish sin, and he doe but that,
how is Death an enemy? First, he was an enemy in invading Christ, who was not in his Commission, because he
had no sin; and still he is an enemie, because still he adheres to the enemy. Death hangs upon the edge of every
persecutors sword; and upon the sting of every calum-
niators, and accusers tongue. In the Bull of Phalaris, in the
Bulls of Basan, in the Buls of Babylon, the shrewdest Buls
of all, in temporall, in spirituall persecutions, ever since
God put an enmity between Man, and the Serpent, from
the time of *Cain* who began in a murther, to the time of
Antichrist, who proceeds in Massacres, Death hath adhered to the enemy, and so is an enemy.

Death hath a Commission, *Stipendium peccati mors est,* [Rom.
The reward of sin is Death, but where God gives a Super- 6.23]
sedeas,[10] upon that Commission, *Vivo Ego, nolo mortem,* [Ezek.
As I live saith the Lord, I would have no sinner dye, not 33.11]
dye the second death, yet Death proceeds to that execution: And whereas the enemy, whom he adheres to, the
Serpent himselfe, hath power but *In calcaneo,* upon the
heele, the lower, the mortall part, the body of man, *Death* **Jer. 9.21**
is come up into our windowes, saith the Prophet, into our

9. *Wiseman:* Solomon.
10. *Supersedeas:* countermand.

best lights, our understandings, and benights us there, either with ignorance, before sin, or with senselesnesse after: And a Sheriffe that should burne him, who were condemned to be hanged, were a murderer, though that man must have dyed: To come in by the doore, by the way of sicknesse upon the body, is, but to come in at the window by the way of sin, is not deaths Commission; God opens not that window.

So then he is an enemy, for they that adhere to the enemy are enemies: And adhering is not only a present subministration of supply to the enemy (for that death doth not) but it is also a disposition to assist the enemy, then when he shall be strong enough to make benefit of that assistance. And so death adheres; when sin and Satan have weakned body and minde, death enters upon both. And in that respect he is *Ultimus hostis*, the last enemy, and that is *Sextum vestigium*, our sixth and next step in this paraphrase.

Novissimus hostis

Death is the last, and in that respect the worst enemy. In an enemy, that appeares at first, when we are or may be provided against him, there is some of that, which we call Honour: but in the enemie that reserves himselfe unto the last, and attends our weake estate, there is more danger. Keepe it, where I intend it, in that which is my spheare, the Conscience: If mine enemie meet me betimes in my youth, in an object of tentation, (so *Josephs* enemie met him in *Putifars* Wife) yet if I doe not adhere to this enemy, dwell upon a delightfull meditation of that sin, if I doe not fuell, and foment that sin, assist and encourage that sin, by high diet, wanton discourse, other provocation, I shall have reason on my side, and I shall have grace on my side, and I shall have the History of a thousand that have perished by that sin, on my side; Even Spittles[11] will give me souldiers to fight for me, by their miserable example against that sin; nay perchance sometimes the vertue of that woman, whom I sollicite, will assist me. But when I lye under the hands of that enemie, that hath reserved himselfe to the last, to my last bed, then when I shall be able to stir no limbe in any other measure then a Feaver or a Palsie shall shake them, when everlasting darknesse

11. *Spittles:* hospitals.

shall have an inchoation in the present dimnesse of mine
eyes, and the everlasting gnashing in the present chatter-
ing of my teeth, and the everlasting worme in the present
gnawing of the Agonies of my body, and anguishes of
my minde, when the last enemie shall watch my remedilesse body, and my disconsolate soule there, there, where
not the Physitian, in his way, perchance not the Priest in
his, shall be able to give any assistance, And when he hath
sported himselfe with my misery upon that stage, my
death-bed, shall shift the Scene, and throw me from that
bed, into the grave, and there triumph over me, God
knowes, how many generations, till the Redeemer, my Redeemer, the Redeemer of all me, body, aswell as soule,
come againe; As death is *Novissimus hostis,* the enemy
which watches me, at my last weaknesse, and shall hold
me, when I shall be no more, till that Angel come, *Who* [Rev.
shall say, and sweare that time shall be no more,* in that 10.5–6]
consideration, in that apprehension, he is the powerfullest,
the fearefulest enemy; and yet even there this enemy
Abolebitur, he shall be destroyed, which is, *Septimum
vestigium,* our seventh and last step in this paraphrase.

This destruction, this abolition of this last enemy, is *Abolebitur*
by the Resurrection; for this Text is part of an argument for the Resurrection. And truly, it is a faire intimation, and testimony of an everlastingnesse in that state of
the Resurrection (that no time shall end it) that we have
it presented to us in all the parts of time; in the past, in
the present, and in the future. We had a Resurrection in
prophecy; we have a Resurrection in the present working
of Gods Spirit; we shall have a Resurrection in the finall
consummation. The Prophet speaks in the future, *He will* Esay 25.8
swallow up death in victory,* there it is *Abolebit:* All the
Evangelists speak historically, of matter of fact, in them it
is *Abolevit.* And here in this Apostle, it is in the present,
Aboletur, now he is destroyed. And this exhibites unto us
a threefold occasion of advancing our devotion, in considering a threefold Resurrection; First, a Resurrection
from dejections and calamities in this world, a Temporary
Resurrection; Secondly, a Resurrection from sin, a Spirituall Resurrection; and then a Resurrection from the
grave, a finall Resurrection.

1 *A*
calamitate
A calamitate; When the Prophets speak of a Resurrection in the old Testament, for the most part their principall intention is, upon a temporall restitution from calamities that oppresse them then. Neither doth *Calvin* carry those emphaticall words, which are so often cited for a proofe Job 19.25 of the last Resurrection: *That he knows his Redeemer lives, that he knows he shall stand the last man upon earth, that though his body be destroyed, yet in his flesh and with his eyes he shall see God,* to any higher sense then so, that how low soever he bee brought, to what desperate state soever he be reduced in the eyes of the world, yet he assures himself of a Resurrection, a reparation, a restitution to his former bodily health, and worldly fortune which he had before. And such a Resurrection we all know *Job* had.

In that famous, and most considerable propheticall vision [Ezek. 37] which God exhibited to *Ezekiel,* where God set the Prophet in a valley of very many, and very dry bones, and invites the severall joynts to knit again, tyes them with their old sinews, and ligaments, clothes them in their old flesh, wraps them in their old skin, and cals life into them again, Gods principall intention in that vision was thereby to give them an assurance of a Resurrection from their present calamity, not but that there is also good evidence of the last Resurrection in that vision too; Thus far God argues with them *à re nota;* from that which they knew before, the finall Resurrection, he assures them that which they knew not till then, a present Resurrection from those pressures: Remember by this vision that which you all know already, that at last I shall re-unite the dead, and dry bones of all men in a generall Resurrection: And then if you remember, if you consider, if you look upon that, can you doubt, but that I who can do that, can also recollect you, from your present dispersion, and give you a Resurrection to your former temporall happinesse? And this truly arises pregnantly, necessarily out of the Prophets answer; God asks him there, *Son of man, can these bones live?* And he answers, *Domine tu nôsti, O Lord God thou knowest.* The Prophet answers according to Gods intention in the question. If that had been for their living in the last Resurrection, *Ezekiel* would have answered God John 11.24 as *Martha* answered Christ, when he said, *Thy brother*

OK

Lazarus shall rise again, I know that he shall rise again at the Resurrection at the last day; but when the question was, whether men so macerated, so scattered in this world, could have a Resurrection to their former temporall happinesse here, that puts the Prophet to his *Domine tu nôsti,* It is in thy breast to propose it, it is in thy hand to execute it, whether thou do it, or do it not, thy name be glorified; It fals not within our conjecture, which way it shall please thee to take for this Resurrection, *Domine tu nôsti,* Thou Lord, and thou only knowest; Which is also the sense of those words, *Others were tortured, and accepted* Heb. 11.35 *not a deliverance, that they might obtain a better Resurrection:* A present deliverance had been a Resurrection, but to be the more sure of a better hereafter, they lesse respected that; According to that of our Saviour, *He that* Mat. 10.39 *findes his life, shall lose it;* He that fixeth himself too earnestly upon this Resurrection, shall lose a better.

This is then the propheticall Resurrection for the future, but a future in this world; That if Rulers take counsell against the Lord, the Lord shall have their counsell in Psal. 2.4 derision; If they take armes against the Lord, the Lord shall break their Bows, and cut their Speares in sunder; Psal. 46.9 If they hisse, and gnash their teeth, and say, we have [Job 30.9] swallowed him up; If we be made their by-word, their parable, their proverb, their libell, the theame and burden of their songs, as *Job* complaines, yet whatsoever fall upon me, damage, distresse, scorn, or *Hostis ultimus,* death it self, that death which we consider here, death of possessions, death of estimation, death of health, death of contentment, yet *Abolebitur,* it shall be destroyed in a Resurrection, in the return of the light of Gods countenance upon me even in this world. And this is the first Resurrection.

But this first Resurrection, which is but from temporall calamities, doth so little concerne a true and established 2 Christian, whether it come or no, (for still *Jobs* Basis is *A peccatis* his Basis, and his Centre, *Etiamsi occiderit,* though he kill me, kill me, kill me, in all these severall deaths, and give me no Resurrection in this world, yet I will trust in him) as that, as though this first resurrection were no resurrection, not to be numbred among the resurrections, S. *John* calls that which we call the second, which is from

Apoc.
20.6

John 5.25

sin, the first resurrection: *Blessed and holy is he, who hath part in the first resurrection:* And this resurrection, Christ implies, when he saies, *Verely, verely, I say unto you, the houre is comming, and now is, when the dead shall heare the voyce of the Son of God; and they that heare it shall live:* That is, by the voyce of the word of life, the Gospell of repentance, they shall have a spirituall resurrection to a new life.

S. *Austine*[12] and *Lactantius* both were so hard in be-leeving the roundnesse of the earth, that they thought that those *homines pensiles,* as they call them, those men that hang upon the other cheek of the face of the earth, those Antipodes, whose feet are directly against ours, must necessarily fall from the earth, if the earth be round. But whither should they fall? If they fall, they must fall upwards, for heaven is above them too, as it is to us. So if the spirituall Antipodes of this world, the Sons of God, that walk with feet opposed in wayes contrary to the sons of men, shall be said to fall, when they fall to repentance, to mortification, to a religious negligence, and contempt of the pleasures of this life, truly their fall is upwards, they fall towards heaven. *God gives breath unto the peo-ple upon the earth,* sayes the Prophet, *Et spiritum his, qui calcant illam.* Our Translation carries that no farther, but that *God gives breath to people upon the earth, and spirit to them that walk thereon;* But *Irenæus* makes a usefull difference between *afflatus* and *spiritus,* that God gives breath to all upon earth, but his spirit onely to them, who tread in a religious scorne upon earthly things.

Esay 42.5

Col. 3.5

Is it not a strange phrase of the Apostle, *Mortifie your members; fornication, uncleanenesse, inordinate affections?* He does not say, mortifie your members against those sins, but he calls those very sins, the members of our bodies, as though we were elemented [13] and compacted of nothing but sin, till we come to this resurrection, this mortification, which is indeed our vivification; *Till we beare in our body, the dying of our Lord Jesus, that the life also of Jesus may be made manifest in our body* God may give the other resurrection from worldly miseiy, and not give

2 Cor.
4.10

12. *S. Austine:* St. Augustine, Bishop of Hippo, Donne's favorite au-thority among the Fathers of the Church.

13. *elemented:* composed.

this. A widow may be rescued from the sorrow and solitarinesse of that state, by having a plentifull fortune; there
she hath one resurrection; but *the widow that liveth in*   1 Tim. 5.6
pleasure, is dead while she lives; shee hath no second resurrection; and so in that sense, even this Chappell may be a
Church-yard, men may stand, and sit, and kneele, and
yet be dead; and any Chamber alone may be a *Golgotha*,
a place of dead mens bones, of men not come to this
resurrection, which is the renunciation of their beloved
sin.

It was inhumanely said by *Vitellius*, upon the death of
Otho, when he walked in the field of carcasses, where the
battle was fought; O how sweet a perfume is a dead
enemy! But it is a divine saying to thy soule, O what a
savor of life, unto life, is the death of a beloved sin!
What an Angelicall comfort was that to *Joseph* and *Mary*
in Ægypt, after the death of *Herod, Arise, for they are*   Mat. 2.20
dead, that sought the childes life! And even that comfort
is multiplied upon thy soul, when the Spirit of God saies
to thee, Arise, come to this resurrection: for that *Herod*,
that sin, that sought the life, the everlasting life of this
childe, the childe of God, thy soule, is dead, dead by repentance, dead by mortification. The highest cruelty that
story relates, or Poets imagine, is when a persecutor will
not afford a miserable man death, not be so mercifull to
him, as to take his life. Thou hast made thy sin, thy soule,
thy life; inanimated all thy actions, all thy purposes with
that sin. *Miserere animæ tuæ*, be so mercifull to thy selfe,   [Ecclus.
as to take away that life by mortification, by repentance,   30.24
and thou art come to this Resurrection: and though a man   Vulg.;
may have the former resurrection, and not this, peace in   23 A. V.]
his fortune, and yet not peace in his conscience, yet whosoever hath this second, hath an infallible seale of the third
resurrection too, to a fulnesse of glory in body, as well as
in soule. For *Spiritus maturam efficit carnem, & capacem*   Irenaeus
incorruptelæ; this resurrection by the spirit, mellowes the
body of man, and makes that capable of everlasting glory,
which is the last weapon, by which the last enemy death,
shall be destroyed; *A morte*.

Upon that pious ground that all Scriptures were written   3
for us, as we are Christians, that all Scriptures conduce to   *A morte*
the proofe of Christ, and of the Christian state, it is the

ordinary manner of the Fathers to make all that *David* speaks historically of himselfe, and all that the Prophet speaks futurely of the Jews, if those places may be referred to Christ, to referre them to Christ primarily, and but by reflection, and in a second consideration upon *David*, or upon the Jews. Thereupon doe the Fathers (truly I think more generally more unanimely then in any other place of Scripture) take that place of *Ezekiel* which we spake of before, to be primarily intended of the last resurrection, and but secundarily of the Jews restitution. But *Gasper Sanctius* a learned Jesuit, (that is not so rare, but an ingenuous Jesuit too) though he be bound by the Councel of Trent, to interpret Scriptures according to the Fathers, yet here he acknowledges the whole truth, that Gods purpose was to prove, by that which they did know, which was the generall resurrection, that which they knew not, their temporall restitution. *Tertullian* is vehement at first, but after, more supple. *Allegoricæ Scripturæ,* saies he, *resurrectionem subradiant aliæ, aliæ determinant:* Some figurative places of Scripture doe intimate a resurrection, and some manifest it; and of those manifest places he takes this vision of *Ezekiel* to be one. But he comes after to this, *Sit & corporum, & rerum, & meâ nihil interest;* let it signifie a temporall resurrection, so it may signifie the generall resurrection of our bodies too, saies he, and I am well satisfied; and then the truth satisfies him, for it doth signifie both. It is true that *Tertullian* says, *De vacuo similitudo non competit;* If the vision be but a comparison, yet if there were no such thing as a resurrection, the comparison did not hold. *De nullo parabola non convenit,* saies he, and truly; If there were no resurrection to which that Parable might have relation, it were no Parable. All that is true; but there was a resurrection alwaies knowne to them, alwaies beleeved by them, and that made their present resurrection from that calamity, the more easie, the more intelligible, the more credible, the more discernable to them.

Let therefore Gods method, be thy method; fixe thy self firmly upon that beliefe of the generall resurrection, and thou wilt never doubt of either of the particular resurrections, either from sin, by Gods grace, or from worldly calamities, by Gods power. For that last resurrection is the

ground of all. By that *Verè victa mors,* saies *Irenæus,* this
last enemy, death, is truly destroyed, because his last
spoile, the body, is taken out of his hands. The same body,
eadem ovis, (as the same Father notes) Christ did not
fetch another sheep to the flock, in the place of that which
was lost, but the same sheep: God shall not give me another, a better body at the resurrection, but the same
body made better; for *Si non haberet caro salvari, neuti-* Idem
quam verbum Dei caro factum fuisset, If the flesh of man
were not to be saved, the Author of salvation would never
have taken the flesh of man upon him.

The punishment that God laid upon *Adam, In dolore* Gen. 3.19
& *in sudore, In sweat, and in sorrow shalt thou eate thy
bread,* is but *Donec reverteris, till man returne to dust:*
but when Man is returned to dust, God returnes to the
remembrance of that promise, *Awake and sing ye that* Esay 26.19
dwell in the dust. A mercy already exhibited, a promise
allready performed unto us, in the person of our Saviour
Christ Jesus, in whom, *Per primitias benedixit campo,*
(saies S. *Chrysostome*) as God by taking a handfull for
the first Fruits, gave a blessing to the whole field; so he
hath sealed the bodies of all mankind to his glory, by pre-
assuming the body of Christ to that glory. For by that
there is now *Commercium inter Cœlum & terram;* there Bernard
is a Trade driven, a Staple[14] established betweene Heaven
and earth; *Ibi caro nostra, hic Spiritus ejus;* Thither have
we sent our flesh, and hither hath he sent his Spirit.

This is the last abolition of this enemy, Death; for after
this, the bodies of the Saints he cannot touch, the bodies
of the damned he cannot kill, and if he could, hee were
not therein their enemy, but their friend. This is that
blessed and glorious State, of which, when all the Apostles
met to make the Creed, they could say no more, but
*Credo Resurrectionem, I beleeve the Resurrection of the
body;* and when those two Reverend Fathers, to whom it
belongs, shall come to speake of it, upon the day proper
for it, in this place, and if all the Bishops that ever met in
Councels should meet them here, they could but second
the Apostles *Credo,* with their *Anathema,* We beleeve, and
woe be unto them that doe not beleeve the Resurrection

14. *Staple:* commerce.

[Exod.
6.12, 30] of the body; but in going about to expresse it, the lips of
an Angell would be uncircumcised lips, and the tongue of
an Archangell would stammer. I offer not therefore at it:
but in respect of, and with relation to that blessed State,
according to the doctrine, and practise of our Church,
we doe pray for the dead; for the militant Church upon
earth, and the triumphant Church in Heaven, and the
whole Catholique Church in Heaven, and earth; we doe

[B.C.P. pray that God will be pleased to hasten that Kingdome,
Order for that we with all others departed in the true Faith of his
the Burial holy Name, may have this perfect consummation, both of
of the body and soule, in his everlasting glory, *Amen.*
Dead]

DEATHS DUELL, OR, A CONSOLATION TO THE SOULE, AGAINST THE DYING LIFE, AND LIVING DEATH OF THE BODY

VOLUME X: NUMBER 11[1]

*Delivered in a Sermon at White Hall,
before the Kings Majesty, in the beginning
of Lent, 1630.*

To the Reader.

This *Sermon was, by Sacred Authoritie, stiled*[2] *the Authors owne funeral Sermon. Most fitly: whether wee
respect the time, or the matter. It was preached not many
dayes before his death; as if, having done this, there remained nothing for him to doe, but to die: And the matter
is, of Death; the occasion and subject of all funerall Sermons. It hath beene observed of this Reverend Man, That
his Faculty in Preaching continually encreased: and, That
as hee exceeded others at first; so, at last hee exceeded*

1. *Number 11*: Donne's last sermon, first published as No. 26 in *XXVI
   Sermons* (London, 1660).
2. *stiled:* called.

himselfe. This is his last Sermon; I will not say, it is there-
fore his best; because, all his were excellent. Yet thus
much: A dying Mans words, if they concerne our selves;
doe usually make the deepest impression, as being spoken
most feelingly, and with least affectation. Now, whom
doth it not concerne to learn, both the danger, and benefit
of death? Death is every mans enemy, and intends hurt to
all; though to many, hee be occasion of greatest goods.
This enemy wee must all combate dying; whom hee living
did almost conquer; having discovered the utmost of his
power, the utmost of his crueltie. May wee make such use
of this and other the like preparatives, That neither death,
whensoever it shall come, may seeme terrible; nor life
tedious; how long soever it shall last.

R.

Psa. 68. vers. 20. In fine. *AND UNTO GOD THE*
LORD BELONG THE ISSUES OF DEATH. i.e.
FROM DEATH.

Buildings stand by the benefit of their *foundations* that
susteine and *support* them, and of their *butteresses* that
comprehend and *embrace* them, and of their *contignations*[3]
that knit and *unite* them: The *foundations* suffer them not
to *sinke*, the *butteresses* suffer them not to *swerve*, and
the *contignation* and knitting suffers them not to *cleave*.
The body of our building is in the former part of this
verse: It is this, hee that *is our God* is the *God of salvation;*
ad salutes, of salvations in the plurall, so it is in the originall; the *God* that gives us spirituall and temporall salvation too. But of this *building*, the *foundation*, the *but-*
teresses, the *contignations* are in this part of the *verse*,
which constitutes *our text*, and in the three divers *ac-*
ceptations of the words amongst our expositors, *Unto God*
the Lord belong the issues of death. For *first* the *founda-* Of
tion of this *building*, (that our *God* is the *God of all sal-*
vations) is laid in this; That *unto* this *God the Lord* belong *the issues of death*, that is, it is in his power to give
us an *issue* and deliverance, even then when wee are
brought to the jawes and teeth of death, and to the lippes

3. *contignations:* joints

of that whirlepoole, the grave. And so in this acceptation, this *exitus mortis*, this *issue of death* is *liberatio à morte*, *a deliverance from death*, and this is the most obvious and most ordinary acceptation of these words, and that upon which our *translation* laies hold, the *issues from death*. And then *secondly*, the butteresses that comprehend and settle this building, That hee that is *our God*, is the *God* of all *salvation*, are thus raised; unto *God the Lord belong the issues of death*, that is, the disposition and *manner of our death*: what kinde of *issue*, and *transmigration* wee shall have out of this world, whether prepared or sudden, whether violent or naturall, whether in our perfect senses or shaken and disordered by sicknes, there is no condemnation to bee argued out of that, no Judgement to bee made upon that, for howsoever they dye, *precious in his sight is the death of his saints*, and with him are *the issues of death*, the *wayes* of our *departing* out of this life are in his *hands*. And so in this *sense* of the *words*, this *exitus mortis*, the *issue of death*, is *liberatio in morte*, *A deliverance in death*; Not that God will *deliver* us *from dying*, but that hee will *have a care* of us in the *houre of death*, of what kinde soever our passage be. And this *sense* and acceptation of the *words*, the naturall frame and contexture doth well and pregnantly administer unto us. And then *lastly* the *contignation* and knitting of this building, that hee that is *our God* is the *God of all salvations*, consists in this, *Unto this God the Lord belong the issues of death*, that is, that this *God* the *Lord* having *united* and knit *both natures in one*, and being *God*, having also *come* into this *world*, in our *flesh*, he could have no other meanes to save us, he could have no other *issue* out of this world, nor *returne* to his former *glory*, but by *death*; And so in this sense, this *exitus mortis*, this *issue of death*, is *liberatio per mortem*, a *deliverance by death*, by the death of this *God* our *Lord Christ Jesus*. And this is Saint *Augustines* acceptation of the words, and those many and great persons that have adhered to him. In all these three lines then, we shall looke upon these words; *First, as the God* of *power*, the *Almighty Father* rescues his servants from the *jawes* of death: *And then*, as the *God* of *mercy*, the glorious *Sonne* rescued us, by taking upon himselfe this *issue of death: And then* betweene these two, as the *God*

[Psal. 116.15]

of *comfort*, the *holy Ghost* rescues us from all discomfort by his blessed impressions before hand, that what manner of death soever be ordeined for us, yet this *exitus mortis* shall bee *introitus in vitam*, our *issue in death*, shall be an *entrance into everlasting life*. And these three consider- ations, our deliverance *à morte*, *in morte*, *per mortem*, *from death*, *in death*, and *by death*, will abundantly doe all the offices of the *foundations*, of the *butteresses*, of the *contignation* of this our *building*; That he that is our *God*, is the *God of all salvation*, because *unto this God the Lord belong the issues of death*.

A morte, in morte, per mortem Founda- tion, butteresses and con- tignation

First, then, we consider this *exitus mortis*, to bee *liberatio à morte*, that with *God*, the *Lord* are the *issues of death*, and therefore in all our deaths, and deadly calamities of this life, wee may justly *hope* of a good *issue* from him; and all our *periods* and *transitions* in this life, are so many passages *from death* to *death*. Our very *birth* and entrance into this life, is *exitus à morte*, an *issue from death*, for in our mothers *wombe wee are dead so*, as that wee doe *not know* wee *live*, not so much as wee doe in our *sleepe*, neither is there any *grave* so close, or so *putrid* a *prison*, as the *wombe* would be unto us, if we stayed in it *beyond* our time, or dyed there *before* our time. In the *grave* the *wormes* doe not kill us, wee *breed* and *feed*, and then *kill* those wormes which wee our selves produc'd. In the wombe the dead *child* kills the *Mother* that conceived it, and is a murtherer, nay a *parricide*, even after it is dead. And if wee bee not dead so in the *wombe*, so as that being dead, wee kill her that gave us our first life, our life of *vegetation*,[4] yet wee are dead so, as *Davids Idols* are dead. In the *wombe* wee have *eyes and see not, eares and heare not;* There in the wombe wee are fitted for *workes of darkenes*, all the while deprived of light: And there in the *wombe* wee are taught *cruelty*, by being *fed with blood*, and may be *damned*, though we be *never borne*. Of our very making in the *wombe*, *David* sayes, *I am wonderfully and fearefully made*, and, *Such knowl- edge is too excellent for me*, for even that *is the Lords do- ing, and it is wonderfull in our eyes. Ipse fecit nos, it is hee that hath made us, and not wee our selves*, no, nor

1 Part *A morte*

Exitus à morte uteri

Psal. 115 vers. [5,] 6

Psal. 139.14 [ver. 6]
Ps. 118.23
100.3 [2 in Vulg.] 10.8

---

4. *vegetation:* physical existence.

comparing birth / womb (tomb)
with being dead

our parents neither; *Thy hanas have made me and fashioned me round about,* saith *Job,* and, (as the *originall
word* is) *thou hast taken paines about me,* and yet, sayes
he, *thou doest destroy me.* Though I bee the *Master peece*
of the greatest *Master* (*man* is so,) yet if thou doe no
more for me, if thou leave me where thou madest mee,
destruction will follow. The *wombe* which should be the
house of life, becomes *death* it selfe, if *God* leave us there.
That which God threatens so often, the *shutting of the
womb,* is not so *heavy,* nor so discomfortable a *curse* in
the *first,* as in the *latter* shutting, nor in the shutting of
barrennes, as in the shutting of *weakenes,* when *children
are come to the birth,* and there is not *strength to bring
forth.*

Esa. 37.3

It is the *exaltation* of *misery,* to *fall* from a *neare hope*
of *happines.* And in that vehement *imprecation,* the
Prophet expresses the *highth* of *Gods* anger, *Give them
ô Lord, what will thou give them? give them a mis-carying
wombe.* Therefore as soone as wee are men, (that is,
inanimated, quickned in the womb) thogh we cannot our
selves, our parents have reason to say in our behalf,
wretched man that he is, who shall deliver him *from this
body of death?* for even the *wombe* is a *body of death,*
if there bee no deliverer. It must be he that said to *Jeremy,*[5]
*Before I formed thee I knew thee, and before thou camest
out of the wombe I sanctified thee.* Wee are not sure that
there was no kinde of *shippe* nor *boate* to *fish* in, nor to
passe by, till *God* prescribed *Noah* that absolute *form* of
the *Arke.* That word which the *holy Ghost* by *Moses*
useth for the *Arke,* is common to all kinde of *boates,
Thebah,* and is the same word that *Moses* useth for the
boate that he was *exposed* in, that *his mother layed him
in an arke of bulrushes.* But we are sure that *Eve* had no
Midwife when she was *delivered* of *Cain,* therefore shee
might well say, *possedi virum à Domino, I have gotten a
man from the Lord,* wholly, entirely from the Lord; It is
the *Lord* that *enabled* me to *conceive, The Lord* that *in-
fus'd* a *quickning soule* into that conception, the *Lord*
that *brought into the world* that which himselfe *had
quickened;* without all this might *Eve* say, My *body had*

Ose. 9.14

Ro. 7.24

1.5

Exo. 2.3

Gen. 4.1

5. *Jeremy:* Jeremiah.

bene but *the house of death*, and *Domini Domini sunt exitus mortis*, to God the Lord belong the issues of death.

But then this *exitus a morte*, is but *introitus in mortem*, this *issue*, this deliverance *from* that *death*, the death of the *wombe*, is an *entrance*, a delivering over to *another death*, the manifold deathes of this *world*. Wee have a winding sheete in our Mothers wombe, which growes with us from our conception, and wee come into the world, wound up in that *winding sheet*, for wee come to *seeke a grave;* And as prisoners discharg'd of actions may lye for fees;[6] so when the *wombe* hath discharg'd us, yet we are bound to it by *cordes* of flesh, by such a *string*, as that wee cannot goe thence, nor stay there. We celebrate our owne funeralls with cryes, even at our birth; as though our *threescore and ten years of life* were spent in our mothers labour, and our *circle* made up in the first point thereof. We begge one Baptism with another, a sacrament of tears; And we come into a world that lasts many ages, but wee last not. *In domo Patris*, says our blessed *Saviour*, speaking of *heaven*, *multæ mansiones*, there *are many mansions*, divers and durable, so that if a man cannot possesse a *martyrs* house, (he hath shed no blood for *Christ*) yet hee may have a *Confessors*, he hath bene ready to glorifie God in the *shedding of his blood*. And if a woman cannot possesse a *virgins* house (she hath embrac'd the *holy state of mariage*) yet she may have a *matrons* house, she hath brought forth and brought up *children in the feare of God. In domo patris, in my fathers house*, in heaven there *are many mansions;* but here upon earth *The Son of man hath not where to lay his head*, sayes he himselfe. *Nonne terram dedit filiis hominum?* how then hath God given this earth to the *sonnes of men?* hee hath *given* them *earth* for their *materialls* to bee made of earth, and he hath given them *earth* for their *grave* and sepulture, to *returne* and resolve to *earth*, but not for their *possession: Here wee have no continuing citty*, nay no *cottage* that continues, nay no *persons*, no bodies that continue. Whatsoever moved Saint *Jerome* to call the journies of the *Israelites*, in the *wildernes*, Mansions, the *word* (the word is *Na*-

Exitus à mortibus mundi

Joh. 14.2

Mat 8.20

[Ps. 115.16]

Heb. 13.14

Exo. 17.1

6. *fees:* Acquitted prisoners may be compelled to remain in prison because of fees owed to the jailer.

sang) signifies but a *journey*, but a peregrination. Even the *Israel of God* hath no mansions; but journies, pilgrimages in this life. By that measure did *Jacob* measure his life to *Pharaoh*, *The daies of the years of my pilgrimage.* And though the *Apostle* would not say *morimur*, that, whilest wee *are in the body* wee *are dead*, yet hee sayes, *Peregrinamur*, whilest wee are *in the body*, wee are but in *a pilgrimage*, and wee are *absent from the Lord;* hee might have sayd *dead*, for this whole *world* is but an *universall church-yard*, but our *common grave;* and the life and motion that the greatest persons have in it, is but as the shaking of buried bodies in their graves by an *earthquake.* That which we call life, is but *Hebdomada mortium, a week of deaths*, seaven dayes, seaven periods of our life spent in dying, *a dying seaven times over;* and there is an end. *Our birth dyes in infancy*, and our *infancy* dyes in *youth*, and *youth* and the rest dye in *age*, and *age* also dyes, and *determines all.* Nor doe all these, youth out of infancy, or age out of youth arise so, as a *Phœnix* out of the *ashes* of another *Phœnix* formerly *dead*, but as a *waspe* or a *serpent* out of a *caryon*, or as a *Snake* out of *dung.* Our *youth* is *worse* then our *infancy*, and our *age worse* then our *youth.* Our *youth* is *hungry and thirsty*, after those *sinnes*, which our *infancy knew not;* And our *age* is *sory* and *angry*, that it *cannot pursue* those *sinnes* which our *youth* did. And besides, al the way, so many deaths, that is, so many deadly calamities accompany every condition, and every period of this life, as that death it selfe would bee an ease to them that suffer them. Upon this sense doth *Job* wish that *God had not given him* an *issue* from the *first death*, from the *wombe*, *Wherefore hast thou brought me forth out of the wombe? O that I had given up the Ghost, and no eye had seen me; I should have been, as though I had not been.*

And not only the impatient *Israelites* in their murmuring (*would to God wee had dyed by the hand of the Lord in the land of Egypt*) but *Eliah*[7] himselfe, when he *fled* from *Jesabell*, and went for his life, as that text sayes, under the juniper tree, requested that *hee might dye*, and sayd, *It is enough, now O Lord, take away my life.* So

Gen 47.9

Cor. 5.6

10.18

Exo. 16.3

1 Reg. 19.4

---

7. *Eliah:* Elijah.

Jonah justifies his impatience, nay his anger towards *God* himselfe. *Now ô Lord take, I beseech thee, my life from mee, for it is better for me to dye then to live.* And when *God* asked him, *doest thou well to be angry for this,* and after, (about the Gourd) *dost thou well to be angry for that,* he replies, *I doe well to be angry, even unto death.* How much worse a death then death, is this life, which so good men would so often change for death? But if my case bee as Saint *Paules* case, *quotidiè morior,* that *I dye dayly,* that something heavier then death fall upon me every day; If my case be *Davids* case, *tota die mortifica-mur, all the day long wee are killed,* that not onely every day, but every houre of the day some thing heavier then death fall upon me, though that bee true of me, *Conceptus in peccatis, I was shapen in iniquity, and in sinne did my mother conceive me,* (there I dyed one death,) though that be true of me (*Natus filius iræ*) I *was borne* not onely the child of sinne, but *the child of wrath,* of the wrath of *God* for sinne, which is a heavier death; Yet *Domini Domini sunt exitus mortis,* with *God the Lord are the issues of death,* and after a *Job,* and a *Joseph,* and a *Jeremie,* and a *Daniel,* I cannot doubt of a deliverance. And if no other deliverance conduce more to his glory and my good, yet he hath the *keys of death,* and hee can let me out at that dore, that is, deliver me from the manifold deaths of this world, the *omni die* and the *tota die,* the *every dayes death* and *every houres death,* by that *one death,* the *final dissolution* of body and soule, the end of all.

But then is that the end of all? Is that dissolution of body and soule, the last death that the body shall suffer? (for of spirituall death wee speake not now) It is not. Though this be *exitus à morte,* it is *introitus in mortem:* though it bee an *issue from* the manifold *deaths* of this *world,* yet it is an *entrance* into the *death of corruption* and *putrefaction* and *vermiculation*[8] and *incineration,* and dispersion in and from the *grave,* in which every dead man dyes over againe. It was a *prerogative* peculiar to *Christ,* not to dy this death, *not to see corruption.* What gave him this priviledge? Not *Josephs* great proportion[9] of *gummes*

4.3

[v. 9]

1 Cor.
15.31
Psa. 44.22

[Psa.] 51.5

[Eph. 2.3]

Apoc.
1.18

Exitus à morte inci-nirationis

---

8. *vermiculation:* consumption by worms.
9. *proportion:* portion.

and *spices*, that might have preserved his body from corruption and *incineration* longer then he needed it, longer then *three dayes*, but it would not have done it for ever. What preserved him then? did his exemption and *freedome from originall sinne* preserve him from this corruption and *incineration?* 'Tis true that original sinne hath induced this corruption and *incineration* upon us; if wee had not sinned in *Adam*, *mortality had not put on immortality*, (as the *Apostle* speakes) nor *corruption had not put on incorruption*, but we had had our *transmigration* from this to the other world, without any *mortality*, any *corruption at all*. But yet since *Christ* tooke *sinne* upon him, so farre as made him *mortall*, he had it so farre too, as might have made him see this corruption and *incineration*, though he had no *originall sinne* in himself. What preserv'd him then? Did the *hypostaticall union*[10] of both natures, *God* and *Man*, preserve him from this corruption and *incineration?* 'tis true that this was a most powerfull *embalming*, to be embalmd with the *divine nature* it selfe, to bee embalmd with *eternity*, was able to preserve him from corruption and *incineration* for ever. And he was embalm'd so, embalmd with the *divine nature* it selfe, even in his *body* as well as in his *soule;* for the *Godhead*, the *divine nature* did not depart, but remained still *united* to his *dead body* in the grave; But yet for al this powerful *embalming*, this *hypostaticall union* of both natures, we see *Christ* did *dye;* and for all this *union* which made him *God* and *Man*, hee became no man (for the *union* of the *body* and *soule* makes the man, and hee whose soule and body are separated by death, (as long as that state lasts) is properly no man.) And therefore as in him the dissolution of *body* and *soule* was no *dissolution* of the *hypostaticall union;* so is there nothing that constraines us to say, that though the *flesh* of *Christ* had *seene corruption* and *incineration* in the grave, this had bene any *dissolution* of the *hypostaticall union*, for the *divine nature*, the Godhead might have remained with all the *Elements* and *principles* of *Christs* body, aswell as it did with the two *constitutive* parts of his *person*, his *body* and his *soul*. This

10. *union:* The reference is to the mysterious union of divine and human natures in Christ.

incorruption then was not in *Josephs gummes* and *spices*, nor was it in *Christs* innocency, and *exemption* from *originall sin*, nor was it (that is, it is not necessary to say it was) in the *hypostaticall union*. But this *incorruptiblenes* of his *flesh* is most conveniently plac'd in that, *Non dabis,*   Psal. 16.10 *thou wilt not suffer thy holy one to see corruption.* We looke no further for *causes* or *reasons* in the *mysteries of religion*, but to the *will* and pleasure of *God: Christ* himselfe limited his *inquisition* in that *ita est, even so Father,*   Mat. 11.26 *for so it seemed good in thy sight. Christs* body did *not see corruption,* therefore, because *God* had *decreed* it shold not. The humble soule (and onely the humble soule is the religious soule) rests himselfe upon *Gods* purposes, and his decrees; but then, it is upon those purposes, and decrees of *God,* which he hath declared and manifested; not such as are *conceived* and imagined in our selves, though upon some probability, some *verisimilitude.* So, in our present case, *Peter* proceeded in his *Sermon* at *Jerusalem,* and so   Acts 2.31 *Paul* in *his* at *Antioch.* They preached *Christ* to have *bene*   13.35 *risen* without seeing *corruption,* not onely because *God* had *decreed* it, but because he had *manifested* that *decree* in his *Prophet.* Therefore doth Saint *Paul* cite by special number the *second Psalme* for that *decree;* And therefore both Saint *Peter* and S. *Paul* cite for it that place in the 16.   Vers. 10 *Psalme,* for when *God* declares his *decree* and purpose in the expresse words of his *Prophet,* or when he declares it in the reall execution of the decree, then he makes it ours, then he manifests it to us. And therfore as the *Mysteries* of our *Religion,* are *not* the *objects* of *our reason,* but *by faith we rest* on *Gods decree* and purpose, (It is so, ô *God,* because it is *thy will,* it should be so) so *Gods decrees* are ever to be considered in the *manifestation* thereof. All *manifestation* is either in the *word* of *God,* or in the *execution* of the *decree;* And when these two concur and meete, it is the strongest *demonstration* that can be: when therefore I finde those *markes* of *adoption* and *spirituall filiation,*[11] which are delivered in the *word* of *God,* to be upon me, when I finde that reall *execution* of his *good purpose* upon me, as that *actually* I doe *live* under the *obedience,* and under the *conditions* which are *evidences*

11. *filiation:* sonship.

of *adoption* and *spirituall filiation*; then, and so long as I
see these *markes* and live so, I may safely comfort my
selfe in a *holy certitude* and a *modest infallibility* of my
adoption. *Christ* determines himself in that, the purpose
of *God*; because the purpose of *God* was manifest to him:
S. *Peter* and S. *Paul* determine themselves in those two
wayes of knowing the *purpose* of *God*, the *word* of *God*
before, the *execution* of the *decree* in the *fulnes of time*.
It was *prophecyed before*, say they, and it *is performed
now*, *Christ is risen* without seeing corruption.

Now this which is so singularly peculiar to him, that
his flesh should not see corruption, at his *second coming*,
his coming to *Judgement*, shall extend to all that are then
alive, their *flesh* shall not *see corruption*, because (as the
Apostle saies, and saies as a secret, as a mystery, *behold
I shew you a mystery*) *wee shall not all sleepe*, (that is,
not continue in the state of the dead in the grave,) *but
wee shall all be changed*. In an instant we shall have a
dissolution, and in the *same instant* a *redintegration*, a
recompacting of *body* and *soule*, and that shall be truely
a death and truely a resurrection, but no sleeping, no corruption. But for us that dye now and sleepe in the state of
the dead, we must al passe this *posthume* death, this *death*
after *death*, nay this death after buriall, this *dissolution*
after *dissolution*, this *death of corruption* and *putrifaction*,
of *vermiculation* and *incineration*, of *dissolution* and *dispersion* in and *from* the grave. When those bodies that
have beene the *children* of *royall parents*, and the *parents*
of *royall children*, must say with *Job*, *to corruption thou
art my father*, and *to the Worme thou art my mother
and my sister*. *Miserable riddle*, when the *same worme*
must bee *my mother*, and *my sister*, and *my selfe*. *Miserable incest*, when I must bee *maried* to my *mother* and my
sister, and bee both *father* and *mother* to my *owne mother*
and *sister*, *beget*, and *beare* that *worme* which is all that
miserable penury; when my *mouth* shall be *filled* with
dust, and the *worme* shall *feed*, and *feed sweetely* upon me,
when the *ambitious* man shall have *no satisfaction*, if the
poorest alive tread upon him, nor the *poorest* receive any
contentment in being made *equall* to *Princes*, for they
shall bee equall but *in dust*. One dyeth at his full strength,
being wholly at ease and in quiet, and another dyes in the

1 Cor.
15.51

17.14

24.20

Job 21.23

devt.
episalizes

fear of
losing ones physicality

bitternes of his soul, and never *eates* with *pleasure*, but
they lye downe *alike* in *the dust*, and the *worme covers
them;* The worm covers them in *Job*, and in *Esay*,[12] it [Isa.] 14.11
covers them and is spred under them, the worme is spred
under thee, and the worme *covers thee;* There's the *Mats*
and the *Carpets* that *lye under*, and there's the *State*[13] and
the *Canapye*, that *hangs over* the greatest of the sons of
men. Even those bodies that were *the temples of the holy
Ghost*, come to this *dilapidation*, to ruine, to rubbidge, to
dust: even the *Israel of the Lord*, and *Jacob* himselfe hath
no other specification, no other denomination, but that
vermis Jacob, thou *worme of Jacob.* Truely the considera- Esa. 41.14
tion of this *posthume death*, this death after buriall, that
after *God*, (with whom are the *issues of death*) hath delivered me from the *death* of the *wombe*, by bringing mee
into the *world*, and from the manifold *deaths* of the *world*,
by laying me in the *grave*, I must dye againe in an *Incineration* of this *flesh*, and in a dispersion of that dust: That
that *Monarch*, who spred over many nations alive, must in
his dust lye in a corner of that *sheete of lead*, and there,
but so long as that lead will laste, and that privat and
retir'd man, that thought himselfe his owne for ever, and
never came forth, must in his dust of the grave bee published, and (such are the *revolutions* of the *graves*) bee
mingled in his dust, with the dust of every high way, and
of every dunghill, and swallowed in every puddle and
pond: This is the most inglorious and contemptible *vili-
fication*, the most deadly and peremptory *nullification* of
man, that wee can consider. *God* seemes to have caried
the declaration of his *power* to a great height, when hee
sets the *Prophet Ezechiel* in the *valley of drye bones*, and [37.1]
sayes, *Sonne of man can these bones live?* as though it
had bene impossible, and yet they did; The *Lord* layed
Sinewes upon them, and flesh, and breathed into them, and
they did live: But in that case there were *bones* to bee
seene, something visible, of which it might be sayd, can
this thing live? But in this death of *incineration*, and dispersion of dust, wee see *nothing* that wee can call *that
mans;* If we say, can this dust live? perchance it *cannot*,

12. *Esay:* Isaiah.
13. *State:* canopy.

it may bee the meere *dust* of the *earth*, which never did live, nor never shall. It may be the dust of that mans worms which did live, but shall no more. It may bee the dust of *another* man, that concernes not him of whom it is askt. This death of *incineration* and dispersion, is, to naturall *reason*, the most *irrecoverable death* of all, and yet *Domini Domini sunt exitus mortis*, unto God the Lord belong the issues of death, and by *recompacting* this *dust* into the *same body*, and *reanimating* the *same body* with the *same soule*, hee shall in a blessed and glorious *resurrection* give mee such an *issue from* this *death*, as shal never passe into any other death, but establish me into a life that shall last as long as the *Lord of life* himselfe. And so have you that that belongs to the *first acceptation* of these words, (*unto God the Lord belong the issues of death*) That though from the *wombe* to the *grave* and in the grave it selfe wee passe from *death* to *death*, yet, as *Daniel* speakes, *The Lord our God is able to deliver us, and hee will deliver us.*

And so wee passe unto our *second accommodation* of *these words* (*unto God the Lord belong the issues of death*) That it *belongs* to *God*, and *not* to *man* to *passe a judgement* upon us at our death, or to conclude a dereliction on *Gods* part upon the manner thereof.

2 Part
*Liberatio
in morte*

Those *indications* which the *Physitians* receive, and those *presagitions*[14] which they give for *death* or *recovery* in the *patient*, they receive and they give out of the grounds and the *rules of their art*: But we have no such rule or art to give a *presagition* of *spirituall death* and damnation upon any such *indication* as wee see in any *dying man;* wee see often enough to be sory, but not to despaire; for the *mercies* of *God* worke *momentarily* in minutes, and many times *insensibly* to *bystanders* or any other then the party departing, and wee may bee deceived both wayes: wee use to comfort our selves in the death of *a friend*, if it be testified that he went away like a *Lambe*, that is, without any *reluctation*.[15] But, *God* knowes, that may bee accompanied with a *dangerous damp* and *stupefaction*, and *insensibility* of his *present state*. Our blessed *Saviour* suf-

14. *presagitions:* presages.
15. *reluctation:* reluctance.

fered *colluctations*[16] with *death*, and a *sadnes even in his soule to death*, and an *agony* even to a *bloody sweate* in his *body*, and *expostulations* with *God*, and *exclamations* upon the crosse. He was a *devout man*, who said upon his death bed, or death-turfe (for hee was an *Heremit*) *septuaginta annos Domino servivisti, & mori times? hast thou served a good Master threescore and ten yeares, and now art thou loath to goe into his presence?* yet *Hilarion* was loath. He was a *devout* man (an *Heremit* too) that sayd that day hee died, *Cogita te hodie cœpisse servire Domino, & hodie finiturum. Consider this to be the first days service that ever thou didst thy Master*, to glorifie him in a Christianly and a constant death, *and if thy first day be thy last day too, how soone dost thou come to receive thy wages?* yet *Barlaam*[17] could have beene content to have stayd longer for it: Make no *ill conclusions* upon any mans *loathnes* to *dye*. And then, upon *violent deaths* inflicted, as upon malefactors, *Christ* himselfe hath forbidden us by his owne death to make any *ill conclusion;* for his owne *death* had those impressions in it; He was *reputed*, he was *executed* as a *malefactor*, and no doubt many of them who concurred to his death, did beleeve him to bee so. Of *sudden death* there are scarce examples to be found in the *scriptures* upon *good men*, for *death* in *battaile* cannot be called *sud[d]en death;* But *God* governes not by *examples*, but by *rules*, and therefore make no *ill conclusion* upon *sudden death* nor upon distempers neyther, though perchance accompanied with some *words of diffidence*[18] and distrust in the *mercies of God*. The *tree lyes as it falles;* 'Tis true, but yet it is *not* the *last stroake* that *fells* the *tree*, nor the *last word* nor *gaspe* that *qualifies* the *soule*. Stil *pray* wee for a *peaceable life* against *violent death*, and for *time* of *repentance* against *sudden death*, and for *sober* and *modest assurance* against *distemperd* and *diffident death*, but never make *ill conclusions* upon persons overtaken with such deaths; *Domini Domini sunt exitus mortis, to God the Lord belong the issues of death.* And *he* received *Sampson*, who went out of this world in

Hilarion

Barlaam

[Eccles. 11.3]

---

16. *colluctations*: conflicts.
17. *Barlaam*: a hermit in medieval legend.
18. *diffidence*: doubt.

such a manner (consider it *actively*, consider it *passively*, in his *owne death*, and in those whom he *slew* with him-selfe) as was subject to interpretation hard enough. Yet the *holy Ghost* hath moved S. *Paul* to celebrate *Sampson* in his *great Catalogue*, and so doth all the *Church*. Our *criticall* day is *not* the *very day* of our *death:* but the whole course of our life. I thanke him that *prayes* for me when my bell tolles, but I thank him much more that *Catechises* mee, or *preaches* to mee, or *instructs mee how to live. Fac hoc & vives*, there's my *securitie*, the mouth of the *Lord* hath sayd it, *doe this and thou shalt live:* But *though I doe it*, yet *I shall dye too*, dye a bodily, a naturall death. But *God* never mentions, never seems to consider that death, the bodily, the naturall death. *God doth* not say, Live well and thou shalt dye well, that is, an easie, a quiet death; But *live well here*, and thou shalt *live well for ever.* As the first part of a sentence peeces wel with the last, and never respects,[19] never hearkens after the *paren-thesis* that comes betweene, so doth a *good life* here flowe into an *eternall life*, without any consideration, what *manner* of *death* wee dye: But whether the *gate of my prison* be *opened* with an *oyld key* (by a gentle and *pre-paring sicknes*) or the gate bee *hewen downe* by a *violent death*, or the gate bee *burnt downe* by a *raging* and *fran-tique feaver, a gate into heaven I shall have*, for *from the Lord* is the *cause of my life*, and *with God the Lord are the issues of death*. And further wee cary not this *second acceptation* of the *words*, as this *issue of death* is *liberatio in morte, Gods care* that the *soule* be *safe*, what *agonies* soever the *body suffers* in the *houre* of death; but passe to our *third part* and last part; as this *issue of death* is *liberatio per mortem, a deliverance by the death* of another, by the *death* of *Christ*.

Sufferentiam Job audiistis, & vidistis finem Domini, sayes Saint *James* 5.11. *You have heard of the patience of Job*, says he, All this while you have done that, for in every man, calamitous, miserable man, a *Job* speaks; Now *see the end of the Lord*, sayth that *Apostle*, which is not that end that the *Lord* propos'd to himselfe (*salvation to*

19. *respects:* refers to.

us) nor the end which he proposes to us (*conformitie to him*) but *see the end of the Lord*, sayes he, The end, *that the Lord* himselfe came to, *death*, and a painefull and a shamefull death. But why did he dye? and why dye so? *Quia Domini Domini sunt exitus mortis* (as Saint *Augustine* interpreting this *text* answeres that question) because to this *God our Lord belong'd the issues of death. Quid apertius diceretur?* sayes hee there, what can bee more obvious, more manifest then this sense of these words? In the former part of this verse, it is sayd, *He that is our God, is the God of salvation, Deus salvos faciendi*, so hee reads it, the *God* that must save us: Who can that be, sayes he, but *Jesus?* for *therefore* that *name* was *given him*, because he was to *save us*. And to this *Jesus*, sayes he, this *Saviour, belongs the issues of death; Nec oportuit eum de hac vita alios exitus habere quam mortis.* Being come into this life in our mortal nature, he could not goe out of it any other way then by Death. *Ideo dictum*, sayes he, *therefore it is sayd, To God the Lord belong the issues of death; ut ostenderetur moriendo nos salvos facturum, to* shew *that his way to save us was to dye.* And from this *text* doth Saint *Isiodore* prove, that *Christ* was *truely Man*, (which as many *sects* of *heretiques denyed*, as that he was *truely God*) because to him, though he were *Dominus Dominus* (as the *text* doubles it) *God* the *Lord*, yet to *him*, to *God the Lord belong'd the issues of death. Oportuit eum pati*, more can not be sayd, then *Christ* himselfe sayes of himself, *These things Christ ought to suffer;* hee had no other way but by death. So then *this part* of our *Sermon* must needes be a *passion Sermon;* since all his *life* was a *continuall passion*, all *our Lent* may well bee a *continuall good Fryday. Christs* painefull life tooke off none of the paines of his death, hee felt not the lesse then for having felt so much before. Nor will any thing that shall be sayd before, lessen, but rather inlarge your devotion, to that which shall be sayd of his passion at the time of the due *solemnization* thereof. *Christ* bled not a droppe the lesse at the last, for having bled at his *Circumcision* before, nor wil you shed a teare the lesse then, if you shed some now. And therefore bee now content to consider with mee how to *this God the Lord belong'd the issues of death.*

De civitate
Dei lib. 17.
c. 18

Mat. 1.21

Lu. 24.26

Potuisse
Mori
Exod. 14.21
Jos. 10.12
[Dan. 3.19]
[Dan. 6.22]

That *God*, this *Lord*, the *Lord* of *life could dye,* is a strange contemplation; That the *red Sea* could bee *drie,* That the *Sun* could *stand still,* That an *Oven* could be *seaven times heat* and *not burne,* That *Lions* could be *hungry* and *not bite,* is strange, *miraculously strange,* but *supermiraculous* that *God could dye;* but that *God would dye* is an *exaltation* of that. But even of that also it is a *superexaltation,* that *God shold dye, must dye,* and *non exitus* (said *S. Augustin*) *God* the *Lord* had *no issue but by death,* and *oportuit pati* (says *Christ* himself) all this *Christ ought to suffer,* was bound to suffer. *Deus ultionum Deus* says *David, God* is the *God of revenges,* he wold *not passe* over the sin of man unrevenged, unpunished. But then *Deus ultionum liberè egit* (sayes *that place*) The *God of revenges workes freely,* he *punishes,* he *spares whome he will.* And wold he *not spare himselfe?* he would not: *Dilectio fortis ut mors, love is strong as death,* stronger, it drew in death that naturally is not welcom. *Si possibile,* says *Christ, If it be possible, let this Cup passe,* when his *love expressed in a former decree* with his *Father,* had *made it impossible. Many waters quench not love, Christ* tryed many; He was *Baptized* out of his *love,* and his love determined[20] not there; He wept over *Jerusalem* out of his love, and his love determined not there; He *mingled blood* with *water* in his *agony* and that determined not his love; hee *wept pure blood,* all his blood at all his eyes, at all his pores, in his *flagellation* and *thornes* (*to the Lord our God belong'd the issues of blood*) and these *expressed,* but these did *not quench his love.*

Psal. 94.1
Voluisse
Mori

Cant. 8.6

[Mat. 26.39]
Vers. 7

Oportuisse
Mori

Hee *would not* spare, nay he *could not spare himselfe.* There was nothing more free, more voluntary, more spontaneous then[21] the death of *Christ.* 'Tis true, *liberè egit,* he *dyed voluntarily,* but yet when we consider the *contract* that had passed betweene his *Father* and *him,* there was an *oportuit,* a kind of *necessity* upon him. All this *Christ ought to suffer.* And when shall we *date* this *obligation,* this *oportuit,* this *necessity?* when shall wee say *that* begun? Certainly this *decree* by which *Christ was to suffer*

20. *determined:* concluded.
21. *then:* than.

all this, was an *eternall decree*, and was there any thing before that, that was eternall? *Infinite love, eternall love,* he pleased to follow this home, and to consider it seriously, that what liberty soever wee can *conceive* in *Christ,* to dye or not to dye; this *necessity of dying,* this *decree* is as *eternall* as that *liberty;* and yet how small a matter made hee of this *necessity* and this *dying?* His *Father* cals it but a *bruise,* and but a *bruising of his heele (the serpent shall* Gen. 3.15 *bruise his heele)* and yet that was, that the *serpent* should *practise* and *compasse* his *death.* Himselfe calls it but a *Baptisme,* as though he were to bee the better for it. *I have a Baptisme to be Baptized with,* and he was in paine till Luk. 12.50 it was accomplished, and yet this *Baptisme* was *his death.* The *holy Ghost* calls it *Joy (for the Joy which was set* Heb. 12.2 *before him hee indured the Crosse)* which was not a *joy* of his reward after his passion, but a joy that filled him even in the middest of those torments, and arose from them. When *Christ* calls his passion *Calicem, a Cuppe,* and no worse, *(Can ye drink of my Cuppe?)* he speakes not Mat. odiously, nor with detestation of it: Indeed it was a *Cup,* 20.22 *salus mundo, a health to all the world.* And *quid retribuam,* Psal. says *David, what shall I render to the Lord?* answere you 116.12 with *David, accipiam Calicem, I will take the Cup of salva-tion;* take it, that *Cup of salvation,* his *passion,* if not into your *present imitation,* yet into your *present contempla-tion.* And behold how that *Lord* that was *God,* yet *could dye, would dye, must dye,* for your *salvation.*

That *Moses* and *Elias talkt with Christ* in the *trans-* Mat. 17.3 *figuration,* both Saint *Mathew* and Saint *Marke* tel us but Mar. 9.4 what they talkt of, onely S. *Luke, Dicebant excessum ejus,* Luc. 9.31 says he, *they talkt of his decease, of his death* which *was to be accomplished* at *Jerusalem.* The *word* is of his *Exodus,* the very word of our Text, *exitus,* his *issue by death. Moses* who in his *Exodus* had *prefigured* this *issue of our Lord,* and in passing *Israel* out of *Egypt* through the *red Sea,* had foretold in that actua¹ *prophesie, Christs passing* of *mankind through* the *sea* of his *blood,* and *Elias,* whose *Exodus* and *issue out of* tnis *world* was a *figure* of *Christs ascension,* had no doubt a great satisfaction in *talking* with our *blessed Lord de excessu ejus,* of the *full consummation* of *all this* in *his death,* which was to bee *accomplished* at *Jerusalem.* Our *meditation* of his *death* should be more *viscerall* and affect us more because it is of a thing already done. The ancient *Romanes* had a certain tenderness, and detestation of the name of death, they cold not name death, no, not in their wills. There they could not say *Si mori contigerit*, but *si quid humanitus contingat*, not if, or when I dye, but when the course of nature is accomplished upon me. To us that speake dayly of the *death* of *Christ*, (he was *crucified, dead and buried*) can the memory or the mention of our owne *death* bee yrkesome or bitter? There are in these latter times amongst us, that name death freely enogh, and the death of *God*, but in *blasphemous oathes* and *execrations*. Miserable men, who shall therefore bee sayd never to have named *Jesus*, because they have named him *too often;* and therfore heare *Jesus* say, *Nescivi vos, I never knew you*, because they made themselves *too familiar* with him. *Moses* and *Elias* talkt with *Christ* of his *death*, only in *a holy* and *joyfull sense* of the *benefit* which *they* and *all* the world were to *receive by that.* *Discourses* of *Religion* should not be *out* of *curiosity*, but to *edification.* And then they talkt with *Christ* of his *death* at that time, when he was in the greatest *height* of *glory* that ever he admitted in this world, that is, his *transfiguration.* And wee are afraid to speake to the *great men* of this world of their *death*, but nourish in them a *vaine imagination* of *immortality*, and *immutability.* But *bonum est nobis esse hic* (as Saint *Peter* said there) *It is good to dwell here*, in this *consideration* of his *death*, and therefore *transferre* wee our *tabernacle* (our *devotions*) through some of those *steps* which *God* the *Lord* made to his *issue of death* that *day.*

Take in the *whole day* from the *houre* that *Christ received* the *passeover* upon *Thursday*, *unto* the *houre* in which hee *dyed* the *next day.* Make *this* present *day* that *day* in thy *devotion*, and consider what *hee did*, and remember what *you have done.* Before hee *instituted* and *celebrated* the *Sacrament*, (which was *after the eating of the passeover*) hee proceeded to that *act* of *humility*, to *wash his disciples feete*, even *Peters, who* for a while *resisted* him; In thy *preparation* to the holy and blessed *Sacrament*, hast thou with a sincere *humility* sought a *reconciliation* with all the *world*, even with those that have beene *averse* from it, and *refused* that *reconciliation*

[Mat. 7.23]

Conformitas

live through Christs death as vividly as possible

from thee? If so (and not else) thou hast spent that *first part* of this his *last day*, in a *conformity* with him. After the *Sacrament* hee spent the time till night in *prayer*, in *preaching*, in *Psalmes;* Hast thou considered that a *worthy receaving* of the *Sacrament* consists in a *continuation* of *holinesse after*, aswell as in a *preparation* before? If so, thou hast therein also *conformed* thy selfe to him, so *Christ* spent his time till night. *At night* hee *went into the garden* to *pray*, and he prayed *prolixius;* he spent *much time* in prayer. How much? Because it is literally expressed, that he *prayed there three severall times*, and that *returning to his Disciples* after his *first prayer*, and *finding them a sleepe* sayd, *could ye not watch with me one houre*, it is collected that he *spent three houres* in *prayer*. I dare scarce aske thee *whither* thou *wentest*, or *how* thou *disposedst* of *thy self*, when it *grew darke* and after *last night:* If that time were spent in a *holy recommendation* of thy selfe to *God*, and a *submission* of *thy will* to *his*, it was spent in a *conformity* to him. In that *time* and in those *prayers* was *his agony* and *bloody sweat*. I will *hope* that thou didst *pray;* but not *every ordinary* and *customary prayer*, but *prayer actually* accompanied with *shedding of teares*, and *dispositively* in a readines to *shed blood* for *his glory* in *necessary cases*, puts thee into a *conformity* with him. About midnight he was *taken* and *bound with a kisse*, art thou not *too conformable* to him in that? Is not that *too literally*, too exactly *thy case?* at *midnight* to have *bene taken* and *bound with a kisse?* From thence he was *caried back* to *Jerusalem*, first to *Annas*, then to *Caiphas*, and (as late as it was) then hee was *examined* and *buffeted*, and *delivered over* to the custody of those *officers*, from whome he received all those *irrisions*,[22] and *violences*, the *covering of his face*, the *spitting upon his face*, the *blasphemies of words*, and the *smartnes of blowes* which that *Gospell* mentions. In which compasse fell that *Gallicinium*, that *crowing of the Cock* which *called up Peter* to his *repentance*. How thou passedst all that time last night, thou knowest. If thou didst any thing then that needed *Peters teares*, and hast *not shed them*, let me be thy *Cock*, doe it now, Now thy *Master* (in the unworthi-

22. *irrisions:* jeerings.

est of his servants) *lookes back upon thee,* doe it now.
Betimes, in the morning, so soone as it was day, the *Jewes
held a counsell in the high Priests hall,* and *agreed upon
their evidence* against him, and then caried him to *Pilate,*
who was to be his *Judge.* Diddest thou *accuse* thy selfe
when thou *wakedst this morning,* and wast thou content
to admit even *false accusations* (that is) rather to *suspect
actions* to have beene sin, which were not, then to
smother and *justify* such as were *truly sins?* then thou
spentst that *houre* in *conformity* to him. *Pilate* found
no evidence against him, and therefore to ease himselfe,
and to passe a *complement* upon *Herod, Tetrarch of Gali-
lee,* who was at that time at *Jerusalem* (because *Christ*
being a *Galilean* was of *Herods jurisdiction*) *Pilat sent
him* to *Herod,* and rather as a *madman* then a *malefactor,
Herod* remaunded him (*with scornes*) to *Pilat* to proceed
against him; And this was about *eight* of the *clock.* Hast
thou been content to come to this *Inquisition,* this exami-
nation, this agitation, this cribration,[23] this pursuit of thy
conscience, to *sift* it, to follow it from the *sinnes* of thy
youth to thy *present sinnes,* from the *sinnes* of thy *bed,*
to the *sinnes* of thy *boorde,* and from the *substance* to the
circumstance of thy *sinnes?* That's *time spent* like thy
Saviours. Pilat wold have *saved Christ,* by using the
priviledge of the *day* in his behalfe, because that *day* one
prisoner was to be delivered, but they chose *Barrabas;*
hee would have *saved* him *from death,* by *satisfying their
fury,* with *inflicting* other *torments* upon him, *scourging*
and *crowning with thornes,* and *loading* him with many
scornefull and *ignominious contumelies;* But this redeem'd
him not, they pressed a *crucifying.* Hast thou gone about
to *redeeme thy sinne,* by *fasting,* by *Almes,* by *disciplines*
and *mortifications,* in the way of *satisfaction* to the *Justice*
of *God?* that will not serve, that's not the right way, *wee
presse* an utter *Crucifying* of that *sinne* that governes
thee; and that *conformes* thee to *Christ.* Towards *noone
Pilat* gave *judgement,* and they made such *hast*[24] to execution, as that *by noone* hee was *upon the Crosse.* There
now hangs that *sacred Body* upon the *Crosse, rebaptized*

23. *cribration:* sifting.
24. *hast:* haste.

in his owne *teares* and *sweat*, and *embalmed* in his *owne blood alive*. There are those *bowells of compassion*, which are so conspicuous, so manifested, as that you may *see them through his wounds*. There those *glorious eyes* grew faint in their light: so as the *Sun ashamed* to survive them, *departed with his light too*. And then that *Sonne of God*, who was *never from us*, and yet had now come a *new way unto* us in *assuming our nature*, delivers that *soule* (which was *never out* of his *Fathers hands*) by a *new way*, a *voluntary emission* of it into his Fathers hands; For though to this *God our Lord*, *belong'd these issues of death*, so that considered in his owne contract, he *must* necessarily *dye*, yet at *no breach* or *battery*, which they had made upon his *sacred Body*, issued his soule, but *emisit*, hee *gave up the Ghost*, and as *God breathed a soule into* the *first Adam*, so this *second Adam breathed his soule into God, into the hands of God*. There wee leave you in that *blessed dependancy*, to *hang* upon *him* that *hangs* upon the *Crosse*, there *bath*[25] in his *teares*, there *suck* at his *woundes*, and *lye downe in peace* in his *grave*, till hee vouchsafe you a *resurrection*, and an *ascension* into that *Kingdome*, which hee *hath purchas'd for you*, with the *inestimable price* of his *incorruptible blood*. AMEN.

25. *bath*: bathe.

Index
OF TITLES AND
FIRST LINES

MODERN LIBRARY COLLEGE EDITIONS

302

as if we made a scalpel fail in loss
we know we could be
It's impossibility is far the weed
same source as its applied

crazy thing is it true
it is only an abstract our presents
us believe

resurrection: most beautiful idea

Rewrite: there is a difference we made by using
to gov process, 365, "logistics"
human life vs. human spirit

laughing